The German Left
and the Weimar Republic

Historical Materialism Book Series

The Historical Materialism Book Series is a major publishing initiative of the radical left. The capitalist crisis of the twenty-first century has been met by a resurgence of interest in critical Marxist theory. At the same time, the publishing institutions committed to Marxism have contracted markedly since the high point of the 1970s. The Historical Materialism Book Series is dedicated to addressing this situation by making available important works of Marxist theory. The aim of the series is to publish important theoretical contributions as the basis for vigorous intellectual debate and exchange on the left.

The peer-reviewed series publishes original monographs, translated texts, and reprints of classics across the bounds of academic disciplinary agendas and across the divisions of the left. The series is particularly concerned to encourage the internationalization of Marxist debate and aims to translate significant studies from beyond the English-speaking world.

For a full list of titles in the Historical Materialism Book Series available in paperback from Haymarket Books, visit:
www.haymarketbooks.org/category/hm-series

The German Left and the Weimar Republic

A Selection of Documents

Translated and Introduced by
Ben Fowkes

Haymarket Books
Chicago, IL

First published in 2014 by Brill Academic Publishers, The Netherlands
© 2014 Koninklijke Brill NV, Leiden, The Netherlands

Published in paperback in 2015 by
Haymarket Books
P.O. Box 180165
Chicago, IL 60618
773-583-7884
www.haymarketbooks.org

ISBN: 978-1-60846-486-9

Trade distribution:
In the US, Consortium Book Sales, www.cbsd.com
In Canada, Publishers Group Canada, www.pgcbooks.ca
In the UK, Turnaround Publisher Services, www.turnaround-uk.com
In all other countries, Publishers Group Worldwide, www.pgw.com

Cover design by Ragina Johnson.

This book was published with the generous support of
Lannan Foundation and the Wallace Global Fund.

10 9 8 7 6 5 4 3 2 1

Library of Congress Cataloging-in-Publication data is available.

Contents

3 Communism and Insurrection   71

Introduction   71

Documents   79

Preface

Despite its brief presence on the historical stage, a mere 14 years, the Weimar Republic has been an endless source of interest to observers not only of political systems but also of cultural and intellectual development. The philosopher and social theorist Theodor Adorno, himself a product and survivor of the Weimar epoch, wrote in 1963 that 'there is a great fascination for the ideas of Weimar, perhaps because of the inadequacy of what came after Hitler'.[1] Another reason for this interest, in addition to the disillusionment with the post-1945 world to which Adorno refers here, is the tremendously broad spectrum of Weimar politics, stretching from the authoritarians and racialists on the extreme Right to the revolutionary anarchists on the extreme Left. This is matched by the equally broad range of Weimar culture, from the rarefied high art of the abstractionists to the mass proletarian art of the communists, from the intellectualism of the university mandarinate to the choral and gymnastic activities of the working classes, from the macho militarism of the Free Corps to the gentle persuasion of the advocates of sexual reform. There is ample material here for a multi-volume enterprise covering the overall Weimar experience.

The aim of the present collection of documents is more modest. It is to offer a glimpse into the mass of published and in some cases unpublished material which bears on the history of the political Left in Weimar Germany. The book may thus be seen as a complement to the magnificent, all-embracing volume recently produced by Anton Kaes and his collaborators,[2] who, perhaps because they aspired to present a complete picture of Weimar in all its facets, offered the reader what was in fact a rather sketchy treatment of the political scene. There are, it is hardly necessary to add, many German-language collections of documents on Weimar, and their content overlaps this volume to some extent,[3] but there is nothing comparable available in English.

The present work is divided into 12 chapters, and I have endeavoured to provide helpful introductions to each one. My comments can only be an indication of the main lines taken by research, and no claim is made to completeness. I have concentrated on the policies of the two main parties of the Left towards the issues that came up during the course of the Weimar Republic, although there is one chapter at the end on dissident leftists. The trade union movement, important as it is, has not been given a large place here as this is a study of the political Left rather than the German working-class movement as a whole. I have included questions of gender and sexual reform (Chapter Nine) but there are no specific documents on the Weimar Left's relation to cultural and artistic matters, because these will be treated in a companion volume.

---

1   In a letter of 17 December 1963 to Siegfried Kracauer (Schopf 2008, p. 627).
2   Kaes, Jay and Dimendberg 1994.
3   For example: Michalka and Niedhart 1992; Lönne 2002; Flemming 1979; Longerich 1992, Luthardt 1978 and Huber 1966.

Acknowledgements

I would like, first and foremost, to thank Dr. Norman Laporte of the University of Glamorgan for his advice and encouragement. I would also like to thank the following scholars for giving permission to translate extracts from certain documents printed by them and included in the present collection: Professor Dr. Dr.h.c. Hermann Weber of the University of Mannheim, Professor Hagen Schulze of the Freie Universität, Berlin; and Dr. Hans Woller of the Institut für Zeitgeschichte. I have also received permission to translate a number of items from Verlag Neue Gesellschaft/Verlag J.H.W. Dietz Nachfolger, Bonn, and from Karl Dietz Verlag, Berlin. Despite my best efforts, it has not been possible to locate some copyright holders. I welcome correspondence from any legitimate right holder.

Abbreviations

AAU	General Workers' Union
ADGB	General German Trade Union Confederation
AfA	Cooperative Union of Free Salaried Employees' Associations
ARSO	Working Group of Social and Political Organisations
AUCP (B)	All-Union Communist Party (Bolsheviks)
AVAVG	Law on Labour Exchanges and Unemployment Insurance
BVP	Bavarian People's Party
DBB	German Union of Officials
DDP	German Democratic Party
DVNP	German National People's Party
DVP	German People's Party
ECCI	Executive Committee of the Communist International
FAUD (S)	Free Workers' Union of Germany, Syndicalists
IfA	Association for Workers' Culture
IKD	International Communists of Germany
KAG	Communist Working Group
KAPD	Communist Workers' Party of Germany
KPD (O)	Communist Party of Germany (Opposition)
KPD	Communist Party of Germany
MSPD	Majority Social Democratic Party of Germany
NSDAP	National Socialist German Workers' Party
OHL	Supreme Army Command
RCP (B)	Russian Communist Party (Bolsheviks)
RFB	League of Red Front Fighters
RFMB	League of Red Women and Girls
RGO	Revolutionary Trade-Union Opposition
SAP	Socialist Workers' Party
SPD	Social Democratic Party of Germany
USPD	Independent Social Democratic Party of Germany
VKPD	United Communist Party of Germany
VSPD	United Social Democratic Party of Germany
ZAG	Central Association for Cooperation

General Introduction

There were many differences between the two parties which constituted the political Left for most of the Weimar period, the SPD (Social Democratic Party of Germany) and the KPD (Communist Party of Germany). Their nature will, I hope, become clearer in the course of this book of documents. I should like to begin, however, by highlighting one very clear divergence in political approach, which followed from the different perspectives they had of the future. In their heart of hearts, whatever Marxist theory might say, the Social Democrats (or at least the most influential Social Democrats, those who determined the course of party policy) thought that capitalism was a permanent fixture, and that society would remain divided into classes for the foreseeable future. The correct approach for a working-class party was therefore to try to promote democracy and the interests of the workers (these two things went together) and to secure piecemeal improvements, which were possible even under capitalism. The communists thought that capitalism and bourgeois rule were doomed, that they had already been overthrown in Russia, and that the task was to prepare the socialist revolution, which would arrive sooner rather than later; piecemeal improvements were at best a waste of time and at worst a dangerous diversion. Hence the SPD was a party of government, whether alone or in coalition with other parties, whereas the KPD did not expect to form a government until after (or perhaps in the course of) the revolution, and was never a part of the German government at the Reich (in other words the national) level. At the next level down, the 18[1] individual states which made up the German Reich, and still further down the scale, in the institutions of local self-government, the differences between the two parties were not so great: although the communists had serious reservations about the desirability, or the usefulness, of becoming involved in bourgeois institutions, they did form governments locally. They had to enter coalitions with the SPD to do this, as they were nowhere powerful enough to govern on their own. This happened in Saxony and Thuringia in October 1923, the most significant case, which we touch on in Chapter Three, but there were others.[2] Most discussions of the

---

1   17 after 1928, when the tiny state of Waldeck was incorporated into the largest state, Prussia.
2   Communist party involvement in local government has been examined thoroughly by Wünderich 1980 and Herlemann 1977. The SPD's activities in local government are a much bigger subject and there is no overall study of them, though there are plenty of studies of individual states. For Prussia see, among others, Schulze 1977 and Orlow 1986 and 1991.

KPD, however, and the majority of the documents translated here, have nothing to do with governmental activities.

For the Social Democrats (or, more accurately at this time, the Majority Social Democrats, MSPD) the opposite is true. The documents in Chapter One are intended to illuminate the SPD's role in government at a national level in the early years of the Weimar Republic. They had a dominant role in the Council of People's Representatives, which took over in November 1918 from the old imperial government which had been overthrown by the November Revolution. The USPD People's Representatives left that body in December 1918, leaving the SPD in exclusive control. The leaders of the SPD firmly believed that they should take no major reforming steps until a constituent assembly had been elected on a democratic vote; they considered themselves to be a caretaker government. Once the first elections had taken place (January 1919) the way was open for a coalition government, which the SPD set up in February 1919 alongside the Centre Party and the German Democratic Party. The Social Democrats continued in office until June 1920, and thus for sixteen months they were in a position to organise the return of the country to peacetime conditions. This involved in particular the demobilisation of the armed forces, and the re-integration of millions of men into peaceful economic activities. As the new Social Democratic President of the country, Friedrich Ebert,[3] told the German parliament, the Reichstag, to the accompaniment of jeers from the Right: 'We did everything we could to restore economic life' (1.6).

There were people in the Party who would have liked to do much more than this. There was initially strong pressure in favour of taking the major industries of the country into public, or state, ownership, which was after all part of the Marxist programme to which the SPD was in theory committed. The first SPD government, headed by Philip Scheidemann,[4] reacted to this in March 1919 by issuing a framework law for the 'socialisation', or 'nationalisation' of industry. Although the law reached the statute book it was never actually put into effect (1.9). Instead a 'Socialisation Commission' was set up to examine the possible ways of doing this and of course also to look at the objections. The commission dissolved itself in April 1919, after many interesting discussions, but no concrete achievements. There were also other proposals that need mention-

---

3   Friedrich Ebert, chair of the Council of People's Representatives 1918–19 and President of Germany 1919–25.

4   Philipp Scheidemann (1865–1939), SPD, joint party chair since 1917, member of the Council of People's Representatives 1918–19, Reich Prime Minister 1919, Mayor of Kassel 1920–25.

ing. Rudolf Wissell,[5] who was both a high-ranking trade unionist and an SPD leader, advocated the introduction of economic planning, and the involvement of both sides of industry in this process, through 'organised associations' with a 'communal economic basis' (1.11), an idea which had its precedents in the wartime planned economy. Max Cohen,[6] one of the leading figures in the group around the revisionist journal *Sozialistische Monatshefte*, felt, although he was on the right of the Party, that the workers' councils which emerged all over Germany in November 1918 and were regarded by most of his party colleagues as purely temporary organisations doomed to disappear once democratically elected national and local governments were in place, nevertheless had some positive features and should be allowed to continue, albeit in a different form. In his conception, they would exist side by side with the official government of the country. This idea was not rejected out of hand by the party majority, but was transformed into a system of 'Factory Councils', which became law in 1920 (2.16, 2.18). There would have been much more support within the SPD for daring ideas of reform at this time if it had not lost its more radical members to the USPD during the First World War. The spectrum of opinion within the Party was fairly narrow before 1922. What changed was the re-entry of the remnant of the USPD into the Party in that year. From then on there was a strong and vociferous left-wing minority, led by the ex-Spartacist Paul Levi until his death, which endeavoured to push the Party towards a more confrontational stance towards its coalition partners and greater efforts to stimulate a mass movement to defend workers' interests.

In most areas of policy the SPD operated a bipartisan approach with its coalition partners. We present documents on SPD foreign policy in Chapter Seven and SPD military policy in Chapter Eight. As Jeffrey Verhey has written, it was impossible for the SPD to develop a distinctive line here because it was still committed to the 'spirit of 1914': it continued to 'align itself with existing national symbols'.[7] It had voted for the war credits in August 1914, and continued to do so throughout the War. Friedrich Ebert, as head of the government, welcomed the troops home in December 1918 with the words 'I salute you, who return undefeated from the field of battle'. The Party continued to regard the Versailles Treaty as a completely unjust act of brutality against a

---

5 Rudolf Wissell (1869–1962), SPD, trade unionist, People's Representative 1918–19, Reich Economics Minister 1919, Reich Minister of Labour 1928–30.
6 Max Cohen (1876–1963), SPD, normally referred to as Max Cohen-Reuss to distinguish him from others of the same name. He chaired the Central Council of the German Socialist Republic while it existed.
7 Verhey 2000, pp. 207–8.

defeated nation. In this it was entirely in line with the rest of the political spectrum except the USPD. In addition, the perceived need to defend Germany
against the Bolshevik threat coming from the east in 1918 meant that the Party
was unable to confront the old military rulers of the country, and called on
them instead for their help. Later attempts to remedy this situation, such as
Scheidemann's complaints about the way the *Reichswehr* was acting as a 'state
within a state', came far too late to achieve anything.

In foreign policy, the SPD was always strongly in favour of international
reconciliation and general disarmament (7.12, 7.14), but it was unable to gain
majority support within the country for these principles, and it therefore
fell back in the mid-1920s on supporting the policies of Gustav Stresemann,[8]
which promised 'at least a partial achievement of socialist objectives'.[9] At the
same time the Party presided when in government over an army which was
rapidly rearming in secret, and, like its coalition partners, it never gave up hope
of revising the Versailles Treaty, though this would be done by peaceful means.
The Party has been criticised for its 'general passivity' and 'helplessness' in foreign affairs,[10] but its lack of influence in the foreign policy sphere should be
emphasised. As Stefan Feucht has pointed out, its 'room for manoeuvre in foreign policy was exceedingly limited' and after 1920 there were even fewer possibilities to pursue an active and specifically social democratic foreign policy.[11]
What was most important for the SPD was always the need to keep the Weimar
coalition in being, in the interests of the workers, and also of democracy.

After the Party's disastrous performance at the June 1920 elections, when its
proportion of the vote fell from 38 percent to 22 percent, the issue of coalition
with the non-socialist parties became very important. Had the SPD lost votes to
its left-wing rival, the USPD, precisely because of the coalition? Would the best
approach be to start attacking the 'bourgeois' parties (the Social Democrats
may not have been Marxists but they never abandoned Marxist language)
and to reject the idea of coalition with them? Within a single year the SPD
changed its mind twice on the permissibility of a coalition with the furthest
right of those parties, the conservative DVP (German People's Party), one
wing of which was associated with heavy industry. The DVP would have preferred a restoration of the monarchy, but was prepared to accept the Weimar

---

8   Gustav Stresemann (1878–1929), head of the Association of Saxon Industrialists, founder
         and chair of the DVP 1919, Reich Chancellor 1923, Reich Foreign Minister 1923–29.
9   Feucht 1998, p. 113.
10   See Matthias 1954, p. vii.
11   Feucht 1998, p. 113.

Republic for lack of any alternative.[12] In 1920 the Social Democratic party congress voted against a coalition, and in 1921 it voted in favour. There was a continuous dispute throughout the whole period between the right and left of the Party, and sometimes within the right wing itself, over the advisability of coalition. Chapters Four and Five treat this issue from various different angles. The issue of coalition was very much bound up with that of the defence of working-class interests, and the preservation of democracy and the Republic itself was seen as a major working-class interest by most of the SPD, though never by the KPD. This could only be achieved, it was claimed, by keeping on the right side of the bourgeoisie (4.7, 4.8), and by avoiding actions which might undermine the (sometimes explicit, sometimes implicit) coalition with the two moderate parties, the DDP and the Centre (with the addition of the DVP at critical points). After Ebert's death in 1925 this approach implied supporting the moderate bourgeois parties' presidential candidates instead of the SPD's. Thus the SPD supported the Centre politician Wilhelm Marx[13] in 1925 (only to see him defeated by Paul von Hindenburg,[14] the candidate of the Right) and it supported von Hindenburg himself in 1932 (with the aim of keeping Hitler out of the presidency). It also implied support for the anti-democratic and anti-proletarian policies of von Hindenburg's Chancellor Heinrich Brüning,[15] because this seemed to be the only way of keeping the Nazis out of power: this was the politics of the 'lesser evil' (4.13).[16]

The other major party of the German Left, the KPD, took a very different line on all these matters. The KPD was born out of the November Revolution and the associated Council movement of 1918–19, and it was committed to achieving a socialist revolution in Germany on Marxist lines, following the example set by the Bolsheviks in Russia in 1917. Whether this revolution would be identical in all respects with what had happened in Russia, and whether the same route to revolution needed to be followed, were questions over which there was

---

12 Social Democratic suspicion of the DVP was partly a question of perception. The DVP's unwillingness to oppose the Kapp putsch made it seem clear that it was opposed to the republic, but in fact its leader, Stresemann, was able through his personal authority to pull it towards the left, and towards cooperation with the SPD, despite opposition from its right wing (Winkler 1985, p. 454).

13 Wilhelm Marx (1863–1946), Centre Party, member of the Reichstag 1920 to 1932, German Chancellor 1923–25 and 1926–28, presidential candidate 1925.

14 Paul von Beneckendorff und Hindenburg (1847–1934), Field Marshal, head of the General Staff of the army 1916–18, President of Germany 1925–34.

15 Heinrich Brüning (1885–1970), Centre Party, member of the Reichstag 1924–33, leader of the Party in the Reichstag 1929–30, Reich Chancellor, 1930–32.

16 Winkler 1990, pp. 205–27.

initially some disagreement. There were several different revolutionary ideas in competition with each other in Germany in the immediate postwar period. The idea of rule by councils (or 'soviets', to use the Russian word) was one of them, but this could take several different forms. It could be combined with the existence of a revolutionary political party, or it could replace it entirely. Councils might also replace trade unions. Trade unions might replace political parties. The dissident communists who were expelled in 1919 and set up the KAPD (Communist Workers' Party of Germany) in 1920 favoured the establishment of 'One Big Union' on syndicalist lines although they maintained that a political party was also needed (12.3) The left of the USPD favoured rule by the councils alone (12.1, 12.2). Even within the KPD itself there were differing opinions at first on these issues. Above all, they disagreed on the question of the communist uprising. Was an immediate insurrection desirable? Would it be, on the contrary, a disastrous mistake? Chapter Three contains several documents about the attempted risings of March 1921 and October 1923. Another major issue in dispute was the meaning of the 'united front tactic', first put forward in 1921 and continued, at least in words, for the remainder of the Weimar Republic. To what extent were alliances with other parties permissible? How far should the Party go in softening its line to make such alliances possible? Then there was the question of the Party's relations with the rest of the international communist movement. Should the Party develop its policies independently or submit in all cases to the directives issued by the Executive Committee of the Communist International? It was several years before a hard and fast view congealed on all these points, in part under the pressure of the Soviet Bolsheviks, in part simply through following their example and in part as a result of developments within Germany. Chapter Six, entitled 'The Moscow Connection', is intended to illustrate these processes.

Much of the discussion within the KPD was inevitably dominated by the question of revolution. Had it ever been possible? Were mistakes made in preparing an uprising? Or in setting the time for an uprising? These matters continued to be discussed long after they were of any real significance, but more mundane issues tended to take centre stage after 1925. The Party was forced to co-exist with the institutions of the German state and the system of German and international capitalism. It also needed to find a relationship with the SPD, with the working class in general and it needed to try gradually to increase support for the Party through the 'united front' tactic. The ultimate objective was still revolution, but that was in the future. In the short term, the Party's perspective was to use the 'united front' tactic to discredit the SPD among its more active members by showing that Social Democracy was far too inclined to compromise with the capitalist class to engage in a serious struggle against it. Whether this implied agreements at the summit ('united front from above') or at the base alone ('united front from below') or a combination of the two methods was a matter of disagreement, and the answer to the question, which varied from year to year, was ultimately given at the highest level, in the Executive Committee of the Communist International (ECCI), based in Moscow. A further constraint on the KPD's ability to decide its tactical line independently was the Party's second and equally important objective: to defend and support the Soviet Union. This meant for instance supporting the secret military cooperation of the 1920s between the German armed forces, the Reichswehr, and the Red Army, while denying that it existed. The dissident left communists, who had broken with the Party in the mid-1920s, took a certain malicious pleasure in siding with the SPD in December 1926 when that Party stood alone in its attempt to bring the facts about the army's secret links with the Soviet military into the open (8.7).

Once it was tacitly assumed that capitalism, and the Weimar system, would survive, it became necessary to work out policies that took account of this. Both the SPD and the KPD put forward proposals for changing tax policy, as early as 1922. They called for the requisitioning of material assets, as the only way of taxing the rich. There was no point in taxing their cash reserves because money was rapidly losing all value in a period of high inflation, which by 1922 was running completely out of control (5.7, 5.9). Later on, in 1926, the two parties jointly called for the expropriation of the former princely houses (5.14). This final period of cooperation did not last long. After 1928 the KPD changed course abruptly, and the SPD began to be abused as a 'Social Fascist' party more dangerous even than the 'National Fascists' of the Hitler movement. Why this happened is still disputed. Was the left turn preceded by a 'radicalisation' from below? Or was it entirely imposed upon the KPD's members from outside?[17] While it is clear that the Comintern did change course at this time, and that the 'general line' of the communist movement was set by the ECCI, this does not in itself explain the popularity of the 'Social Fascist' line among local party members and functionaries. The fact that the SPD was in power both nationally (the Müller[18] government of 1928 to 1930) and locally (the Braun[19] government, which held office in Prussia almost continuously from 1920 to 1932) was

---

17   See Laporte 2003, pp. 238–62 for a discussion of these issues within the Saxon context.

18   Hermann Müller, sometimes referred to as Hermann Müller-Franken (1876–1931), member of the SPD executive 1917–29, joint SPD chair 1919–27, Reich Foreign Minister 1919–20, Chancellor 1920 and 1928–30.

19   Otto Braun (1872–1955), member of the SPD leadership 1917–20, 1921–22, Prussian Minister of Agriculture 1918–21, Prussian Prime Minister 1920–21, 1921–25, 1925–33.

one reason. Even after Hermann Müller had been removed from the office of Chancellor (March 1930) the SPD continued to run Prussia, hence a demonstrator struck by a policeman's baton or wounded by a bullet could blame those who appeared to control the police, the Social Democrats. The 'bloodbath' of May 1929, when 33 people were killed by the Berlin police in the course of several days of street fighting arising out of the SPD decision to ban all political demonstrations owing to the risk of bloodshed, appeared to ordinary communist party members to justify the new 'Social Fascist' line.[20]

There were other reasons as well. In periods of economic downturn the KPD's members tended to be hit more severely than those of the SPD. They were also harder hit by the process of rationalisation of German industry, which the SPD generally approved of. In 1924, 70 percent of the Party's members were unemployed. This situation improved somewhat during the mid-1920s. By 1927 this figure had fallen to 21.6 percent; still a substantial proportion.[21] From then on it increased steadily. By 1932 only 11 percent of party members were employed in industry.[22] This sociological fact reduced opposition to the left course of the Party, and may even have encouraged it. Moreover, most of the Party's trade unionists tended to be on the 'right', in the sense that they wanted to engage in joint struggles against capital with non-communist trade unionists. Hence the removal of 'rightists' from the Party in 1928 meant the decimation of the Party's trade union element: the Party 'separated itself from its trade union supporters' at this time.[23] This also lessened opposition to the left course. The groups of trade unionists who remained in the Party, particularly miners and chemical workers, were ready to follow the leadership's course of setting up a separate trade union organisation, the RGO.[24] The basic aim of the new organisation was to politicise wage demands, because 'traditional trade union wage claims were no longer adequate to the changed situation of the working class'.[25] It should also be said, finally, that hostility to Social Democracy was nothing new for the communists. The new course was in fact a reversion to the line pursued in 1924 and 1925, and even in 1927, at the 11th Party Congress, held at the height of the renewed united front policy, the SPD was described as 'one of the main

---

20   Hoppe 2007, p. 146.
21   Schöck 1977, pp. 57 and 228.
22   Mallmann 1996, p. 103. The Party did not give figures on unemployment after 1927, but this statistic gives some indication of the situation.
23   Stolle 1980, p. 268.
24   Schöck 1977, p. 177.
25   Heer-Kleinert 1983, p. 333.

props of the foreign policy of the imperialist German bourgeoisie' and the fight against the 'Left SPD' as 'the main enemy within the SPD' was stressed.[26]

During the next few years, when actual Fascism was on the increase in the shape of Hitler's NSDAP, the Social Democrats continued to be referred to as 'Social Fascists' (6.13), although there was some disagreement in communist circles about whether they were more or less dangerous to the working class than the Hitler movement. Almost at the last moment, in May 1932, the KPD unveiled its plan for an 'Anti-Fascist Action' to 'bar Hitler Fascism from taking the path to power'. This looked like a reversal of policy, and there were even scenes of fraternisation between communists and social democrats in Berlin,[27] but the guidelines issued immediately afterwards made it plain that 'the decisive strategic orientation remains to strike the main blows within the working class against Social Democracy' and that the only permissible form of united front was the 'united front from below'. The SPD executive responded by rejecting the united front offer and warning that 'the so-called Anti-Fascist Action is in reality nothing other than an Anti-Social Democratic Action.'[28] So the whole idea came to nothing.

We have not limited ourselves to questions of high politics in this collection of documents. After all, both the SPD and the KPD wanted in their different ways to promote the welfare of ordinary people, and this meant taking up the cause of the working class as a whole and agitating in favour of various particularly oppressed groups within it. This category includes the unemployed, the old, the sick, the disabled veterans of the War, and the agricultural workers. The SPD was somewhat handicapped in this respect because it was a party of government and had to take into account its coalition partners, and also the financial situation. As Matthew Stibbe has written, the SPD 'burned its bridges with the poorest members of society, not least because of its association with Weimar housing and welfare policies, especially at local level'.[29] This is perhaps too harsh a judgment; one should not forget that until the onset of the Depression local SPD councillors and officials made 'painstaking and persistent efforts'[30] to promote social welfare. After 1929 they were forced by sheer lack of money to cut down on the support they gave to welfare claimants. The KPD had fewer constraints on the policies it put forward. In some ways the leftist, 'third period', 'class against class' policy adopted after 1928 freed the Party to

---

26 Fowkes 1984, pp. 142–3.
27 Drechsler 1965, p. 260.
28 Mallmann 1996, p. 378.
29 Stibbe 2010, p. 112.
30 Crew 1998, p. 226.

seek out and make use of 'even the smallest instances of protest by the masses against exploitation',[31] since its aim was in the immediate term to gain as much support as possible from discontented groups and in the longer term not to reform the system but to smash it. Working-class women continued to suffer disproportionately under Weimar and there were numerous causes the Party could take up in this connection. The KPD was able to take an approach that was more in line with feminist ideas than the SPD on issues like abortion, the free availability of birth control, sex education, equality in the workplace, and equal opportunity to gain employment, but there were also many women in the SPD who would have liked their Party to take a stronger line on issues like the dismissal of women manual workers after 1918 to make room for returning soldiers (9.3, 9.7) or on equality within the Party (9.8, 9.11). They were less keen on decriminalising abortion than the KPD, which in 1931 fought a high-profile campaign to get rid of paragraph 218 of the penal law, which prohibited abortion. It was also the only party to advocate the complete abolition of the law which made homosexual acts a criminal offence (paragraph 175), although the SPD did vote in favour of restricting its scope considerably.

Another objective both parties shared was to raise the cultural level of the workers, through socialist education and through the organisation of leisure activities. People participated enthusiastically in these, sometimes too enthusiastically for the functionaries of the KPD. Eric Weitz quotes a report of 1926 to the Central Committee complaining that party members spent too much time singing in choirs, playing chess and riding their bicycles and too little time doing party work.[32] The press and various periodicals made perhaps a greater contribution to socialist education. One aspect of this was the fight against bourgeois ideology, conducted very strenuously by the KPD but not entirely ignored by the SPD. The promotion of a secular outlook and the replacement of church burial by cremation was one aspect of this, initially conducted by organisations of 'free thinkers' not attached to either party (11.5, 11.6), until the communists decided in 1929 to split all the broad-based workers' cultural organisations, a move that met with resistance from some party members who preferred to stay in the old ones.[33]

With the appearance of a strong mass movement of the extreme right, which can be dated from as early as 1923, self-defence started to be a priority for both parties. As mentioned earlier, one way the SPD defended itself

---

31   The words of a resolution on the tasks of communist parties issued by the Eleventh ECCI
       Plenum in 1931 (Carr 1982, pp. 37–8).
32   Weitz 1998, p. 282.
33   See the evidence presented in Mallmann 1996, p. 179.

was by seeking agreements with parties to the right of it. This did not exclude self-defence, however. The *Reichsbanner Schwarz-Rot-Gold* (National Flag of Black, Red and Gold) was set up in that year as an organisation of democratic war veterans (11.5). It was intended to include supporters of Weimar democracy in general, although in practice its members were largely Social Democrats. In some areas, such as Saxony, the *Reichsbanner* had violent confrontations with the Nazis, but its main activities were peaceful demonstrations and marches. A more effective method of defending democracy was the general strike. This was used once, and very successfully, against the Kapp[34] putsch in 1920 (4.1, 4.2, 4.3, 4.4) but the experiment was not repeated. At a number of key moments in the early 1930s the leaders of the Party and the Free Trade Unions discussed the possibility of a general strike, but they decided that it was inappropriate as well as physically impossible given the high level of unemployment (4.15). They preferred to fight elections, in the hope that the democratic parties together would gain enough seats to keep the republic in existence by majority vote. The reduction in the Nazi vote at the November 1932 elections appeared to give some justification to this. As is well known, however, the forces which manipulated the aging President Hindenburg were not really interested in preserving democracy. The SPD was therefore unable to prevent the collapse of the Weimar Republic and the coming to power of Adolf Hitler.

Both the SPD and the KPD were mass parties, and questions arising from this are examined in Chapter Ten. How did they gain and retain support? Did they appeal to particular groups, or have strongholds in particular regions of the country? Was support consistent or variable? How were the parties organised? Were they embedded in a milieu? Was there a single 'left proletarian' milieu which embraced supporters of both parties, or did political divisions eventually create social divisions? In particular, did communists and social democrats live unconnected lives in separate communities? There is much dispute about the milieu question, with the main recent protagonists being Hermann Weber, Klaus-Michael Mallmann and Andreas Wirsching. The answer perhaps lies in a more nuanced examination of local conditions. Germany was still a big country, even after the territorial losses of 1918–19, and each region had its own characteristics. The local character of the parties and their adherents reflected these divergences. There are a number of local studies which bring out the differences both between regions and within the regions themselves. The situation of the proletarian enclave of Penzberg in southern Bavaria as

---

34   Wolfgang Kapp (1858–1922), right-wing nationalist politician, founded the Fatherland
        Party in 1917, mounted the Kapp putsch in 1920, fled, returned to Germany, was arrested,
        died before his trial, and was posthumously amnestied by President Hindenburg in 1925.

an island in a sea of small farmers is one example.[35] Another is the contrast in Saxony between the small textile workshops of the Erzgebirge, with their weakly developed socialist milieu organisations and the big factories of the north-west and the centre of the province with their strongly implanted socialist groups which were much more resistant to the rise of Nazism in later years.[36] Many other examples could be given.

The documents printed here are intended to stand by themselves, although I have added explanatory notes to individual documents where I thought it necessary. I have also included short biographies of leading figures on the Weimar Left at appropriate points in the text. In the present selection the endeavour has been made to give due representation to the different viewpoints taken in both the SPD and the KPD on a whole range of issues, from the prospects for revolution right through to the social and legal consequences of sexual activity.

---

35   Tenfelde 1982.
36   Laporte 2003, pp. 35–6.

CHAPTER 1

Social Democracy in Government: Measures of Reform in Theory and Practice

Introduction

The German Social Democrats (SPD) were in government nationally[1] for a total of five years out of the 14 years of the Weimar Republic's uneasy survival.[2] They were also in office locally[3] for much longer than that, particularly in Prussia. Their ability to pursue their own distinctive policies, however, was restricted for most of the time by the presence of non-socialist coalition partners. Nevertheless, in the first two years after the November Revolution of 1918 they

---

1 In other words, at the level of the German Reich as a whole. One of the features of the compromise that founded the Weimar Republic was the retention of the word 'Reich' to describe the whole country, although the 'Second Reich' ceased to exist with the establishment of the Republic.

2 The SPD participated in the following Reich cabinets during the Weimar period: November 1918 to February 1919: Council of People's Representatives (SPD alone or in coalition with the USPD); February 1919 to June 1919: Scheidemann Cabinet (SPD-DDP-Centre coalition); June 1919 to March 1920: Bauer Cabinet (SPD-DDP-Centre coalition); March to June 1920: First Müller Cabinet (SPD-DDP-Centre coalition); May to October 1921: First Wirth Cabinet (Centre-SPD-DDP); October 1921 to November 1922: Second Wirth Cabinet (Centre-SPD-DDP); August 1923 to October 1923: First Stresemann Cabinet (DVP-Centre-DDP-SPD); October 1923 to 3 November 1923: Second Stresemann Cabinet (DVP-Centre-DDP-SPD); June 1928 to March 1930: Second Müller Cabinet (SPD-Centre-BVP-DDP-DVP).

3 Local politics is a very wide field, which I have not tried to treat in detail. It covers everything below the national (Reich) level, in other words from the largest sub-unit, the State (Land) (there were 18 of these) down through the Province (Provinz), the District (Regierungsbezirk), the County (Kreis), and the City (Stadt) to the smallest, the Rural District (Gemeinde). The SPD was in government locally during much of the Weimar period in Prussia, Saxony, Hamburg, Baden, Hesse, and many smaller states as well, and was therefore often able to appoint the officials who controlled the smaller units. It also had a majority in many elected city councils. The Party achieved a great deal at this local level in areas such as social welfare, health, education and training, although the onset of the Great Depression after 1929 undermined many of these achievements. On welfare, see Crew 1998 and Young-Sun Hong 1998 and on education, see Lamberti 2002. Whether housing should be added to this list is doubtful. It has been suggested that the many new dwellings built by SPD-run municipalities in the 1920s were simply too expensive for the ordinary working-class person (Silverman 1970, pp. 112–39).

had greater room for manoeuvre because defeat in the First World War and the collapse of the old ruling system led to a temporary loss of confidence on the part of their 'bourgeois'[4] colleagues and opponents. There was also greater pressure than later from forces to the left of them, both inside and outside the Party. Hence many more Social Democratic measures of reform were passed, or at least adumbrated, in these two years than at any later time.

The unifying theme in this first chapter, which deals essentially with Social Democracy's first two years in government after 1918, is provided by the interplay between the responsibilities of power and the pressure of mass action from below. This process can be summed up in general terms as a conflict between Majority Social Democracy (MSPD)[5] and the parties to the left of it for the allegiance of the working class. Under Weimar (as well as in the transitional pre-Weimar situation of the rule of the Council of People's Representatives between the end of the War and February 1919) the SPD saw itself as a party of government, with all the compromises and modifications of socialist principles that that implied, but it still contained many people who were unhappy with its governmental role and who hankered after the greater political purity afforded by opposition. In contrast to this, its rival the Communist Party of Germany (KPD)[6] was identified with mass revolutionary action, but at this early stage it was not the only candidate for the title of 'the party of the revolution'. Until autumn 1920 it was politically overshadowed by the Independent Social Democrats (USPD).[7] Within two years, however, the Independents disintegrated, partly because they combined a number of contradictory elements, but also because of the evaporation of their initial hope that the spontaneous, unorganised elements of socialism which were growing out of the economic conditions of the time would gain a victory over the old

---

4 *Bürgerlich*: this word was almost always used by SPD members to refer to their non-socialist colleagues (Wilhelm Keil was an exception: see 7.15). It implies that a political line can be identified with membership of a particular social class, and presupposes a Marxist or Marxist-influenced perspective; the 'bourgeois' politicians did not generally return the compliment by referring to their SPD colleagues as 'working class'. I use the word in the documents that follow as the most convenient and appropriate translation.

5 *Mehrheitssozialdemokratische Partei Deutschlands* (Majority Social Democratic Party of Germany). This was their official title, adopted after the 1917 split so as to distinguish them from the Independent SPD (USPD). It was retained until reunification with the USPD remnant in September 1922. Since most authors refer to the MSPD simply as the SPD I shall also do this from now on, where possible.

6 *Kommunistische Partei Deutschlands* (Communist Party of Germany).

7 *Unabhängige Sozialdemokratische Partei Deutschlands* (Independent Social Democratic Party of Germany).

system. This spontaneous move towards a kind of socialism, with which the various councils of workers and soldiers were associated, was not identified with any particular party, and its objectives were very unclear, but it played a highly significant part in the history of the first few years after the fall of the German Empire. We shall present the Council System in more detail in Chapter Two of this book. Its main achievement was to force various measures of socialisation[8] on an unwilling SPD government, which was also put under strong pressure in this direction by the 1919 movement for workers' control among the coalminers of the Ruhr (see 1.5, 1.8, 1.9).

It was a fixed principle with the SPD leaders that reforms must come through constitutional, parliamentary action and in no other way. As Friedrich Ebert[9] said shortly after the November Revolution: 'Democracy is the only rock upon which the working class can erect the edifice of Germany's future'.[10] The first and most important task, in the SPD's view, was to establish a fully democratic[11] parliamentary constitution, in collaboration with the liberals. It was possible to include in the constitution certain references to elements of socialism, although it remained to be seen whether these would be put into effect. Constitutionalism naturally implied rejecting communist attempts to impose socialism by force, and thus 'defence against Bolshevism was the strongest tie that bound together the men of the old and new regimes in Germany'.[12] It is something of a paradox that the heyday of reform through parliament came at the outset of the Weimar period, and coincided with the most violent phenomena of mass agitation and semi-civil war. The contradiction in the SPD's position under Weimar was that only a lively mass movement (of which it was

---

8   The word 'socialisation' (*Sozialisierung*, also sometimes *Vergesellschaftlichung*) was generally used at this time to cover what in English would be described as 'nationalisation', and I have adopted it as it reflects its supporters' objective of bringing industries under the control of society, as distinct from the state.

9   Friedrich Ebert (1871–1925) started work as a saddler. Trade unionist and SPD member. General Secretary of the SPD 1905–13. Chair of the SPD 1913–19. Member of the Council of People's Representatives 1918–19. President of Germany 1919–25.

10 Speech of 16 December 1918. (*Deutscher Geschichtskalender* 1919, 35.1.1, pp. 153–4, 202–3.)

11 Universal suffrage was introduced in 1919 for elections to all national and local assemblies in Germany, but it should be noted that top local officials in Prussia continued to be appointed by the government and not elected, and also that by 1929 only 4 out of 12 Provincial Governors and 6 out of 32 District Directors were Social Democrats (Runge 1965, p. 201)

12 Miller 1979, p. 196. This book is the most thorough treatment of the SPD's early years in government.

highly suspicious) could provide the impulse and generate the necessary terror among the middle classes for radical reform to be implemented. Once the mass movement had been liquidated there was no further reason to tolerate socialist interference in the economy, or anywhere else. For this reason, the reforms of 1918–19 proved impossible to defend in the long run. By 1924 it was difficult for the workers to see in the Weimar Republic the state they had brought into existence by revolutionary means in November 1918'.[13] Later on, in Chapters 4 and 5 of this collection, we shall cover the attempts made by the Social Democrats to defend early achievements such as the right to work, the eight-hour working day, the democratic system, and indeed the Weimar Republic itself, against the resurgent traditionalist Right which wanted in essence to restore the pre-1918 system, and the New Right represented by Hitler's Party the NSDAP[14] which had other far more sinister ideas.

In 1920 the SPD left the government, and although it returned to office as a coalition partner in bourgeois governments several times in subsequent years, it no longer exerted a decisive influence on them. In 1928, however, after achieving improved electoral results, the SPD was again able to form a government, in coalition with the largely Roman Catholic Centre Party, the left liberals (DDP)[15] and the liberal-conservatives (DVP).[16] This cabinet was headed by Hermann Müller. Although the coalition parties agreed on foreign and defence policy, conflicts quickly arose over taxes and unemployment. The SPD Finance Minister, Rudolf Hilferding,[17] wanted to raise taxes to cover a budget deficit; but the most right-wing party in the coalition, the DVP, wanted to deal with the problem by reducing social expenditure instead. It was a classic left-right disagreement, which worsened from 1929 onwards with the onset of the economic crisis.[18] The Foreign Minister, Gustav Stresemann, the leader of the DVP, was able to compel his Party to compromise with the SPD while he was alive, but he died in October 1929, just after brokering one final compromise, over changes in the Unemployment Insurance Law.[19] The coalition did not last much longer. We shall examine its break-up in Chapter 5.

---

13   Winkler 1985, p. 731.

14   *Nationalsozialistische Deutsche Arbeiterpartei* (National Socialist German Workers' Party).

15   *Deutsche Demokratische Partei* (German Democratic Party).

16   *Deutsche Volkspartei* (German People's Party).

17   Rudolf Hilferding (1877–1941), USPD 1917–22, then SPD. Finance Minister in 1923 and 1928–29. In SPD top leadership 1922–29, 1931–33.

18   See in detail Leuschen-Seppel 1981.

19   See Chapter 5 for the break-up of the Müller coalition cabinet.

Documents

1.1   *Proclamation of the Council of People's Representatives,*
       12 November 1918

To the German People!

The government which has emerged from the revolution, the political leadership of which is purely socialist, has set itself the task of putting into effect the socialist programme. We hereby proclaim the following points, which will enter into immediate legal effect:

1 The state of siege is abolished.
2 The right of association and assembly is no longer subject to any restriction, even for officials and those who work for the state.
3 There is to be no censorship. Theatre censorship is also abolished.
4 The expression of opinion in speech and writing is free of restriction.
5 Freedom of religious observance is guaranteed. No one may be compelled to take part in a religious activity.
6 An amnesty is granted for all political offences. All proceedings pending on account of such offences are hereby quashed.
7 The law on auxiliary service for the Fatherland is abrogated, with the exception of the provisions relating to the settlement of disputes.
8 The Agricultural Servants' Ordinances are set aside, as also the exceptional laws against rural workers.
9 The provisions to protect labour, which were suspended at the beginning of the war, are hereby brought into effect once again.

Further ordinances in the field of social policy will be published shortly. A maximum working day of eight hours will enter into force on 1 January 1919 at the latest. The government will do everything it can to make sure there are enough opportunities to secure work. We have prepared a set of rules for the maintenance of the unemployed. It divides the burden between the Reich, the States and the municipalities.

As regards insurance against sickness, the obligatory level of insurance is to be raised above the previous limit of 2,500 Marks. We shall combat the housing shortage by providing new dwellings.

We shall work towards securing an orderly supply of food for the people. The orderly flow of production will be maintained by the government, property will be protected from attacks by private persons, and the liberty and safety of the individual will be protected. All elections to public bodies are henceforth to take place on the basis of proportional representation with equal, secret, direct and universal suffrage for all male and female persons who are at least twenty years old. This electoral law is also valid for the Constituent Assembly, for which more specific regulations will later be issued.

Ebert, Haase, Scheidemann, Landsberg, Dittmann, Barth

Source: Deutsches Reich 1918, *Reichsgesetzblatt 1918*, p. 1303.

Note: The Council of People's Representatives (*Rat der Volksbeauftragten*) ruled Germany from the November Revolution of 1918 until February 1919. It began as a coalition between the Majority Social Democrats (MSPD) and the Independent Social Democrats (USPD, which had emerged as separate parties from the former SPD after the split of 1917. Each party had three representatives, Friedrich Ebert, Philipp Scheidemann and Otto Landsberg[20] for the MSPD, Hugo Haase,[21] Wilhelm Dittmann[22] and Emil Barth[23] for the USPD. On 29 December 1918 the three USPD representatives withdrew from the Council in protest against the MSPD's decision to call on the military forces of the old army to suppress a sailors' mutiny (See Section Two). They were replaced by two members of the MSPD: Gustav Noske[24] and Rudolf Wissell.

1.2 *The Agreement for Co-Operation Made on 15 November 1918 Between 21 Employers' Associations and 7 Trade Unions*

The major employers' associations have arrived at the following arrangements with the trade unions of the workforce:

1 The trade unions are recognised as the qualified representatives of the workers
2 All restrictions on the freedom of male and female workers to form trade unions are impermissible

---

20 Otto Landsberg (1869–1957), SPD, People's Representative 1918–19, Reich Minister of Justice 1919, German Ambassador to Belgium 1920–24, member of the Reichstag 1924–33.

21 Hugo Haase (1863–1919), USPD chair, 1917–19. People's Representative November-December 1918, murdered 1919.

22 Wilhelm Dittmann (1874–1954), USPD 1917–22, member of the Council of People's Representatives 1918–19, member of the SPD executive from 1922 onwards.

23 Emil Barth (1879–1941), Revolutionary Shop Steward 1918, USPD 1918–22, member of the Council of People's Representatives 1918, SPD 1922.

24 Gustav Noske (1868–1946), SPD, Governor of Kiel in 1918, in charge of military forces in Berlin 1919, Reich Minister of Defence 1919–20, Governor of the Prussian province of Hanover 1920–33.

3 The employers and the employers' associations will henceforth no longer either directly or indirectly support the labour unions (*Werkvereine*),[25] the so-called industrially peaceful unions, completely leaving them to their fate.

4 Immediately after reporting back from military service, all workers have the right to take up again the job that they had before the War started. The employers' associations and trade unions participating in this agreement will work to ensure that this obligation can be fulfilled to its full extent, by procuring raw materials and signing labour contracts.

5 The labour exchanges are to be regulated jointly, and administered on a basis of equality.

6 The conditions of labour for all male and female workers are to be fixed in accordance with the situation prevailing in the relevant trade by means of collective agreements with the workers' professional associations. Negotiations on the point are to be begun without delay, and brought to a conclusion as quickly as possible.

7 A Factory Committee is to be set up in every enterprise with a labour force of at least 50 employees, to represent them, and to make sure, together with the employers, that the conditions prevailing in the enterprise are regulated in accordance with the collective agreements.

8 The collective agreements are to provide for committees or offices for the settlement of disputes, such committees to consist of representatives of the workers and the employers in equal numbers.

9 The maximum length of the normal working day is fixed at eight hours for all enterprises. No reduction in earnings is to take place on account of this shortening of working time.

10 The employers' and workers' organisations participating in this agreement will set up a Central Commission, on a basis of parity in numbers, and with subsections organised according to profession, for the following purposes: to implement the present agreement, and to settle the further measures to be taken for demobilisation, for the maintenance of economic life, and for securing the workers' ability to make a living, especially the severely war-wounded.

11 The Central Commission will further be responsible for deciding questions of principle, to the extent that they emerge, as for example from the collective regulation of wages and working conditions. It will also be responsible for the peaceful settlement of disputes affecting

---

25 *Werkvereine*: alternative, non-striking trade unions set up by the employers, often referred to disparagingly as 'Yellow Unions'. They continued to exist throughout the Weimar period despite this promise. See Mattheier 1973.

several professional groups simultaneously. Its decisions will be binding on employers and workers if they are not contested within a week by one or other of the professional associations involved in the dispute, on either side.

12 This agreement enters into the force on the date of signature. It is valid, subject to legal regulations made elsewhere, until further notice, such notice to be given by either side three months in advance of termination. It is also intended to be valid, analogously, for the relationship between the employers' associations and associations of salaried employees (*Angestelltenverbände*).

Berlin, 15 November 1918

[There follows a list of 21 employers' associations in the iron and steel, textile, chemistry, coalmining, electrical goods and other industries, and 7 trade unions, headed by the General Commission of the Trade Unions of Germany, with the signatures of accredited representatives of all these bodies.]

Source: Deutsches Reich 1918, *Reichsanzeiger* No. 273, 18 November 1918.

Note: The origins of this remarkable agreement lie in the summer of 1918, when certain industrialists, aware of Imperial Germany's impending military defeat, decided to make contact with the top trade union leaders to discuss ways of easing the transition to peacetime labour conditions. The latter were happy to concur with the suggestion that they cooperate with the other side of industry, and barely a week after the November 1918 Revolution the negotiations resulted in an agreement between the major industrial firms and the three trade union confederations, the Free Trade Unions (ADGB),[26] the Christian (Catholic) and the Hirsch-Duncker (Liberal) trade unions. The Council of People's Representatives unanimously accepted this. Ebert and Haase issued a statement requesting the directors of all state and communal enterprises to comply with it. It was clear that the trade unions had now achieved full recognition, at least on paper, as equal partners in negotiations over wage contracts. The trade union leaders regarded the body set up in the agreement, the Central

---

26   *Allgemeine Deutscher Gewerkschaftsbund* (General German Trade Union Confederation). This, by far the largest trade union confederation, was in theory neutral and independent of political parties, but in practice it was close to Social Democracy. Its leaders were overwhelmingly Social Democrats, and 80 percent of its members voted for the SPD at elections (Hunt 1964, p. 169).

Association for Cooperation (ZAG)[27] as an effective counter to the Council movement which threatened them from below, and as a means of drawing more layers of the population into their orbit through the evident success of their policy of cooperation.

This cooperation between employers and trade unions was, however, strictly temporary. It could only last while the post-war boom smoothed over any conflicts over the distribution of profits. Once the squeeze came, with the stabilisation of the Mark and the end of the inflation, in November 1923, the ZAG lost its value for the employers. They began to set harsher and harsher conditions for continued cooperation, until finally the trade union side pulled out of the Association in protest against the abandonment of the principle of parity between employers' and workers' representatives (1924). From that time onwards, the employers settled their affairs by direct negotiations with the relevant trade unions outside the kind of formal collaborative framework represented by the ZAG. Not everyone on the Left regretted this outcome. The parties to the left of the SPD had always opposed the ZAG (which they referred to disparagingly as the 'Stinnes-Legien Agreement') as an example of class collaboration, and there were more and more complaints even from moderate SPD-inclined trade union leaders as the consequences of compromise with the employers became ever clearer. When in 1926 the industrialist Paul Silverberg proposed the renewal of the ZAG the trade unions were very sceptical of the idea.[28] In any case Silverberg was unable to overcome the opposition of his colleagues in the mining industry.

1.3 Demobilisation Office Ordinance Establishing a Maximum Working Day of Eight Hours for Industrial Workers, 23 November 1918 (extract)

This regulation covers industrial workers in all industrial enterprises including mining. It includes enterprises owned by the Reich, the States, the town councils and the associations of town councils, even where they are not conducted with the aim of making a profit. It also covers workers employed in agriculturally-related enterprises of an industrial kind.

The regular daily working time, exclusive of breaks, is not permitted to exceed eight hours in duration. If a different arrangement has been made by agreement through a reduction of working hours on the evenings preceding Sundays and holidays, the missing working hours on those days can be distributed among the remaining working days.

---

27 German: *Zentralarbeitsgemeinschaft*.
28 See for example Lothar Erdmann's article in the main trade union journal (Erdmann 1926, pp. 641–52).

Source: Deutsches Reich 1918 *Reichsgesetzblatt 1918*, p. 1334.

Note: A further regulation, issued on 18 March 1919, introduced the eight-hour working day for office employees as well. Both regulations were issued by the Demobilisation Office, which had been set up to facilitate the reintegration of demobilised soldiers into the workforce, and were thus strictly temporary. Discussions over the next four years failed to produce a lasting agreement between workers and employers' organisations on the length of the working day. The trade unions were in practice strong enough to hold on to the eight-hour day until the crisis of 1923. Then, on 21 December 1923 a provisional Decree on Hours of Work was issued, retaining the eight-hour day, but allowing so many exceptions that the restriction on hours lost all practical significance.[29]

1.4 'Up with Social Democracy!' The Editorial of 8 December 1918 in the Social Democratic Newspaper Vorwärts (extract)

A Sunday has dawned, the like of which Berlin has never yet experienced. A dull feeling of tension dominates the giant city, which awaits the coming events like a patient sacrificial victim. Even at this moment we should like to avoid giving up the hope that tomorrow the population will heave a liberating sigh of relief, and that the *tranquillity*, the *composure*, which have always distinguished the proletariat of Berlin will be maintained today as well.

It is senseless to employ violence, because it cannot change anything in the existing relations of power. A counter-revolutionary *putsch* and a Spartacist coup are equally senseless, because they can only lead to a fresh loss of human life without attaining their goal. The adventurers who made Berlin unsafe on Friday, and whose guilt no one wishes to belittle or gloss over, could think of nothing better to do than to offer comrade Ebert a promotion which he declined with thanks.[30] The supporters of Spartacus know, however, to the extent that they have retained a grain of common sense, that an attempted coup would have no prospect of success, and that even in the wholly improbable event of its succeeding, a Liebknecht-Luxemburg government wouldn't even last three days because it would have the whole nation against it.

---

29   Preller 1949, p. 275.
30   On Friday 6 December 1918 a group of soldiers, acting on the orders of Count von Stumm, of the German Foreign Office, attempted to proclaim Ebert President of Germany; at the same time another group stormed the House of Deputies and arrested the members of the Greater Berlin Executive Council of Workers' and Soldiers' Councils, a USPD-dominated body. The whole thing in effect amounted to an attempted putsch in favour of the Majority Socialists with the aim of driving the Independents out of the government.

The declaration of the Reich government which was affixed to the columns yesterday gives in brief the results of the investigation made of Friday's events. It emerges from this that a *couple of petty officials of the Foreign Office* with high-sounding aristocratic names set in motion this impertinent pseudo-coup. They are the ones who led the soldiers astray. One hardly knows what to be more amazed at: these gentlemen's lack of scruples or their incomprehensible stupidity. The harm they have done is immense. The Social Democratic government is taking pains to work in cooperation with the officials of the old régime, and an obvious prerequisite for this is naturally those officials' *obedience* to superior authority. But these two minor characters have boldly pursued an adventurist policy on their own authority and with sovereign indifference to the criminal law, thereby bringing their whole caste into disrepute. They have only themselves to blame for the consequences. Such stupidity deserves no mercy.

The tragic events in the Chausseestrasse are still in need of an explanation.[31] But in contrast to the *Freiheit*,[32] which steps protectively in front of Spartacus, the whole of the bourgeois press finds the treatment of that group by the Social Democrats and the *Vorwärts* much too gentle. The bourgeois press seems to us still to be far too much caught up in the habits of thought of the old days. It is also very much inferior to English liberalism in placing its faith in the power of the police and the military to bring universal salvation. We regard the freedom of all citizens as a possession so precious that for its sake even certain dangers and inconveniences must be taken on board. What we have never conceded, however, and never will, is the right of a minority to rule over a majority by force. Where an attempt is made to set up such a system of government you will find us in the front rank of the resistance to it, whereas the bourgeoisie, always more cautious, will perhaps slip quietly away ...

On 9 November the workers of Berlin learned to their great joy that the two socialist tendencies had joined together for *common action*, that the *fratricidal conflict was going to come to an end*. We are, and we remain, the upholders of the idea of unity, but we reject any cooperation with elements who have abandoned the ground of the Social Democratic programme, who want to treat the German people as an immature mass without a will of its own, and to impose their own domination by force. Let them see today how few they are in number, and how many there are of us! We demonstrate for peace, freedom,

---

31   This is a reference to an incident on 6 December when a detachment of soldiers armed with machine-guns fired on a crowd of unarmed Spartacist demonstrators in the Chausseestrasse in Berlin, killing sixteen on them.

32   The main press organ of the Independent Social Democrats (USPD).

and bread, for the consolidation of the achievements of the revolution, *for the democratic order and for socialism*. Forward with the masses!

Source: *Vorwärts* No. 337, 8 December 1918

1.5   *Rudolf Hilferding's Speech at the First Congress of Workers' and Soldiers' Councils Arguing against the Immediate Socialisation of Industry, 18 December 1918 (extracts)*

It is our deeply tragic fate to have come to power at a moment when our inheritance has been despoiled and ruined. We must take over an economy that has been bled white and is short of raw materials. Its productive capacity is practically in ruins, and its working class has been weakened by undernourishment and crippled by the War. All these circumstances render the task of socialisation[33] uncommonly difficult. This does not mean that the undertaking is impossible; but it does mean that we need longer to complete it. Our first task is to set the economy in motion again. On the one hand, certain areas of the economy must be excluded at the outset from socialisation: agricultural production by peasant farms, and export industries, for we need the latter to restore foreign trade and bring in raw materials from abroad. But, on the other hand, socialisation will have to extend to all the areas where capitalist concentration through cartels and trusts has prepared the way for an organised socialist economy.

When we speak of socialisation we must be clear as to what we mean by this. It does not mean that the workers take over the factories directly. That would give rise to a series of factory associations but it would not alter the character of capitalist society. The idea of producers' associations goes back a long way in Germany, but it has been completely discredited. Socialisation can only mean that the whole of production is transferred gradually to the community so that it is at its disposal. Which branches of industry should come first? If we ask which branches are ripe for socialisation, we can answer that they are ripe if they (1) provide articles of mass consumption (2) are at a high level of technical and economic concentration, and (3) are of great economic importance owing to the kind of commodities they produce. All these conditions are fulfilled in the mining industry, including the extraction of coal, iron and potassium from the ground, and the initial stages of the manufacture of iron.

What other areas can be taken over? In Russia the banks were taken over first, relying on my own arguments in *Finance Capital*[34] about their power. But we need the credit the banks provide so as to resuscitate industry, and we

---

33   See above, note 8.
34   Originally published in 1910 as *Das Finanzkapital*.

cannot take over the whole of industry at one stroke. The activity of the banks is therefore indispensable.

Should we confiscate or compensate? I am convinced that the idea of simple confiscation would be incorrect. If we cannot immediately organise the whole of production in a socialist way, a wide range of inequalities would arise: some capitalists would be expropriated, other would carry on privately. Large-scale property would conceal its own possessions by splitting them up into small parts and evading confiscation. A wealth tax would yield copious amounts, and it would achieve as much as we might attain, unevenly and incompletely, by confiscation.

A political revolution is an act which lasts a relatively short time. Not so the replacement of one economic formation by another. Economic formations do not disappear in one day or one month. It is clear that a socialist society can only be set up in an organic fashion, and this requires a fair amount of time. It would be a completely topsy-turvy idea to think that this process could be arbitrarily accelerated, and enterprises could simply be handed over to certain categories of worker. What is at stake here is not the handing over of wealth but the re-organisation of whole branches of industry. Time is needed. But the proletariat can spare the time.

Socialism is something more elevated than a movement for a pay increase. Socialism happens when a new spirit seizes hold of humanity, when people no longer ask themselves 'How can I live, eat, drink today?' but humanity instead concerns itself with the grand problems. It happens when the animal in us is replaced by the spiritual, by the ideal.

Source: Allgemeiner Kongress der Arbeiter- und Soldatenräte Deutschlands 1918., *Vom 16. bis 21. Dezember 1918 im Abgeordnetenhause zu Berlin. Stenographische Berichte*, Berlin, 1919, cols. 312–321, 9th. session, 18 December 1918, morning.

Note: Hilferding was contradicted later in the debate by his USPD colleague Emil Barth, who called for 'socialisation not in months but in a few short days'. Nevertheless, a resolution in line with Hilferding's conception of socialisation was passed unanimously. It called on the government to begin without delay the socialisation of all industries considered ripe for this, mining in particular.

1.6 *Friedrich Ebert's Address to the Opening Session of the Constituent National Assembly, 6 February 1919*

Ladies and Gentlemen, the government of the Reich, through me, greets the Constituent Assembly of the German Nation. In the Revolution the German people rose up against the violent rule of an outdated and collapsing system.

(Vocal assent from the left; violent disagreement from the right).[35] This National Assembly is the supreme and the sole sovereign in Germany. The old kings and princes by the grace of God will never return. The German people are free, will remain free, and will rule themselves in the future, forever. Freedom is the only consolation left to the German people, the only strong point which makes it possible to work our way out of the bloodstained swamp of war and defeat. We have lost the War. This fact is not a consequence of the Revolution. (Violent disagreement from the right). The Revolution rejects all responsibility for the misery into which the German people have been thrown by the mistaken policies of the old authorities and the arrogance of the militarists. It is also not responsible for the severe food shortage.

The armistice conditions are unbelievably harsh. Alsace is treated as French land without any discussion. Germans have been driven out of the territory, German possessions have been taken into administration. Even though we have long been in no condition to start the War again, 800,000 of our war prisoners have still not been returned to us. These acts of violence do not indicate a spirit of reconciliation. We warn our opponents not to push us to the limit. A German government might one day be forced to give up working on the peace negotiations. We are presented with the fateful choice between starvation and humiliation. Even a socialist government, or indeed precisely a socialist government, must stick to the principle: better the heaviest sacrifice than dishonour (Storms of applause) ... We have fought to achieve our right of self-determination within the country. We cannot abandon the hope of uniting the whole German nation within one Reich. (Bravo!) German-Austria must be united with the motherland for all eternity. Our comrades in race and destiny may be assured that we greet them with open arms in the new Reich of the German nation. They belong to us, and we belong to them. No boundary-post should stand between us. Germany cannot be allowed to fall victim again to the tragedy of fragmentation and constriction. Many tribes and many dialects are united together in Germany, but they form a single nation and speak a single language.

Ladies and gentlemen, the Provisional Government took over a very disagreeable inheritance. We were in the true meaning of the phrase the 'trustees in bankruptcy' of the old régime: all the barns were empty, all supplies were on the verge of running out, credit had collapsed, morale was very low. We exerted all our strength, supported and encouraged by the Central Council of Workers'

---

35   All the words in parenthesis are taken from the stenographic report of Ebert's speech.

and Soldiers' Councils[36] (laughter on the right) to combat the dangers and the misery of the period of transition. We have not sought to anticipate the decisions of the National Assembly. But where time was short and the need was great we endeavoured to fulfil the most urgent demands made by the workers.

We have done everything we could to restore economic life (repeated objections from the right)... and you (turning to the right) are apparently completely ignorant of what had to be done to set the economy going again. If we were not as successful as we might have hoped, the circumstances that prevented this must in justice be borne in mind. (Cries of 'Very true!' from the Social Democrats). Many employers, spoiled by the giant national market of the wartime economy and the elevated and certain profits conceded to them by the monarcho-militarist state, have forgotten how to develop the necessary initiative (Very good!). We therefore urgently appeal to them to promote the restoration of production with all their strength.

Equally, we call on the working class to exert all its strength in labour. This is the only thing that can save us (Lively shouts of approval from the Social Democrats; dissent from the USPD). We understand the emotional reaction of those who now seek relaxation after the excessive expenditure of vital forces during the War. We know how difficult it is for those who have spent years on the field of battle to find their way back to a peaceful life of labour. But this must happen. We must work and create value, otherwise ruin faces us. Socialism is in our opinion only possible if production is carried on at a sufficiently high level of efficiency. For us, socialism is organisation, order and solidarity, not unilateral action, egoism and destruction. Even the old state could not avoid extending its role in the economy to cover the immense war debts. In a time of universal need like the present, there should be no more room for private monopolies and profits gained without effort. We want to remove the profit element in a planned way where economic development has made an industry ripe for socialisation.

The future is full of care. But we place our trust, despite everything, in the inextinguishable creative force of the German nation. Here in Weimar we must make the change from *imperialism* to *idealism*... Now the spirit of Weimar, the spirit of the great philosophers and poets, must again fill our lives. (Objections from the USPD; cries of 'Bravo!' from the DDP). Let us set to work, with our great goal firmly fixed before our eyes, the goal of maintaining the rights of the

---

36   This refers to the institution set up on 19 December 1918 under the name Central Council of the German Socialist Republic. It had a purely MSPD membership as the USPD boycotted it.

German people, anchoring a strong democracy in Germany, and imbuing it with a truly social spirit and socialist deeds.

Source: Nationalversammlung 1920, *Stenographische Berichte über die Verhandlungen der verfassunggebenden deutschen Nationalversammlung*, vol. 326, 6 February 1919, pp. 1–3.

Note: Ebert's defence of the actions of his Party in November 1918 has been taken up by many subsequent historians. It was indeed true, as he said, that supplies of vital necessities were running out, and that it was essential to restore the functioning of the economy. It is, however, also possible to take the view that the SPD showed excessive timidity in 1918 in deciding to make as few changes as possible to the existing system and to leave the bureaucracy, the military and the judiciary, relatively untouched, out of a fear that otherwise, chaos would result.[37]

1.7 The Government Programme of 13 February 1919, Presented to the National Assembly by the SPD Reich Chancellor, Philipp Scheidemann

The Constituent German National Assembly is the sole repository of authority in the Reich. The unity of the Reich is to be firmly established through the creation of a strong central authority. Foreign policy, including foreign economic policy, will be conducted in a unified manner.

I   Foreign Policy
1 Immediate peace on the basis of the principles put forward by the President of the United States. Any imposed peace is to be rejected.
2 The restoration of Germany's colonial territories.
3 The immediate return of German prisoners of war.
4 Entry into the League of Nations with equal rights. Immediate mutual disarmament. Obligatory courts of arbitration for the prevention of future wars. The abolition of secret diplomacy.

II   Domestic Policy
1 A democratic administration. The ending of preferential treatment in appointments to official positions. The enlistment of women into the public services in accordance with the increased responsibility of women in all spheres of life.

---

37   For a useful summary of these discussions, see Gallus 2006, p. 149.

2 The raising of the general educational standard of the people by the greatest possible development of the school system, from the ground up.

3 The creation of a people's army built up on democratic foundations for the protection of the Fatherland. Every detachment of troops is to elect a Committee of Representatives to participate in the provision of food supplies, the granting of leave, and the organisation of accommodation, and to bring forward complaints. All soldiers at present in barracks are to be sent home. The military authorities which were established purely for the purposes of the war are to be abolished. Maintenance is to be provided for formerly active officers and NCOS.

4 Adequate provision is to be made for war widows and war-wounded servicemen.

5 A uniform foundation is to be laid for the reconstruction of economic life. The Reich must enter into the closest contact with the relevant groups and intervene to ensure that German economic life develops for the welfare of the whole people.

6 Rationing and limits on prices are to be retained initially in relation to the necessary means of subsistence, especially where these are in short supply.

7 Branches of the economy which have assumed the character of private monopolies, owing to their nature and the stage of development they have reached, are to be subjected to public control. Where they are suitable for overall control by society (this applies in particular to mines and the energy-producing industries) and are accordingly ripe for uniform regulation by society ('socialisation') they are to be taken over and run by the Reich, the States or the local authorities.

8 The universal right of association is to be established in the Constitution. Wages and working conditions are to be settled by agreement between the organisations of employers, workers and office employees. Representatives of the workers and employees are to supervise the implementation of such agreements. The whole of the law governing labour is to be adapted to the new circumstances.

9 In the field of social policy, a start should be made with the planned improvement of public health, protection of mothers, and care of children and young people. Labour exchanges are to be established as public institutions, with parity of representation, and provision is to be made for the unemployed where work cannot be procured for them.

10 State officials are to have professional and civil rights, including the right of association. Salaries and pensions are to be regulated anew in a manner appropriate to the present epoch. A liberal code of discipline is to be introduced.

11 Agricultural production is to be increased in small peasant, peasant and all other economically valuable forms of agricultural enterprise, particularly through the encouragement of the cooperative system. New land is to be obtained for settlement, both by improving the soil and by drawing on the resources of the large landed properties, if necessary through the application of a right of pre-emption or through confiscation.

12 Wartime profits are to be taxed heavily, and a super-tax is to be levied. Existing private wealth is to be utilised to lessen the debt burden of the Reich, with exemption for the owners of small-scale property. Income tax is to be placed on a uniform basis and extended according to social and popular principles. Inheritance tax is to be extended in the direction of a confiscation of large-scale property, taking into account the amount of property already possessed by the heir.

The personal and civil rights of individuals are to be guaranteed. There is to be freedom of conscience and religious observance, freedom of expression in speech and writing, freedom of the press, science and art, and freedom of assembly and association.

Source: Sozialdemokratische Partei Deutschlands 1919, *Protokoll über die Verhandlungen des Parteitages der Sozialdemokratischen Partei Deutschlands, abgehalten in Weimar vom 10. bis 15. Juni 1919*, pp. 57–9.

1.8   'Socialisation is Here!'. Proclamation of 4 March 1919 by the Scheidemann Government

The Coal Syndicate is to be socialised immediately. In this way the Reich, that is to say the whole of the people, will gain a decisive influence on the whole of mining and heavy industry even before the socialisation of the mines themselves.

The socialisation of potassium mining is being prepared with the utmost rapidity. The framework law on socialisation, which has been laid before the National Assembly,[38] will provide a foundation for the Communal Economy[39] for Germany in place of the previous unrestricted private economy.

---

38   For the text of this document, see below, section 1.9.

39   *Gemeinwirtschaft*: a middle way between socialism and capitalism, to be achieved by establishing administrative bodies for each individual branch of the economy, staffed jointly by the entrepreneurs, representatives of the work force, and consumers. It was favoured by Rudolf Wissell, who was Economics Minister for part of 1919.

The Reich, in other words all of us, will control this German communal economy. The Reich will take care that the economy is run everywhere in the common interest, and nowhere in the private interest of the capitalists.

And that is socialism.

The Government of the Reich

Source: *Soziale Praxis*, vol. 28, p. 401.

Note: This proclamation was issued by the Scheidemann government to coincide with the critical point of the Berlin general strike of March 1919 and thereby take the sting out of its demands. It was never implemented, for a number of reasons. (See the Note to 1.9.)

1.9   *The 'Socialisation Law' of 23 March 1919*

I

Every German, notwithstanding his personal liberty, has the moral duty to exert his mental and physical powers in the manner required by the welfare of the whole people. Labour-power, as the highest economic good, enjoys the special protection of the Reich. Every German should be given the possibility of maintaining his or her existence through economically productive labour. Where the opportunity to work cannot be provided, care will be taken for his or her necessary maintenance. These matters will be determined in more detail for specific fields by the legislation of the Reich.

II

The Reich is empowered, by way of legislation, and in return for adequate compensation,

> 1 to transfer into the Communal Economy[40] those industrial undertakings which are suitable for socialisation, in particular industries extracting the treasures of the earth and utilising the forces of nature
> 2 in case of urgent need, to regulate the production and distribution of economic wealth through the Communal Economy.

The laws to be issued by the Reich in specific fields will contain precise regulations on compensation.

---

40   The text of the law carefully avoids using the word 'state'.

III

The tasks of the Communal Economy are to be settled by law. These tasks will be the responsibility of either the Reich, or its member states, or the local councils or associations of local councils, or the self-governing bodies of economic administration. The self-governing administrative bodies are under the supervision of the Reich. The Reich may call on the services of the authorities of its member states to implement this supervision.

IV

In exercising the powers provided for in Paragraph II specific Reich laws will determine the use of coal, lignite, briquettes, coke, water power and other natural sources of energy, and the use of the energy arising from them from the standpoint of the Communal Economy. A law regulating the coal industry enters into force simultaneously with this present law.

V

This law enters into force on the date of its proclamation.

Signed: The Reich President Friedrich Ebert
The Reich Minister for the Economy Rudolf Wissell

Source: Deutsches Reich 1919, *Reichsgesetzblatt 1919*, No. 68, pp. 341–42.

Note: This law did not socialise anything in particular. Its aim was to provide a framework for possible future socialisation measures. Two successive Socialisation Commissions[41] were set up by the government to examine the mining industry, but neither was able to achieve anything, partly because of the fierce resistance of the mineowners, partly because of the fear that socialised property would be seen as a source of reparations payments by the victorious allies and confiscated. By February 1921 'the government, the parties and trade unions were all agreed that a socialisation of the mining industry could not be carried out in the existing foreign policy situation'.[42] The same thing applied to all the other measures of socialisation suggested at this time.

---

41   The first commission sat between November 1918 and April 1919, the second between March 1920 and February 1921.

42   Wulf 1977, p. 96.

1.10   *Karl Kautsky's Speech*[43] *on 'The Socialisation of Economic Life' at the Second Congress of Councils, April 1919*

The Russian method – act first and think later – has not produced very pleasing economic results. It has worsened the misery of the Russian proletariat and the proletarians have paid heavily for their lesson. The Russian comrades themselves warn us to learn from their mistakes, and we have every reason to do so. Full, complete socialisation is an empty slogan; but if it is not possible, the aspiration to render all capitalist production impossible is not less ruinous. This completely topsy-turvy approach, namely the endeavour to accelerate socialisation by encouraging the workers to make demands which necessitate either producing at a loss or raising prices so high that the market for the goods disappears, is not the socialisation of *production* but the socialisation of *bankruptcy*. This does not mean, however, that capitalism is for us a flower that cannot be touched.

The present government does not enjoy people's confidence. Its attitude arouses the impression that it does not want to grant any more socialisation than it absolutely must. For a determined socialist government, the practical difficulties of socialisation could only be challenges, leading it to devote to this task twice as much attention, twice as much work. For the present government, in contrast, these difficulties only produced the commonplace prudence of a warning against all experiments. The most dangerous experiment of all, however, would be the attempt to return to the old capitalism. The government called into existence a Socialisation Commission,[44] but merely as an advisory body and it narrowed its sphere of competence so far as to make it insignificant, whereupon its members felt that they had to resign. What we need is a Central Socialisation Office, composed not just of bureaucrats but of theorists and practical people who have shown their capacity and determination to proceed with socialisation. A Socialisation Office with far-reaching powers, on the model of the one just set up in German Austria[45] is needed, along with rights of expropriation for the local authorities and an immediate takeover by the state

43   Karl Kautsky (1854–1938, leading SPD theorist, member of the USPD from 1917–22), was ill at the time, and the speech was delivered by his wife, Luise Kautsky.

44   On 18 November 1918 the Council of People's Representatives established a Socialisation Commission, which included leading politicians and trade unionists. As Kautsky notes, the Commission dissolved itself in April 1919.

45   *Deutschösterreich*. This was the official name of Austria, the state which emerged in 1918 from the ruins of the old Habsburg Monarchy.

of the big private forests and entailed estates, plus the socialisation of the coal mines. These would be the first steps.

Source: Centralrat der Sozialistischen Republik Deutschlands 1919, *II. Kongress der Arbeitern, Bauern- und Soldatenräte Deutschlands am 8. bis 14. April 1919 im Herrenhaus zu Berlin. Stenographisches Protokoll*, pp. 229–30.

1.11 *Rudolf Wissell's Speech of June 1919 to the SPD Party Congress Criticising the Record of the Government of Which He Was a Member*
It is asserted that the failure to put into effect our economic programme caused the slide towards the left[46] (interjection: very true!). I therefore consider it my duty to give a thorough explanation of the reasons for this slow advance of the economic reforms. Political, economic and ethical factors have prevented the implementation of socialisation. My remarks on this point are naturally not made in my official capacity.[47] I am speaking as a Party comrade and I want to say what is actually the case.

Let me turn first to the obstacles of a political nature. We transferred the National Assembly to Weimar because we wanted to express the fact that Germany's policies would henceforth be imbued with the Weimar spirit. I believe that the National Assembly will live on in history as a second edition of the National Assembly of 1848.[48] What has the government done, what has it been able to do? That is the main question. A programme was agreed in February,[49] but it was a compromise programme with all its attendant weaknesses. Moreover, in the decisive questions (particularly the economic ones) it often rendered the coalition government almost incapable of acting.[50] Despite the Revolution, the people have been disappointed in their expectations. We have extended formal political democracy further, to be sure. But we have still done nothing more than continue the programme already initiated by the Imperial German government of Prince Max of Baden.[51] We could not satisfy

---

46 A reference to the rising popularity of the USPD.

47 In June 1919 Wissell was still the Minister for the Economy in the Scheidemann cabinet. He resigned from Gustav Bauer's cabinet on 12 July in protest against his colleagues' rejection of his proposals for a planned economy. He was replaced by Robert Schmidt, who opposed his ideas.

48 Not a compliment. The Frankfurt National Assembly of 1848 was a byword for its weakness and hesitancy.

49 The programme of 13 February 1919. See above, 1.7.

50 The Scheidemann cabinet was a coalition between the SPD, the Centre Party and the DDP.

51 Prince Max of Baden's government programme, read out to the Imperial Reichstag on 5 October 1918, had promised the conversion of Germany into a parliamentary democracy, though without removing the Emperor.

the indistinct murmurings of the masses, who had an instinctive urge to higher forms of life, because we had no proper programme.

In essence, we have retained the old forms of life of our state. We have been able to breathe only a little of the new spirit into these forms. And the people believe that the achievements of the Revolution have a purely negative character, that one form of military and bureaucratic domination has been replaced by another, and that the government's principles do not differ essentially from those of the old regime.

Behind the scenes, a struggle is going on: it is the burning conflict between the communal-socialist economy and the old economy of the free play of forces. Attempts are being made to intervene in this fight with any method available. Now or never, is what it says in the bourgeois press. Let us make no mistake about our strength and what we can achieve. Only under the impact of the street fighting in Berlin were we able to push through the Socialisation Law.[52] Now the supporters of the old economy are on the attack and the struggle is made easier for them because broad masses of workers have been infected by the profit motive: they see in socialism only the economic improvement, not the moral principle as well. We too are guilty in this regard. In our agitation we have concentrated exclusively on the economic driving forces of socialism, not the ethical elements that are contained within it. We must find a formula to unleash the moral and spiritual forces within the people. We have not yet done so, and this has driven great masses to the Left. Not because the Left has the correct formula. Oh, no. On the Left, the masses are flattered, and deceived with the plausible suggestion that the dictatorship of the proletariat will satisfy all their needs.

That our economic life cannot today be socialised without further ado will be agreed by most people. A full socialisation, that is to say the conversion of economic enterprises into the property of the Reich, would cost resources no responsible person could think of laying out. The Reich must pay compensation to previous owners, even according to extreme socialists like Kautsky, Hilferding and the rest. I am myself ready to go in this direction, but only if we create the necessary foundation in the shape of a tax on wealth. Our theoreticians have all assumed that economic enterprises will become ripe for taking over by society through their increased concentration, at a time of excess supply of commodities and a high level of production. We do not have this, but on the contrary an almost inconceivable immiseration of our country.

---

52   See above, 1.9. The street fighting which took place between 3 and 8 March 1919 in Berlin was sparked off by a general strike.

What should be done? We shall only be able to exist when we develop our economy in a planned way. Not private interest but the general interest must be the decisive factor. The Communal Economy (*Gemeinwirtschaft*) makes possible a gradual advance to socialism. For all branches of the economy, socialist principles can be advanced by means of organic association on a communal economic basis. Economic life must not receive its impulse merely from the individual's profit motive. Economic activities must be under the influence of society, they must be subjected to the requirements of the moral law.

Source: Sozialdemokratische Partei Deutschlands 1919, *Protokoll über die Verhandlungen des Parteitages der Sozialdemokratischen Partei Deutschlands, abgehalten in Weimar vom 10. bis 15. Juni 1919*, pp. 363–6.

Note: At this Congress Wissell was in effect speaking for an oppositional minority, which was struggling against the complacency of the official Party leadership. He was supported by perhaps 3 to 5 percent of the delegates. Within the government, his cabinet colleagues continued to oppose his ideas of planning, and he soon resigned. He returned to office in 1928, but now the situation was completely different: the four SPD ministers were in a coalition cabinet sitting alongside eight bourgeois representatives, and Wissell's main concern was to defend existing social legislation, not to pass fresh measures.

1.12   *Eduard David (SPD) Praises the Weimar Constitution, July 1919*

Let me say a few words in evaluation of this work. By voting through the constitution the National Assembly has performed the second great task set for it. The first one was to establish peace. Only with the ending of the War did it become possible to establish peace at home. The purpose of the constitution is first and foremost to serve this peace. With the constitution the internal political life of our people has found a firm new legal form. A well thought-out construction on a stable constitutional basis now replaces the temporary dwelling quickly hammered together in the stormy days of the Revolution. The national existence of our people should be able to settle down more within its walls, and our people will again be able to go happily to work in well-regulated circumstances.

The new constitution has been criticised sharply on the Right and the Extreme Left. But it also does justice to you, gentlemen of the opposition. It does not prevent you from advancing your political objectives, it gives you the opportunity of achieving its alteration by a legal route, provided you can win over the necessary majority of the people to your views. This means there is no need for political violence. From now on, the will of the people is the supreme law . . . It will be objected that there is only a semblance of political democracy as long as economic dependency prevents millions of the propertyless from exerting their political will. People point to the antagonism between the interests of capital and those of the workers, people say an economic struggle arises out of this which excludes any real internal pacification. No one can close his eyes to this source of sharp political antagonisms and conflicts.

But the new constitution should point the way to peace in this respect too. Not only political democracy but *economic democracy* is anchored in it. The system of economic organisation which is laid down in it and should shortly find legal expression points the way to an organisation of the economy which will overcome the hostile antagonism between capital and labour. The intention of these provisions of the constitution is to end the domination of the law of the jungle in the economy as well. It can be characterised as the constitution of a *social democracy.*

The Germans are the first people to have adopted this idea, this signpost to social peace, in their fundamental laws. There was no model to follow. It is the achievement of the Germans themselves, of the best German spirit, the spirit of Weimar, which has such a high reputation in the intellectual and cultural history of the world . . . We are certain that the judgment of tendentious newspaper reports to the effect that the Germans are only playing out a comedy of democracy before the world will collapse through its own superficiality. Nowhere in the world has democracy been more consistently put into effect than in the new German constitution. I need only point to the democratic electoral law covering all legislative bodies; I need only point to the supreme power which is ascribed to the will of the people exerted directly. Finally, I need only point to the fact that women in Germany have achieved full civic equality. From now on, the *German republic* is the *most democratic democracy in the world.*

We have built a new national house, with modern furnishings and a tremendous view . . . Let it not only secure the cohesion of the German national community within the boundaries of the Reich, but also nourish the idea and the wish to belong to the motherland among Germans outside the Reich, 'as far as the German tongue resounds'.[53]

Source: Heilfron 1919, *Die Deutsche Nationalversammlung im Jahre 1919, in ihrer Arbeit für den Aufbau des neuen deutschen Volksstaates*, Bd. 7, p. 453.

---

53   A deliberate reference to the slogan used by those who advocated the political unification of all German speakers in the 1848 Revolution.

1.13 *Rudolf Wissell Argues in Favour of a Planned Economy, October 1919*
It is no longer permissible for our national economy to be conducted under the sign of anarchic commodity production. We must arrive at a consciously planned organisation of social production. And our economy must be conducted with due regard to the welfare of the people. Not the individual, but the general, social interest must be the decisive factor. If we want to raise ourselves up to a better existence with our work the whole people must be guided by the sense that the individual is subordinate to the totality. The economy should no longer be merely a means to the maintenance and advancement of the individual, it must become a social duty of the individual towards the whole.

Legislation must show the way. It must lay down the fundamental principles. I made the first attempt in this direction in the Law on Socialisation by laying on every German the moral obligation to use his mental and physical powers as required by the welfare of the whole. This was only possible with a planned insertion of the individually based economy into the framework of the German Communal Economy [*Gemeinwirtschaft*], a subordination of the private economic principle to the requirements of the total economy. This should be done, not through police-state methods of central regulation, but through the planned establishment of self-governing entities in each of the economic groups. These should be created *from the bottom up* in the individual enterprises and enterprise groups, and they should be closely interlocked so that they become an embodiment of the economy as a whole. The state should be restricted to general supervision and the settlement of conflicts of interest, which cannot be ironed out by the self-governing entities themselves.

This is the sole way of ordering the economy, which allows us to lay the foundations of the economic system envisaged by socialism. Socialism is nothing other than the planned regulation of all the forces dominating our economy, which are at present locked in mutual combat. This approach does not rule out the handing over (where possible and appropriate) of individual branches of the economy or enterprises to the whole society, either as represented by the Reich, a state, or a local authority. But my proposals are not limited to the socialisation of single branches of our economy, since they intend to embrace the whole economy and not let parts of it continue as a battleground for the free play of forces. Finally, it is only possible to apply self-government to the economy with the participation, on the basis of equal rights, of both workers and consumers.

Source: *Die Neue Zeit*, 38/1/1, 3 October 1919, pp. 3–5.

1.14   *The SPD Leadership Calls its Cabinet Ministers to Order in*
November 1919

Philipp Scheidemann informs the *Fraktion*[54] confidentially of a memorandum
by the Party leadership sent to the Social Democratic members of the government. The increasing danger of a reactionary rising has called forth this intervention by the Party leadership. We demand a change in the course pursued
by the government, in relation to the following: the banning of newspapers,
the arrest of individuals, the prohibition of meetings, the giving of promotions
and decorations to objectionable characters, the conditions prevailing in the
Reichswehr, the arming of peasants, landowners and security guards, and the
imposition of a state of siege.... The memorandum of the Party leadership was
discussed with the ministers yesterday. The *Fraktion* has to decide whether it
approves the step taken by the Party leadership.

Source: Potthoff and Weber (eds.) 1986, *Die SPD-Fraktion in der Nationalversammlung 1919–1920*, No. 95, 21.11.1919 Evening Sitting p. 190.

Note: According to Scheidemann, the SPD Chancellor, Gustav Bauer,[55] angrily
accused him of being behind this memorandum. None of the demands made
in it was in fact met by the Social Democratic ministers, partly because of the
need to consider the views of their coalition partners.

1.15   *Wilhelm Keil, SPD Minister of Labour,*[56] *Recalls his Difficulties*
with the Eight-Hour Day

As Minister of Labour I was faced with an important issue of social and economic policy, namely whether or not to ratify the Washington Agreement on
the Eight-Hour Day.[57] The German trade unions supported ratification, the
employers opposed it. Apart from their disinclination towards this measure
in principle, there was also the objection that the German economy would
become incapable of competing in the world market if it had to keep strictly to
the Eight-Hour Day, and if, in addition, Germany had to bear the gigantic cost

---

54   *Fraktion*: the group of SPD deputies in the German parliament.

55   Gustav Bauer (1870–1944), SPD, trade unionist, Chancellor of Germany June 1919 to March
      1920, with other ministerial appointments earlier and later.

56   Wilhelm Keil (1879–1938), SPD, president of the Württemberg Constituent Assembly in
      1919, was Minister of Labour and Food Supply in the state of Württemberg between 1921
      and 1923.

57   This is the Convention adopted at the International Labour Conference which was held
      in Washington, D.C. during October and November 1919.

of war reparations. I was unable to accept the employers' opinion. The Eight-Hour Day had been established by law in Germany,[58] and I naturally held firm on that point. But there were reasons for objecting to an international obligation under the given circumstances. I therefore had a proposal drafted to agree to ratification only on certain conditions.

I proved that I was not afraid to make critical remarks in public about the eight-hour day with my speech to the committee that was organising Württemberg's participation in the Frankfurt Trade Fair. I underlined the advantages of the eight-hour day from the social, hygienic, cultural and family points of view, but I emphasised just as strongly that under the given economic conditions (we were at the height of a boom, and there was a labour shortage) a rigid, mechanical implementation of the law was not advisable. A certain differentiation between light and heavy work was permissible, I said. The bourgeois press issued sensational reports about my 'heresy' and predicted that I would be attacked for my views by my own Party. I was not.

Source: Keil 1948, *Erlebnisse eines Sozialdemokraten*, vol. 2, pp. 254–56.

1.16   *The Unreality of Power, 1928–1930: Rudolf Wissell Explains why the SPD Government of 1928–30, of Which He Was a Member, was Unable to Implement the 1927 Measures of Social Legislation*

I regard it as very important for our movement to create clarity over what obstructive forces a socialist Minister of Labour has to reckon with in present circumstances ... as well as critics in our own ranks who are inclined to minimise a number of conflicts, which has led them to view the break-up of the 'grand coalition' on account of differences over unemployment insurance as perhaps not urgently necessary.

What was the situation at the end of June 1928 when Social Democracy entered the government of the Reich? Four socialist ministers confronted eight bourgeois ministers in the cabinet, a circumstance which was not always borne in mind by some socio-political hotheads who expected immediate and fundamental progress. When I took over the office of Minister of Labour I entered into a very burdensome inheritance. The year 1927 was very favourable for social policy. The economic crisis of 1926 had been overcome and the labour market was in good shape.

In the optimistic atmosphere of 1927 the overwhelming majority of the Reichstag, from the German Nationalists to the Social Democrats, adopted

---

58   See above, 1.1.

the Law on Labour Exchanges and Unemployment Insurance (AVAVG).[59] This law, which closed a gap in the existing system of social insurance, always painfully felt, fulfilled an old working-class demand. But experience shows that the Reichstag is only capable of passing a great piece of social legislation from time to time. There was the danger that the Reichstag would feel 'saturated' and that the proposals I made would be postponed to the distant future. It was clear to me that with the growth of countervailing forces it would be impossible to continue raising wage levels and extending social insurance at the previous tempo. I also realised the difficulties that would pile up if the economic climate turned unfavourable, as many signs were indicating even at the beginning of 1928. Indeed, from mid-1928 onwards this development really set in.

The fact that the AVAVG came into force in the favourable atmosphere of 1927 is the germ of the difficulties with which I had to contend later on. An average figure of 700,000 unemployed was taken as the basis for calculating the financial resources needed to insure them. This calculation later turned out to be completely at variance with the facts. The SPD and myself were of course entirely free from blame for the incorrect basis used to evaluate how the labour market would develop in the winter of 1928/29. Even so, the mistake made by others in setting up the unemployment insurance scheme was exploited by people agitating against the alleged 'exaggerations' of our social policy, and later on it hindered my work considerably.

In the winter of 1928/29 the number of unemployed, particularly in seasonal occupations, shot up to a quite unforeseeable extent, and I had first to ward off the complete collapse of the scheme by establishing what I called 'Special Provisions for Occupationally Determined Unemployment'. These special arrangements for the seasonally unemployed could not prevent the erosion of the insurance scheme's financial basis. The Siberian severity of that winter, and the downward trend of the labour market associated with it, skewed all our financial calculations, compelling us to seek a large loan from the Treasury. The situation for unemployment insurance became critical. The public was deluged with a mass of stories (some of them true) about inefficiency and corruption in this area. I felt obliged to protect the unemployment insurance scheme

---

59   *Arbeitsvermittlung- und Arbeitslosenversicherungsgesetz.* This passed the Reichstag on
16 July 1927 by 356 votes to 47. Only the NSDAP, the KPD and some German Nationalists
voted against it. The law entered into force on 1 October 1927. The non-socialist parties
were ready to accept the measure, having just made sure, against the votes of the liberals
and the Left, and the opposition of the trade unions, that the length of the working day
could be varied by overtime, paid at a rate of 25 percent extra (under the 8 April 1927 Law
on Working Time).

by making legislative changes. A new unemployment insurance law had to be issued at a moment when the question of further finance for it had not been clarified, and the slogan of a 'clean up' of the insurance system was being put out by 'economic circles'. What dangers this inevitably conjured up for us!

I don't understand why some parts of the democratic press are astonished that I did not agree to the Brüning-Meyer compromise. It was not a *solution* of the difficulties but the *postponement* of a solution. It also pointed unmistakably in the direction of a reduction in unemployment benefit. If I had signed this, the responsibility for cutting benefits would have been ascribed to Social Democracy. Now, with Social Democracy again in opposition, the Centre Party will not and cannot reduce benefits…Social Democracy will ensure, even in opposition, that the system of unemployment insurance, and indeed the whole of Germany's social policy, remains intact.

Source: Wissell 1930, 'Einundzwanzig Monate Reichsarbeitsminister', *Die Arbeit*, 7, 1930, pp. 218, 225, 227–28.

Note: Wissell proved to be far too optimistic about the future of social policy during the final crisis of the Weimar system, and also far too sanguine about the influence of Social Democracy on events as an opposition party in the Reichstag.

The Council Idea: Workers' Councils and Factory Councils

Introduction

None of the Majority Socialists saw the Workers' and Soldiers' Councils that emerged in 1918 as alternatives to the parliamentary system. Most of them viewed the Councils as a temporary and regrettable phenomenon, considering that they would cease to have any function at all once a properly constituted parliament-based government had taken over, which happened in February 1919. The SPD Executive wanted to turn the Workers' Councils into Factory Councils, with the job of 'controlling and jointly determining the economic process'.[1] The trade union leaders, who were usually members of the SPD, and exerted a considerable influence on the Party, were strongly opposed to the idea. They thought institutions of this type would usurp their rightful function of collaborating with the employers in determining the functioning of the economy.

There was, however, a minority trend within the SPD, led by Max Cohen, and centred around the journal *Sozialistische Monatshefte*, which did see a place for the Workers' Councils (not, of course, for the Soldiers' Councils, because they did not want to undermine army discipline) as a form of representation of the workers on corporatist lines, existing side by side with parliament, though certainly of inferior status. Cohen first put forward this idea at the First Congress of Councils, held in December 1918. He claimed that the Workers' Councils 'could do a tremendous amount of good in developing production.'[2] This conception lay at the heart of the idea of Chambers of Labour, which was adopted by a majority at the Second Congress of Councils in April 1919,[3] and later bore fruit in the institution of the National Economic Council (*Reichswirtschaftsrat*). This council brought together three groups – representatives of the workers, the employers and the consumers – and the Social Democratic Minister for the Economy, Rudolf Wissell, hoped to use it influence the running of the economy even when his party was out of office after 1920. In practice, however, the

---

1 This was the description used in the SPD executive's resolution of 1 March 1919.
2 Allgemeiner Kongress 1919, p. 223.
3 See document 2.16.

National Economic Council never amounted to more than a forum for the discussion of economic and social questions between the more liberal employers and the moderate wing of the workers' movement.

The idea of Workers' and Soldiers' Councils found its strongest support among the left of the USPD. In the last months of the War, starting with the big strike wave of January 1918, a radical wing had grown up in the USPD, around the Berlin group known as the Revolutionary Shop Stewards (*Obleute*). They dreamed of establishing a socialist republic, with institutions analogous to, but not identical with, the Russian Soviets. There is no evidence that Workers' and Soldiers' Councils actually existed before the outbreak of the Revolution of November 1918, but once they did emerge the USPD played the leading part in the Berlin ones. They were able to gain control of the Greater Berlin Executive Council (*Vollzugsrat*) of Workers' and Soldiers' Councils, and they hoped that this would be as important in Germany as the Petrograd Soviet had been in Russia a year before. The German situation was different, however, in a number of important respects. The Soldiers' Councils were strongly inclined to the SPD if anything, and outside Berlin the SPD had a majority in most of the Workers' Councils.[4] The First Congress of Councils (16 to 21 December 1918), which represented Councils from all over Germany, did not want to take power; rather the reverse, it was anxious to give away what power it possessed to the Council of People's Representatives and to get Germany onto a parliamentary footing as soon as possible. Before this happened, though, the USPD-dominated Berlin Executive Council made several efforts to assert its own sovereignty, relying on the largely imaginary precedent of the events of 10 November, when the SPD People's Representatives had graciously consented to let themselves be invested with authority by it. Georg Ledebour[5] argued in his speech of 18 November that this proved the Executive Council's right to appoint and dismiss the People's Representatives.[6] The SPD did not feel strong enough yet to controvert him, and an agreement was reached on 22 November conceding political power in appearance to the Workers' and Soldiers' Councils.[7] The real views of the SPD's leader, Friedrich Ebert, which his colleagues shared, were

---

4   This was exhaustively demonstrated by Eberhard Kolb in his path-breaking book on the Workers' Councils (Kolb 1962, pp. 99–113).

5   Georg Ledebour (1850–1947), founder member of the USPD 1917, and a 'Revolutionary Shop Steward' in 1918. He remained with the USPD after the 1920 split, and between 1922–32 he led the remnant of the USPD which refused to rejoin the SPD (after 1924 it adopted the name 'Socialist League') He helped to set up the SAP (Socialist Workers' Party) in 1932.

6   See Document 2.2.

7   See Document 2.3.

clear from his statement of 13 December that the Councils were 'advisory bodies or nothing.'[8]

The provinces were a useful counterweight to 'Red Berlin'. They helped
to emasculate the Workers' and Soldiers' Councils. At a conference of all the
German states on 25 November, 23 out of the 25 assembled chief ministers voted
to summon a Constituent Assembly. This was the first nail in the Councils' cof-
fin. The second was driven in by the First Congress of Councils, that 'political
suicide-club' (as Däumig called it). The Congress rejected Laufenberg's[9] proposal that it seize power (2.7); it voted on party lines (SPD against USPD) by 344
to 98 not to substitute itself for the Constituent Assembly; and on 18 December
it formally transferred power to the Council of People's Representatives, pending the election of a proper government by the forthcoming Constituent
Assembly (2.9). The one radical step taken by the First Congress was to pass
the Seven Hamburg Points, a bill of rights for soldiers aimed at democratising
the army (8.4) but even this came to nothing owing to the preference of the
Majority Social Democrats for reconstructing the army in collaboration with
the former high command.

The collapse of all their hopes made it tempting for the three USPD members
of the Council of People's Representatives to withdraw from a government in
which they were now powerless. They were under pressure to do this from the
more radical left-wingers in their Party, in particular from the Spartacists, and
the incident of 24 December tipped the balance. On that day the rebellious
sailors of the People's Naval Division were bombarded by troops brought back
from the front under the command of General Lequis. This seemed to show
that the moderates of the SPD were perfectly prepared to spill blood with the
help of the old military leaders where disorder was likely, and the USPD People's
Representatives concluded that they must return to the work of agitation from
outside the government (2.10). Subsequent efforts by the USPD to maintain
the Councils in the face of the determination of the SPD to deprive them of
all influence were doomed to failure. A minority of Berlin workers rose up in
revolt on 6 January 1919 in response to appeals from the left of the USPD and
Karl Liebknecht and Wilhelm Pieck of the Spartacist League (now the KPD) to
defend the achievements of the revolution.[10] But the military forces of the old

---

8   See Document 2.5.

9   Heinrich Laufenberg (1872–1932), Hamburg Left Radical leader in 1918. Chair of the
       Hamburg Workers' and Soldiers' Council 1918–19, he joined the KPD in 1919, was expelled
       and joined the KAPD in 1920. Later in that year he was expelled from the KAPD for
       advocating 'National Bolshevism'.

10   Müller 1925, pp. 32–6.

régime had already recovered sufficient strength by January 1919 to suppress them. A desperate joint appeal for a general strike on 9 January by the Greater Berlin USPD, the KPD and the Revolutionary Shop Stewards (3.1) did not meet with success, and Berlin was reconquered by force in the next few days.

The next stage in the decline of the Councils was the Central Council's surrender of its powers. This organisation had originally been set up by the First Congress of Councils in December so as to provide a permanent national representation for the local Councils in the intervals between Congresses. All of its members were Majority Socialists, so it was not surprising that in February 1919 it formally handed over its authority to the newly elected National Assembly (2.12). It also cancelled the elections for new Workers' Councils, which had been planned for October 1919. The Second Congress of Councils, held in April 1919, was dominated by the SPD, with 146 seats to the USPD's 56, and it voted to set up 'Chambers of Labour' side by side with the Reichstag. (2.16). It disbanded without providing any mechanism to elect a successor.

In Bavaria, meanwhile, a severe political conflict had developed in the early months of 1919 between the local Workers' Council, which dominated the city of Munich, and most of the rest of the former kingdom, which was predominantly agricultural, and deeply suspicious of the urban working class. The assassination of the well-liked leader of the local USPD, Kurt Eisner, in February 1919, brought the conflict to a head. The parliamentarians in the newly elected Bavarian Diet fled from Munich to Bamberg, where they felt safer, leaving the Workers' Council in control. Although it initially pursued a path of compromise, with the elected Bavarian Diet and the Councils essentially sharing power, the situation deteriorated and a group of revolutionaries (anarchists rather than communists) acting jointly with the Soldiers' Council, which was more Social Democratic in political complexion, seized power on 7 April 1919 and proclaimed a 'Bavarian Council Republic'. (2.15), It only lasted for three weeks, since the exiled government in Bamberg was able to call on the help of local Bavarian Freikorps units, which marched into Munich on 1 May 1919 and quickly suppressed all resistance. They took a bloody revenge.

The Workers' Councils continued to exist at a local level, but they gradually lost influence in 1919 to the state bureaucracy. In some cases they were strong enough to resist this process, but not for long. The central government of the Reich responded by sending troops to suppress them by force. By the summer all that was left of the Workers' and Soldiers' Councils was the promise to anchor the Council system in the Weimar constitution, a promise fulfilled in part by the establishment of the National Economic Council (*Reichswirtschaftsrat*) and in part by the legal recognition of Factory Councils. The latter came to birth, after a long gestation period in government offices, with the law of 4 February 1920 (2.18).The Factory Councils created by this law had more in common with the joint consultation machinery set up by the Imperial Government in December 1916 to strengthen the war effort than with the revolutionary institutions of Russia in 1917 or Germany in November 1918. Their purpose (as during the War) was to secure social peace and the efficient running of the factories through cooperation between the workforce and the employers. The Factory Councils did not possess even a shadow of power, since the management was free to accept or reject their recommendations. The parties of the extreme Left, the USPD and the KPD, were naturally hostile to the proposal, and a demonstration in protest against the passing of the law was dispersed by the police with copious use of firearms (this was to become known as the 'bloodbath of 13 January 1920').[11] The disappearance of the Workers' Councils meant the end of the USPD's distinctive 'middle way' between proletarian dictatorship and bourgeois democracy: soon afterwards the Party split, and the majority of its members joined the KPD (Communist Party of Germany), leaving a large minority to return eventually to the SPD (in 1922). The council idea remained an integral component of the KPD's programme, but the communists attached a different meaning to it: the councils advocated by the KPD were 'political Workers' Councils', exercising political power. They were, in other words, intended to be soviets, on the Russian model.

---

11   42 demonstrators were killed, and 105 wounded. As one might expect, there are different views about how this slaughter happened. Heinrich August Winkler, for example, states that the demonstrators 'obviously fired first' although 'the forces of order fired back immediately without warning' (Winkler 1985, p. 289). Hans-Ulrich Wehler, on the other hand, asserts that the police alone fired, but they did so 'because the demonstrators wanted to penetrate into the Reichstag building' (Wehler 2003, p. 401). At the time, the USPD and the KPD maintained that this was an entirely peaceful demonstration. Hartfrid Krause adopts the sensible intermediate position that 'the mass demonstration lacked any leadership which might have brought it to an appropriate conclusion. People stood around outside the building for hour after hour. Incidents occurred, perhaps set off by provocateurs. Then the military intervened.' (Krause 1975, pp. 167–8).

Documents

2.1   Ernst Däumig[12] Advocates the Council System and Argues Against Summoning a Constituent Assembly, 16 November 1918

The old system of government collapsed on the 9th of November. It must be replaced by the system of Workers' and Soldiers' Councils. This is where power must lie, the power that we have conquered for ourselves. If we proceed from this assumption, Germany can be reconstructed on the basis of the governmental power created by the Revolution, the Workers' and Soldiers' Councils. We call it a 'socialist republic' but as yet that is merely a decorative title. We no longer have a monarchy, but we don't yet have a republic. The socialist state formation still needs to be created. We must be clear about this too. What we have done so far is only the first step. The class struggle is not in abeyance. We absolutely must get clear today what position we take up on the first and most important question, namely whether what we have fought for is to be a bourgeois-democratic or a socialist republic.

We cannot support a Constituent National Assembly. The institution of Workers' and Soldiers' Councils must remain the legislative and executive body. The government of the Reich must be subordinated to us, the Workers' and Soldiers' Councils. At present the government appoints Secretaries of State without asking us; it issues proclamations etc. about which we are completely in the dark. These are all things we cannot tolerate.

Let us be clear about what this means: if the Executive Committee[13] adopts the view that a National Assembly must be summoned, it will have passed its own death sentence. The present activity of the Workers' and Soldiers' Councils would then be merely provisional, and the struggle we have so far conducted would be merely a childish game. We must therefore make a clear decision: do we want to extend the achievements of the revolution any further, through the Workers' and Soldiers' Councils, or do we want to follow the old, bourgeois system? If we desire the latter, then we must expect the following to occur: the National Assembly may well be summoned within two months. At that moment, the Workers' and Soldiers' Councils will cease to exist. They will no longer be able to play any political role.

Look closely at the bourgeois strata. In the first few days of the revolution the bourgeoisie was too terrified to do anything. Now it is emerging from all

---

12   Ernst Däumig (1866–1922), USPD, Revolutionary Shop Steward 1918, KPD 1920, left the KPD in September 1921 and joined Paul Levi's group the KAG.

13   He means the Executive Council of the Workers' and Soldiers' Council of Greater Berlin, which is the body he is addressing.

corners. Every day one reads of the setting up of bourgeois political parties. If a National Assembly now enters the picture, the proletarian republic will not be victorious. The bourgeoisie would then enter the new government as a very strong force. It is pretty safe to assume that the right-wing Social Democrats also stand for the National Assembly. The bourgeois democratic republic would then turn its attention to ensuring that the capitalist economy was retained.

Source: Däumig 1918, 'Sitzung des Vollzugsrats der Arbeiter- und Soldatenräte, 16. und 17.11.1918', in Institut für Marxismus-Leninismus beim ZK der SED 1968, *Beiträge zur Geschichte der Arbeiterbewegung*, 10, 1968, p. 139.

Note: All of Däumig's predictions were fulfilled very quickly, except for the 'very strong force of the bourgeoisie' in the 'new government'. This would happen a couple of years later, after the 1920 elections.

2.2   *Georg Ledebour Defends the Authority of the Berlin Executive Council at a Joint Session with the Council of People's Representatives, 18 November 1918*

The present situation can only be a short-lived, provisional one. We must call a delegate conference of all the Workers' and Soldiers' Councils of the Republic as soon as possible and form therefrom an Executive Council of the Republic. This will have to take over the control functions which have grown up around the Workers' and Soldiers' Councils as a whole in the course of the revolution. Until this is done, however, the Greater Berlin Executive Council must fulfil this function provisionally but completely. Herr Landsberg's assertion that all sovereign rights have been as it were delegated to the cabinet by its appointment bears witness to a total misunderstanding of the relation in which we stand to the cabinet as representatives of the Councils. We have confirmed the cabinet of the Republic and the cabinet of the Prussian government in their functions in the same manner as previous holders of sovereignty did. When we appointed the cabinet, we did not give up the right to dismiss the cabinet from office.

We have already made preparations for calling together the Central Council of Workers' and Soldiers' Councils. Only one body can take a decision on the question of the Constituent Assembly: the Executive Council of the Republic, which has yet to be created. The [Greater Berlin] Executive Council has the right to appoint and dismiss the People's Representatives.[14] We must also make

---

14   He means the Council of People's Representatives, the six men, three from the SPD, three from the USPD, who in theory governed Germany at the time.

this area of competence of the Executive Council clear to the gentlemen of the
government, as we have been informed that representatives of the government
have been making quite different statements in private. Under-State Secretary
Baake[15] has been telling representatives of the radio operators that they will
soon get rid of the Executive Council. I would like to point out that the gentlemen of the government should restrain themselves on this matter, and not try
to undermine the authority of the Executive Council.

Source: Miller and Potthoff (eds.) 1969, *Die Regierung der Volksbeauftragten
1918/19*, vol. 1, pp. 88–90.

Note: Ledebour's demand for the calling of a 'delegate conference' of Workers'
and Soldiers' Councils from all over Germany to elect an Executive Council
for the whole German republic was met by point 2 of the 22 November agreement (2.3). But when this body met in December, as the First Congress of
Workers' and Soldiers' Councils, it turned out to be much less radical than he
and the USPD had expected, and the Central Council it elected was dominated
by the SPD.

**2.3   Agreement between the Council of People's Representatives and the
          Berlin Executive Council, 22 November 1918**
The Revolution has created a new constitutional law. For the immediate period
of transition the new legal situation finds expression in the following agreement between the Executive Council of the Workers' and Soldiers' Council of
Greater Berlin and the Council of People's Representatives:

1 Political power lies in the hands of the Workers' and Soldiers' Councils of the
German Socialist Republic. It is their task to maintain and extend the achievements of the revolution as well as to hold down the counter-revolution.
2 Until an assembly of delegates of the Workers' and Soldiers' Councils selects
an Executive Council of the German Republic, the Berlin Executive Council
will perform the functions of the Workers' and Soldiers' Councils of the
German Republic in agreement with the Workers' and Soldiers' Councils of
Greater Berlin.

---

15   Kurt Baake (1864–1938), SPD journalist and editor, head of the Reich Chancellery and
      Under-State Secretary 1918–19, chaired the League of People's Theatre Associations
      1920–33.

3 The appointment of the Council of People's Representatives by the Workers' and Soldiers' Council of Greater Berlin constitutes a transfer of the executive power in the Republic.
4 The appointment and recall of decision-making members of the cabinet of the Republic is to be done by the Central Executive Council, which also has the right to supervise their conduct. Until the relation of the individual states to the Reich has been definitively regulated this is also to apply to Prussia.
5 The Executive Council's views are to be ascertained before the appointment of specialist ministers by the cabinet.

An assembly of delegates of the Workers' and Soldiers' Councils from the whole of the Reich will be held as soon as possible.[16] The current agreement fixes the fundamental relationship between the Workers' and Soldiers' Councils and the government of the Reich. It will be supplemented with Guidelines for the Workers' and Soldiers' Councils, which will be issued as soon as possible.[17]

Source: Ritter and Miller (eds.) 1975, *Die deutsche Revolution 1918–1919. Dokumente. Zweite Auflage*, p. 119.

Note: This agreement was regarded by the Spartacists as a surrender on the part of the Berlin Executive Council, leading Rosa Luxemburg to refer to that body as 'a shadow, a nothing' which had allowed power to slip out of its hands through its 'innate indolence' and which was now condemned to 'complete powerlessness'.[18]

2.4   *Heinrich Cunow (SPD) Opposes the Council System, 22 November 1918*
The goal millions have striven for, the *German Socialist Republic*, has been attained and there is every prospect that it will soon include German Austria as well. Now we have to secure and make firm what has been achieved. We have to give it a broad legal foundation and thereby anchor it in the people's consciousness. The path to this is the summoning of a National Assembly, based on universal, equal, free elections, which will give the Great German Republic

---

16   This refers to the First Congress of Workers' and Soldiers' Councils, which was held between 16 and 21 December 1918.
17   These Guidelines were issued the next day by the Executive Council. They prescribed, among other things, that where the old officials had placed themselves in the service of the new régime they were to be left to carry on the administration, and the Workers' and Soldiers' Councils were not to 'hinder their work by interfering'.
18   In an unsigned article in *Die Rote Fahne*, 11 December 1918.

its democratic constitution. It is therefore to be greeted with satisfaction that the section of the Independents (the USPD) which expressed reservations against the rapid creation of a parliament appears to have abandoned those reservations... The present German revolution has in many places borrowed the language, the arguments and the form of organisation of last year's Russian revolution, and to some extent put on Russian garments. But the conditions in which the German and Russian republics have developed, and their histori-cally given economic and cultural situations, are so different that the wearing of this costume can only be superficial and external. The German revolution cannot adopt the political organisation of the Russian republic, with its dic-tatorship of one single socialist party to the exclusion of all other popular ele-ments. Even less can it appropriate the theoretical arguments brought forward by Bolshevik speakers to justify their party dictatorship and their terrorist practice...

Kautsky is right to say that Marx never understood the expression 'dictator-ship of the proletariat' to mean the rule of a minority party and the abolition of democracy. It is therefore hard to understand that some radical German social-ists have taken over Lenin's theory of dictatorship and rejected the calling of a constituent National Assembly. What had a certain justification under Russian social and political conditions would be completely senseless under German conditions... It would mean basing the new government on a mere act of force, ignoring the general will of the people and its legal expression... *The result could not be anything other than continuously increasing terrorism.* It is there-fore to be welcomed that the newly-arisen Workers' and Soldiers' Councils, as well as a whole series of individual German states, have already come out in favour of the earliest possible summoning of a constituent National Assembly. *Only the constituent National Assembly can give the German republic the neces-sary democratic legal foundation and help it to secure general recognition.*

Source: Cunow 1918, 'Die Diktatur des Proletariats', in *Die Neue Zeit. Wochenschrift der Deutschen Sozialdemokratie* 1.8. 22 November 1918, pp. 170–7.

2.5 *Discussion in the Council of People's Representatives about Relations with the Berlin Executive Council, Afternoon Session, 13 December 1918*

Friedrich Ebert (President): Things cannot go on like this. We are making our-selves ridiculous in the face of history and the whole world. We must submit the following resolution to the Reich Conference.[19] The conduct of the Reich's

---

19   Ebert is referring here to the First Congress of Workers' and Soldiers' Councils.

affairs is exclusively a matter for the government. If this is accepted, then the committee of the Reich Conference can receive parliamentary authority to hear reports at particular times, as the Reichstag Committee used to do in the past.[20] But a sharp demarcation is necessary. We bear the responsibility. Workers' and Soldiers' Councils all over the country must stop interfering and poking around in government matters. They are advisory bodies, and nothing more. If this view is not accepted we must withdraw from the Cabinet. We can take no responsibility for pranks that belong in the madhouse.

Wilhelm Dittmann (USPD): From the very beginning, constant contact between our two chairs and the chair of the Executive Council has been necessary. We must enter into contact with the Central Council[21] from the outset. After all, we do not want to rule in an absolute fashion. Let us now leave the Executive Council in peace, and say what we want in the Central Council. The Central Council also has more authority in the country as a whole than the Executive Council. The right of supervision, however, must be present, in the same way as it was with the Reichstag Committee.

Ebert: Not a word has been said against the right of supervision.

Haase (USPD): The comparison with the Reichstag Committee is appropriate. However, neither the Central Council nor any local Soldiers' Councils may intervene in the activities of any branch of the administration whatsoever. Equally, it should not be overlooked that the Workers' and Soldiers' Councils have often exercised a very fruitful supervision over the administration as local control commissions. If we are talking about excesses, this should not lead us to forget that army officers have also committed excesses.

Landsberg (SPD): With the officers it is a matter of a few stubborn individuals, whereas with the Workers' and Soldiers' Councils we have the organisation of disorder. And the comparison with the Reichstag Committee is not entirely correct. The Reichstag Committee was composed of parliamentarians who had been elected, twice. In the Executive Council, in contrast, there are a lot of unsuitable people. Whether it will be different in the Central Council is doubtful.

Ebert: If we stand together, we can change things very easily. All our differences on specific matters must be disregarded in the face of this great task.

Philipp Scheidemann (SPD): What must be supervised will be supervised by us. What has the Executive Council to do with the main post office, the

20   In 1916 the Budget Committee of the Reichstag was granted the right to meet in the intervals between parliamentary sessions to discuss questions of wartime policy.

21   The Central Council (*Zentralrat*) did not exist yet. It was due to be elected by the forthcoming Congress of Councils.

telegraph agency or the radio station? How does the Executive Council come to be distributing leaflets and conducting agitation? If an immediate change is not brought about, I will no longer be able to tolerate it. These are all people without the slightest trace of a sense of responsibility.

Haase (USPD): If we are united, we can still save the situation. Reason and unreason are represented equally among both Parties in the Executive Council.

Ebert: The technicians are the worst of the lot.

Source: Miller and Potthoff (eds.) 1969, *Die Regierung der Volksbeauftragten 1918/19* Vol. 1, pp. 374–6.

2.6 *People's Representative Friedrich Ebert Calls on the Central Council of Workers' and Soldiers' Councils to Establish Democracy and the Rule of Law in Germany, 16 December 1918*

You have come together, representatives of the workers of all parts of Germany, and of soldiers from all regiments. *Your union must guarantee that a united Germany stays together*. Your union must secure unity among the people and in the government of the Reich for the next few weeks. You must set up the new law-governed state (*Rechtsstaat*) on the basis of the power of the Revolution. In future there can only be the rule of law in Germany that is the wish of the whole German people. That was the meaning of the Revolution. The rule of force has brought us to ruin, and now we shall *no longer tolerate any kind of rule by force*, whoever wants to impose it. The sooner we manage to place our German state on the firm foundation of the will of the whole nation, the sooner will the German republic be healthy and strong, and the sooner will it be able to take in hand the fulfilment of its great socialist goals.

The victorious proletariat sets up no class domination. It overcomes the old class domination and replaces it with the equality of all that bears a human countenance. That is the grand ideal of democracy... Democracy and the National Assembly offer lasting guarantees that arbitrary rule will definitively be brought to an end. That must be our main concern. Only on the bedrock of democracy can the working class place the edifice of Germany's future. Workers and soldiers! Perform here a great work of freedom and democracy, and the German people's republic will master all dangers and move towards a prosperous future.

Source: Deutscher Geschichtskalender 1919, *Deutscher Geschichtskalender 35, Ergänzungsband 1.1. Die Deutsche Revolution. Erster Band. November 1918–Februar 1919*, p. 203.

2.7   *Heinrich Laufenberg's Resolution Calling on the First Congress of*
       Councils to Take Power, 16 December 1918

The revolutionary proletariat, united with the revolutionary army, overthrew the old order. Thanks to the victorious conclusion of the uprising, supreme power fell to the Workers' and Soldiers' Councils. This Congress, as the representative of the Workers' and Soldiers' Councils of the whole of Germany, hereby takes possession of political power and takes over the exercise of that power. As the repository of sovereignty in the Reich it has the right of control, appointment and dismissal over the executive. The Congress demands the immediate departure of the bourgeois members of the government.

Source: Allgemeiner Kongress der Arbeiter- und Soldatenräte Deutschlands 1919, *Allgemeiner Kongress der Arbeiter und Soldatenräte Deutschlands vom 16. bis 21 Dezember 1918 Stenographische Berichte*, col. 176

2.8   *Heinrich Laufenberg Defends His Resolution of 16 December 1918*

Comrades! Russian Bolshevism doubtless adopts methods of struggle which are not appropriate to the German situation. It is clear that Russian social relations are not the same as those of Germany, and that as a result entirely different methods come into question for Eastern Europe from those for Central Europe. If this is all Comrade Cohen[22] is saying there is no reason to disagree. But if it is intended to set up Bolshevism as a scarecrow for reactionary purposes in Germany, then I must object most strongly. (Cries of: Very true!).

On the question at issue, whether to have a National Assembly or a Council System, this has actually already been decided by yesterday's acceptance of Severing's[23] proposal, which is clearly and unambiguously in favour of a National Assembly. It is contradictory to ask the proletariat to give away political power it has not even exercised. The fact is that until now we have not had political power. We have had two governments in Berlin, two governing bodies, and the actual government has a large number of bourgeois members. The proletariat does not have political power in Germany, and the Congress has also not shown that it is at all ready to seize political power to its full extent. In Comrade Cohen's view, the Workers' and Soldiers' Councils should disappear from the centre, from Berlin. I ask you, what does the working class then retain from the revolution that has taken place? If the Workers'

---

22   Max Cohen-Reuss had raised the spectre of Bolshevism in a previous speech.

23   Karl Severing (1875–1952), SPD, State Commissioner for Westphalia 1919–20; Prussian Minister of the Interior 1920–21, 1921–26, 1930–32; Reich Minister of the Interior, 1928–1930.

and Soldiers' Councils disappear from the centre, this will destroy the resistance of the Workers' and Soldiers' Councils in the rest of the country, with very few exceptions.

Source: Allgemeiner Kongress der Arbeiter- und Soldatenräte Deutschlands 1919, *Allgemeiner Kongress der Arbeiter und Soldatenräte Deutschlands vom 16. bis 21 Dezember 1918. Stenographische Berichte*, cols. 243–4.

2.9 Resolution of the First Congress of Councils on the Respective Areas of Competence of the Central Council and the Government, 18 December 1918

1 The Reich Congress of Workers' and Soldiers' Councils of Germany, which represents the supreme political authority, hereby transfers *the legislative and executive powers* to the Council of People's Representatives, until further regulation by the National Assembly.
2 The Congress further appoints a Central Council of Workers' and Soldiers' Councils,[24] which is to carry out *parliamentary supervision* of the German and Prussian cabinets. It has the right to appoint and recall the People's Representatives governing the Reich, and also the People's Representatives governing Prussia until the definitive regulation of the affairs of the States.
3 The Council of People's Representatives will assign adjuncts to the Secretaries of State for the purpose of *supervising the conduct of business* in the offices of the Reich. Two adjuncts will be dispatched to every office of the Reich, such persons to be chosen from both Social Democratic parties. The views of the Central Council are to be heard before the specialist ministers and their adjuncts are appointed.

Source: Allgemeiner Kongress der Arbeiter- und Soldatenräte Deutschlands 1919, col. *Allgemeiner Kongress, der Arbeiter und Soldatenräte Deutschlands vom 16. bis 21 Dezember 1918. Stenographische Berichte*, col. 182.

2.10 The USPD Members of the Council of People's Representatives Announce their Resignation in Protest against the Central Council's Declaration of 28 December 1918

We are withdrawing from the government, and we have taken this step for the following reasons:

---

24   It was given the grandiose title of 'Central Council of the German Socialist Republic' when elected. The minutes of its proceedings are printed in full in Kolb and Rürup 1968.

1 The guilt for the bloodbath of 24 December 1918 lies with the People's Representatives Ebert, Scheidemann and Landsberg[25] because they gave the Prussian War Minister[26] unlimited powers for the application of military force. Such an instruction was neither necessary nor appropriate to the purpose of freeing Wels.[27] His life was itself highly endangered by the bombardment of the building in which he was held.

The People's Representatives Ebert, Scheidemann and Landsberg took no steps throughout the whole of this time to supervise the way in which their instructions were carried out, instructions which were equivalent to a blank cheque. We cannot accept responsibility for handing to a representative of the old power system the right to dispose at will of the lives of his fellow creatures. The road of negotiations ought not to have been abandoned at any stage of the proceedings. In opposition to this view of ours, the Central Council has approved the attitude of Ebert, Scheidemann and Landsberg.

2 The dangerous nature of the instructions given to the War Minister is shown by the fact that the Central Council explicitly stated its disapproval of the way the instructions were carried out.

3 The answer to our third question[28] is equally unsatisfactory to us as it does not require the immediate and unreserved implementation of the decisions of the Congress of Workers' and Soldiers' Councils but merely contains an invitation to put forward regulations governing their implementation.

4 Questions 5, 6 and 7 are of decisive significance for the conduct of internal and external politics in the spirit of the revolution. As the Central Council has postponed its answers to these fundamental questions despite the thorough discussion that took place during the negotiations, it is our conviction that the achievements of the revolution are also in danger in this area.[29]

---

25 In other words, the three SPD members.

26 General Lieutenant Heinrich Scheüch (1864–1946), who held the post from 9 October 1918 to 3 January 1919. He was thus retained in office by the People's Representatives after the November 1918 Revolution.

27 Otto Wels (1873–1939), a top leader of the SPD, was appointed City Commandant of Berlin after the November Revolution. He was taken prisoner by rebellious sailors on the 23rd December, and Ebert instructed the War Minister to force his release, which he endeavoured to do on 24th December. In fact he failed, and the government had to secure Wels' release by negotiation. Wels himself went on to be joint chair of the Party from 1919–33 and a member of the Reichstag from 1920–33.

28 The USPD had asked whether the government was implementing the section of the Seven Hamburg Points which called for the removal of insignia of rank, and prohibited officers from bearing weapons when off duty.

29 The Central Council was asked by the USPD whether it approved of the proposed transfer of the seat of government from Berlin to Weimar (question 5); whether it agreed with the

5 The reply to the question about the immediate socialisation of industries ripe for this, as demanded by the Congress of Workers' and Soldiers' Councils, absolutely fails to secure the realisation of the intentions of the Congress.

6 As we are now leaving the government, we no longer need to answer the question posed of us as People's Representatives by the Central Council.[30]

Source: Miller and Potthoff (eds.) 1969, *Regierung der Volksbeauftragten*, pp. 137–38.

2.11   *Views of Dr. August Müller[31] on the Economic Disadvantages of the Council System at the Cabinet Session of 21 January 1919*

Dr. August Müller: For economic reasons it is necessary to set up a powerful state as soon as possible, to guard against external and internal violence. We are faced with immediate, catastrophic breakdown. Owing to the coal shortage, industry no longer exists. Recently, unemployment benefit has been raised, with the result that a large family receives the salary of a top civil servant as unemployment benefit. I would be in favour of the forcible deportation of the unemployed to the countryside if we could carry this out, but we do not have the power. The system of Workers' and Soldiers' Councils must come to an end. The provision of food supplies has been disrupted, and fishing cannot be conducted in the Baltic Sea because the people refuse to clear the mines.[32] The agreement in the Ruhr is an utter capitulation by the government to the Workers' and Soldiers' Councils.[33] Our economic position is so hopeless that catastrophe is staring us in the face.

---

    decision not to disband the standing army but merely to reduce its size (question 6) and whether it agreed with the Independents that 'the government of the socialist republic cannot and should not depend for military support on the old standing army but should instead build up a new volunteer People's Army on democratic principles'.

30   The Central Council had asked, as a counterblast to the USPD's questions, whether the People's Representatives, including the USPD members, were ready to uphold public order against violent attacks, and in particular to defend property.

31   August Müller (1873–1946), SPD, Under-State Secretary in the government of Prince Max von Baden, 1918, head of Reich Economics Office 1918–19, fierce opponent of measures of socialisation.

32   The crews of mine-sweeping vessels were refusing to clear mines until they were given a bonus payment for doing so.

33   On 28 December 1918 an agreement was made at Mülheim between striking workers and the firm of Thyssen, by which they received 80 million Marks in compensation for loss of earnings.

Source: Miller and Potthoff (eds.) 1969, *Regierung der Volksbeauftragten* vol. 2, pp. 285–6.

Note: Dr. Müller held the position of State Secretary in the Reich Economics Office from November 1918 until February 1919.

2.12 *Proclamation by the Central Council of the German Socialist Republic Handing Over its Power to the National Assembly, 4 February 1919*

To the German National Assembly in Weimar.[34]

1 The political and economic development of the German Reich had already made it clear before the Revolution that there was an urgent need for the conversion of the Reich into a unified state.

2 The revolution of the workers and soldiers has fully confirmed this need, demonstrating that the removal of all the obstacles presented by the individual states to the political, economic and social development of the German republic is one of its most important tasks, after the removal of Prussian domination.

3 Similarly, the transition to a unified state is the inescapable prerequisite for the systematic utilisation of the revolutionary organisations (Workers' and Soldiers' Councils), forces working unitedly for the complete reconstruction of Germany, in definitively shaping the social republic.

4 Recently the former federal states have made such strong claims to rights of sovereignty in the new Republic that the development towards a unified state appears to be in serious danger. The fragmentation of Germany into separate states threatens to work against the most rapid possible recovery of the country from the blows inflicted both by the World War and the likely shape of the peace treaty.

5 Alongside the incorporation of the Workers' and Soldiers' Councils into the future constitution of the Reich, so as to strengthen the representation of the workers and their interests as producers,[35] and to shape the military system in a democratic manner, their most important immediate task appears to be the fight against this harmful restoration of the individual states' rights of sovereignty.

---

34 The National Assembly did not reply to this communication, thereby indicating that it did not recognise the authority of the Central Council.

35 Paragraph 165 of the Weimar Constitution of August 1919 provided for the setting up of Councils of Factory Workers, but when set up these would bear little relation to the Workers' and Soldiers' Councils of the revolutionary period.

6 It is the responsibility of the National Assembly to prepare the political and economic reconstruction of Germany. It must not be restricted in this task by any other body, in particular the National Assemblies of the individual states.

7 The Central Council hereby transfers the power handed over to it by the Reich Congress of Workers' and Soldiers' Councils[36] into the hands of the German National Assembly, in the expectation that that body will implement its sovereignty in full

8 The Central Council will carry out the functions assigned to it, in particular the function of highest court of appeal for the Soldiers' Councils, which has been assigned to it by the new law on the regulation of the power of command[37] until the National Assembly has transferred these functions to another body.

Source: Kolb and Rürup (eds.) 1968, *Der Zentralrat der deutschen sozialistischen Republik 19.12.1918–8.4.1919*, doc. 77, pp. 544–6.

Note: The Communist Party's main newspaper commented on this proclamation with bitter irony, but not inaccurately: 'The Central Council has crowned its work of treachery to the Workers' and Soldiers' Councils. It proceeds on the basis of the plenitude of power transferred to it in order to throw the power away. It deprives the Workers' and Soldiers' Councils of their head by dissolving into thin air'. (*Die Rote Fahne*, 6 February 1919)

2.13   *The USPD Appeals 'to the Revolutionary Proletariat' to Defend the Workers' Councils, 11 February 1919*

The government is exerting all its strength to get rid of the Workers' and Soldiers' Councils, the instruments and guardians of the Revolution. In so doing, it is obeying the orders of the capitalists and the generals. They want the system of Workers' and Soldiers' Councils to shrink down to nothing. It is the task of the proletariat to frustrate this attack. The Workers' Councils are economically indispensable for the establishment of democracy in the factories. They must be given legal rights, so that they are incorporated into economic

---

36   See document 2.9. The First Congress of Councils did not in fact hand over power to the Central Council. It was dominated by the SPD, and it aimed to keep as much power as possible in the hands of the Council of People's Representatives. The Central Council was given a right of 'supervision' and 'appointment and dismissal of ministers' but no executive or legislative power.

37   This was an exaggeration. Paragraph 6 of the Ordinance of 19 January 1919 on the Power of Command provided that Soldiers' Councils could appeal against General Staff decisions to the government, but 'they may also turn to the Central Council at any time'.

life as instruments of social policy, as supervisory bodies for the management of enterprises, and as organs for implementing the socialisation that is to come in the future. The Soldiers' and Sailors' Councils are equally necessary, to keep down the spirit of militarism and to secure democracy in military affairs. We demand that political guarantees for the Workers' and Soldiers' Councils be included in the constitution of the Reich.

The Central Authority of the Workers' and Soldiers' Councils[38] must receive the right to veto the decisions of the National Assembly, with the subsequent settlement of disputed issues by plebiscite. In order to make sure that the revolution continues until the realisation of socialism, the Central Authority of the Workers' and Soldiers' Councils must have the further right to introduce its bills into the National Assembly independently. The USPD will act with all its strength to secure these demands. It is conscious that their implementation depends on the resolute will of the whole German working class. Only when the working class adopts a purposeful policy, aimed directly at socialism without opportunistically taking the bourgeoisie into account, will it be possible to make the socialist republic a reality despite all obstacles.

Weimar, 8 February 1919

Source: Unabhängige Sozialdemokratische Partei Deutschlands 1919, *Die Freiheit* no. 74, 11 February 1919.

2.14   *Demands of the Berlin Workers' and Soldiers' Councils, 3 March 1919*

A   Political Demands

1 Recognition of the Workers' and Soldiers' Councils.

2 Immediate implementation of the Hamburg Points[39] relating to the powers of military commanders.

3 Release of all political prisoners, especially Comrade Ledebour,[40] ending of all political trials; abolition of military jurisdiction; transfer of all military cases to the civil courts, and in particular the immediate abolition of all courts martial. Immediate arrest of all persons who have taken part in political murders.

4 Immediate establishment of a revolutionary Workers' Defence Force.

---

38   In other words, the Central Council, which had just transferred the powers it claimed to the National Assembly.

39   For the Hamburg Points, see 8.4 of this collection.

40   The left USPD leader Georg Ledebour had just been arrested.

5 Immediate disbandment of all Volunteer Units which have come into existence through recruitment.[41]

6 Immediate establishment of political and economic relations with the Russian Soviet government.

B   Economic Demands

The Workers' Councils are the appropriate form of representation for the working population. Their task is to secure and extend the new order of things in Germany. Their task is also to look after the interests of the workers, employees and officials, both male and female, in private firms and in municipal and state enterprises, and to exert a thorough supervision (*Kontrolle*) over those enterprises. The goal of their activity must be the rapid socialisation of economic and state life. The General Assembly of the Workers' Councils, in association with the Soldiers' Councils, is the highest authority for the Workers' Councils and their activities. It is the duty of the working population to make sure that their decisions prevail.

Source: Sozialistische Einheitspartei Deutschlands Zentralkomitee 1958, *Dokumente und Materialien zur Geschichte der deutschen Arbeiterbewegung, Reihe II: 1914–1945, Band 3* no. 115, pp. 289–90.

2.15   *The Proclamation of the Bavarian Council Republic, 7 April 1919*

To the people of Bavaria!

The decision has been made. Bavaria is a Council republic. The working people are masters of their destiny. The revolutionary working class and peasantry of Bavaria, including all our brothers who are soldiers, are no longer divided by any party disagreements and are all agreed that from now on any kind of exploitation or oppression must come to an end. The purpose of the dictatorship of the proletariat, which is now a fact, is to bring into existence a truly socialist community, a just socialist-communist economy, in which every working person may take part in public life.

The Diet, that barren creation of the bourgeois-capitalist age which has now come to an end, is dissolved and the government appointed by it has resigned. Commissars appointed by the Councils of the working people and responsible

---

41   This refers to the various Free Corps units which emerged from the old imperial army after Germany's defeat, and were used by Gustav Noske, SPD Minister of Defence, to suppress revolutionary disorders in 1919. See document 8.6.

to them now receive emergency powers. Tried and trusted men from all the tendencies of revolutionary socialism and communism will be their assistants; we appeal to the numerous capable elements of the bureaucracy, particularly the lower and middle-ranking officials, to cooperate energetically in running the new Bavaria. But the bureaucratic system will be eradicated without delay.

The press will be socialised. A red army will be set up immediately. A revolutionary court will immediately and ruthlessly punish all attacks on the Council Republic. The Bavarian Council Republic follows the example of the Russian and Hungarian nations. It immediately forms a fraternal bond with these nations. In contrast to this, it rejects any cooperation with the despicable government of Ebert, Scheidemann, Noske, and Erzberger because they are continuing the shameful imperialist, capitalist and militarist activities of the collapsed German empire under the flag of a socialist republic.

We call on all our German brothers to go the same way as us. The Bavarian Council Republic offers its greetings to all proletarians, wherever they are fighting for freedom and justice, for revolutionary socialism, in Württemberg and in the Ruhr district, in the whole world.

The seventh of April is declared a national holiday as a mark of our joyful expectation of a happy future for the whole of mankind. On Monday, 7 April 1919, as a sign that we are starting to leave behind the accursed age of capitalism, work will stop in the whole of Bavaria unless it is necessary for the life of the working people. More detailed instructions are simultaneously issued on this point.

Long live free Bavaria! Long live the Council Republic! Long live the world revolution!

The Revolutionary Central Council of Bavaria:
Niekisch, Gustav Landauer, Erich Mühsam, Gandorfer (Peasant Council)
Dr. Franz Lipp, Albert Schmid.
For the Revolutionary Soldiers' Council:
Kohlschmid, Johann Wimmer, Max Mehrer.

Source: Deutscher Geschichtskalender 1919, *Geschichtskalender, Ergänzungsband. Die deutsche Revolution. Band 2*, p. 206.

2.16 *SPD Resolution on the Question of Councils, Adopted in April 1919 by the Second Congress of Councils*

I

1 The basis of the socialist republic must be socialist democracy. Bourgeois democracy evaluates the population according to mere numbers. Socialist democracy must supplement this by seeking to embrace the population on the basis of the kind of work it does.

2 This can best be done through the setting up of Chambers of Labour. In elections to these Chambers all working Germans will have the right to cast their votes, in separate sections divided according to occupation.

3 Every trade is to form an Economic Council to which the specific categories of employee (including the managers of enterprises) are to send their representatives (the Councillors). Agriculture and the free professions are to form analogous representative bodies.

4 Every Economic Council elects delegates to the Chambers of Labour, which thus originate from the smallest economic unit.

5 This is the parish or municipality. Parishes which from a single economic unit will be joined together.

6 The Economic Councils of the Districts, Provinces, States and finally the Republic of Germany are to elect delegates to the relevant Chamber of Labour. Everywhere there will be a general People's Chamber and a Chamber of Labour.

7 Every law requires the agreement of both Chambers, but a bill which is passed in three-successive years by the relevant People's Chamber without alteration gains the force of law.

8 Each of the Chambers has the right to demand an election.

9 As a rule all bills of an economic character (above all, socialisation proposals) will go first to the Chamber of Labour ... The People's Chamber will usually be the first to deal with bills of a general political and cultural character.

II
1 The Trade Unions are the representatives of the workers in all walks of life. The executive organs of the trade unions in the factories are the Factory Councils.

2 Wages and working conditions are to be settled between organisation and organisation, hence between the relevant trade union and the employers' association.

3 While the Workers' Councils represent the workers in the Economic Council in respect of questions of production, the organs for the regulation of wages

and working conditions as well as other occupational questions are the *Arbeitsgemeinschaften* (Working Associations) which have been set up so far. The trade unions and the employers' associations will work together in these institutions.

4 The Economic Councils represent production, and production is in the joint hands of the workers and the employers. The workers are represented in this context by the Workers' Councils. The Economic Council is the infrastructure for socialisation.

Source: Centralrat der Sozialistischen Republik Deutschlands 1975, *II.Kongress der Arbeitern, Bauern- und Soldatenräte Deutschlands am 8. bis 14. April 1919 im Herrenhaus zu Berlin. Stenographisches Protokoll*, p. 267.

Note: The corporatist approach of Max Cohen-Reuss (SPD) and the group around the journal *Sozialistische Monatshefte* is clearly visible in this document. Their objective was to combine the direct representation of the workers in the Workers' Councils which had emerged from the November Revolution with the institutions of parliamentary democracy. The language used is slightly confusing, in that the 'People's Chamber' (*Volkskammer*) is in fact the Reichstag, or analogous bodies in the individual German states. Cohen's ideal was voluntary cooperation between employers and workers in the organisation and running of production. The USPD representatives at the Congress opposed this. The reasons were given by Otto Brass, who represented the industrial district of Remscheid: 'This resolution recognises the parliamentary form of the state and attempts to force the Council Organisation into a lasting cooperation with the parliament. In the economic sphere the SPD resolution gives the capitalist entrepreneurs equality of representation. To give them equality of rights within the Councils is to commit a violent assault on the proletarian Council idea'.

2.17   The Communists and Independents (KPD and USPD) Oppose the Passing of the Factory Council Law, 12 January 1920

The counter-revolution is endeavouring to destroy all the achievements of the Revolution, one after another. With the strangling of the Soldiers' Councils power in military affairs reverted to the old soldiery (under new leadership). After this there followed the annihilation of the Workers' Councils, the repository of the revolutionary proletariat's political hopes. Now the counter-revolution wants to set the seal on its activities by using legislation to break the influence of the workers in the factories. The Factory Council Law is intended finally to destroy any thought of a social revolution. It will... be rejected by revolutionary workers by hand or brain as an impudent deception.

This law tears the proletariat apart. It renews the division between the workers and the office employees. It converts the workers' right to determine their own employment and dismissal into a hollow sham, by merely granting the right to complain about dismissal after the event and not providing any means of enforcing the complaint.

It completely excludes the workers and office employees from exerting any supervision over the management and running of the enterprise. It makes the Factory Councils mere foremen in the service of the capitalist entrepreneurs... The confusion in the economy is now worse than ever. The limitless upward surge of prices goes hand in hand with the growth of the counter-revolution's political influence. Only a transformation of the mode of production from the ground up can prevent a general collapse and make possible the reconstruction of the economy. This beneficial transformation of the mode of production in the direction of socialism requires the enthusiastic cooperation of all workers by hand or brain and their representatives in the factories. Only Factory Councils possessing the necessary rights are in a position to do this.

We therefore demand a full right of control over the running of the factories. The productive people, the workers and employees, must determine through their representatives whether factories may be closed down or not, what can be produced in them and in what quantities, what prices should be charged, how coal and other raw and accessory materials should be distributed, and what is to be exported or imported.

The fight for revolutionary Factory Councils must be pushed forward or taken up again in all factories. The next few days will bring this struggle to a culmination, with the parliamentary decision over the Factory Council Law. The counter-revolution's action in parliament must meet with every imaginable resistance, not only in parliament but in the country, thereby setting off mass actions of ever greater intensity.

Zentrale of the Factory Councils of Germany

USPD

KPD (S)

Source: *Die Rote Fahne*, 13 January 1920, reprinted in Sozialistische Einheitspartei Deutschlands Zentralkomitee 1958, *Dokumente und Materialien zur Geschichte der deutschen Arbeiterbewegung, Reihe II: 1914–1945*, vol. VII, part 1, Berlin, 1967, nr. 91, pp. 173–4.

Note: This joint appeal by the USPD and the KPD led to the mass demonstration of 13 January 1920 in Berlin, to coincide with the parliamentary discussion of the bill, which was suppressed by the security forces with considerable loss of life (42 deaths). See below for the law itself.

2.18   *The Factory Council Law of 4 February 1920*

1 Factory Councils are to be established in all factories which employ at least 20 workers, in order to look after the common economic interests of the employees (the workers and office employees) in relation to their employer, and also to give support to the employer in achieving the aims of the factory.

...

6 All factories where there are Factory Councils are to set up Workers' Councils and Councils of Office Employees, with the aim of looking after the common economic interests of the workers and office employees.

...

8 The powers of the economic associations of workers and office employees[42] in relation to the protection of the interests of their members are not to be affected by the provisions of this law.

...

66 These are the tasks of the Factory Councils:
    1 to give advice to the factory management
    2 to cooperate in the introduction of new methods of work
    3 to negotiate with the employer on labour regulations, within the framework of existing wage contracts
    4 to take note of complaints by the Workers' Council and to work towards dealing with them in joint negotiations with the employer.[43]

---

42   This refers to the trade unions.

43   This section of the law reproduces section 34 of the 16 August 1919 draft, but with an important omission: the Factory Council originally had the extra prerogatives of 'collaborating in the fixing of wages, working conditions, methods of payment of wages, working hours, especially the extension and reduction of the regular period of work, holiday periods, organising apprenticeships and collaborating in the appointment and dismissing of workers'. For this text see *Nationalversammlung* 1920, Bd. 338, Anlagen, Nr. 928.

...

71 To enable it to carry out its tasks, the Factory Council has the right to demand from the employer that he give information about all events in the factory which affect the workers' conditions of service and activity, and that he lay before the Factory Council the materials required for the implementation of existing wage contracts. Furthermore, the employer must issue a quarterly report on the situation and progress of the enterprise and the branch of industry of which it forms a part, as well as the performance of the factory and in particular the expected labour requirements.

72 Where a factory employs more than 300 workers, the Factory Councils are entitled to demand to see an annual profit and loss account for the past business year, which is to be issued not later than six months after the end of that business year.[44]

Signed: Ebert (President)
Schlicke[45] (Reich Labour Minister)

Source: Deutsches Reich 1920, *Reichsgesetzblatt* Nr. 26, pp. 147–74.

Note: This final version of the Factory Council Law took account of the objections raised against the government's draft of 16 August 1919 by the non-socialist parties in the National Assembly. The original preamble stated that 'the Factory Council has the task of asserting the influence of the employees on production and all other purposes of the factory'. It was cut out and replaced by paragraph 1 as given above. Even the 16 August draft, however, had very little in common with the more radical objectives of the factory council movement which sprang up in the immediate aftermath of the November Revolution.[46]

2.19   *The KPD Puts its View of the Tasks of the Factory Councils*

The tremendous shortage of all commodities needed to preserve life makes it necessary to replace the anarchic capitalist economy of profit with the planned communist economy for need ... It is therefore the task of the Factory Councils to implement supervision (*Kontrolle*) over the whole of the production, transport

---

44   In the Draft Law this provision applied to factories employing upwards of 50 workers.

45   Alexander Schlicke (1863–1940), chair of the Metalworkers' Union 1895–1919, Minister of Labour in Württemberg 1919, in the Reich 1919–20.

46   Oertzen 1963, p. 155.

and distribution of goods. For this purpose the individual Factory Councils must immediately get into contact with the other Factory Councils of the same industry or craft and also the Councils in agriculture. In the same way all the Factory Councils of every economic region which forms a coherent whole must meet together, for these tasks can only be accomplished through the joint labour of the associated Councils. For the tasks of the Factory Councils the following guidelines are applicable:

1 The workers by hand and brain associated together in the Factory Councils must find out the type and amount of production, trade and transport that is being carried on. The most important thing is to establish the quantity of available raw materials and the possibility of procuring more, and the amount and type of labour-power which can be applied.

2 They must supervise the procurement of the means of production (coal, machines, tools).

3 They must supervise industrial equipment and the employer's legal right of disposition over productive property, in order to prevent the sale abroad of the industrial equipment necessary for the national economy, and also supervise capitalist property in general.

4 They must participate in the calculation of prices in order to prevent the employers from overcharging the consumer.

5 They must exercise control over the marketing of products. In order to preserve the life of society, necessary products must not be exported without compelling reasons. There must therefore be strict supervision over all imports and exports and the exchange of useful and necessary goods for less useful or unnecessary ones must be prevented. The import and export trade must be focused on the most urgent needs, so as to promote the reconstruction of economic life.

6 They must supervise the firm's credit procurements and bring to light the system of credit it operates. They must keep watch over its relations with the banks and over the activities of the banks themselves . . .

7 They must supervise the employment and dismissal of workers.

8 They must exert influence over methods of work, the duration of work and payment for work in association with the trade unions, in order to prevent the introduction of methods of payment such as piece-wages, which destroy the solidarity of the working class and make possible the use of sweated labour.

9 The same supervision as industry must take place in agriculture through the Estate Councils and the Small Peasants' Councils.

10 Both groups of Councils, the urban and the rural, must be in constant communication so as to promote the exchange of industrial for agricultural products.

11 The Factory Councils must exert a determining influence on the distribution of products, so as to secure a minimum level of nourishment, clothing, living accommodation and heating for every member of society whether working
or unfit for work.

12 The dangers which threaten the health of the population, particularly its
working part, make it the duty of the Factory Councils to set up and effectively
implement adequate factory legislation.

Source: Kommunistische Partei Deutschlands 1920, 'Zu den Betriebsrätewahlen',
Die Rote Fahne No. 24, 7 March 1920.

Communism and Insurrection

Introduction

The Communist Party of Germany (KPD)[1] was formed at a congress held between 30 December 1918 and 1 January 1919 out of two divergent components: the Spartacus League and the Bremen and Hamburg Left Radicals. The Spartacists, the most prominent of whom were Rosa Luxemburg[2] and Karl Liebknecht,[3] emerged from the left wing of pre-war Social Democracy. When a section of the Party broke with official Social Democracy in 1917 over its continued support for the German war effort, and formed the rival Independent Social Democratic Party of Germany (USPD) the Spartacists decided to join that group. The Left Radicals, led at this time by Karl Radek[4] and Johann Knief,[5] thought this was a mistake. They considered that a separate communist party should be set up, on the lines of the Bolshevik Party in Russia, and they were already using the word 'communist' in the name of their group, the International Communists of Germany (IKD) which was set up on 23 November 1918. Both sides, the Spartacists and the Left Radicals, were enthusiastic about the October Revolution in Russia, and both wanted something similar in Germany, but they had different views about the way to get there. The Spartacist leaders, Rosa Luxemburg above all, thought the coming

---

1 The Party in fact bore the title KPD (S) (Communist Party of Germany (Spartacus League) for the first two years of its existence. See note 15 for further name-changes.

2 Rosa Luxemburg (1870–1919), eminent Marxist theorist and revolutionary prominent on the left of the SPD before 1914, founder-member of the Spartacus League 1916, led the KPD for some weeks until her murder in January 1919 by officers of the Free Corps.

3 Karl Liebknecht (1871–1918), revolutionary activist, prominent on the left of the SPD before 1914, founder-member of the Spartacus League 1916, led the KPD along with Rosa Luxemburg and Leo Jogiches for a few week until his murder in January 1919 by officers of the Free Corps.

4 Karl Radek (1885–1939), after a varied career on the left of pre-war Social Democracy, went to Russia and was elected a member of the Bolshevik Central Committee. He did not return to Germany until December 1918, but he retained a connection with the Bremen Left Radicals throughout the war. He was later involved closely in German affairs until 1924 on behalf of the ECCI.

5 Johann Knief (1880–1919), leader of the Bremen Left Radicals, then the International Communists of Germany (IKD), founder-member of the KPD, proclaimed the short-lived Bremen Council Republic in January 1919.

revolution should be the achievement of the whole working class and would take time to prepare; the Left Radicals on the other hand called for an immediate insurrection on Bolshevik lines organised by the Communist Party. At the founding congress of the KPD the Left Radicals appeared to be in the minority (there were 94 Spartacist delegates and only 29 from the IKD), but in fact their views prevailed on the issue of participation in the forthcoming elections to the Constituent National Assembly, an indication that many of the Spartacist delegates had also been influenced by leftist ideas. In the words of Chris Harman, 'the majority of the delegates were far from accepting Rosa Luxemburg's conviction that it was necessary to win the masses ... before trying to take over the government'.[6] The congress decided by a large majority (62 to 23) to boycott the parliamentary elections. It also refused to agree that communists should stay in, or enter, the existing trade unions; on this issue the leadership had to temporise by setting up a commission to discuss the question. Paul Levi,[7] who became the leader of the Party after the murder of Luxemburg and Liebknecht in January 1919, had to fight hard to overcome this tendency to ultra-leftism. The leftists opposed participation both in parliaments and trade unions, and favoured a loose federal organisation. In fact some of them rejected the idea of a communist political party in favour of a combined politico-economic 'unity organisation', on Syndicalist lines.[8] At the second congress of the Party, held in October 1919, Levi was able to push through a Declaration of Communist Principles and Tactics, which affirmed the need for parliamentary and trade union participation, and a centralised political party (3.4). Delegates who did not accept Levi's theses were immediately expelled, an extreme step which indicates how dangerous Levi and his associates considered the threat from the left to be.[9] At the same congress theses approving participation in parliament and in trade union activity were also adopted (3.5 and 3.6).

Despite the title of this chapter, communism was not synonymous with armed insurrection.[10] Communists did believe, however, that power could

---

6   Harman 1997, p. 66.

7   Paul Levi (1883–1930), lawyer, joined the Spartacus League in 1916, founder-member of the KPD 1918, leader of the KPD 1919–21, expelled 1921, set up the Communist Working Group (KAG), entered the USPD with his group April 1922, brought his group into the SPD September 1922, led the left opposition in the SPD until his death in 1930.

8   These divergences are clearly brought out in Bock 1993.

9   For this reason, Klaus-Michael Mallmann, in his recent controversial study of the KPD, presents Levi as a Stalinist *avant la lettre* who was 'even more rigorous than the Central Committee under Thälmann' (Mallmann 1996, p. 64).

10   In fact, once the revolution had ceased to be an immediate prospect, local members of the KPD devoted themselves to promoting workers' day-to-day interests through their

only be wrested from the bourgeoisie and given to the working class by a violent uprising as had happened in Russia. This could not happen if the situation was not ripe for it. It seems unlikely that Rosa Luxemburg would have supported the risings of March 1921 and October 1923 (except after the event, out of revolutionary solidarity, as she did in January 1919). Her views were made clear in these words: 'Revolutions are not "made", and great popular movements are not produced with technical recipes from party offices'.[11] The so-called Spartacist Rising of January 1919 was a case in point: its aim was to defend the conquests of the November Revolution, not to go further and overthrow capitalist rule (3.1), and it was in no sense a planned communist insurrection. But the Spartacists themselves contributed to the misunderstanding 'by not making clear that they regarded the movement as having strictly limited objectives'.[12] The driving force of the movement was not the communists but the Revolutionary Shop Stewards, who were members of the USPD, and the immediate impulse for their action was the dismissal of Emil Eichhorn, their party colleague, from the post of Berlin Police Chief.

The suppression of the so-called 'Spartacist rising' of January 1919 by no means brought an end to the post-war upheavals. For the first four years of the Weimar Republic a socialist revolution appeared to be a possibility. There was, first of all, the short-lived episode of the Bavarian Council Republic of April to May 1919 (2.15) which the Munich KPD initially refused to support, but was later drawn into out of motives of revolutionary solidarity. After that there was the resistance to the Kapp putsch of March 1920. This was, it has been argued, the closest the country ever came to revolution.[13] But despite the existence of a 'Red Army of the Ruhr' possibly 50,000 strong according to some estimates, the movement lacked any real direction, given the extreme weakness of the Communist Party at that stage, and ultimately suffered a catastrophic defeat.[14] Though the workers held power locally the question of a national insurrection was not really posed at that stage. In any case, communists held very divergent opinions about the conditions under which the expected revolution might

---

positions in local government. This sort of activity was seen as carrying with it the danger of rightism. We have not dealt with the very large subject of communist local politics. See in detail Wünderich 1980.

11   Luxemburg 1974, pp. 148–9.

12   Harman 1997, p. 91.

13   The *putsch* against the German republic mounted by right-wing politician Wolfgang Kapp (1858–1922), who founded the German Fatherland Party in 1917, and was close to the DNVP after 1918. After the failure of his *putsch* he fled to Sweden, then returned to Germany. He was arrested, but died before he could be brought to trial.

14   Harman 1997, p. 180.

take place, and whether or not it would be advisable to push an insurrection-
ist movement forward if it began under its own momentum. This was one of
the issues in March 1921, when what was now the 'united communist party'
(VKPD)[15] had to decide whether to try to turn the spontaneous resistance of
the workers of Central Germany to provocative police tactics into a genuine
revolution or to dampen down the movement. A critical situation had been
developing for some time in the Halle-Merseburg area of Prussian Saxony, with
constant conflicts between the mineworkers and their employers. The SPD
governor of the province, Otto Hörsing,[16] announced on 17 March 1921 that he
would mount a police occupation of the area, with the aim of disarming the
workers, some of whom had retained the weapons they picked up the year
before during their resistance to the Kapp putsch the year before.

   Hörsing's announcement came at exactly the right time for the advocates of
an uprising within the VKPD. They were supported by the three emissaries of
the Executive Committee of the Communist International (ECCI), Béla Kun,[17]
József Pogány[18] and Felix Kleine (Guralsky)[19] who had been sent from Moscow
with instructions to stir up revolutionary activities in Central Europe if at all
possible so as to take the pressure off the Bolsheviks at a moment which, as
Karl Radek pointed out in his letter of 14 March (6.3a), was very critical. The
supporters of the revolutionary offensive also had the advantage that the previous month the more moderate faction of the party leadership, led by Paul Levi,
had resigned from the *Zentrale*[20] in protest against what they called 'a policy of

---

15   VKPD: United Communist Party of Germany. This name was adopted by the KPD after
      it was joined by the Left USPD at the Sixth (Unification) Congress held in Berlin in
      December 1920. It was retained until July 1921 when the Party became simply the KPD.

16   Otto Hörsing (1874–1937), SPD, governor (*Oberpräsident*) of the Prussian province of
      Saxony from 1920 to 1927. It was on his initiative that the pro-republican war veterans'
      organisation the *Reichsbanner Schwarz-Rot-Gold* (Black-Red-Gold Association for the
      Republic) was set up in 1924.

17   Béla Kun (1886–1937?), founder of the Hungarian Communist Party, 1919. Commissar for
      Foreign Affairs in the Hungarian Soviet Republic of 1919. Subsequently in exile, and active
      in various Comintern functions until his arrest.

18   József Pogány (1886–1939), Hungarian communist, exercised functions of agitation and
      propaganda in the Comintern until 1929.

19   August Kleine (Samuel Haifiz, also known as A.Guralsky) (1890–1960?), member of the
      Bund until 1919, then joined the Bolshevik Party, Comintern functionary, ECCI special
      representative in Germany 1922–1924, member of the KPD *Zentrale* 1923–24. Represented
      the Comintern in Paris, 1924–25, supported the Zinoviev opposition to Stalin in 1926,
      represented the Comintern in South America from 1930, recalled to Moscow 1933 and
      arrested, but survived his imprisonment.

20   *Zentrale*: the name used at the time for the KPD's central committee.

creating purer parties by the method of mechanical splits' which had just been applied in Italy and which they feared might happen in Germany too.[21] On the evening of 17 March the VKPD *Zentrale* voted in favour of Heinrich Brandler's[22] call for immediate action. The workers themselves were not too enthusiastic, and the action had to be promoted by 'artificial methods', including blowing up a workers' cooperative society headquarters in Halle and blaming the explosion on the police. All this later came out into the open accidentally when reports from two local leaders of the March Action fell into the hands of the Social Democrats, who published them in their newspaper (3.7). A general strike finally broke out on 23 March in Prussian Saxony and Hamburg, though it proved impossible to extend it to cover the whole of Germany. The only genuinely insurrectionary element in the March Action was the movement inspired by Max Hölz,[23] a dissident communist previously expelled from the KPD, in the Mansfeld area. His band of 2,500 rebels engaged for a week in a campaign which involved plundering shops, robbing banks, dynamiting railway lines and fighting the Security Police. But by the end of March it was all over. On 1 April the *Zentrale* was finally forced to admit defeat and call off the action. Yet the leading group in that body continued to claim that revolution was on the agenda: the proletariat would act if it was galvanised by some bold stroke.

Paul Levi, who had led the VKPD until February 1921, disagreed with this analysis, considering that the March Action was an unmitigated disaster. When it became clear that the majority faction in the Party would not shift its views, he took the fateful step of publishing a pamphlet, entitled *Unser Weg* (Our Path) in which he laid bare the background of the decision to engage in the March Action. In this pamphlet he denounced the Party's leaders, using his tremendous oratorical powers and biting wit to great effect. He showed the text to Clara Zetkin,[24] another former Spartacist, who had resigned from the *Zentrale* along with him in February 1921. She agreed that the pamphlet

21   Kommunistische Partei Deutschlands 1921, *Die Rote Fahne*, 28 February 1921.
22   Heinrich Brandler (1861–1967), leader of the KPD 1922–24. Countermanded the planned communist uprising of October 1923. Removed from party functions in Germany as 'Rightist' in 1924 and sent to the Soviet Union. Returned to Germany in 1929 and founded the KPO (Communist Party Opposition).
23   Max Hölz (1889–1933), USPD 1918, KPD 1919, KAPD 1920 KPD 1921. Conducted guerrilla activities during the March Action of 1921. Caught and imprisoned. Released in 1928. Later lived in the Soviet Union until his death by drowning, possibly accidental.
24   Clara Zetkin (1857–1933), long active on the Left of the pre-war SPD, founder member of the Spartacus League in 1916, then the KPD in 1919, member of the KPD *Zentrale* 1919–24, member of the KPD Central Committee 1927–29, member of the ECCI 1921–33. Regarded as on the 'Right' of the Party after 1924 but tolerated as a figurehead.

should be published, but with the excision of the most wounding passages, which she indicated with a blue pencil. She particularly disliked the reference to the ECCI's three emissaries as 'the Turkestanis...who would do less harm if they tried their tricks in Turkestan'.[25] Levi ignored her advice and published the pamphlet exactly as he had written it.

The basic argument of *Unser Weg* was that the Party had allowed itself to be dragged into an adventure of an anarchist type, described by Levi as 'the greatest Bakuninist putsch in history so far'. He claimed that the abrupt shift from passivity to putschism displayed by the Party in March 1921 was not caused by a change in the German situation, and that none of the conditions set by Lenin for a seizure of power in 1917, which were regarded as classic in communist circles, obtained in the Germany of 1921. These conditions were (1) the growth of the revolution on a country-wide scale (2) the complete moral and political bankruptcy of the old government, and (3) extreme vacillation in the camp of all middle groups, i.e. those who do not *fully* support the government any more. What had happened, he said, was that three Moscow emissaries had arrived, and that one of them, who 'hadn't the slightest understanding of German conditions' (Levi didn't mention Kun by name but he was clearly meant) dreamed up the March Action. The acting leader of the Party, Heinrich Brandler, far from opposing this, supported it 'by talking nonsense for which he deserved to be sent to the cellars of a mental health clinic for a cold-water cure'. As for Hugo Eberlein,[26] another party leader, he 'had no place in a communist party' because he believed that 'one could drive the workers into action with dynamite or beatings'. This referred to Eberlein's role as the Party's military expert,

---

25 Turkestanis: it is hard to guess what Levi meant by this curious expression, with its xenophobic undertones. The plural would suggest that he was referring to the ECCI's representatives in general, rather than Béla Kun in particular. There is no evidence that Kun was ever in Turkestan. Some authors allege that he was sent there in 1921 because Lenin was allegedly outraged by his brutal actions at the end of 1920 in the Crimea at the time of the capitulation of General Wrangel's White forces, but the detailed account of his activities by Borsány (1993, pp. 231–45) rules this out. He went straight from the Crimea to Moscow then was immediately sent by the Comintern to Germany. Nor did the other ECCI agents have any connection with Central Asia. The most likely explanation for Levi's choice of this word is that he used it as a shorthand description of a 'remote' and 'obscure' Eastern place in Soviet Russia, from which the ECCI sent emissaries to the West to make decisions on matters about which they were ignorant.

26 Hugo Eberlein (1887–1944). Spartacist, KPD leader after 1919, represented the KPD at the First Comintern Congress in March 1919, member of the KPD *Zentrale* 1919–1924. Readmitted to the top leadership of the KPD in 1927. Removed from the leadership in 1928. Died in the Soviet Union.

COMMUNISM AND INSURRECTION

which led him to take the measures of provocation we mentioned earlier. Finally, and perhaps most insulting of all, Levi described the ECCI's emissaries as 'not people of top quality'. The Bolsheviks needed their best cadres urgently at home, so they sent 'second-raters, miniature statesmen, of whom one has the impression that they want to show off their brilliance'. And, he added, in a final rhetorical flourish: these people 'work like a Cheka[27] projected abroad'.[28]

Levi was immediately expelled from the VKPD for his breach of party discipline. The leading comrades of the ECCI did not disagree with this decision at the time, but by mid-1921 the mood had changed in Moscow: Levi's criticisms of the March Action were now seen as valid, although his disobedience was unacceptable. At the Third Comintern Congress, held in June and July 1921, the 'theory of the offensive' was condemned and the accent was placed on the need to secure mass support before taking any further revolutionary action. Trotsky's evaluation of the March Action was expressed in this striking phrase: 'the leadership confused the fifth month of pregnancy with the ninth'.[29]

It seemed for two years as if the post-war wave of revolution had come to an end in Europe. This was the background to the adoption of the 'united front' idea by the Communist International. The theory behind this was that communists and social democrats, despite their fundamental disagreements, could cooperate on partial issues where the interests of the working class could be advanced by joint action, and that the communists, by taking part in these struggles more consistently, unreservedly and actively, would gain the support of social democratic workers and thereby achieve a dominant role in the working-class movement. The Party pursued this policy with some success between 1921 and 1923. Yet in 1923 another crisis blew up in Germany which led many communists, both at home and in the Soviet Union, to believe that a German revolution was once again a possibility.[30] They only reached this conviction very gradually. Even in May 1923 the view was still that 'the German communists are in no state to set up a dictatorship of the proletariat because no desire for revolution yet exists among the majority of proletarians'.[31]

---

27   Cheka: The earliest Soviet state security force, a forerunner of the GPU, NKVD and KGB. Its full title was: Extraordinary Commission for Struggle with the Counter-Revolution.

28   I have not included any extracts from Levi's pamphlet *Unser Weg* in this collection, because it is now available in a complete English translation by David Fernbach (Levi 2011, pp. 119–65.)

29   Trotsky 1996, p. 113.

30   There is now detailed documentation available in German on the policy of the KPD, the Comintern and the Soviet leaders in 1923. See Bayerlein 2003, with explanatory notes.

31   This was Radek's view on 18 May 1923. See Fayet 2004, p. 443.

Not until the late summer of 1923 did the Soviet leaders decide that it would be worth making the attempt. They viewed the impending revolution as a combined political and military operation. Soviet advisers were sent to help on the military side, and the leader of the KPD, Heinrich Brandler, was called to Moscow to discuss the political preparations for an uprising scheduled to take place in October. He rather unwillingly agreed to the plan, which involved his entry into a coalition government with the SPD in Saxony (a parallel coalition was set up in next-door Thuringia) with the sole aim of gaining access to weapon supplies. There was also considerable pressure from below for a revolt, but it was not sufficient to persuade the leaders of the Saxon SPD to join in the general strike proposed by the communists (3.9). Brandler felt that the communists did not have the strength to go it alone. So he decided at the last moment that there was no prospect of success, and countermanded the action. This decision was also supported by Brandler's party colleagues, including Karl Radek, the representative of the Communist International. Whether they were right to retreat in this way has long been disputed.[32] In any case, Brandler's instructions failed to reach the communists in Hamburg, so they rose in revolt in that one place, and were easily defeated. Two weeks later the army was sent in to enforce the removal of the communist ministers from their positions in Saxony and Thuringia and the suppression of the 'Proletarian Hundreds' on which the Party had placed its hopes as a revolutionary striking-force. The position of strength the KPD had built up in the previous months was thereby completely liquidated.

In the post-mortem on the German October, held in Moscow in January 1924, the Brandler leadership was severely, and somewhat unfairly, criticised, and replaced by the most prominent members of the leftist faction of the Party, Ruth Fischer[33] and Arkady Maslow,[34] who appeared to talk a much more revolutionary language. The Hamburg rising, and its local leader, Ernst Thälmann,[35] achieved legendary status among communists, and attempts were immediately made to draw 'military lessons' from the Hamburg experience in view of a possible second attempt (3.13) But after the failure of the 'German October' of

---

32   Chris Harman has given a clear account of the various explanations for the failure of the 'German October' (Harman 1997, pp. 292–300).

33   Ruth Fischer (née Elfriede Eisler) (1895–1961) headed the Berlin branch of KPD, leader of leftists in KPD 1921–24, member of KPD *Zentrale* 1923–25. Expelled from the Party in 1926.

34   Arkady Maslow (Isaak Chereminsky) (1891–1941) headed Berlin KPD and led leftists along with Ruth Fischer, in KPD *Zentrale* 1924–25. Expelled from the Party in 1926.

35   Ernst Thälmann (1886–1944), USPD, then KPD. Chaired the Party from 1925. Candidate for President of Germany 1925 and 1932. Murdered in prison 1944.

1923 and the restoration of relative calm in Germany and internationally, insurrection was no longer seriously envisaged by the communists, despite their verbal radicalism. The idea of setting up an illegal 'military-political' party apparatus under Hans Kippenberger was launched but very little was achieved outside Berlin. As one of Kippenberger's subordinates later recalled, 'it formed an infinitesimally tiny group in the party' and it was 'very limited in extent' while 'the responsibility for these tasks often existed merely on paper'.[36] From that time onwards the distinctiveness of German communism lay not in any concrete plan to seize power but in its total opposition to the Weimar system and its unquestioning support for the Soviet Union, although it continued to be committed in theoretical terms to the violent overthrow of capitalism.

Documents

3.1 A Call to Revolt by the Spartacists and the Revolutionary Shop Stewards, 9 January 1919

General Strike! To Arms!
Workers! Comrades! Soldiers!

Boundless has been the forbearance of the revolutionary workers of Germany; measureless their patience with Ebert and Scheidemann, both stained with the blood of their brothers. The crimes of these traitors to the proletariat, these miserable underlings of capitalist intrigue, these embodiments of the counter-revolution, have long been infamous. The shooting down of defenceless men on leave and soldiers from the front on the 6th December, the shelling of the revolutionary sailors on the 24th December, these were the first bloody deeds of the Judases in the government. Their aim was to break the power of the revolution, and extinguish the blazing indignation of the worker and soldier masses. Yet the revolutionary spirit triumphed; the Scheidemanns and Eberts stood branded and despised before the whole world. But these murderers, condemned by the people's verdict, have not given up their villainous game. They belong in prison, or on the scaffold. But instead they intend to establish their domination on the very corpses of their victims, and to create a violent regime resting on bayonets, machine guns and cannons, a military citadel from which to overawe the revolutionary workers, a regime based on the exploiters and oppressors, the industrial bosses, the Junkers, the baying pack of officers and the volunteer Guards regiments.

---

36   Feuchtwanger 1981, p. 530.

They wanted to drive out Eichhorn,[37] the Police Chief: a despicable theft of this important revolutionary strongpoint was the intention. Then the fury of the Berlin worker masses blazed forth again in gigantic demonstrations. They threw up an impenetrable wall around his office. For they knew that there, in the office of the Berlin Police Chief, a mortal blow was about to be struck against the revolution itself. The masses tried to protect themselves from the infamous slanders of their deadly enemies by taking from their blood-stained hands the main instruments of incitement.[38] The Scheidemanns and Eberts did not hesitate. In their megalomania they lusted for fresh blood. On Monday[39] large numbers of sacred human lives fell victim to their fierce hatred for the revolutionary proletariat. The time was finally ripe for judgement to overtake them.

But the revolutionary proletariat had such unheard-of forbearance and patience that, despite this, it entered into negotiations with them, and appealed yet one more time to the conscience of those scoundrelly assassins in order to avoid further bloodshed. The scoundrels cunningly agreed to entertain these proposals, while insulting the representatives of the workers with impertinent demands and ambiguous turns of phrase. Craftily wearing the mask of peace, they dragged out the negotiations over two days, using those two days for busy military preparations. They brought in counter-revolutionary troops from outside Berlin; they bribed, confused and lulled to sleep the soldiers who had previously been revolutionary; they armed their own supporters and the bourgeoisie; and they feverishly worked to strengthen these military forces. Yesterday, Wednesday evening, when they thought they had made sufficient preparations, they broke off the negotiations, in crude reliance on their brutal strength.

The revolutionary workers have displayed unheard-of forbearance, patience, magnanimity and readiness for a peaceful solution. But the Eberts and Scheidemanns want not peace but war, civil war. They want to wade in the workers' blood, to drown the social revolution in it. They want to feed the starving people, who are trying to free themselves from the chains of capital, on a diet of blue beans[40] and to smash them to the ground.

Workers! Comrades! The situation is clear now. The last traces of mist have been blown away! What is at stake is everything! Our whole happiness, our whole future, the whole of the social revolution!

---

37 Emil Eichhorn (1863–1925) USPD Berlin Police Chief 1918–19, KPD 1920.
38 The reference is to the press.
39 6 January 1919.
40 Bullets (*blaue Bohnen*).

The Scheidemanns and Eberts have publicly called their supporters and the bourgeoisie to arms against you proletarians. The right of self-defence itself compels you to reply in kind. There is no choice! We must fight to the last! Destiny has issued its inexorable summons to every proletarian and every revolutionary soldier: onward to the last decisive struggle!

Leave the factories, you working men and women! Your first reply to Ebert and Scheidemann must be a general strike covering every enterprise! All wheels must come to a halt. Get out, out of the factories and into the street!

Show the scoundrels your strength! Take up arms! Use your weapons against your deadly enemies, the Eberts and Scheidemanns! Forward to the struggle, to the annihilating blow which must smash the blood-befouled Ebert and Scheidemann! The destruction of the revolution and the slaughter of the proletariat, or the destruction of the Eberts, the Scheidemanns and all the other deadly enemies of the proletariat: these are the alternatives.

Be armed, be ready, take action, take action, take action! Long live the proletariat! Long live the socialist revolution of the German proletariat! Long live the world socialist revolution!

Workers! Comrades! Come out of the factories! Forward to the general strike! Out onto the streets for the final battle, for victory!

> The Revolutionary Shop-Stewards and representatives of
> the big factories of Greater Berlin; the Central Leadership
> of the Independent Social Democratic electoral organisations
> of Berlin and surrounding districts; the *Zentrale* of the Communist
> Party of Germany (Spartacus League).

Source: Sozialistische Einheitspartei Deutschlands Zentralkomitee 1958, *Dokumente und Materialien zur Geschichte der deutschen Arbeiterbewegung, Reihe II: 1914–1945, Band 3* (Berlin, Dietz Verlag: 1958), Nr. 16, pp. 33–5.

Note: This proclamation was certainly inflammatory; but it was not a call for insurrection. What was intended was a general strike and a protest demonstration against the removal of Emil Eichhorn. The Revolutionary Shop Stewards took the lead, and the KPD felt that it could not hang back where the masses were clearly in movement.

3.2   *'Despite Everything'. Karl Liebknecht's last article, 15 January 1919*

General onslaught on Spartacus! Through the streets there echoes the cry: 'Down with the Spartacists. Hit them, whip them, stab them, shoot them, run them through, trample them down, tear them to pieces!' The atrocities of German troops in Belgium during the War are put in the shade by those now being committed. 'Spartacus has been faced down!' This is the jubilant cry which runs all the way from *Die Post*[41] to *Vorwärts*. 'Spartacus overpowered!' And the sabres, revolvers and carbines of the restored Old Germanic police and the disarming of the revolutionary workers will set the seal on the defeat... The elections to the National Assembly – a plebiscite for Napoleon-Ebert – will be conducted under the bayonets of Colonel Reinhardt,[42] and the machine-guns and cannons of General Lüttwitz.[43]

'Spartacus overwhelmed!' Yes! The revolutionary workers of Berlin were defeated. Hundreds of their best people were slaughtered. Hundreds of their most faithful supporters were thrown into prison. The workers were defeated because they were abandoned by the sailors, the soldiers and the People's Militia[44] on whose help they had confidently relied. And their strength was reduced by the indecision and weakness of their own leadership. And they were drowned in the immense flood of counter-revolutionary slime welling up from the backward sections of the people and the possessing classes... They have been beaten, and it was decreed by history that they would be. For the time was not yet ripe. Even so, the struggle was unavoidable. For to abandon the Police Headquarters, that palladium of the revolution, to Ernst[45] and Hirsch[46] without a fight would have been to accept a dishonourable defeat. This fight was imposed on the proletariat by the Ebert gang, and the Berlin masses surged forth in elemental fashion, overcoming all doubts and reservations.

Yes, the revolutionary workers of Berlin were defeated... But some defeats are victories, and some victories are more fatal than defeats. The vanquished of this bloody January week have striven for great things, for the noblest goal of suffering humanity, the spiritual and material redemption of the toiling

---

41 *Die Post*: newspaper affiliated to the German Conservative Party.
42 Walther Reinhardt (1872–1930), Colonel in 1919, later General, Prussian Minister of War 1919–20, later military commander of Thuringia.
43 Walther Freiherr von Lüttwitz (1859–1942), general commanding the Third Army Corps in 1918, and all troops in Berlin in 1919, military organiser of the 'Kapp *putsch*' of March 1920. In exile in Hungary after its failure; returned to Germany in 1921, drew his full military pension, and was not put on trial.
44 The People's Militia (*Volkswehr*) was more an idea than a reality at this time. See 8.3.
45 Eugen Ernst (1864–1954), SPD, Prussian Minister of the Interior 1918–19, replaced Eichhorn as Berlin Police Chief in January 1919. Dismissed in 1920 for failing to oppose the Kapp putsch.
46 Paul Hirsch (1868–1940), SPD, Prussian Prime Minister 1918–20. Removed from office in 1920 for negotiating with Kapp. Mayor of Dortmund 1925–33.

masses; they have poured out their blood and thereby sanctified it. And from every drop of this blood there will arise avengers of the fallen, from every mutilated fibre there will emerge new fighters for the noble cause, which is as eternal and imperishable as the firmament.

The defeated of today will be the victors of tomorrow. For they will learn the lesson of this defeat. The German proletariat still lacks a revolutionary tradition and revolutionary experience. And it is only through hesitant attempts, youthful mistakes and painful reverses and disasters that it can gain the practical training which will guarantee success in the future.

And what of today's victors? They did their vicious, bloody work on behalf of a vicious cause. To defend the authorities of a past epoch, the deadly enemies of the proletariat. But the victors are already themselves defeated! For they are already the prisoners of those they thought to use as their instruments. Their sign still hangs in front of the shop, but they have very little time left before their demise. They have already been pilloried by history. Never have there been such Judases. Official German Social Democracy, which sank lower than any other political party in August 1914, now presents the most repulsive picture of all, in the light of the dawning social revolution.

The French bourgeoisie had to recruit the butchers of June 1848 and May 1871 from its own ranks. The German bourgeoisie, however, does not need to lift a finger: 'Social Democrats' perform the dirty, despicable, bloody and cowardly work. Noske, a German 'worker', is the German bourgeoisie's Cavaignac, its Gallifet . . .[47]

They are sowing dragon's teeth! The proletariat of the world has already begun to turn away, shuddering with horror, from people who dare to stretch out their hands, reeking with the blood of the German workers, to the International! They stand before the world besmirched, expelled from the company of honourable human beings, whipped out of the International, detested and cursed by every revolutionary proletarian. Oh, their domination cannot last long now; a brief respite, and they will be judged . . . The revolution of the proletariat, which they could drown in blood, will rise up over them in its full immensity. Its first words will be: Down with the murderers of the workers! Down with Ebert-Scheidemann-Noske!

Those who have been defeated today . . . have been cured of the delusion that they can find salvation in the help of confused masses of troops; or that they can rely on leaders who have shown themselves to be powerless and incapable;

---

47   General Louis-Eugène Cavaignac (1802–1857) was the French Minister of War in charge of suppressing the workers' insurrection of June 1848; General Gaston de Gallifet (1830–1909) had the job of suppressing the Paris Commune in 1871.

cured too of their faith in the Independent Social Democrats, who left them in the lurch like despicable scoundrels. In the future they will fight their battles and win their victories by relying on themselves alone. And the saying that the emancipation of the working class can only be done by the working class itself has won a new and deeper meaning through the bitter lesson of the past week.

'Spartacus overwhelmed!' Come off it! We have not fled, we have not been defeated. And even if they put us all in chains, we are here, and here we remain. And the victory will be ours. For Spartacus means the fire and the spirit, the soul and the heart, the will and the deed of the proletariat's revolution. Spartacus signifies all the class-conscious proletariat's need, all its yearning for happiness, all its fighting resolve. Spartacus means socialism and world revolution.

The calvary of the German working class has not yet come to an end, but the day of redemption is drawing near. It is the day of judgment for Ebert-Scheidemann-Noske and the capitalist potentates who are still hiding behind them at the present. The storm of events casts the waves up to a tremendous height, and we keep on being thrown from the summit to the depths. But our ship keeps a straight course, sailing firmly and proudly to its destination. Whether we are alive when the goal has been reached or not, our programme will live on; it will dominate the world of redeemed mankind. Despite everything!

Like the trumpets of the Last Judgment, the roar of the approaching economic collapse will awaken the sleeping bands of proletarians, and the bodies of the murdered fighters will rise up and demand that they take revenge upon the accursed foe. Today we hear only the underground rumbling of the volcano; tomorrow it will erupt and bury them all in burning ash and streams of lava.

Source: Liebknecht 1919, *Die Rote Fahne*, Nr. 15, 15 January 1919.

3.3   *Paul Levi's Fight against Putschism in June 1919*
(1) It is not the task of the proletariat to make any attempt to get to power itself and thus take away from the bourgeoisie the frightful responsibility for the Peace Treaty (of Versailles). In this situation any action that would signify a struggle for power must be unconditionally avoided ...

(2) A putsch from the Right in response to Versailles is more likely than one from the Left. It would be wrong for the Spartacists to attempt a revolution at this time. Revolution is not a mad, blind process of running amok but a clear weighing up and examination of the given social forces ... To undertake isolated local putsches would be merely to provide victims for the butcheries of

the military dictatorship. That is the clear lesson from the events of the past months...

(3) Now is not the moment for the proletariat to enter into action...Hold back! Do not let yourselves be provoked!...

(4) The workers can wait calmly, despite all provocations, until the day has come. The only revolutionary action that is justifiable is a historically necessary offensive of the proletariat.

Source: (1): *Nachlass Paul Levi* (*NPL*), 19/1, circular from the Central Secretariat, 11 June 1919; (2): *NPL*, 50/16, circular from the Central Secretariat, 13 June 1919; (3): *NPL*, 50/13, circular from the Central Secretariat, 19 June 1919; (4): *Kommunistische Räte-Korrespondenz*, 5, 20 June 1919.

3.4   *Declaration of Communist Principles and Tactics drawn up by Paul Levi and adopted by the Second Congress of the KPD (S), October 1919*

1 The revolution, born out of the economic exploitation of the proletariat by capitalism and its political oppression by the bourgeoisie aimed at maintaining the relationship of exploitation, has a twofold task: the removal of political oppression and the abolition of the relationship of capitalist exploitation.

2 The prerequisite for the replacement of the relationship of capitalist exploitation by the system of socialist production is the removal of the political power of the bourgeoisie and its replacement by the dictatorship of the proletariat.

3 In all the stages of revolution which precede the seizure of power by the proletariat, the revolution is a political struggle by the proletarian masses for political power. This struggle will be conducted with all political and economic means. The KPD is conscious of the fact that this struggle can only be brought to its victorious conclusion by the use of very large-scale political methods (the mass strike, mass demonstrations, uprising).

But the KPD cannot in principle abandon any political methods which might serve to prepare the way for these gigantic struggles. Participation in elections also comes into consideration as a method of this kind, whether the elections are to parliaments, to local councils, to legally recognised Factory Councils, and so on.

These elections are, however, subordinate to the revolutionary struggle as being merely a means of preparing for it. It is therefore possible, in certain highly specific political situations, to dispense with the employment of methods of this kind. This applies particularly when revolutionary actions are in progress and heading towards the decisive moment. In that case, the employment of parliamentary methods may become temporarily or permanently superfluous.

The KPD therefore rejects both the Syndicalist conception of the superfluity or harmfulness of political methods and the USPD view that revolutionary achievements can also be brought about by the route of parliamentary resolutions or negotiations with the bourgeoisie.

The question of participation or non-participation in elections must be determined in a uniform manner for the whole Reich by a Conference or a Congress of the Party.

4 Even before the conquest of power, the greatest stress must be laid on extending the existing [Workers'] Council organisations and creating new ones. In this connection it should of course be borne in mind that [Workers'] Councils and Council organisations cannot be created, nor can they be maintained, by statutes and electoral regulations. They owe their existence rather to the revolutionary will and the revolutionary action of the masses alone, and they are for the proletariat the ideological and organisational expression of the will to power, just as a parliament expresses the bourgeoisie's will to power.

For this reason, the Workers' Councils are also the given instruments of the revolutionary action of the proletariat. Members of the KPD must join together to form factions within these Workers' Councils and endeavour by using appropriate slogans to raise them to the height of their revolutionary mission and to win the leadership of the Workers' Councils and the masses of workers.

5 The revolution, which is not achieved at a single stroke but is the long and stubborn fight of a class oppressed for millennia and therefore not fully conscious from the outset of its task and its strength, is subject to ups and downs, and ebbs and flows. It alters its methods according to the situation. Sometimes it attacks capitalism from the political side, sometimes from the economic side, and sometimes from both sides. The KPD opposes the view that an economic revolution is a substitute for a political one.

Economic methods of struggle are of particular significance because to a very considerable degree they open the eyes of the proletariat to the actual causes of its economic and political misery. The more the proletariat grows to understand that these economic methods of struggle also serve the political goals of the revolution, the greater the value of these methods.

It is the task of the political party to secure to the proletarians the unhindered use of these economic instruments, and to free them from the shackles of a counter-revolutionary trade-union bureaucracy, even at the price of the destruction of the traditional form of the trade union and the creation of a new form of organisation.

The opinion that mass movements can be created by virtue of a particular form of organisation, and that the revolution is therefore a question of organisational reform, is rejected as being a relapse into a petty-bourgeois utopia.

6 The economic organisation is the place where the broad masses assemble together. This is the location of an important part, even if not the only part, of the mass movement which engages in the revolutionary struggle. The political party, in contrast, is called upon actually to lead the revolutionary mass struggle. The most advanced and purposeful elements of the proletariat, who are called upon to take the lead in revolutionary struggles, are assembled together in the communist party. This leading stratum must be united together in the political party in the interests of uniformity, intellectual training and mutual harmony.

There is a Syndicalist opinion that the unification of the most conscious proletarians into a single party is not necessary, that instead the party must disappear in the face of the economic organisations of the proletariat, or be dissolved into them, or that the communist party should give up its leadership of revolutionary actions to the factory organisations et cetera, and restrict itself to propaganda. This opinion is counter-revolutionary, because it aims at replacing the clear understanding possessed by the vanguard of the working class with the chaotic urges of the agitated masses.

The party can only do justice to its task in revolutionary epochs if it is united together on the basis of the strictest centralisation. At such times federalism is merely a hidden way of negating and dissolving the party, because in reality federalism paralyses the party. Moreover, the strictest centralisation is as necessary for the economic as it is for the political organisations. Federalism in economic organisations makes united action by the workers impossible. The KPD rejects federalism.

7 Members of the KPD who do not share these views on the nature, the organisation and the activity of the party must resign from it.

Source: Kommunistische Partei Deutschlands 1919, *Bericht über den 2.Parteitag der KPD (Spartakusbund), 20–24 Oktober 1919*, pp. 60–2.

3.5 *Theses on Parliamentarism, Laid Before the 2nd.Congress of the KPD (S), 23 October 1919*

1 Parliament ... is a means by which the ruling classes exert and maintain their political power. The proletariat fights against this political instrument of the bourgeoisie.

2 Once political power has been conquered, parliament must be destroyed, just as the bureaucracy, the courts etc. must be destroyed. Parliament will be destroyed permanently. Its functions will be completely replaced by the Workers' Councils. In the first phase after the seizure of power – the epoch of proletarian dictatorship – the proletariat requires the Council Organisation as

the clearest expression of the proletariat's will to power. Then, in the second phase, the phase of classless society, the existence of parliament, as an instrument of class rule, is entirely unthinkable.

3 At the present time the fight for political power must be waged *using all means*. This includes participation in elections and parliamentary activities.

4 In no case can political power be attained through parliament and majority voting. The decision can only be brought about through the large-scale actions of the masses, namely demonstrations, the mass strike and the uprising.

5 That is the difference between the attitudes of the USPD and the KPD over the question of parliament. The USPD participates in parliament in order to achieve success *within* parliament. The USPD expects to achieve something through parliamentary decisions, for example it expects to anchor the Councils in the Constitution.

Source: Kommunistische Partei Deutschlands 1919, *Bericht über den 2. Parteitag der KPD (Spartakusbund), 20–24 Oktober 1919*, p. 45.

Note: These theses were adopted by 17 votes to 13 The anti-parliamentary minority of 13 is remarkably large, given that this vote was actually taken after the expulsion of the 25 irreconcilable opponents of parliamentary participation who went on to found the KAPD.[48]

3.6 Theses on Trade Union Questions, Laid Before the 2nd. Congress of the KPD (S), 23 October 1919

1 With the collapse of German imperialism, the trade-unionist policy of small reforms and wage rises has become completely impracticable. Any attempt to prevent extreme exploitation threatens to bring down the whole capitalist economic system.

2 The bourgeoisie now places its political power directly in the service of economic exploitation. Strike-breakers organised by the state are an example.

3 Every economic struggle is now political and revolutionary. The German trade unions' policy of political neutrality and purely economic struggles has been cast aside by events.

4 The unity of political and economic struggle by no means implies a unified political and trade union organisation. The political organisation brings

---

48 KAPD: *Kommunistische Arbeiterpartei Deutschlands* (Communist Workers' Party of Germany). See below, Section 12.

together the *most advanced* elements of the proletariat, whereas the economic organisation assembles the *whole* proletariat.

5 It was possible to form the political party [i.e. the communist party] through the separation of the most advanced elements of the SPD and the USPD from those parties. But the separation of the most advanced elements from the trade unions weakens the striking force of the masses and removes from the trade unions the material that acts as a leaven ...

7 The trade unions are at present a tool of the bourgeoisie and the counter-revolution. This reflects the fact that the proletariat is unclear about its own class situation. The only effective way of changing this is ceaseless agitation and enlightenment *within* the organisations of the proletariat. This task can only be carried out if members of the KPD remain in close contact with the masses. The resignation of individuals from the trade unions is a harmful act.

8 The KPD recommends a struggle against the trade union bureaucracy with the aim of isolating it from the masses. For this, communists within the local branches must organise as a faction and lead the struggle within, and, if it turns out to be necessary, outside, the trade union.

9 Where a single trade union covers a single professional branch, as for example among the mineworkers of Rhineland-Westphalia, or on the railways, this struggle can be combined with the struggle for a new form of organisation, the *factory organisation*. Where factories are very large, this form of organisation can be introduced immediately. But in other areas, where there are many trades, this can only be used as a *platform* for the struggle.

10 We must fight against the trade unionist theory and practice of 'purely economic struggles', the rejection of political mass action.

11 Those parts of the trade unions which separate off are to be organised within economic areas into Workers' Unions, organised either by trade or by factory. The aim is an organisation of workers for the whole *Reich*.

Source: Kommunistische Partei Deutschlands 1919, *Bericht über den 2. Parteitag der KPD (Spartakusbund), 20–24 Oktober 1919*, p. 55.

3.7   *The* 'Vorwärts Revelations'. *The Reports of Lemke and Bowitzky to the VKPD Zentrale, 8 April 1921 and 12 April 1921*
        Lemke's Report to the VKPD Zentrale, 8 April 1921
20 March 1921: A session of the District Directorate was held in Halle. The mood, it was reported, was so bad and so pessimistic that artificial measures would be needed to bring matters to a head.

23 March 1921: Eberlein arrived in Halle. He suggested that comrades Lemke and Bowitzky should get themselves arrested in order to entice the Halle workers out into the streets. Attempts should be made to whip up tension among the workers so as to pull them into the struggle ... There were, he said, two wagons full of grenades in Halle railway station. They should be dynamited. They next day we should announce in *Klassenkampf* that the counter-revolution had let its own ammunition blow up through carelessness, and that workers' dwellings had been flattened with the loss of hundreds of lives. It would be possible to withdraw the statement a few days later when it proved untrue ... At an evening session of the directorate with Eberlein present, Schumann objected to driving the Action forward any more. But most comrades agreed with Eberlein, and it was decided to blow up the munitions depot.

Bowitzky's Report to the VKPD leadership, 12 April 1921

I arrived from Halle on 18 March with the direct mission of *immediately* starting the Action. The occasion was supposed to be the occupation of Central Germany by *Sipos* and *Schupos* ... On 22 March Comrade Hugo [Eberlein] appeared. He had been sent from Berlin as the representative of the *Zentrale* with the purpose of driving the Action forward in Central Germany and directing its course. He made concrete proposals as to how the Action should be conducted, and he had with him an instruction from the *Zentrale* that the call should come from Central Germany, which would then decisively stimulate the Action in the rest of the Reich. This was extraordinarily difficult, because the occupying forces behaved with extreme moderation despite all provocations. Even in the Mansfeld district it proved impossible to entice them out of their attitude of reserve ... They played cards, smoked their pipes and took great pleasure in doing nothing ... Up to that point not one factory had been occupied by the *Sipo* and contrary reports about the Leuna Works are completely untrue. The Leuna Works were only occupied on 30 March.

On 22 March Eberlein proposed that the munitions depot in Seefen should be blown up, as well as the newly-acquired building of the Producers' Cooperative Society. For technical reasons it was impossible to carry out either of these plans. The Cooperative Society was not blown up because of a shortage of detonators ... Lemke and I were also supposed to disappear so that the news could be put out that we had been wounded and arrested by a *Sipo* unit and taken to an unknown place ... Eberlein repeated the order to blow up the Cooperative Society on two further occasions; the third time the District Directorate of the Party energetically resisted this madness ... If the building had gone up during daytime twenty of our best comrades would have been killed.

Source: *Vorwärts*, No. 556, 25 November 1921, morning edition.

3.8   *Theses on the March Action, Adopted by the KPD* Zentrale *on 7 April 1921*

I

[This section is a general introduction on the political situation at home and abroad in the month of March 1921, culminating in the sentence 'The SPD-USPD alliance delivered the German workers into the hands of the bourgeoisie of Germany and the Entente'.]

II

This general situation urgently demanded from the German working class the snapping of the chains which bound them to the broken-down carriage of the bourgeoisie ... it required the sharpest class struggles, *it required the working class to seize the revolutionary initiative* ... and to summon its forces for independent action, to confront the counter-revolution with a powerful counter-attack ... Whether passively to accept the counter-revolution's decisions, or, acting in a revolutionary manner, to make its own decisions independently, and anticipate the counter-revolution by taking the initiative: this is how the question was posed for the German working class.

III

In all previous crises of the German bourgeoisie ... the Communist Party informed the masses of the need to sharpen the crisis and independently set in motion the revolutionary solution. The KPD(S), however, was not strong enough to do more than exploit these crises in a propagandist way.

In contrast to this, the VKPD, by virtue of its strength, was obliged to go beyond mere propaganda and agitation. It had to lead the working class into action, it had to show the proletariat, at the time when the proletariat was called upon to fight, that it was ready and willing to take the lead in that struggle.

It had to make the attempt to pull the masses along with it, even running the risk that at first it would only draw a narrow circle of workers with it into the fight.

IV

[This section recalls the failure of parliamentary action to secure an alliance between Germany and Soviet Russia, adding that this made necessary 'a transition to mass action, to a mass offensive'.]

V

The mass action (which was required, as indicated above) was unleashed by Hörsing's impertinent offensive against the Mansfeld workers ... The VKPD had to offer to lead the counter-attack with the whole of its strength; it was impossible to hesitate. Hence the Party called for a general strike all over Germany [24 March].

VI

This attempt to seize the revolutionary initiative was opposed by a part of the working class, people who were under the influence of the SPD, the USPD and the trade-union bureaucracy. The better-paid workers thought they could wait, without having to fight. In contrast to this, there was an increase in the number of unemployed and short-time workers, who were unable to wait, because of their increasing misery . . . Acts of despair by individuals and small groups occurred . . . An understanding of serious struggles, and a readiness to engage in them, has grown among the revolutionary vanguard. It is impossible to preserve the strength of these strata of the revolutionary vanguard, and to maintain the will to fight which arises out of increasing misery, by gearing the VKPD to mere propaganda, and avoiding action until one believes victory is an absolute certainty. The VKPD cannot wait until revolutionary propaganda by itself brings to an end the mass passivity of the economically better off and the ideologically backward strata . . . In times of political tension, actions like this one, even if they lead to a temporary defeat, are a prerequisite for victory in the future. They are the only possible way a revolutionary party can win the masses for itself, and produce in the minds of the indifferent masses an awareness of the objective political situation . . . Action is itself a factor in unleashing revolutionary mass feeling.

VII

This revolutionary offensive ended with a defeat for the VKPD, viewed from outside. The VKPD is temporarily isolated from broad sections of the working class. But in truth this result contains the fruitful germs of new, broader revolutionary actions. The fortifications have been breached; revolutionary propaganda can enter through the gaps, and in the final analysis the action must strengthen the confidence of the workers in the VKPD and with it the revolutionary impetus of the working class . . . Whereas in 1918 and 1919 the revolutionary vanguard conducted a defensive struggle, it is now on the offensive. That is a tremendous advance. The March Action is the first step the VKPD has taken in leading the German working class towards the revolutionary offensive.

[Section VIII enumerates a number of achievements arising out of the March Action, including a 'demonstration to the Entente that the suggestion of a united front between the German proletariat and the bourgeoisie is an impertinent lie'; Section IX distinguishes between acts of terrorism and the method of revolutionary mass struggle: the VKPD rejects the former and favours the latter.]

X

The VKPD must correct the organisational and technical mistakes made in this first attempt. If it wants to fulfil its historical task, it must hold fast to the line of the revolutionary offensive, which lies at the basis of the March Action, and continue decisively and with certainty along this path.

XI

In this situation the VKPD has a duty to heighten all the conflicts which are suitable for bringing the masses into movement and activity. If partial actions (*Teilaktionen*) arise the Party's task is to sharpen and spread these actions.

XII

The ZA sees the March campaign of the Party as an action corresponding to this tactical situation, an action which was necessary ... if the Party wanted to become a party of revolutionary action rather than a party of revolutionary communist phrase-making. The ZA therefore approves the political and tactical position of the *Zentrale* and *condemns with the utmost severity the passive and active opposition of certain comrades during the Action.* It invites the *Zentrale* to place the organisation on a footing of the greatest possible fighting strength and to implement all the organisational measures required for this.

Source: Kommunistische Partei Deutschlands Zentrale 1921, *Die Internationale*, pp. 122–7.

Note: These theses, worked out by the *Zentrale* and usually attributed to Thalheimer[49] were presented to the 7/8 April 1921 session of the ZA (Central Commission) of the VKPD. They are a very clear statement of the theory of the 'revolutionary offensive', which was used to justify the March Action retrospectively. They were adopted by 26 votes to 14. The opposition minority was led by Clara Zetkin.

---

49   August Thalheimer (1884–1948) joined the Spartacus League in 1916, founder-member of
     the KPD in 1919. One of the Party's leading theoreticians. He was a leftist at first, though
     later, after the defeat of 1923, he advocated more moderate policies and was associated
     with Brandler on the right of the Party. He co-founded the KPO with Brandler in 1929.

3.9   *The Proceedings of the Chemnitz Conference of 21 October 1923,*
       as Reported by the SPD's Main Newspaper
Dresden, 22 October

The economic conference called in Chemnitz by Ministers Graupe,[50] Heckert[51] and Böttcher[52] was extremely well attended. The following representatives were present: 79 from the Control Commissions, 26 from the Consumers' Associations, 102 from the trade unions, 16 from the unemployed, 20 trade union local officials, 140 from the Factory Councils and 15 from the Action Committees. In terms of party representatives, there were seven people from the VSPD, 66 from the KPD and one from the USPD. Labour Minister Graupe...indicated the seriousness of the situation and the misery of the population. The Minister of Economics, Heckert, provided information about the emergency relief operation which was in progress to supply the needy population with bread, potatoes and coal. He emphasised the government's firm intention to carry out this relief effort despite sabotage on the part of the industrialists and bankers. Minister of Finance Böttcher gave an account of the catastrophic financial situation of the Reich and the States. It was absolutely necessary to bring the possessing classes to make emergency sacrifices...After the three ministers had spoken there was an extensive discussion, in which the need to take up the fight immediately, especially against the military dictatorship,[53] was underlined again and again. One speaker after another demanded that the government openly intervene and proclaim a general strike against the state of emergency and the military measures. Brandler, the communist who was Ministerial Director of the State Chancellery,[54] proposed that an immediate decision be taken on the proposal to proclaim a general strike. It was obvious, he said, that a decision of this nature could only be meaningful it were taken *unanimously.* Labour Minister Graupe said that this conference was not competent to make such a decision; moreover, if there were any

---

50   Georg Graupe (1875–1959), SPD, Minister of Labour in the government of Saxony in 1923, member of the Saxon Diet 1919–1930.

51   Fritz Heckert (1884–1936), KPD. In KPD *Zentrale*, 1920–24, and KPD Political Bureau, 1925–36.

52   Paul Böttcher (1891–1975), USPD, KPD from 1920, in KPD *Zentrale* 1921–24, Saxon Finance Minister October 1923, expelled as 'rightist' in 1929, joined the KPO.

53   A state of emergency had been proclaimed on 27 September 1923, thereby placing executive power in the hands of the Minister of Defence. The local commander, General Alfred Müller, was thus the 'military dictator' in Saxony.

54   Heinrich Brandler was in fact the national leader of the KPD as well as being a member of the Saxon government.

further discussion of a general strike he himself would be unable to continue his participation in the proceedings. He proposed that the general issue be left to a committee. After a short discussion a committee was set up, consisting of three members of the VSPD and three of the KPD. After an interval this committee returned with a proposal to designate an Action Committee, consisting of five members of the VSPD and five of the KPD, with the task of conducting negotiations immediately with the leadership of the trade unions and the [Saxon] government on the proposal to proclaim a general strike for the protection of Saxony against military dictatorship. If the trade-union leaders and the government rejected this demand the Action Committee would have the right to carry through the general strike on its own authority. This proposal was adopted almost unanimously. Its only opponents called for an immediate general strike. It was stated on behalf of the Communist Party that it regarded an immediate struggle, using the instrument of a general strike, as necessary, and that it only agreed to its postponement with the strongest reservations. But the Party was absolutely determined to preserve a united front, even at the cost of heavy sacrifices. The Action Committee was then immediately elected by the meeting... It had the twofold task of trying to form a socialist-communist government and immediately issuing a joint appeal to the proletariat of Saxony and Germany.

Source: *Vorwärts*, No. 495, 23 October 1923.

Note: This account of the Chemnitz Conference, after which the KPD *Zentrale* called off the planned insurrection of October 1923, was later confirmed by Thalheimer,[55] who adds that Brandler's proposal for a general strike met with an 'icy' reception. The setting up of an Action Committee, in Thalheimer's view, constituted a 'third-class funeral' for the idea of a general strike. This face-saving compromise was soon overtaken by greater events, namely the Hamburg rising of 23 October, and the forcible removal of the Zeigner[56] government in Saxony by General Müller on 29 October. The general strike idea resurfaced in an attenuated form as a three-day protest strike against Zeigner's removal (proclaimed on 29 October), but he resigned from office the next day, thereby rendering the strike pointless.

---

55   In his pamphlet *1923: Eine verpasste Revolution?* (Berlin 1931), p. 26.
56   Erich Zeigner (1886–1949), SPD, Saxon Prime Minister in 1923. Mayor of Leipzig after 1945.

3.10   *Resolution Issued by the KPD Zentrale on the Impending Clash of Revolution and Counter-Revolution, [28] October 1923*[57]

1 The social and political antagonisms are becoming more and more acute with every day that passes. Any day may bring great, decisive struggles between the revolution and the counter-revolution.

2 The vanguard of the working class (the Communists and a section of the Social Democratic workers) is pressing for the struggle to be taken up; but the mass of the workers, despite their great bitterness and misery, are not yet ready to fight.

3 The reserves of the proletariat must therefore be drawn towards the vanguard by resolute agitation. The Party must work in particular to get into contact with those strata of the proletariat which are especially relevant for the struggle (the metal workers, miners, railway workers, agricultural workers and office employees). The work of technical preparation must be carried on with all possible energy. Immediate central and local negotiations with the Social Democrats must be put in hand to unify the proletariat for the struggle: this will have the result of either compelling them to enter the fight or separating the Social Democratic workers from their treacherous leaders.

4 In view of this situation it is necessary for the Party to hold back the comrades from armed struggle as long as possible, so as to gain time for its preparation. If, despite this, great spontaneous struggles of the working class should break out, the Party will support them with all the means at its disposal. The Party must also ward off the blows of the counter-revolution by using the means of the mass struggle (demonstrations and political strikes). In these struggles, the use of weapons is to be avoided as much as possible.

5 The Party in the whole country must call for a protest strike against Stresemann's ultimatum,[58] in connection with which armed conflicts are to be avoided. If the SPD in Saxony does not take up the fight against Stresemann's

---

57   The source gives the date as 26 October 1923. Wenzel (2003 p. 253) gives 25 October. The most likely date, however, is 28 October, owing to the reference to 'Stresemann's ultimatum'. See the next note.

58   This may possibly refer to the ultimatum sent by General Müller on 17 October to Zeigner, the Prime Minister of Saxony, calling on him to disavow statements by the Minister of Economics, the Communist Paul Böttcher, calling for the arming of the Proletarian Hundreds. It is far more likely, however, that it refers to Stresemann's 24-hour ultimatum sent to Zeigner on the 27th October calling for the resignation of his cabinet and published on 28 October. The draft text of this ultimatum is printed in Erdmann and Vogt 1978, pp. 860–2. There is no evidence for an earlier ultimatum by Stresemann to Zeigner, and this would suggest that the KPD resolution printed here was not in fact issued until 28 October at the earliest.

ultimatum, our comrades must break with the Saxon government and go over to the fight against it.

Source: Communist International Executive Committee 1924, *Die Lehren der deutschen Ereignisse. Das Präsidium des Exekutivkomitees der Kommunistischen Internationale zur deutschen Frage, Januar 1924*, pp. 7–8 (Radek's speech).

Note: The immediate circumstances of this declaration need to be outlined here. When the news of the defeat of the Hamburg rising arrived in Berlin (23 October) the *Zentrale* and Radek discussed what the Party should do next. There were three rival proposals. Ruth Fischer called for a mass strike which would take place on 25 October and 'pass over into an armed insurrection'; Radek called for a strike without an armed uprising; and there was a further proposal for the Party to take no action at all. All of these resolutions were rejected, and instead a Commission of Seven was set up. The fruit of its deliberations was this resolution, the context of which was Stresemann's letter of 27 October to Zeigner demanding that within one day he get rid of his communist ministers and reconstruct the cabinet without them, failing which a *Reichskommissar* would be sent to Saxony to take over the state. Zeigner's first reaction was to defy this ultimatum (28 October). Hence on 29 October President Ebert authorised Chancellor Stresemann to dismiss the Zeigner government and appoint Dr. Rudolf Heinze[59] as *Reichskommissar* for Saxony. The ministries in Dresden were occupied by troops. Zeigner resigned the next day, and on 31 October the Saxon Diet elected Dr. Alfred Fellisch,[60] a moderate member of the SPD, as the next prime minister. Radek tried to get some action going on the lines of the 28 October resolution, but his suggestion of holding a protest march defended by armed (and now illegal) Proletarian Hundreds[61] was rejected by Ruth Fischer, on the basis that the masses were too discouraged after the defeats in Saxony and Hamburg to come into the streets. So the idea was dropped, and nothing at all was done to put the resolution into effect.

---

59 Rudolf Heinze (1865–1928), chair of DVP parliamentary group, Minister of Justice 1920–21 and 1922–23.

60 Alfred Fellisch (1884–1973), SPD, Saxon Prime Minister and Minister of Economics from October 1923 to January 1924.

61 Proletarian Hundreds: organs of working-class self-defence which emerged in March 1923 in Saxony and quickly spread with the encouragement of the KPD to many German cities. Prohibited by the SPD government of Prussia in May 1923, and in other German states except Saxony and Thuringia, where they flourished and were expected to be the striking force in the impending insurrection. They were prohibited there too after October 1923.

3.11   *KPD Resolution on 'The Victory of Fascism over the November*
         Republic and the Tasks of the KPD', 3 November 1923[62]

1   The End of the November Republic

Over the whole territory of unoccupied Germany[63] the November Republic
has been delivered over to Fascism. Power is in the hands of the military,
and they are making it their deliberate task to annihilate the achievements
of the working class, namely the Eight-Hour Day and the Factory Councils,
and finally to establish the unrestricted rule of the bourgeoisie on the backs
of the defenceless proletariat. By taking an axe to the roots of the social
achievements of the November Revolution the government has itself abolished its historical essence, which consisted in the attempt to pretend to the
working class that capitalism in Germany could be restored while democracy
was retained and careful attention continued to be paid to the social interests
of the workers ...

       The victory of Fascism over bourgeois democracy occurred in a form which
was different from that expected by the working class, and therefore this fact
did not become clear to them immediately. The working class saw Bavaria as
the centre of Fascism, but the Fascist headquarters was established in Berlin
itself, in the shape of the dictatorship of General Seeckt[64] ... While the working class was had its eyes fixed on Munich, where the white dictatorship was
proclaimed with trumpets and banners ... the Social Democrat Ebert and the
cabinet of the Grand Coalition appointed General Seeckt as dictator ... The
presence of 400 parliamentary deputies in that beer hall called the Reichstag
cannot conceal the fact of Fascism's seizure of power.

2   The Social Democrats as Accomplices of Fascism

The responsibility for the victory of Fascism falls completely on the leaders of
the SPD ... There can only be a life and death struggle with these leaders ... In
order to stop the growing opposition of the working class from turning into a
revolutionary struggle ... the leaders of Social Democracy have left the Fascist
government. This is so that they can deck themselves out in the finery of oppo-

---

62   These are the theses drawn up by the Brandler *Zentrale* and adopted by the ZA (Central
       Commission) of the KPD by 40 votes to 16, in preference to the Left Opposition's theses,
       which sharply condemned Brandler's conduct of affairs. See Bayerlein 2003, p. 303.

63   The Ruhr was still under French and Belgian occupation at this point.

64   Hans von Seeckt (1866–1936), General, head of the German Army Command 1920–26,
       DVP member of the Reichstag 1930–32.

sition, as they did under Cuno[65] ... As for the Left Social Democrats, as long as they do not make an open and clear political and organisational break with the right-wing leaders of Social Democracy they remain their accomplices.

3   The Working Class and the Collapse of the November Republic

The proletariat could not fight to save the corpse of the November Republic. The hatred for the November Republic with which a section of the proletariat is imbued has eased the path for the Fascists.

State power in the hands of the Fascist gangs means the proletariat is in danger of being fettered, strangled and enslaved. Fascism's seizure of power therefore signifies the beginning of a decisive life and death struggle for the proletariat. An armed uprising stands on the agenda as its inescapable task. The KPD therefore calmly, resolutely and with iron self-belief declares a war to the death against the Fascist dictatorship. This struggle must begin with the resistance of the working class against the introduction of the ten-hour day, against unemployment, against the state of siege and the muzzling of the working-class press, and for peace-time real wages. It will develop into an onslaught of the proletariat against the basis of arbitrary Fascist rule. The working class will tear the power away from the hands of the Fascist dictatorship. The KPD proclaims that it will not rest until the proletarian dictatorship becomes a reality. *Only the destruction of the Fascist power apparatus by revolutionary proletarian struggle can open the door to proletarian dictatorship.* The task of the revolutionary workers in the next period will be to prepare this struggle.

The Fascist bourgeoisie wanted to provoke the proletariat into an uprising[66] when it was weakened and confused by the treachery of Social Democracy and when its preparations had as yet hardly started. *In the awareness that the time to fight for the proletarian dictatorship will not be long in coming, the KPD will enter into preparations for this event with all its energy.* The Party has tried to secure a united front by negotiation with the leaders of Social Democracy. It made the sacrifice of entering the Saxon government, but the treachery of the Social Democratic leaders brought this to nothing. Now the united front will be set up from below. There will be a break with the betrayers of the proletariat and a unification and a gathering together around the flag of the KPD.

---

65   Wilhelm Cuno (1876–1933), director of the Hamburg-America Line, ex-DVP non-party Reich Chancellor 1922–23.

66   A reference to Ebert's decree of 29 October dismissing the Zeigner government and appointing a *Reichskommissar* to govern Saxony.

4   Fascist Dictatorship, the Last and Weakest Bourgeois Government
           of Germany

The German bourgeoisie is at the end of its tether. The fact that it is not even capable of feeding the people now that it has capitulated to the foreign foe constitutes a death blow. Under Fascist rule the middle class will be driven to the side of the working class by despair ... The Fascist government will probably legalise the separatist forces [in Bavaria and the Rhineland]: it will hand the German nation over to France and international capital. This will be repellent to all the vigorous and honourable elements of the nationalist masses. Germany will enter the proletarian camp. In Germany the fight for social liberation is indissolubly connected with the fight for national liberation. The Party of the dictatorship of the proletariat will become the Party of national salvation.

Source: Kommunistische Partei Deutschlands 1923, *Internationale Pressekorrespondenz*, 3: 172, 7 November 1923, pp. 1457–60.

3.12   *The ECCI's Resolution on the Lessons of the German Events, 19 January 1924*[67]

[After a preamble and sections on 'united front tactics' and 'the revolutionary crisis in Germany' the resolution passes directly to Section III.]

III   The October Retreat and its Causes

In October 1923 the KPD was still consciously attuned to the revolutionary struggle for power, despite all its weaknesses. If, despite the revolutionary situation and despite the efforts of the Communist International and the KPD, there were neither revolutionary struggles nor mass political struggles, this was the result of a series of errors and weaknesses, which in part involved opportunist deviations:

1 Weaknesses in evaluating revolutionary development. The fact that a revolutionary situation had matured in Germany was recognised too late by the Party ... The Party did not realise soon enough the significance of the mass struggles in the Ruhr and Upper Silesia, which were signs of the growing political activity of the working masses ...

2 Tactical errors. The Party failed to link its transitional demands with the final objective ... it neglected the Factory Council movement ... and it did

---

67   This should read 21 January 1924, as it is the final version, agreed at the ECCI Presidium's meeting in Moscow between 19 and 21 January 1924.

not make use of other organs of the united front (Action Committees, Control Committees, Fighting Committees).

3 Politico-organisational weaknesses. The Party failed to realign its apparatus for the struggle for power, and it failed to arm the Proletarian Hundreds to any significant extent.

IV   The Saxon Experiment and the Hamburg Struggles

The sharpening of class antagonisms in Germany occasioned the ECCI and the KPD to undertake the experiment of the entry of communists into the Saxon government. The meaning of this step, in the ECCI's view, consisted in the fulfilment of a specific military and political task, which was precisely stated in an instruction worded as follows:

'As we evaluate the situation the decisive moment will arrive not later than four, five or six weeks from now; hence we think it necessary immediately to occupy every position which can be of direct assistance to us. On this basis one must in practice pose the question of entry into the Saxon government. On condition that the Zeigner people are ready genuinely to defend Saxony against Bavaria and the Fascists, we must go in. Implement the immediate arming of 50–60,000 people. Ignore General Müller.[68] The same thing goes for Thuringia'.[69]

Originally this decision to enter a government would have corresponded with the decisions of the Fourth Congress [of the Communist International] ... Entry into the government should have had the backing of mass movements. But instead the communists failed to mobilise the masses. The Saxon experiment therefore did not become a stage in the struggle; rather than an act of revolutionary strategy it turned out to be an un-revolutionary parliamentary combination with the 'Left' Social Democrats.

At the Chemnitz Conference, although the general strike was supposed to be proposed, no attempt was made to turn the meeting towards exclusive concentration on the defence of Saxony against the intervention of the Reich authorities. These were mistakes which doubtless made it easier for the Left SPD leaders to play their treacherous game.

The *Hamburg uprising* was at the opposite pole to Saxony. Hamburg showed how resolute fighting groups can overcome their opponent militarily by taking the offensive when he is least expecting it. But what was also evident was that

---

68   General Alfred Müller (1866–1925), commander of the Reichswehr troops in Saxony in 1923.

69   As appears from Zinoviev's speech to the meeting of the ECCI Presidium (Communist International Executive Committee 1924, p. 60) this instruction is a telegram he sent to the *Zentrale* of the KPD on 1 October 1923, in the name of the ECCI.

an armed struggle of this kind is condemned to failure if it remains *isolated* and is not borne along by a Council movement developing on the spot.

V   The Role of Social Democracy and the Turn in the United
            Front Tactic in Germany

The leading layers of German Social Democracy are at present nothing other than a faction of German Fascism under a socialist mask. They have handed over state power to the representatives of capitalist dictatorship in order to save capitalism from the proletarian revolution . . . There are shades of difference between Ebert, Seeckt and Ludendorff . . . But the German communists must never forget that in the struggle between capital and labour the SPD leaders are united with the White generals in life and in death . . . This circumstance induces us to subject the tactic of the united front in Germany to a modification. *There can be no negotiating with the hired mercenaries of the White dictatorship* . . . Yet more dangerous than the right wingers, however, are the Left SPD leaders, that last illusion of the betrayed workers . . . The KPD rejects negotiations with the SPD, and also with the 'Left' SPD leaders until they have the guts to break with the SPD party leadership. The turn in tactics is therefore expressed in the words: United Front from Below!

VI   The Party's Immediate Tasks

The fundamental estimation of the situation in Germany which was given in September [1923] by the ECCI remains essentially the same . . . The KPD must not strike off from its agenda the question of the uprising and the conquest of power . . . However great the partial victories of the German counter-revolution, they solve none of the critical problems of capitalist Germany . . . The Party's agitation must bring home to the broad masses that *only the dictatorship of the proletariat* can save them . . . The *arming of the workers* and the technical preparations for the decisive struggles must be pursued with stubborn insistence. *Proletarian Hundreds* must be created in reality, not just on paper . . . Only when the working masses find the protection of the Hundreds in demonstrations and strikes will the Hundreds meet with wholehearted mass support . . . The Communist Party is the only revolutionary party; it is strong enough to prepare and achieve the victory of the masses of the proletariat *against all other parties*. This conviction must be firmly implanted in every member of the Party.

Source: Communist International Executive Committee 1924, *Die Lehren der deutschen Ereignisse*, pp. 95–109.

Note: Section IV of this resolution is an attempt to have it both ways: the KPD was instructed to enter the governments of Saxony and Thuringia in October 1923 for a military purpose, not to apply the united front tactic. Once the KPD ministers were in the governments, they failed to achieve their military purpose; yet here they are condemned both for this and for failing to operate the united front tactic correctly. Heinrich Brandler was very bitter about this accusation, first raised by the ECCI at the end of 1923 in a letter to the KPD. 'You converted the united front into a banal parliamentary combination with the Social Democrats. No, comrades, that is not the way one prepares a revolution'.[70] Section V, at this surprisingly early date, anticipates the theory of 'Social Fascism' applied to the Social Democrats after 1928. Combined with the assertion that the KPD is strong enough to achieve its aims against all other parties, the resolution appears to render the united front in its previous form not only harmful but unnecessary. Section VI is an attempt to pretend that nothing untoward has happened, and that revolution is still on the agenda: an unrealistic view by January 1924.

3.13   *Military Lessons of the October 1923 Struggles in Hamburg*
Most important lesson: adequate armaments, at least for the striking force. Incorrect to take up fixed positions at specific points, such as police stations, barracks etc., because this makes it easy for the opponent to mount an enveloping attack. Where necessary the entrances of police stations and barracks can be controlled by marksmen positioned on the roof.

Maximum mobility of small-armed groups, appearing unexpectedly. It was made very clear in Hamburg that a military opponent accustomed to definite rules of combat is worn down most effectively by the unexpected emergence of individual sharp-shooters, now in the rear, now to either side. The fighting worker must be nowhere and everywhere, he must appear unexpectedly, and disappear again, always remaining out of reach. In this way the enemy in Hamburg became uncertain, was worn down by the losses we inflicted, and was never able to gain a clear picture of the strength of the opposing force of the workers.

The taking of photographs in this battle zone must in all circumstances be avoided. The battle zone is to be transferred to the bourgeois districts if at all possible, so that these people too may have some experience of the struggle. There must be an immediate house-to-house search for weapons in these districts.

---

70   *Internationale Pressekorrespondenz* 1924, 4.16, 4 February 1924, p. 169.

The area of combat must be extended as quickly as possible by sending reserves to the periphery of the battle zone. At the outskirts of the city all means of access must be blocked off, so as to prevent any additional enemy forces from reaching the main battle zone. This can be done by interrupting rail connections, setting up barricades on access roads, cutting telephone links and securing the installations that have been cut off by stationing marksmen, so as to make repairs by the *Teno*[71] impossible.

Another important lesson is that an attempt must be made to ensure uninterrupted communication between the leadership and the fighting troops. Furthermore, the leadership must have at its disposal a properly functioning information service, so that it is constantly kept in the picture about the strength of the opponent, the mood of the population, and so on. Communications and information make good leadership possible.

The greatest stress must be laid from the outset on the need to secure adequate printing facilities in the battle zone.

May the skirmish that took place in the revolutionary outpost at the water's edge[72] soon be followed by the decisive battle and the victory of the German proletariat.

Source: *Vom Bürgerkrieg*, No.6 [published at the end of 1923], pp. 3, 6–7, in Weber (ed.) 1963, *Der deutsche Kommunismus: Dokumente*, pp. 81–2.

Note: These generally sensible pieces of advice on urban guerrilla warfare printed in the KPD's illegal military journal had ceased to be relevant by the time they were issued. The era of communist insurrection in Germany had reached its conclusion by the end of 1923. Out of the ruins of the Proletarian Hundreds there emerged in 1924 another organisation, the Red League of Front Fighters (RFB).[73] Its purpose, however, was not to rise in revolt but to protect party members and engage in street demonstrations. These sometimes ended in pitched battles against other paramilitary groups (the German Nationalists'

---

71   *Teno*: abbreviation for *Technische Nothilfe* (Emergency Technical Corps), a body set up in 1919 under the Ministry of the Interior to keep vital services going in case of a strike. The Free Trade Unions regarded them as strike-breakers (they were even used to break strikes of agricultural workers), but successive SPD governments continued to make use of them.
72   The reference is to the Hamburg uprising of October 1923.
73   *Roter Frontkämpferbund*: founded in July 1924, prohibited in 1929. See chapter 11.

Stahlhelm, the Nazis' SA, and even at times the SPD's *Reichsbanner*).[74] There was some conspiratorial activity until the middle of 1924; but plots to assassinate General Seeckt are not to be confused with organised insurrection. After 1929 the economic crisis and the rise of Nazism obviously raised the level of political violence, but no serious preparations for insurrection were undertaken again, even under the threat of a Nazi seizure of power.

74　*Reichsbanner Schwarz-Rot-Gold* (Black-Red-Gold Association for the Republic). This organisation, founded in February 1924, was in theory meant to bring together supporters of all the pro-republican political parties, but 90 percent of its members were Social Democrats, and it had an SPD chair (Otto Hörsing) and vice-chair (Karl Höltermann).

In Defence of Democracy

Introduction

There were three main issues for socialists in this context: firstly, whether to defend Weimar democracy or to see it as merely a cover for the continuation of the previous regime of the big landowners and capitalists. This dilemma was present right from the start (4.2) and it continued to be posed throughout the Weimar Republic. The KPD was usually opposed to defending Weimar democracy, while the SPD always saw itself as the upholder, in fact perhaps the sole consistent upholder, of the democracy established under the 1919 Constitution. Secondly, once the decision had been made to defend Weimar democracy there was a choice of constitutional or extra-constitutional methods. When the opponents of democracy had broken the constitution the answer seemed to be clear: reply to force with force, as in the general strike of 1920 against the Kapp putsch (4.1). Then the defence of democracy might well turn into something more. In this case it sparked off the rising of the workers of the Ruhr, which Barrington Moore has described as 'the most significant uprising by industrial workers that has so far taken place in any modern industrial country'.[1] In more moderate Social Democratic circles it also gave rise to the idea of a 'workers' government', which was advocated by the Free Trade Unions in 1920 (4.4). The third issue was this: was it necessary, in order to defend democracy, to extend and deepen it, to establish a more all-embracing democratic system by democratising the various state institutions such as the judiciary, the civil service and the army which the Weimar Republic had essentially taken over unchanged from Imperial Germany? These were the main issues at stake in the arguments over democracy within Social Democracy in the late 1920s.[2] There was also a fourth issue, affecting both Social Democrats and communists: was it possible to unite temporarily to defend and deepen democracy?

Was there ever a possibility that the two big working-class parties of the Weimar Republic might join together in a genuine alliance? The call for an alliance against 'Fascism', and more specifically the National Socialist movement, was made particularly urgently in the 1930s by smaller groups which had

---

1   Moore 1978, p. 328.
2   See in more detail Fowkes 1989, pp. 247–64.

split off from the SPD or the KPD. But it never eventuated during the lifetime
of the Republic. There were many obstacles in the way, and these had existed
from the very beginning. There was a deep mutual hatred. The SPD leaders
have often been blamed for causing, or at least worsening this, by their harsh
repression of revolutionary movements in 1919 and 1920, made even harsher by
their preference for using the Free Corps, the revived forces of the old imperial
order, to do the job. The reply of Arthur Crispien[3] to Müller's invitation to join
the government in 1920[4] is a characteristic reflection of the feelings of USPD
members, many of whom (though not Crispien himself) were to enter the KPD
later in the year.

In addition to emotional reactions of this type there were many other
obstacles, both ideological and practical. Ideologically, the SPD's aims were
no longer what they had been in the early 1890s, namely the achievement of
socialism through revolution. The Görlitz Programme of 1921 represented a
belated victory for the revisionists, who had tried and failed to alter the Erfurt
Programme in the late 1890s. This meant that any alliance had to be an agreement for practical cooperation for specific political or social objectives, to be
achieved within the framework of the capitalist system. The KPD could only
agree to this idea by re-describing it as an attempt to demonstrate the incom-
patibility of such agreed objectives with capitalism. In effect they said to the
SPD: 'Let us go ahead with these proposals of yours, but you are quite wrong
to think that there is a chance of success. What they will achieve is to raise
the consciousness of the masses, and their understanding that such demands
can only be realised under socialism'. A second reason for the communists'
readiness at certain times to enter into a temporary alliance was the hope that
the Social Democrats' supporters would abandon their Party and join the KPD
when they saw both the half-heartedness of Social Democratic campaigning
and the determined resistance of the bourgeoisie.

For the SPD leaders there was very little reason to go along with offers which
seemed to be directed at undermining their own position. Yet they occasionally did so. Examples of this are the campaign in 1921 for the taxation of material assets and the defence of the Republic against the right-wing assassination
gangs who murdered Rathenau and later Erzberger; the campaign of 1926 for
the expropriation of the former princely houses, the campaign of 1928 against
the building of Armoured Battle Cruisers. But each time cooperation began to
look as if it would last, both sides took fright, the SPD both because it spent

---

3 Artur Crispien (1875–1946), joint chair of USPD 1917–22, member of SPD leadership 1922–33.
4 See below, 5.1.

much of the time looking over its shoulders at its parliamentary coalition allies further to the right, for whom communism was anathema, and because it feared it might lose control of its followers if it made the KPD look respectable by joining its campaigns; the KPD because it also had to look over its shoulder, both at leftists within the Party (until 1924) and, particularly in the later period, at the ECCI in Moscow, which had the final say on all questions of communist strategy, including how to apply what was called 'the united front tactic'.

Although a coalition at the national level was out of the question, if only because the two parties never constituted a majority in the Reichstag, there were some coalitions at state level, particularly in Saxony and Thuringia. There the left wing of the SPD was dominant in the early years, between 1921 and 1923, and it is in those states that the 'united front' policy bore fruit most effectively. In most other parts of the country, the local SPD was more likely to go for a coalition with the Centre Party and the DDP. Indeed, in 1927 in Hamburg, when elections produced an arithmetical 'red majority', the SPD, rather than join with the KPD, preferred a coalition with the DVP, the more conservative wing of the liberals.[5]

When the threat to democracy was indirect or did not appear to be too serious there were two possible responses: to play a waiting game in political isolation or to join hands with bourgeois parties in a parliamentary coalition. The first answer was given by the socialists of the USPD, while it existed as a mass party, and also later on by a left wing which grew up within the reunited SPD, largely though by no means entirely based on former Independents. The second answer was that usually given by the SPD leadership, though differences of view could arise where genuinely democratic bourgeois coalition partners were missing from the scene. Apart from the DDP, and the Centre Party in its earlier years, the bourgeois parties were somewhat lukewarm on the question of democracy. They were, in the famous phrase, *Vernunftrepublikaner*, in other words republicans of the head and not the heart. They were unwilling to make any social concessions which might damage the interests of the groups they represented in order to secure a coalition with the SPD. Hence voices were often heard in the Party, arguing against continuing in coalitions simply in order to defend democracy. Social Democrats asked themselves: How much should one swallow to achieve this? It all depended on the perception of danger. Until the autumn of 1930 the SPD leaders did not regard the threat posed to democracy by the National Socialists as particularly serious. If anything,

5   Mallmann 1996, p. 273.

Chancellor Heinrich Brüning was seen as more of a threat, with his use of Article 48 of the constitution to override Reichstag majorities against the new budget. On 18 July 1930, for instance, the SPD gained a majority for a motion annulling the emergency decree which the Chancellor had pushed through the budget; he immediately replied by dissolving the Reichstag, calling fresh elections, and re-issuing the decree on the authority of the president.

The SPD leaders clearly did not expect the disastrous outcome of the September 1930 election (nor did Brüning). Otherwise they would not have been in such a hurry in July to gain a meaningless parliamentary victory. It should be said in their defence that it took some time to get used to the complete transformation of the political spectrum which resulted from the impact of the Great Depression on Germany. Fear of the Nazis was not yet the dominant emotion, despite the NSDAP's local election victories in the spring and summer of that year, and despite the warning issued in May by the Prussian Ministry of the Interior.[6] After September 1930 everything changed. In the desperate situation of 1931 and 1932, the negative task of keeping Hitler out of power led the SPD to accept policies it would previously have fiercely opposed. For two years the Party pursued a 'policy of toleration' (Tolerierungspolitik) towards the cabinet of Heinrich Brüning, which rested on the support of the German president, von Hindenburg,[7] rather than a parliamentary majority. Any kind of extra-parliamentary action was ruled out. As Erich Ollenhauer[8] said in 1931, 'the use of the vote is the only way to fight Fascism which is in line with the traditions of Social Democracy.'[9] There was a danger that this policy would lead to complete capitulation to the right-wing parties, in the vain hope that the Right would resist Hitler and the Nazis.[10] The documents in this section trace the gradual slide of the SPD leaders in this direction (4.13–4.15). When

---

6   Büttner 2008, pp. 404–5.

7   Paul von Beneckendorff und Hindenburg (1847–1934), Field Marshal, head of the General Staff of the army 1916 to 1918, President of Germany 1925–34.

8   Erich Ollenhauer (1901–63), SPD. Chair of the Socialist Youth International 1923, Chair of the SPD Youth Movement 1928–30, member of the party leadership in 1933, party chair from 1952.

9   Sozialdemokratischer Parteitag 1931, p. 204.

10   This highly negative view of the SPD's policy of toleration has been challenged recently, but not very convincingly. The argument (in itself not new) has been put forward that there was no alternative, firstly because to attack Brüning in parliament was to attack the Centre Party, and the governmental position of the SPD in Prussia was dependent on the support of the Centre; and secondly because the extremely high level of unemployment made strike action impracticable. As Rainer Schäfer puts it: 'Social Democratic strategy

presidential elections fell due in March 1932 they supported the re-election of President Hindenburg, in order to keep out Hitler. Some Social Democrats wanted to put up their own man, Otto Braun, as candidate, but in the end almost all the party leaders 'endorsed the man they had bitterly opposed in 1925' so as not to 'split the republican vote'.[11] At the last moment, when it was too late to do anything, they made the opposite mistake: they changed direction once again, adopting an entirely oppositional stance towards Franz von Papen[12] and his successor Kurt von Schleicher.[13] When Schleicher proposed to dissolve the Reichstag, early in January 1933, as part of an attempt to prevent Hitler from coming to power, the SPD leaders reacted in a 'rigidly negative way' (Erich Matthias) towards this.[14]

For the communists, the questions at issue were different. Political isolation was assumed, the Party saw its task as the overthrow of capitalism rather than the defence of democracy. The Social Democratic leaders, with their ingrained reformism, remained the enemy for the communists throughout the period, even during the heyday of the united front. After 1928 (and also in 1924 and 1925) they were seen as the main enemy. Nevertheless, tactical alliances could be made with them, ostensibly for the defence of democracy, but with the ultimate aim of pushing any resulting mass movement in an anti-capitalist direction, or at least securing an increase in communist influence when, as was considered inevitable, the alliance fell apart. These elements are all present in the Open Letter of 8 January 1921 (4.5) and in the 1923 theses on the united front (4.6). Although the united front remained a constant feature of communist politics in subsequent years, its scope varied considerably. After the 1923 debacle the view was taken both in the Executive Committee of the Communist International in Moscow and in the leadership of the KPD in Germany that a united front 'from above', in other words a united front arrived at by agreement with the leaders of the SPD and the Free Trade Unions, was no longer acceptable. The united front could be conducted only 'from below',

---

was oriented towards the real possibilities for the workers' movement' (Schäfer 1990, p. 442). See also Schönhoven 1992, pp. 59–75.

11   Harsch 1993, p. 179.

12   Franz von Papen (1879–1969), right-wing member of the Centre Party, member of the Prussian Diet 1920–28, 1930–32, Reich Chancellor 1932, Vice-Chancellor 1933–34.

13   Kurt von Schleicher (1882–1934), General, Head of the Ministerial Office 1929–1932, Minister of Defence 1932, Reich Chancellor, December 1932–January 1933. Murdered on Hitler's orders 1934.

14   Matthias 1960, p. 146.

by appealing directly to rank-and-file Social Democrats. When in 1925 the line taken in Moscow was slightly modified, so that the slogan again became 'united front both from below and above' it was difficult to impose this on the KPD, which was still dominated by the leftists Ruth Fischer and Arkady Maslow, who had taken control in 1924. Opinion within the Communist Party at this time was if anything to the left of Fischer and Maslow. The direct intervention of the Comintern was needed to overcome this opposition, in the shape of the Open Letter of August 1925. Despite their abject submission, Fischer and Maslow lost influence, and were gradually removed from the leadership. The leftists were marginalised and then expelled in the new two years.[15] The way was now open for a number of agreements with the SPD and the SPD-led trade unions, at least at a local level, between 1925 and 1928.[16]

In 1928, however, the Party line changed again, and the Social Democrats were once again referred to as 'Social Fascists'. The left course was resumed, and the Sixth Comintern Congress held between July and September confirmed that 'the main danger' for communism internationally, and particularly in Germany, was 'the Right deviation', in other words the attempt by leading communists in some of the parties to lessen the harshness of the attacks on Social Democracy. In terms of practical politics this meant that the 'united front from above' was once again out of the question. Even the united front 'from below' was now in doubt. When the KPD resisted Nazism in subsequent years, it did so for most of the time without allies or associates,[17] and under the flag of the revolutionary overthrow of the capitalist order and self-defence against Nazi terror rather than the preservation of the democratic republic. There were some exceptions to this, but they were initiatives by local branches of the Party, undertaken without the approval of the top leadership or the ECCI. In Brunswick in 1931 the KPD supported the SPD in order to prevent the Nazis from taking control of the city council (the two left-wing parties together had a

---

15 See Winkler 1988, pp. 417–44, Weber 1969, vol. 1, pp. 120–85, Laporte 2003, pp. 79–234 and Fowkes 1984, pp. 119–41 for details of this process.

16 For these, see Herlemann 1977, pp. 93–103.

17 Klaus-Michael Mallmann's claim that 'the deadly challenge' posed by the political violence of the Nazis brought the supporters of the SPD and KPD together at the grass roots level (Mallmann 1996, p. 372) has often been challenged, most recently by Joachim Häberlen, who says 'this did not happen in Leipzig' (Häberlen 2010, p 384 n.24). In any case, Mallmann himself concedes later in the book that 'the joy of unity did not last long', with the SPD denouncing the KPD's 'Anti-Fascist Action' proposal of May 1932 as 'an Anti-Social Democratic Action' and the KPD condemning 'opportunist tendencies towards a united front from above' and insisting that 'the main onslaught' must still be directed 'against Social Democracy' (Mallmann 1996, pp. 377–8).

majority there). This highly irregular situation continued until 1932, when the party leadership found out what was happening and put a stop to it.[18] Even so, the party leader Ernst Thälmann gave the impression in June 1932 that he was prepared to envisage 'the application of the united front tactic from below *and* above in the revolutionary sense', while stressing that no *bloc* could ever be formed 'with the Social Fascist leaders'.[19] In the Prussian Diet a little later the communist *Fraktion* went further than this: it supported the Social Democratic candidate for president of the Diet, in order to keep out the Nazi candidate, even though the SPD had rejected the conditions set by the KPD, and drawn up by the ECCI, for their support.[20] This move had not been approved by Moscow, and it was seen as an act of disobedience. It was never repeated.[21]

The SPD was for its part unwilling, even at this late stage, to engage in a united front with its left-wing rival. The KPD's offer of June 1932 put the Party in a difficult position. The Social Democrats feared that the communists would lead them in an unwelcome direction, towards a mobilisation of the masses, which could have incalculable consequences. It would also give von Papen an excuse to intervene in Prussia to remove the SPD state government, which was seen as the Party's chief power-base. The SPD therefore agreed to a united front on one condition: there must be a 'non-aggression pact' by which both parties would ignore their differences, concentrate their fire on National Socialism, and not make hateful comments about each other. Even this was impossible, given the KPD's insistence on retaining the freedom of propaganda: 'under no circumstances is a weakening of our slogans permissible' was the condition made by the Party's Political Bureau.[22] The SPD leaders could conceivably have gone ahead with a united front without making this condition, but Friedrich Stampfer, the influential editor of the party newspaper, pointed out that in that case 'they would be booted out by their own supporters'.[23] Although it finally brought the SPD's long-standing 'policy of toleration' to an end, von Papen's coup of 20 July 1932, by which he removed the SPD state government in Prussia, did not change this attitude. The KPD's proposal for a general protest strike was rejected both by the SPD and the ADGB. Legien, the head of the ADGB,

---

18   Rother 1990, p. 240.

19   Thälmann 1932, pp. 277, 279, 284.

20   On 22 June the KPD agreed to support an SPD or Centre candidate for president of the Prussian Diet without making any conditions (Winkler 1987, p. 624, n. 11).

21   Hoppe 2007, p. 307.

22   Heer-Kleinert 1983, p. 343.

23   Winkler 1987, p. 625, quoting Stampfer's article of 19 June 1932 in *Vorwärts*.

declared that what had to be done now was 'to ensure that the Reichstag elections' scheduled for 31 July 'take place in a calm atmosphere'.[24]

Documents

4.1 *Joint Call by German Trade Unions for a General Strike against the Kapp Putsch, 13 March 1920*

Forward to the general strike!

To all workers, office employees and civil servants.

Men and women! The military reaction has raised its head again, and in Berlin it has actually seized power. Disloyal units of the Reichswehr have marched in here under the command of mutinous officers and they have had the impertinence to set up an illegal authority alongside the government elected by the people. The reactionaries have declared the dissolution of the National Assembly and the Prussian State Assembly and they are preparing to do away with the achievements of the revolution of November 1918.

The German republic is in danger!

They intend to restore absolutism, both in the state and in the factories. They have done away with the right of combination, that indispensable prerequisite of all social progress, and suppressed all freedom of opinion. This means the return of all the reactionary conditions the German people were fortunate enough to sweep away in November 1918. The following are under threat: the Eight Hour Day, the lawful representation of factories and offices, the reform of civil service pay, the extension of legal protection for workers and civil servants, the railway workers' national wage agreements, the right of all employees to participate in social and political decision-making (*Mitbestimmung*) and all the factory laws.

Let no thinking worker, office employee or civil servant be taken in by the unreliable promises of the putschist government! All popular forces must be gathered together in resistance. The people would not be worthy of their freedom ... if they did not defend themselves to the uttermost. We are therefore calling on all workers, office employees and civil servants to go on strike everywhere immediately. All factories must be brought to a standstill. Water installations, hospitals and sick funds are the sole exceptions to this. The local representatives of the workers will decide what other factories may continue in operation, in so far as they are needed for the preservation of life.

---

24   Winkler 1987, p. 670.

The workers must undertake a gigantic and overwhelming fight in their own defence ... Everyone must do their duty. The reaction must be broken by the solid resistance of the people. The instruments of its power will soon crumble away. Victory will be on the side of the working people.

Signed: C. Legien[25] (for the ADGB[26])

S. Aufhäuser[27] (for the AfA[28])

Berlin, 13 March 1920

Source: Sozialistische Einheitspartei Deutschlands Zentralkomitee 1958, *Dokumente und Materialien*, VII, 1, no. 104, 13 March 1920.

4.2   *Proclamation by the KPD* Zentrale *Opposing the General Strike, Issued on 14 March 1920*

In the delivery crisis[29] the Ebert-Bauer government showed itself to be nothing but a speck of dirt stuck to the coat-tails of Ludendorff[30] and Lüttwitz. Now they have shaken off this annoying speck of dirt with the help of a handful of Baltic veterans. These are the very men who were sent by the government to the Baltic to fight against Soviet Russia, who were again offered by the government to the Entente as cannon-fodder, and permitted to retain their weapons and ammunition, in breach of international law.

The Eberts, the Bauers and the Noskes have fallen silently and without resistance into the grave they themselves have dug ... The government which has now been swept away did not dare until the last minute to inform the proletarian masses about its demise and call them into action ... Let us ask, what were the final actions of this government? It filled the prisons and fortresses with thousands of revolutionary workers. Their last action in the economic sphere was the outrageous and sanguinary order issued against the mining workers of

---

25   Carl Legien (1861–1920), chair of the SPD-aligned trade unions from 1890 to 1920.

26   ADGB (*Allgemeiner Deutscher Gewerkschaftsbund*): this was the General German Trade Union Confederation, the umbrella organisation for Social Democratic trade unions.

27   Siegfried Aufhäuser (1884–1969), USPD 1917 SPD 1921 Member of the Reichstag 1921–33. Chair of the office employees trade union, the AfA.

28   AfA (*Arbeitsgemeinschaft freier Angestelltenverbände*): Cooperative Union of Free Salaried Employees' Associations. This organisation represented office employees and was aligned to the SPD.

29   The 'delivery crisis' arose out of the German government's refusal to hand over former leaders of the country regarded by the Entente as war criminals.

30   Erich Ludendorff (1865–1937), General, determined German policy 1916–18, later leading supporter of the extreme right German *völkisch* (Racialist) movement, took part in Hitler's Munich *putsch* November 1923, member of the Reichstag 1924–28.

the Ruhr.[31] Then, at the moment of collapse, this bankrupt group calls on the workers to mount a general strike for the 'salvation of the Republic'. The revolutionary proletariat knows that it will have to enter a life and death struggle against the military dictatorship. But it will not lift a finger for the government of the murderers of Liebknecht and Luxemburg, a government which has collapsed in ignominy and infamy. It will not lift a finger for the democratic republic, which was only a paltry mask for the dictatorship of the bourgeoisie. The bourgeoisie is now exercising its dictatorship directly, through its traditional rulers, the heroes of 1914. That is all that has changed. The democratic republic is irretrievably lost; it is not the republic which has to be saved ... What is needed is to take up the struggle for the proletarian dictatorship, for the republic of Councils. Capitalism or communism? The dictatorship of the military, or the dictatorship of the proletariat? That is now how the question is unavoidably posed.

Should the workers enter into a general strike at this moment? The working class, which was only yesterday still being smashed to pieces by Ebert-Noske, has no weapons to hand, and is under very strong pressure from the employers. It is at present not capable of action. We consider it our duty to say this plainly. The working class will take up the fight against the military dictatorship at the time, and with the methods, that seem appropriate to it. One section of the working class knows the face of this military dictatorship: the Hungarian workers.[32] The great majority of the workers will only find out what it means when instead of whips raining down on their backs they are stung by scorpions, when the returned heroes of 1914 bring back the August of that year, and when renewed threats of war from outside raise their heads to join the iron oppression inside the country. Then will the working class fight to the end with these battle cries:

Down with the military dictatorship!
For the dictatorship of the proletariat!
For the German Communist Republic of Councils!

Zentrale of the KPD (S)
13 March 1920

Source: *Die Rote Fahne*, Nr. 30, 14 March 1920.

---

31   The state of emergency declared on 13 January 1920 by Ebert was applied particularly harshly in the Ruhr. See Hürten 1977, pp. 312–5, 317.

32   The defeat of the Hungarian Soviet Republic in 1919 was followed severe acts of repression directed against its participants.

Note: This statement was drafted by August Thalheimer, but supported by Ernst Friesland (Reuter) of the Berlin organisation.[33] According to a later account by the ECCI's representative in Germany M.J. Braun (Brónski),[34] the KPD's 14 March line on the general strike against Kapp reflected the 'momentary mood of the Berlin workers',[35] and was altered the day afterwards when it appeared that the strike was highly successful and effective, spreading across the whole working population (including communists). On 15 March the *Zentrale* issued another declaration, this time in favour of the general strike, though not in support of the government. The Party continued to demand the replacement of bourgeois democracy with a 'republic of Councils', or, to use the Russian expression, 'Soviets'. 'Orthodox' communists, unlike Social Democrats of the left and right, did not differentiate between these two institutions.

4.3　Paul Levi's Critique of the Line Taken by the KPD Zentrale towards the Kapp Putsch

To the *Zentrale*, from prison, 16 March 1920:

I have just read the leaflets. My judgment: the KPD is under threat of moral and political bankruptcy. It is incomprehensible to me how in the present situation one can write phrases such as 'the working class is at present not capable of action...the state of the class struggle is not directly changed by the mere fact that Lüttwitz and Kapp have replaced Bauer and Noske'.[36] This will be grist to the mills of the most miserable fellows in the working-class movement, those who are always crying 'it's all pointless anyway'. Now they have written confirmation of their views from the KPD. One day (14 March) one denies the proletariat's capacity for action; the next day (15 March) one issues a leaflet proclaiming: 'Now the German proletariat must at last start the struggle for proletarian dictatorship and the communist republic of Councils'. At the same time (even though the general strike has taken the masses out of the factories) one calls for elections to Councils, for a Central Congress of Councils. In short, our 'party bosses' snap the vital spring of the general strike

---

33　Ernst Reuter (Ernst Friesland) (1889–1953), chair of Berlin KPD 1919, replaced Levi as party leader 1921, expelled from KPD 1922, joined SPD, mayor of Magdeburg 1931–33, mayor of West Berlin 1948–53.

34　M.J. Braun (Miechysław Brónski) (1882–1941), Polish Social Democrat till 1917, then Bolshevik. Comintern and Bolshevik emissary to the KPD 1919. Took part in meetings of the KPD leadership under the name M.J. Braun, 1919–21. Recalled to Moscow 1921.

35　Braun 1920, p. 27.

36　This phrase summarises the general tenor of the 14 March declaration, rather than its words, although Levi presents it as a direct quotation.

both organisationally and politically. Morally as well. In my view it is a crime to destroy the present action by writing that 'the proletariat will not lift a finger for the democratic republic'. Do you know what that means? It means you are attacking the greatest-ever action undertaken by the German proletariat from the rear. I always thought we were clear and united about the following point: if an action does come about – even for the stupidest of goals! – we support the action, and endeavour to push it on beyond its foolish objective. We do not cry at the outset 'we will not lift a finger' if the goal does not suit us. Raise the level of the slogans, of course, but do it gradually. 'Republic of Councils' comes last, not first. The only proper slogan at present is: Arm the proletariat ... We must carry on the action jointly with the USPD and the SPD, and the immediate slogan is: No compromise!

These must be the Party's demands: (1) Arming of the proletariat, that is to say the distribution of weapons to the politically organised workers, so as to secure the Republic; (2) Unconditional capitulation of Kapp and Lüttwitz. This demand is of the greatest importance, for sordid attempts at haggling with them are already being made. (3) The leaders of the putsch must be immediately arrested and condemned by an emergency proletarian court. Nothing more. What the *Zentrale* writes in its leaflet of 16 March is unusable. 'A republic of Councils' and 'a congress of Councils' are not demands to stay off work for ... 'Disarming of the Reichswehr'! This is nonsense, because it will drive those parts of the army which oppose the putsch into the opposite camp ... There must be total concentration on the strike demands. If they are achieved the Republic will have to shift to the left ... For if the strike demands are fulfilled the proletariat will be the force holding up the Republic, and its government, whatever name it is given, will then be the advertising billboard for this complete change in the balance of social forces. It would then be a matter of six months of normal development to get from there to the Republic of Councils.

Source: *Die Kommunistische Internationale*, 1920, No. 12, col. 2145–48, p. 147.

4.4 The Nine Point Programme of the ADGB, the AfA and the DBB,[37] 18 March 1920

1 The above-mentioned employees' unions must have a decisive influence on the reconstruction of the governments in the Reich and the states, as well as on

---

37 DBB: *Deutscher Beamtenbund* (German Union of Officials): the largest association of German public officials. It was politically neutral and not aligned with the SPD. In 1922

the changes in legislation on economic and social policy. [The final agreement provided for 'consultation' instead of 'decisive influence', and always subject to the rights of the parliamentary assemblies.]

2 The immediate disarming and punishment of all troops who participated in the putsch, and punishment of all the people who took part in the overthrow of the legal government or placed themselves at the disposal of illegal governments, whether in the Reich, the states or the local councils. [Accepted]

3 The immediate resignation of Reich minister Noske and Prussian ministers Oeser[38] and Heine.[39] [This had already happened by the time the final agreement was signed.]

4 A thorough purge of all reactionary [changed to 'counter-revolutionary'] personalities from all public offices and factory managements, particularly those in leading positions, and their replacement by reliable forces. The reinstatement of all the representatives of trade union organisations in the public services who were dismissed. [Accepted]

5 The most rapid possible democratisation of public administrative offices; in this connection, the economic organisations of the workers, office employees and civil servants are to be consulted and play an equal part in determining the outcome. [Accepted]

6 The immediate extension of existing social laws and the establishment of new laws guaranteeing complete social and economic equality of rights to the workers, office employees and civil servants. The rapid introduction of a code of conduct for civil servants. [Accepted]

7 The immediate socialisation of the mining and energy industries. The Coal Syndicate and the Potassium Syndicate are to be taken over by the Reich. [Socialisation is to be put in hand where a branch of the economy is ripe for this, as determined by a Socialisation Commission. This Commission is to be set up immediately. The Coal and Potassium Syndicates are to be taken over.]

8 The immediate presentation to parliament of a law expropriating landowners who do not dispatch the food supplies they have available, or fail to run their enterprises in the interests of the people as a whole, with a view to ensuring that the productive forces can be used without exception for the production

---

the ADGB and the AfA set up their own SPD-aligned General German Union of Officials (ADB) based mainly on railway employees, which was half as strong as the DBB initially but declined rapidly in membership in the course of the late 1920s.

38 Rudolf Oeser (1858–1926), DDP, Prussian Minister of Public Works 1919–21, Reich Minister of Transport 1923–24.

39 Wolfgang Heine (1861–1944), SPD, Prussian Minister of Justice then Minister of the Interior, 1918–20.

of the means of nourishment. [Possession of available food supplies to be secured effectively; measures against profiteering in town and country to be made more severe.]

9 The dissolution of all counter-revolutionary military formations. The security services are to be taken over by the organised working class.[40] [The disbanded troops are to be replaced by formations from the reliable republican population, especially the organised workers, office employees and civil servants.]

Source: Könnemann, Berthold and G. Schulze (eds.) 1971, *Arbeiterklasse siegt über Kapp und Lüttwitz*, vol. 1, pp. 175–6.

Note: This programme formed the basis for the negotiations between the Trade Unions and the parties of the coalition government. The head of the Free Trade Unions, Legien, played a big part in forcing their acceptance. He threatened that otherwise the government would not be able to return to Berlin.[41] The eventual agreement of 20 March 1920 incorporated all the points except number three, but certain changes in wording, aimed at weakening the force of the original demands, were introduced by the SPD and DDP representatives. These are indicated in parentheses in the document.

4.5 Open Letter of 8 January 1921 from the VKPD to Other Workers' Organisations Calling for United Action

To the ADGB, AfA, AAU,[42] SPD, USPD, and KAPD

The United Communist Party of Germany (VKPD) considers it its duty in this significant and grave moment for the whole German proletariat to turn to all socialist parties and trade union organisations.

The progressive decomposition of capitalism, and the combined impact of the incipient world crisis and the one specific to Germany have had the following consequences: a progressive fall in the value of the currency, a continuing increase in the prices of all the means of nourishment and the requirements

---

40 Hugo Sinzheimer, SPD specialist in labour law, complained that this laid the military basis for a dictatorship of Councils, and Otto Wels and Friedrich Stampfer worked out the more anodyne formula that is added here in parentheses.

41 Winkler 1985, p. 311. Legien's role in pushing for the Nine Point Programme is treated in detail in Potthoff 1979, pp. 267–87.

42 *Allgemeine Arbeiter-Union* (General Workers' Union). Syndicalist trade union founded in August 1919 under the influence of the 'One Big Union' conception held by the American IWW (Industrial Workers of the World).

of everyday living, a rise in unemployment and the impoverishment of the broad masses. All this makes it necessary for the proletarian class as a whole to defend itself. This applies not just to the industrial workers but to all the strata which are now awakening and becoming conscious of their proletarian character.

The proletariat is being kept in this intolerable situation by the advance of the reaction, which is speculating on the workers' disunity and constantly inventing new chains for them, such as the Orgesch,[43] the disgusting assassination campaign and the judicial system which tolerates these killings.[44]

The VKPD therefore proposes that all socialist parties and trade-union organisations should join together on the following basis for various immediate actions to be discussed in detail later:

I

1 Joint struggles over wages are to be started in order to safeguard the existence of the workers, salaried employees and civil servants. The fight of the railway workers, civil servants and miners for higher wages is to be conducted as a joint action with other workers in industry and agriculture.
2 All the annuities and pensions of the war-wounded, widows and elderly people are to be raised in line with the wage increase demanded by the workers.
3 Unemployment benefit is to be regulated uniformly over the whole of Germany on the basis of the earnings of people who are in full employment. The burden of this support is to fall on the Reich and capital alone is to be applied to these purposes. The unemployed are to control this through special Councils of the Unemployed, acting in association with the trade unions.

II

Measures to reduce the cost of living, namely:

1 Food is to be delivered at lower prices to all recipients of wages and low salaries (annuities, widows' and orphans' pensions etc.) with the participation of

---

43   *Orgesch*: *Organisation Escherich*, a paramilitary organisation named after its founder and leader the Bavarian politician Georg Escherich. It was disbanded under Allied pressure in May 1921.
44   The early years of the Weimar Republic were plagued by an assassination campaign carried out by elements of the extreme Right. If caught, the perpetrators were usually treated very mildly by the judges, as opposed to the condign punishments meted out to left-wingers.

the consumers' associations and under the control of the trade unions and Factory Councils. The financial means for this are to be provided by the Reich.
2 All available habitable dwellings are to be confiscated immediately, and a right to compulsory accommodation is to be introduced, as well as the compulsory removal from accommodation of small families occupying large dwellings or indeed houses.

III

Measures to provide food and objects of everyday use:

1 The Factory Councils are to control all available raw materials, coal and fertiliser. All the factories that have been closed are to be put into operation again where they produce objects of daily use; these products are to be distributed in accordance with the principles laid down in section II.1.
2 The Estate Councils and Small Peasants' Councils are to control the cultivation, harvesting and sale of all agricultural products in association with the organisations of agricultural workers.

IV

1 All bourgeois local defence associations (*Einwohnerwehren*)[45] are to be disarmed and dissolved immediately and proletarian self-defence associations are to be formed in all states and local communities.
2 An amnesty is to be granted for all crimes committed for political motives or resulting from the present general state of deprivation. All political prisoners are to be set free.
3 The existing prohibitions on strike action are to be lifted.
4 Trade and diplomatic relations with Soviet Russia are to be established immediately.

While proposing this basis for action, we do not conceal for one moment, either from ourselves or from the working masses, that the demands put forward by us cannot remove their misery and deprivation. Nor do we give up

---

45   These paramilitary organisations were opposed by the Left; but most of the German Right, including some members of the SPD, such as Gustav Noske and Wilhelm Blos, the prime minister of Württemberg, defended them as useful instruments in maintaining law and order (Winkler 1985, p. 339, n. 392). The Western allies regarded them as a breach of the Versailles Treaty and demanded their abolition, which had to be conceded. But they continued to exist unofficially, particularly in Bavaria.

for one moment our endeavours to spread the idea of the struggle for the dictatorship, which is the only road to salvation. Nor shall we desist from summoning the working masses at every favourable moment to the struggle for the dictatorship, and leading them in that struggle. The VKPD is ready, along with the other parties which draw support from the proletariat, to carry out joint actions to achieve the measures indicated above.

We will not hide the differences that divide us from the other parties. We declare instead that we do not want from them lip-service to the proposed basis for action, but action itself. We do not ask the parties whether they regard these demands as justified. We assume this. We ask them rather: Are you ready immediately to undertake an unyielding struggle for these demands, together with us?

We expect this clear and unambiguous question to receive a similarly unambiguous answer. The situation itself requires a rapid answer. We therefore expect a reply by 13 January 1921.

If the other parties and trade unions do not want to take up the struggle, the VKPD will regard itself as duty bound to lead the fight alone, and it is convinced that the working masses will follow it. From this day forward the VKPD addresses itself to all the proletarian organisations in Germany and the masses of workers gathered around them with the call to proclaim publicly their desire for joint defence against capitalism and reaction, and for the protection of their interests.

Zentrale of the VKPD

Source: *Die Rote Fahne*, 8 January 1921.

Note: This appeal for a united front was in line with the tactics pursued by Paul Levi, the leader of the KPD, towards the USPD in 1920, which had arguably allowed the majority of that Party to be won over to communism. It was also approved by Karl Radek, who was in Germany as the representative of the ECCI at the time. It was either written by him alone or jointly with Levi.[46] It was fiercely opposed not just by the communist Left in Germany but also by some influential people in Moscow, such as Zinoviev and Bukharin. In the short run it was overtaken by events (the decision to launch the March Action) but after the Third Comintern Congress in July 1921 it again became official communist policy, and was pursued for the next two years.

46　Radek's most recent biographer thinks the Open Letter was written jointly by Radek and Levi (Fayet 2004, p. 363).

4.6   *The KPD's Theses on the United Front Tactic and the Workers'*
        Government, February 1923

        I

        The United Front Tactic

The fight for working class power can only be victoriously conducted as a mass struggle, a fight of the *majority* of the working class against the rule of the capitalist minority. The conquest of the majority of the proletariat for the struggle for communism is the most important task of the Communist Party.

The greatest obstacle to the development of the united front is the influence of the reformist leaders of Social Democracy ... Through their policy of civil peace with the bourgeoisie (coalitions, *Arbeitsgemeinschaft* with the bosses,[47] national unity) they bind large parts of the proletariat to capitalist politics and prevent any serious struggle. Hence the fight for the united front is today to a considerable degree a fight to detach the masses from reformist tactics and leadership ... In the course of the joint resistance by the workers to the offensive of capital, the tactics of the communists will prove to be superior to those of the reformists. Social Democracy will be crushed ... The united front tactic is not a manoeuvre to unmask the reformists. Rather the reverse: the unmasking of the reformists is the means to building a firmly united fighting front of the proletariat ... In every serious situation, the Communist Party must turn both to the masses and to the leaders of all proletarian organisations with the invitation to undertake a common struggle for the construction of the proletarian united front. The notion that the establishment of the united front is possible only through an appeal to masses to struggle (only 'from below') or only by negotiations with other organisations at the summit (only 'from above') is un-dialectical and rigid ...

Alongside the conquest of the old mass organisations (trade unions, cooperatives) the proletarian united front must create new organs for the achievement of its aims, organs which embrace the whole of the class (Factory Councils, Control Commissions, political Workers' Councils) ... The revolutionary united front for the overthrow of the bourgeoisie, organised in political Workers' Councils, cannot exist at the beginning but only at the end of the fight to win the masses for communism. In Germany's present situation the Factory Council movement is the first step towards a gathering together of the masses who are ready to engage in revolutionary class struggle. The German united front movement has already created its own organs in the

---

47   *Arbeitsgemeinschaft:* a reference to the ZAG (Central Working Association) set up by the
      trade unions and the employers' representatives in November 1918, and still in operation
      at this point.

Factory Councils and Control Commissions which have come together on the lines laid down by the nationwide Factory Council Congress.[48] These organs are capable of giving direction to elemental mass movements and can be led without the consent and against the will of the saboteurs who run the trade union and SPD bureaucracy.

II
The 'Right' and 'Left' Deviations

'Right' deviations: the opportunist tendencies displayed by *Die Rote Fahne* during the Rathenau campaign;[49] the purely defensive propaganda which followed the March Action...

'Left' errors: the 'Left' opposed the requisitioning of physical assets (*Sachwerte*) by the state and advocated instead their seizure from below; they also opposed the New Economic Policy in the Soviet Union.

III
The Fight for a Workers' Government

The workers' government is neither the dictatorship of the proletariat nor a peaceful parliamentary ascent to it. It is an attempt by the working class, within the framework and initially with the instruments of bourgeois democracy, based on proletarian organs and mass movements, to pursue a working-class policy; the proletarian dictatorship, in contrast, consciously bursts the bounds of democracy, destroys the democratic state apparatus and replaces it entirely with proletarian class organs...

A workers' government can only conduct a proletarian policy and put its programme into effect if it is based on the broad masses of the working class,

---

48 This congress took place in November 1922 and was attended by 846 delegates, almost 200 of them non-communists, who defied the ADGB's threat to expel those who took part, on the ground that the congress was not based on the legally recognised network of Factory Councils.

49 Walter Rathenau (1867–1922) was an industrialist who after a varied career founded the DDP in 1919 and became German Foreign Minister. He was murdered in June 1922 by right-wing nationalist extremists for his support of the policy of fulfilling the terms of the Treaty of Versailles. The parties of the Left replied to this with a campaign of demonstrations in defence of the republic, in which the KPD participated jointly with the SPD. The collapse of this alliance led to recriminations by the left opposition in the Party against Ernst Meyer's conduct of the campaign as party leader. These criticisms were supported by Zinoviev in a confidential letter (see below, 6.5), and Meyer was soon dropped from the *Zentrale*. The comment in the text is an indirect attack on Meyer.

on the organs that emerge from the united front movement (Factory Councils, Control Commissions, Workers' Councils) and on the armed workers.

A victory of working-class parties at a parliamentary election can also form the opportunity for the establishment of a workers' government if... strong mass movements are in progress. In struggling to overcome the resistance of the bourgeoisie, the workers' government will be forced to go beyond the democratic framework, and take dictatorial measures... If the working class is not to succumb these struggles will inevitably lead to the destruction of the democratic constitution and the establishment of proletarian dictatorship. If the workers' government were to hesitate to pursue the ruthless policy against the bourgeoisie that is required and fail to put into effect the complete dis-armament of the bourgeoisie, this would inevitably lead to its collapse if the Communist Party was not yet in a position to lead the masses in the struggle for the proletarian dictatorship.

[Our] participation in a workers' government is not a trick or a tactical manoeuvre. It involves readiness to engage in a common struggle alongside the reformist working class parties... The Communist Party must lay down conditions for its entry into a workers' government. The most important of these are the participation of organs of the proletarian united front in leg-islation and the arming of the working class. The workers' government is no more than a point of support, a stage, in the proletariat's struggle for sole politi-cal supremacy. The workers' government is a possible stage in the struggle for political power, not an unconditionally necessary one.

IV
Workers' Governments in the States
The KPD takes part in state governments so as to make them into points of support in the struggle for a workers' government in the Reich as a whole. The workers' governments in the individual states must keep in close contact, and form a red block against the capitalist government of the Reich, which may either be purely bourgeois or rest on a bourgeois-SPD coalition.

Source: Kommunistiche Partei Deutschlands 1923, *Bericht über die Verhandlungen des III (8) Parteitages der Kommunistischen Partei Deutschlands (Sektion der Kommunistischen Internationale), 28 Jan.–1 Feb. 1923*, pp. 415–24.

Note: This programme represents the highpoint of KPD united front poli-tics. The united front is declared to be genuine: it is 'not a trick or a tactical manoeuvre', it is 'not a manoeuvre to unmask the reformists'. It is to happen both 'from above and from below'. It is to be carried as far as the establishment of joint SPD-KPD governments in the German states as a result of success in parliamentary elections. These are 'workers' governments', which are not to be seen as a 'peaceful ascent to proletarian dictatorship'. In putting this forward the Brandler leadership of the KPD was exposing itself to strong attacks from the Left, which garnered 59 votes to the leadership's 118 on the issue. The united front was a great success in its own terms in 1923, but its very success brought fresh dangers: the temptation was to assume, as was assumed in Moscow later in the year, that the SPD would back the KPD's plans for insurrection, under pressure from its rank and file. When this did not happen, the immensity of the disappointment led temporarily to the complete abandonment of the united front by the KPD and the emergence of the phrase that the Social Democrats were 'Social Fascists' (1924) which would be used again after 1928 with fateful consequences.

4.7   Rudolf Hilferding's 1927 Speech on the Importance of the Defence of Democracy for Socialists

Viewed historically, *democracy* has always been *a matter of interest to the proletariat*. I have continually been amazed by the assertion even at this Congress . . . that democracy is a matter for the bourgeoisie. This view denotes a lack of knowledge of the history of democracy, and a wish to extract that history from the writings of a few theoreticians in a colourless, intellectual fashion. In reality there is no sharper political struggle than that of the proletariat against the bourgeoisie for democracy. Not to see that this fight belongs among the great deeds of the proletarian class struggle is to deny the whole past of socialism. It is historically false and misleading to speak of 'bourgeois democracy'. Democracy was *our* cause. We had to wage a stubborn campaign to wring democracy out of the bourgeoisie. What a lot of proletarian blood has flowed to attain universal and equal suffrage, for instance!

But what if the rulers do not respect democracy? Is that a problem for us? Is it not evident that the moment an attempt is made to destroy the foundations of democracy, not only every Social Democrat, but every republican, will employ every means available to maintain those foundations? Then there is the question of the use of force . . . If the foundations of democracy are destroyed, we are *defending ourselves* and we have no choice but to employ all methods of defence . . . We want to defend democracy, and for that reason we are grateful to the *Reichsbanner*[50] for its work . . . If you haven't understood that

---

50   The full name of this organisation is *Reichsbanner Schwarz- Rot- Gold, Bund deutscher-Kriegsteilnehmer und Republikaner* [The National Flag in Black, Red, Gold. League of

the *preservation of democracy and the Republic are in the highest interests of the Party* you have not grasped the ABC of political thinking.

There are people who go around saying: beware of democratic illusions! I am of a very different opinion. The real danger is rather ... that there have been proletarian strata in other countries who have *failed to recognise the importance of freedom, of democracy*. In Italy Mussolini achieved power because the Italian proletariat did not know how good it was to have freedom and democracy ... The danger, not for the Republic – I admit that – but for the *real content and extent of democracy* has been tremendously *heightened* by the very fact that the German Nationalists have kept their monarchist ideas in cold storage for the last two years ... The fight between *the Republic and the monarchy* does not stand in the foreground when formulated directly in those terms; but it has changed into a fight between *fascism and democracy* (interjection: Very true!). We should be committing the worst of mistakes if we said to the proletariat: you don't need to worry much about politics any more, only material questions come into consideration at present ...

Thanks to Otto Braun and Karl Severing the waves of both Bolshevism and fascism have been broken in Prussia. That has been a world-historical achievement. History will eventually record what Severing, that little metalworker from Bielefeld, has achieved for Central Europe, indeed for the whole of Europe ... We were seriously concerned, after Severing's departure,[51] as to whether we could find an appropriate replacement. Our worries were unjustified. Severing's successor [Otto Braun] is an outstanding success. Prussia is a proud stronghold in the camp of the republic and our only task is to make it a proud stronghold in the camp of socialism. But when one reads some of the resolutions put forward here one might think that the most important task of the proletarian class struggle in Germany was to overthrow the Prussian government. No, the most important task of the class struggle is the overthrow of the right-wing government of the German *Reich*.

Source: Sozialdemokratischer Parteitag in Kiel 1927, *Protokoll mit dem Bericht der Frauenkonferenz*, pp. 172–5, 180–1.

4.8   *Siegfried Aufhäuser Replies to Hilferding* (1927)

What stands in our resolution is nothing other than that this government is less a blow against the Republic than a blow against the working class. I take back

---

German War Veterans and Republicans]. It was set up in 1924 as an association of war veterans of republican convictions. See most recently Ziemann 1998, pp. 357–98.

51   Severing ceased to be Prussian Minister of the Interior in 1926.

no word of that. Hilferding plainly stated that the confrontation is not monarchy against republic but capitalism against Social Democracy. Why should we not express this in a resolution? Hilferding and others, who are against this out of regard for building future governments, are showing a considerate attitude towards the Centre Party. But if the Centre Party decides it is appropriate to look for a different coalition in the Reichstag, it will not matter how plainly we describe the situation today. The Centre Party is not as sensitive as some people assume. Moreover, the Centre Party is not at all considerate towards us. They have never attacked us more sharply than in the last few weeks. They have asserted that they are ready for a merciless struggle against Social Democracy within the government ... Why have we been cut out of the government? It is not our fault. It happened for economic reasons. If we want to conquer these positions in our Republic, we must be ready to take up the struggle against the opponents of the Republic and its false friends who rule it ... I therefore protest against the claim that those who want to conduct the struggle mercilessly are inferior republicans to the others, who don't want to express themselves so plainly. It is not true that our resolution weakens the republican idea. We are merely describing the situation, not expressing an opinion, when we say that it is not the form of the state that is decisive for the present bourgeois government (*Bürgerregierung*) but the wishes of powerful economic circles ... We are all equally ready to defend and to extend the People's State. But we do not therefore need to awaken any kind of democratic illusions. Where does it lead, when Hilferding says he refuses to describe present-day democracy as bourgeois? We have learned from Hilferding himself what a difference there is between social and bourgeois democracy ... What use is a purely abstract democracy when one doesn't think about the human beings who have to be prepared for a given goal and a given decision. There are now new proletarian strata, such as employees and professionals. We shall not win these new strata by taking part in the government. We must meet them with our own social democratic programme plainly visible, just as we did previously in the case of manual workers. We shall only win over these strata if we reject responsibility for things Social Democracy cannot tolerate ... We find ourselves in an oppositional position, and the more plainly the Party Congress proclaims this fact to the whole working population the sooner we shall arrive at the great victories Hilferding desires.

Source: Sozialdemokratischer Parteitag in Kiel 1927, *Protokoll mit dem Bericht der Frauenkonferenz*, pp. 198–200.

4.9   *Rudolf Breitscheid[52] (SPD) Suggests in May 1929 that the Party may
        have to Withdraw from the Grand Coalition and Defend Democracy
        from Outside*

Comrade Müller said yesterday that anyone who wanted a crisis ought to find
a better occasion for this than the Armoured Cruiser issue. We do not want a
crisis; but if it should come to a decisive conflict the terrain is more favourable for us if we use the question of unemployment insurance ... The proletariat will understand if we do not go beyond the limits we have drawn, and
the bourgeois parties will have to learn to understand this ... They must recognise that we are the strongest party, not only in the coalition and the government but also outside, in the country. There is a limit to the concessions we
are in a position to make to the coalition and to unfavourable economic circumstances ... Another matter where our readiness to make concessions must
find a limit is tariff policy ... We must mount the strongest possible resistance
to endeavours to increase the cost of living for the masses by further raising
import duties.

We Social Democrats have displayed a sense of responsibility towards the
German state, even though this state is not yet ours. If this government col-
lapses, what comes afterwards? A dissolution of parliament. Fine! But do you
believe that democracy can continue in the long run if one resorts to a dissolution every few years? What is the alternative to a dissolution? Another government, a parliamentary government. Certainly, if we can work the trick of
bringing all the parties from the Democrats to the National Socialists under
one umbrella. Otherwise, a genuine crisis of parliamentarism takes place, with
certain desperadoes ... making use of the certain provisions in the constitution, provisions which give the President rights incompatible with democracy.[53]
Then we should be presented with a kind of cabinet of officials, in itself perhaps a concealed dictatorship. I do not say that we would need to make every
sacrifice to ward this off, I am only warning you to think about this possibility. It
may be that a moment arrives when, even bearing this danger in mind, we have
to say: thus far and no further. But in that case we must naturally be ready to
defend and advocate democracy and parliamentarism outside the parliament.

Source: Sozialdemokratischer Parteitag in Magdeburg 1929, *Protokoll mit dem
Bericht der Frauenkonferenz*, vom 26. bis 31. Mai in der Stadthalle, pp. 165, 170.

---

52   Rudolf Breitscheid (1874–1944), USPD 1917, SPD 1922. Joint chair of SPD Parliamentary
      Party 1928–33.

53   He refers here to the notorious Article 14 of the Weimar Constitution giving the President
      the power to issue emergency ordinances, which was used by governments from 1930
      onwards to bypass the parliament.

4.10   *Julius Leber Reflects in Prison on the Failure of Social Democracy after 1928*

If Hermann Müller had introduced a period of parliamentary, republican reform, as so many people hoped, he would have risen in stature to the level of a political statesman, the picture of German politics would have assumed a different pigmentation, and the light of feudal conservatism, which was merely flickering dimly, would have be extinguished. But the new government neither came to a decision nor committed itself to action. It failed at the most important task of all: the conduct of the affairs of state. It failed to develop a will of its own, and it failed to force through its own desiderata.

The ultimate reason for the complete collapse of this second Social Democratic experiment,[54] and the deepest one, lay as before in the Party's continuing lack of clarity and the ambiguity of its basic political principles ... The great Congress debates of the intervening period[55] had brought neither reform nor clarification. All the splits and confusions had been papered over by compromises of no practical use ... The so-called Left of the Party sharply advocated the thesis that the sole cause of decline and failure was the abandonment of true Marxist principles. This apparently revolutionary catchphrase of unswerving Marxists was an easy way of winning over large sections of the Party's youth ... All attempts to remove doctrinaire obstacles were condemned to absolute hopelessness; they could at most achieve the opposite result to the one hoped for. Everyone therefore fell silent. The Russian example worked in the same direction. The competition from the communists compelled large parts of the Party – in Berlin and Saxony for example – to operate with theories and slogans which indisputably derived from the old and 'well-tried' Marxist cookbook ... But by this time[56] the conflicts over doctrine had assumed quite a different aspect. Now the manoeuvres did not take place on the fine and distant plains of grey theory, no, now it was a matter of decisions which had to be made on practical day-to-day questions ... If one goes to the root of the many problems which unsettled the Party, one keeps on meeting with the fundamental question of its attitude to the state ... In foreign policy everything crystallised around the keel of Armoured Cruiser A.[57] In domestic policy the issues

---

54   The Müller government of 1928–30.
55   The period between 1920 and 1928.
56   After 1928, when the SPD was again in government.
57   The decision of August 1928 by the Müller cabinet to go ahead with the construction of Armoured Cruiser A met with strong opposition from the left of the SPD. The issue was a continuing source of disagreement within the Party for the next three years. The nine parliamentary deputies who defied party discipline to vote against the ship went on to

were connected more with the relation of the Party to the government and the way the government was conducted. This dispute reached its culminating point on 27 March 1930 with the resignation of Hermann Müller... That date will come to be called the black day of Social Democracy, and of German democracy altogether. For on that day the Social Democrats showed that they were still incapable of running the state... Without bothering to think too deeply about the matter, the SPD leadership sailed back into the comfortable waters of dear old opposition.

Source: Leber 1952, 'Thoughts on the Prohibition of German Social Democracy, June 1933', *Ein Mann geht seinen Weg. Schriften, Reden und Briefe*, pp. 218–20, 234.

Note: Julius Leber wrote these reflections on Weimar Social Democracy in prison under the Nazis. They were not published until after the Second World War.

4.11 *The KPD Analysis of the September 1930 Elections*

One question remains to be answered. By deciding to go over to the National Socialists, did the mass electorate of the bourgeois parties express its satisfaction with the existing capitalist system and its acceptance of the domination of finance capital? It is absolutely clear that the reverse of this was the case. Millions of toiling people are voting for the Nazis in order to express their embitterment with capitalist mismanagement and their protest against Young-slavery.[58]

The National Socialists are the paid agents of finance capital, the hired ruffians of the Young Plan. Their whole policy serves to defend capitalism against the threat of a proletarian revolution, to put the Young Plan into effect at the expense of the toiling masses. The Fascists, who have entered the new Reichstag with 107 seats, must inevitably lose the confidence of their 6.4 million electors, they are bound to disappoint their expectations, they have to trample on their demands. Hence Hitler's electoral success bears within itself with inescapable

---

leave the Party and form the left-wing splinter group the SAP (Socialist Workers' Party) in 1931.

58   The Young Plan, an international agreement made in 1929, placed Germany's reparations obligations on a new, and more favourable footing, and for the first time placed a time limit on them. The expiry date was, however, 1988, which many Germans, particularly on the political right, found unacceptable. The KPD also opposed the Young Plan as part of its general opposition to the Versailles Treaty.

certainty the germ of his future defeat. The 14th of September was the highest point of the National Socialist movement in Germany. What comes afterwards can only be decline and fall.

Fascism is the last card played by the German bourgeoisie against the working-class revolution that threatens it. But this card is also the most unreliable. Fascism, whose whole mission is the forcible prevention of the proletarian revolution, and the armed defence of the assistants of capital, constitutes at the same time, in present-day Germany, the living symptom of the dissolution of the bourgeois social order. That is the objective historical contradiction which seals the coming bankruptcy of German Fascism.

Source: *Internationale Presse-Korrespondenz*, 78, 16 September 1930.

Note: The main thrust of this analysis was clearly the assertion that mass support for the Nazis reflected popular hatred of the capitalist system, on which the KPD itself hoped to capitalise in the future. It should, however, be noted that this was combined with a recognition of the nationalist element in Nazi support, since the article also ascribed the Nazis' success to a 'protest against Young-slavery'. The KPD had also hoped to gain support from nationalist opponents of the Young Plan. This was characteristic of the Party's line at the time, as expressed in the Programme for the National and Social Liberation of the German People issued in August 1930 (10.12). To call the Nazis 'hired ruffians of the Young Plan' when they were notoriously opposed to it may seem absurd, but it was completely in line with the instructions issued at the highest possible level, at a joint meeting of the Soviet leadership, including Stalin and Molotov, and representatives of the ECCI, a month earlier. The KPD was to 'expose the National Socialists as elements capable of selling themselves to the makers of the Versailles Treaty, although they oppose it in words' and to stress that 'the liberation of Germany from Versailles is only possible with the overthrow of the bourgeoisie'.[59]

4.12   *Gustav Radbruch*[60] *Looks Back on the 'Excessive Rationalism' of the SPD*

I became a Social Democrat because that Party pursued a rational, careful, responsible policy, not revolutionary at the wrong moment, nor inappropri-

---

59   Politbiuro 2004, No. 388, pp. 626–67.
60   Gustav Radbruch (1878–1949), legal philosopher, SPD, member of the Reichstag 1920–24, Minister of Justice 1921–22, 1923. Promoter of the 'Hofgeismar movement' of 'Young Socialists' on the right of the Party.

ately nationalist, because it possessed precisely those qualities which many people ... customarily scorn as petty-bourgeois.[61] Only a sober policy, neither picturesque nor romantic, could save Germany in the difficult period after 1918 ... This salvation of Germany was the great achievement of that time. The mistake of the Social Democrats was that they did not play the nationalist mood music which would have been the appropriate accompaniment to their national attitude, that they accomplished what the nation needed accomplishing without talking about it and with their teeth clenched. The Party failed to catch the popular imagination ... Since then we have learned that the world is not ruled by reason but by useless knick-knacks, or, to put it in a more stylish way, that every policy needs symbols and an imaginative presentation. When we abolished decorations, titles and particles of nobility in the [Weimar] Constitution we displayed too high an opinion of the people. We were imbued with a deep faith in the power of reason and science ... We could not provide the democratic form of the state with an adequate emotional appeal. The banners carried by the workers' youth movement on demonstrations read: 'Republic gives us little cheer/Socialism is what we want to hear'.[62] We should have said the opposite to the masses: with democracy half of the SPD programme has been achieved, and it is now time to establish solid fortifications around the position that has been won. It should have been brought home to party comrades that democracy wasn't merely the first step to socialism but an achievement of independent value ... The leaders of Social Democracy were not always sufficiently aware that ruling necessarily means losing votes. They were concerned instead to avoid those losses by paying too much heed to what happened to be the attitude of the masses at the time.

During the long period of permanent opposition, Social Democrats learned to feel like members of a sect, and the Party was unable to overcome this sectarian character even when it had come to power. It was necessary to win a broader circle of sympathisers, over and above the narrow group of party members, in other words bourgeois and intellectuals, who might have entered into contact with the Party, without a lasting connection, because of their ideological convictions rather than their proletarian situation. The SPD was unable to persuade even one newspaper (leaving aside its own party press) to promote an interest in socialist ideas among broader circles without fixed party connections.

---

61   Radbruch in fact joined the SPD long before 1918, but his description of it fits the Party better in the period after 1918.

62   German: 'Republik das ist nicht viel / Sozialismus unser Ziel'.

Source: Radbruch 1951, *Der innere Weg*, pp. 177–80.

4.13   *Discussion between the Leaders of the SPD and the German Chancellor, Heinrich Brüning, on their Conditions for Parliamentary Support, 17 March 1931*

On 17 March 1931 the Reich Chancellor, with Minister of Finance Dietrich[63] and Minister of Labour Stegerwald[64] also present, receive the leaders of the SPD parliamentary group, the deputies Dr. Breitscheid, Dr. Hertz,[65] Dr. Hilferding and [Otto] Wels.

Dr. Breitscheid said he must have definite answers on the government's position on (1) whether a surcharge to the income tax will be accepted by it if adopted by the Reichstag, despite the opposition of the German People's Party; (2) whether concessions will be made to the SPD on tariff policy; and (3) whether the money placed at the disposal of the *Osthilfe* by industry will be used for unemployment insurance instead.

The SPD parliamentary group [he added] cannot give a blank cheque to the government for the budget if it does not know its intentions. The prorogation of the Reichstag until November will be very difficult to defend in the SPD group. It cannot be accepted on democratic grounds, because it is incompatible with democracy to cut out parliament for so long that vitally important measures need to be taken in the intervening period. The Brauns[66] Commission on the unemployment problem, in particular, would continue its activity and proceed to dismantle unemployment insurance.

The Chancellor replied that he thanked Dr. Breitscheid for these comments. He was ready to prorogue the Reichstag until October... The government must have peace and quiet to take measures which were in the interests of the nation and the fatherland. The ministers were unable to do the immense amount of work required of them when parliament was in session... The government had reservations about adding a surcharge to the income tax.

---

63   Hermann Dietrich (1879–1954), DDP, member of the Reichstag 1920–33, Minister of Food 1928–30 under Müller, continued under Brüning as Minister of Finance, 1930–32.

64   Adam Stegerwald (1874–1945), Centre Party, leading Roman Catholic trade unionist and chair of the Central Association of Christian Trade Unions 1919–29, Prussian Prime Minister 1921, Reich Minister of Labour 1930–32.

65   Paul Hertz (1888–1961), USPD 1917, SPD 1922, member of the Reichstag 1920–33, secretary of the SPD parliamentary party.

66   Heinrich Brauns (1868–1939), the Centre Party's expert on social policy, Reich Minister of Labour continuously from 1920–28.

Dr. Hilferding expressed his anxiety that the exodus of the right-wing parties[67] would be given political justification by the prorogation of the Reichstag. He suggested a session at Whitsuntide, with a precise agenda laid down in advance. Otherwise the SPD was in a very difficult position as it bore a share of responsibility for the government. As far as the Budget Enabling Act was concerned, they must be certain that no adverse steps in social policy would be taken.

The Chancellor replied that the drastic measures which must be taken needed thorough examination, which was not possible if the Reichstag assembled at Whitsuntide.

Dr. Breitscheid pointed out that the results of the discussion were very meagre for the Social Democrats. The German People's Party (DVP) would not tolerate the imposition of new taxes. From the SPD, on the other hand, much was being expected. The People's Party should be confronted energetically once in a while ... He still could not see why a short session of the Reichstag at Whitsuntide was impossible. One should, after all, also reflect on what it would mean for the SPD if the Reichstag vanished from the scene until October. The SPD would not make any objection to emergency powers, but it must first know the government's intentions. He would be quite unable to present to the parliamentary group such general information as the SPD leaders had been given in today's discussion ... He had the impression that the government was exploiting the weak position of Social Democracy. The effect in the long run would be that the government would be unable to maintain itself [in power]. In view of the [impending] Party Congress he once again urgently requested the government not to make Social Democracy's situation too difficult.

Parliamentary Deputy Wels stressed that it would not be possible to explain to the workers that the Reichstag was going to be prorogued until autumn. One must create a favourable psychological impression to enable the leaders of Social Democracy to achieve a certain degree of success at the Party Congress. The government constantly had regard for the People's Party [but not for the Social Democrats] ... It was unconditionally necessary in the interests of the democratic state that more attention should be paid to the wishes of the SPD parliamentary group. This applied to instance to the question of prorogation of the Reichstag.

The Chancellor again pointed to the great difficulties a Whitsuntide session of the Reichstag would create.

---

67   The boycott of the Reichstag begun in February 1931 by the National Opposition.

Source: Koops (ed.), *Die Kabinette Brüning I u.II, Bd.2.,1.März 1931 bis 10. Oktober 1931* (Akten der Reichskanzlei. Weimarer Republik, herausgegeben für die Historische Kommission bei der Bayerischen Akademie der Wissenschaften von K.D. Erdmann), Harald Boldt Verlag, Boppard am Rhein, 1982, doc. 264, pp. 955–61.

Note: The immediate occasion for this meeting was the vote of 20 March 1931 on Armoured Cruiser B. Despite gaining practically nothing from Brüning, the SPD abstained on the vote in order not to bring down the government. The Reichstag was duly prorogued, as Brüning had insisted, and it did not reassemble until the middle of October. The SPD continued its policy of toleration, although strong misgivings were voiced by Breitscheid and the trade union leaders. A campaign by the left of the Party against cooperating with Brüning only led to disciplinary measures by the SPD executive committee against the offenders, who decided to leave and form their own Party, the SAP (Socialist Workers' Party), for which see Document 12.8.

4.14   *Otto Braun (SPD) Writes from Berlin to Karl Kautsky in Vienna, 19 February 1932 about his Decision to Support Hindenburg as Presidential Candidate*

For months I have been working to bring about a Hindenburg-candidature, in the knowledge that this is the only way of preventing the election of a Nazi as President.

In any case, it is you I have to thank in particular for the good theoretical socialist foundation which provides me with the political and tactical agility required for governing with a coalition. You describe the difficulties involved in a coalition government as accurately as if you had sat in my cabinet for the last 12 years. These consist not only in the need for uniform leadership of the common fighting front, with its highly heterogeneous elements, against the ever stronger onslaught of the opposition, but in the constant struggle within the coalition over every single concession that one has either to make to the coalition partners or to extract from them. On top of the internal conflict with oneself, there are the reproaches of comrades who believe one has betrayed the Party by sacrificing more than was necessary. If I were able to give these people some open indication of the motives guiding my decisions, if I were able on each occasion to reveal the objectives I was aiming at, giving due consideration to the balance of political power, they would be more inclined to comprehend some of my measures. But I usually have to keep silent, to avoid angering my coalition partners and endangering the success of the operation, or to avoid giving our opponents the ready-made wedge with which they would be happy to split the coalition.

But what wears me down most of all is the unsatisfactory, infuriating, exhausting nature of my activities. The frightful financial emergency compels one to dismantle what one has vainly struggled to build up for decades, what one has long fought for and could only achieve in part after the Revolution. From a personal point of view it would be pleasant, but one cannot follow the advice of those friends in the Party who consider that in such a situation one should leave the government, and unload the odium of dismantling the achievements of the Revolution [of November 1918] onto the bourgeois parties. Certainly there is a limit, a point beyond which one should not retreat any further, because otherwise one would do irreparable harm to the movement. But until then one must stay in the government and fight stubbornly for every inch of terrain, so as to retreat not a single step further than the circumstances absolutely require. Above all, one must keep hold of the fragment of political power one has, for this is irreplaceable if the proletariat is to retain the rights and liberties it needs to re-conquer, and even perhaps add fresh conquests to, the political, social and cultural territory lost under the pressure of unfavourable economic circumstances, and, not least, as a result of its own political fragmentation. Shall I live to see the day? I don't know, as my bones are already beginning to creak dangerously, which is something I have to conceal from outsiders as much as possible. One cannot live a life of wearisome labour and remain intact without occasional relaxation amidst family and friends. I lack both.

But I don't want to bother you with my personal troubles, everyone has his share of problems. My wife is spending the winter in Ascona, so that I can devote the whole of my strength and time to the problems we are compelled to solve owing to the way the political situation has developed. The next few months will bring the decision. You must find it strange that ... I have decided to support the candidature of Hindenburg. I must abstain from providing you with a lengthy justification for this. The fact itself will indicate how the balance of political forces stands here at present. The presidential election, which is also an important preliminary to the elections in Prussia, will bring the decision as to whether Germany continues to develop calmly along the lines of the republican constitution,[68] or the German people will have to wade through a Fascist vale of sorrows. With six million unemployed and millions of other people in misery and in despair for the future, this fight for the republic is

68   This seems an unusual way of describing the situation in Germany in 1932.

proceeding under the worst imaginable conditions, the more so as the proletariat is still divided into several rival hosts which are literally engaged in a war
to the knife with each other.

Even so, let us not despair. We shall put forth all our strength in order to
achieve the utmost for the republic that is at all possible, given the confusion
in people's minds here. We are doing this in the awareness that the political
decisions arrived at in Germany and Prussia in the coming weeks will not only
be vital for the fate of the German people themselves, but will probably also
influence the political situation in the whole of Europe.

Source: A letter preserved in the *Nachlass Kautsky* in the International Institute
for Social History, Amsterdam, and printed for the first time as an appendix to
Erich Matthias, article 'Hindenburg zwischen den Fronten', in *Vierteljahrshefte
für Zeitgeschichte*, 8, no. 1, January 1960, pp. 82–4.

4.15   *Otto Wels (SPD) on the Party's Reaction to Papen's Coup of 20 July 1932*

The news had a depressing effect on those present [at a joint conference
of the leaders of the SPD, the *Reichsbanner* and the ADGB held on the day of
the coup]. Not one angry word was uttered, no spontaneous agitation was in
evidence. I had the impression that no one had any idea what to do. When
Leipart[69] asked me for my opinion, I said I was just as surprised by the situation as everyone else, and must be allowed to think aloud. We were faced
with a clear coup d'état. We had always stressed that we would oppose this
with all means at our disposal. Now the question was, what means were there?
What forces stood on our side? The memory of the Kapp putsch sprang clearly
to mind. Do we have the mass of the people behind us an unanimously as in
1920? No. The Communists and the Nazis are against us. The state power, i.e.
the Reichswehr, is equally on the other side, as well as the civil service and
very broad circles of the bourgeoisie. Nevertheless, we must seriously consider
the question of a general strike. Preparations must be made ... Now everything would depend on the railway workers ... They must tell us clearly what
our prospects are. Then there is the question of the intentions of the government ... The whole action could be a provocation of the working class. The
government may intend to inflict a bloody defeat on the workers, so as to bring
democracy to an end.

In ten days there will be elections to the Reichstag. If there were a fight now,
the elections would not take place ... Should we say: 'Above all else, we must
make sure of the Reichstag elections on 31 July?' If it comes to a fight, the Nazis

---

69   Theodor Leipart (1867–1947), chair of the Woodworkers' Union 1908–18, Minister of
       Labour in Württemberg 1919–20, chair of the ADGB 1921–33.

will stand on the side of the reaction. But in recent months, as indeed always, the Communists have shown that they desire our destruction. The workers must not be handed over to their leadership. Despite all these considerations, everything depends on the attitude of the trade unions to the general strike.

Leipart, as head of the trade unions, replied that the correct course was to secure the Reichstag elections, and the *Reichsbanner* representative, Höltermann,[70] agreed. I then went to see Severing at the Prussian Ministry of the Interior and informed him of the results of the meeting. I particularly emphasised to him that I did not believe the trade unions would go for a general strike. Nor did I think it would succeed. Severing replied that a general strike would mean an immediate military dictatorship. The *Schutzpolizei* [who came under Severing's orders as Prussian Minister of the Interior] could not fight the army and most of them would not want to . . . He immediately and very firmly agreed to my suggestion that the slogan 'Safeguard the Reichstag elections of 31 July', should be our reply to the coup.

Source: Wels, 'Note on the 20th July 1932', probably written in 1933. Printed in H. Schulze (ed.), *Anpassung oder Widerstand? Aus den Akten des Parteivorstands der deutschen Sozialdemokratie 1932/33*, (*Archiv für Sozialgeschichte, Beiheft 4*), Friedrich-Ebert Stiftung, Verlag Neue Gesellschaft Gmbh, Bonn-Bad Godesberg, 1975, Doc. 1, pp. 8–10.

4.16   *Rudolf Hilferding (SPD) on the Need to Preserve Parliament and Fight Against Left and Right Simultaneously, November 1932*

Our basic misfortune is the fact that we are viewed by the electors on the fringe of the Party as communists of a particular kind: communists who don't dare to be revolutionary. The main thing, in my opinion, is to show these electors that we are conducting the struggle with the utmost ruthlessness. We must arouse this impression by the principled position we take up against communism. It is not possible to work for parliament and for democracy when it continues to stand before the electors as an absolutely unworkable institution. They do not know why they are voting. We can only overcome this situation by fighting the communists, a fight which must start with questions of principle, namely democracy and the leadership of the German working class, and whether this leadership is to take account of Germany's own needs, or be an instrument of Moscow's policies. That is a decisive question of party tactics . . .

Now for the second issue: our attitude in parliament. It goes without saying that we cannot do anything there that might be interpreted, even in

---

70   Karl Höltermann (1894–1955), SPD, vice-chair of the *Reichsbanner*, member of the
      Reichstag 1932–33.

appearance, as toleration of Papen. What then is the situation in parliament? The Reichstag will most likely be dissolved again at the beginning of next year, so we shall have the opportunity of supporting a vote of no confidence and the abolition of the emergency decrees. There is no doubt about that. The German Nationalists will do everything they can to hinder the activities of parliament. I do not believe that the Centre Party will succeed in replacing the present Papen government with one that is capable of working with parliament. However, do we not have every reason to provide for ourselves a real fighting platform for the next elections, within the parliament? Do we not have every reason to make sure that we can work, even if we are obstructed in this by the German Nationalists? What are we going to tell the electors if this parliament too goes down into the grave?

The government must answer before the parliament. If this debate is conducted energetically and uninhibitedly it will have a powerful impact on the electors. The task is gigantic. The government is in a whole series of blind alleys. It is conducting a financial policy which we can denounce as bringing a danger of inflation. Its commercial policy severely threatens the interests of the workers; its foreign policy deepens Germany's isolation. We should tell this to the government, and not just in the parliamentary committees. Our task must be to follow this up with a plenary debate on the matter. We must be able to shake up the nation with a programme of immediate relevance. That is the basis of our struggle in the next election. The tactics of our deputies in parliament are important because they must help to determine our tactics in the next election. I have no fear that in this situation we may appear to be tolerating Papen. I imagine, on the contrary, that the whole fury of the people will find expression in these debates.

Finally, I should like to say this: we need ruthlessness and rigour if we are to sweep away those statesmanlike considerations that have held us back. These are things that should not stand in our way. If we once again come to a situation where we can seize power, it must be different, for real power must be there, so that we can also make use of it. If it comes to that, it will do us no harm to have spoken a language which, while not threatening to use means we do not possess, extra-parliamentary means, nevertheless leaves no doubt in its political thrust that we are the real fighters for the interests of the German workers, we are their real representatives. We must therefore fight not only against the Right but also the Left.

Source: Hilferding's speech to the SPD Party Committee, 10 November 1932, printed in H. Schulze (ed.) 1975, *Anpassung oder Widerstand?*, pp. 39–41.

CHAPTER 5

The Weimar Left Between Opposition and Coalition: Varied Strategies

Introduction

The SPD was always torn between its traditional function as a party of opposition to the existing system, and its role under Weimar as a party of government. It could be described as a governmental party because of both its frequent participation in government at national and local level and its readiness (in the first few years) to construct and join coalition governments. As Wilhelm Schröder has commented 'in the Weimar Republic the Social Democrats moved out of their enforced ghetto of "negative integration" and began to change into one of the parties that upheld the state'.[1] There was, however, considerable opposition from within the Party to its entry into coalition cabinets with bourgeois parties. At some points even the established leaders of the Party lost patience with the idea. After the SPD's disastrous showing in the elections of 6 June 1920, when its share of the vote fell from the 37.9 percent secured in 1919 to 21.7 percent, largely owing to losses to the USPD, the Chancellor, Hermann Müller, felt obliged to resign because his coalition government no longer had a majority in the Reichstag. President Friedrich Ebert thereupon gave him the mandate to form a new government, which he tried to fulfil by calling on his left-wing rivals to take part. The USPD leader Crispien refused even to discuss a possible coalition, such was the degree of distrust that prevailed between the two parties at this point (5.1). Faced with this, Müller abandoned his task, with some relief, as he explained in detail to a meeting of party leaders (5.1). Later on, at the next party congress, he reaffirmed this position: 'None of us has any desire to re-enter the government. I would point out that the Party Congress has made this declaration: there must be compelling reasons for the SPD to be forced to send comrades into the government again'.[2] Nevertheless, the Party did not stay in opposition for long. It re-entered a government coalition a year later, in May 1921, and stayed there till November 1922. The Social Democrats were also in coalition between August and November 1923 in the situation of national emergency associated with the period of hyper-inflation and threats from both Right and Left against the continued existence of the democratic

---

1 Schröder 2001, p. 78.
2 Sozialdemokratische Partei Deutschlands 1920, pp. 35–6, 270.

republic. It was the refusal of the Stresemann government to employ force against a defiant right-wing government in Bavaria while intervening militarily against the SPD governments in Saxony and Thuringia which led the SPD to withdraw from the coalition in November.

After this, they remained out of office nationally for long periods (between 1924 and 1928, and from 1930 onwards). For much of this time, however, their opposition was hardly irreconcilable. They always 'behaved as a government party if foreign policy required it',[3] because without their votes measures like the Dawes Plan of 1924, the Locarno Treaties of 1925 and the entry of Germany into the League of Nations would not have passed the Reichstag against the combined opposition of the nationalist Right and the communist Left. As regards economic and social policy, the SPD did indeed have a distinctive position, though paradoxically the most successful advances in social policy in the mid-1920s were achieved by non-socialist governments, with the SPD providing support from outside. Moreover, the Party was almost continuously in office between 1918 and 1932 in the largest German state, Prussia,[4] in coalition with the Centre Party, the DDP and sometimes the DVP. It also formed governments in several smaller states. There was, however, a strong trend within the SPD, especially after reunification with the USPD in 1922,[5] which opposed the strategy of coalition with bourgeois parties and demanded resolute opposition to all bourgeois governments (5.16. 5.17). In fact, it has been claimed that the reason why the SPD was able to stay in a well-nigh permanent coalition with the Centre Party and the DDP in Prussia was the absence of any mechanism in Prussia for controlling the Party's leaders from below.[6] The opponents of coalition were never able to win the support of the majority of delegates at the crucial party congresses, but they did make things difficult for the leadership.

---

3   Schönhoven 1989, p. 118.

4   Prussian coalition cabinets led by SPD members: Hirsch cabinet, January 1919 to March 1920; Braun cabinet, March 1920 to April 1921; Braun cabinet, November 1921 to February 1925; Braun cabinet April 1925 to July 1932 (formally until March 1933). There was one coalition cabinet led by Wilhelm Marx (Centre Party) with SPD participation (February 1925 to April 1925). The only period during which there were no SPD ministers in Prussia was between April and November 1921.

5   There was a sizeable group of middle-level former members of the USPD who supported the left opposition after joining the SPD (such as Kurt Rosenfeld, Robert Dissmann, Heinrich Ströbel, Toni Sender, Karl Löwenstein, Siegfried Aufhäuser, Mathilde Wurm, and Lore Agnes). They were joined by the ex-communists of Paul Levi's KAG. But most of the former top leaders of the USPD (such as Crispien, Dittmann and Hilferding) did not support the Left after 1923.

6   See in detail Möller 1985.

It has often been claimed that the SPD failed to compromise sufficiently with the bourgeois parties, because its leaders were constantly having to look over their shoulders both at the left-wing opposition within the Party and the trade unions and at the KPD outside it. In Hans Mommsen's phrase, after 1923 the SPD 'showed little interest in ... bourgeois coalitions'.[7] There is some evidence for this. In November 1922 the SPD Parliamentary Party refused to enter a Grand Coalition with the DVP, because one of the latter's representatives, Hugo Stinnes,[8] had just called on the workers to put in two extra hours of labour a day for no extra payment, as well as demanding that strikes be prohibited in vital industries. The result of what Heinrich Winkler has called 'this short-sightedness' was that a cabinet of experts was appointed under Wilhelm Cuno, which the SPD was in any case forced to support in the Reichstag for foreign policy reasons.[9] A similar situation occurred seven years later. In December 1929 the ADGB responded to the decision by the cabinet of Hermann Müller to reduce unemployment benefit by announcing that it was 'no longer prepared to agree to increases in the burden resting on the propertyless masses'.[10] It was supported in this view by Rudolf Wissell, the SPD Minister of Labour, although the majority of his colleagues continued to support Müller. But by March 1930 the SPD Parliamentary Party had decided that it must dig in its heels. Partly under trade union pressure, it refused to allow Müller and his cabinet colleagues to compromise any further over the issue of benefit payments to the unemployed, and as a result the bourgeois parties withdrew from the cabinet, forcing him to resign.[11] The left-wing of the Party was happy with this decision, but criticism came both from Rudolf Hilferding, one of the respected elder statesmen of the Party (5.16), and from the theorists of the 'Young Right' who gathered around the journal *Neue Blätter für den Sozialismus* (5.17). The attitude of the SPD's partners should not, however, be forgotten: the bourgeois parties were increasingly unwilling to compromise with the SPD. As Hans Fenske has pointed out 'their anti-Marxism steadily gained strength' as time went on. This, he adds, rather than SPD stubbornness, was 'the real germ of the disease in the German party system'.[12]

---

7   Mommsen 1991, p. 43.

8   Hugo Stinnes (1870–1924), wealthy industrialist, founder of the Stinnes Concern, member of the Reichstag (DVP) 1920–24.

9   Winkler 1985, pp. 499–501.

10   *Gewerkschafts-Zeitung* 1929, 21 December 1929.

11   Timm 1953, pp. 150–2.

12   Fenske 1972, pp. 345, 281 and 349.

Documents

5.1   *Letter of 11 June 1920 from the SPD Chancellor, Hermann Müller,*
         to the Chair of the USPD, Arthur Crispien, with Crispien's Reply

I have been presented with the task of forming a government. In order to accomplish this I am turning first of all to the leadership of the USPD. The elections have brought 80 seats to that Party and thereby made it the second strongest group in the future Reichstag. Participation by the USPD in the government is therefore the obvious response to this situation. Moreover, in our young German republic the presence of the USPD in the government appears particularly necessary because only a coalition government strengthened towards the Left can defend our republican institutions against all attacks from the Right, ward off reactionary attempts to undermine the eight-hour day and the post-war achievements in social welfare, and implement a foreign policy which is in line with the republican and pacifist ideas of the overwhelming majority of the German people.

Reply from Arthur Crispien received on either 11 or 18 June 1920

On the instructions of the USPD I hereby present to you the following reply to your invitation of 11 June to a discussion over the entry of members of our Party into the government which is to be reconstructed. The USPD cannot enter a government which has set itself the objective of reconstructing the economy of capitalist exploitation which collapsed in the War. The entry of the USPD into such a government would signify that it was supporting the counter-revolutionary policy it had previously fought on principle. It would constitute an abandonment of the Party's programme and an act of treachery against the interests of the workers, employees, officials, small traders and poor peasants who gave their votes to the USPD in the Reichstag elections, in the confident expectation that it would energetically pursue its policy of ruthless proletarian class struggle with the aim of doing away with the class domination of the capitalists and militarists.

The USPD entered a coalition government with the Socialist Right at the beginning of the Revolution[13] so as to secure the above-mentioned goals. Even though the right-wing socialists had promised to make the Social Democratic programme the basis of government policy, their representatives unceasingly conducted a policy of dependence on and compromise with the old state bureaucracy, the capitalist parties and the old militarism, so that the USPD was

---

13   Three USPD leaders entered the Council of People's Representatives set up in November 1918 and remained in it until the end of December.

compelled to withdraw from the government in order not to share the guilt for bringing capitalism and militarism back to life and implementing a bloody policy of force against the revolutionary working class. The strengthening hold of the reaction cannot be fought by continuing the coalition, which confuses and divides the proletariat, but by a principled, clear and consistent socialist policy, aimed at the seizure of political power by the proletariat, and the retention of sole power until socialism has been achieved.

If the necessity for a socialist government emerges from the development of the Revolution, the sole kind of socialist government the USPD is prepared to consider, as a transition,[14] is a pure one in which the USPD will have a majority and exert the decisive influence, and which will use the USPD's programme as the basis for government policy. In view of all this, you will certainly agree with me that there is no point in engaging in the discussion you have requested.

Source: *Schulthess' Europäische Geschichtskalender, Neue Folge*, Jg. 61, 1920, Part I, p. 156.

5.2   *Hermann Müller's Speech to a Joint Session of the Party Executive, the Party Committee and the Parliamentary Party Explaining Why the Social Democrats Are No Longer in the Government, 13 June 1920*

We did not enter into a coalition government with the bourgeois parties after the elections to the Constituent National Assembly [in 1919] for our own enjoyment. We had no choice, because the result of the elections had not given the two socialist parties a majority, and this was in part because the Independents [USPD] had pushed for the elections to be delayed until January [1919]. If they had taken place earlier we should have had a socialist majority in the National Assembly ... Now we have ruled for one and a half years, and it was to be expected that this would not happen without losses ... From November 1918 we had the leadership in the coalition, and hence in politics. We were the strongest party. But this all lies in the past. The coalition no longer has a majority. If we want to get a majority we have to include the Bavarian People's Party. But the Bavarian People's Party includes not only Bavarians but separatist Rhinelanders, hence we could not get a stable coalition majority in this way. We cannot hand over our Party to Herr Heim[15] and his followers.

---

14   He presumably had in mind a transition to the coming socialist revolution.

15   Georg Heim (1865–1938), Bavarian politician, founded the Bavarian People's Party (BVP) in 1918; opposed the Weimar constitution on federalist grounds; favoured the return of the monarchy to Bavaria; inclined towards Bavarian separatism.

If we wanted to safeguard our republican achievements, it was obvious that we needed to turn to the USPD, also because they were now the second-largest party in the Reichstag. The USPD had already rejected the idea of entering a coalition. Its leaders rushed to declare that they would not enter a coalition alongside any bourgeois party whatever. The more realistic people in the USPD, such as Haase and Wurm,[16] are unfortunately now dead...If we can't form a government with the Independents we must remain in opposition in the future...Once both socialist parties are in opposition, the desire for unification will show itself more strongly than previously among the workers...Where do we have a shining opportunity to anchor democracy? In Prussia...After a strengthening of the coalition to the left proved to be impossible, I considered it my duty to lay down my mandate and ask the President to see if a government of the Right could be formed...This does not mean that we abandon coalition politics. We have no reason to disavow what we have done in the past. We should also not forget that leaving the government will bring disadvantages for us. In government we could hinder the other parties from doing many things they wanted to do, and we could advance our own policies. We also knew exactly what was happening. Moreover, we have every reason to hold onto the positions we have, in the administration, in the individual states and in the *Reichsrat*.[17] We remain very influential in Prussia, Saxony, Thuringia, Hesse, Württemberg, Baden, Anhalt and other places.

But there are also advantages to leaving the government. In the next few months a very severe economic crisis will call for all possible economic and political measures. We have no reason to force ourselves to give backing to these measures, after the voters have made their decision. Attempts to impose wage reductions will lead to counter-measures by the workers and bring disturbances all over Germany...If I believed the Spa negotiations could be concluded successfully, I would use all my oratorical powers to persuade you to stay in the government. But there is no prospect of success, and the right-wing parties when in power will be forced to cut the number of army officers in half, so they will lose all their prestige in military circles. We have no reason to take this responsibility away from them. Perhaps it will be healthy for Germany if a deliberately anti-military policy can no longer be imputed to the Social Democrats...The German people cannot be spared the learning experience of a right-wing government...The people must come to the conviction that elections are not an opportunity to vent your anger against the government,

---

16   Emanuel Wurm (1857–1920), USPD, State Secretary of the Reich Food Office in 1918.

17   *Reichsrat*: the Upper House of the German parliament. Under the Weimar constitution, this consisted of elected representatives of the individual states.

but that everyone has his share of responsibility, and a sense of duty rather than mere irritation should speak loudest.

We cannot enter a right-wing coalition. The electorate would not understand it if we now sit down beside Stresemann and Stinnes...A government along with the DVP would have consequences that we cannot accept. We would have to renounce socialism three times a day, before the cock had crowed – it would be the suicide of Social Democracy. We would suffer the fate of the National Liberals in 1878, though they achieved far more for the bourgeoisie than we have achieved of our socialist programme. Social Democracy must leave it to the bourgeois parties to find their way out of the crisis.

In entering opposition we are still fundamentally different from the Independents. We must conduct our opposition from the angle of the positive work we have to do. In no circumstances can we join in the purely negative policy of the Independents...It is conceivable that we may be forced to enter a coalition as a result of internal disturbances in the country...in that case we should have no alternative, if we want to save the republic and save Germany...But at present the main task is to keep the Party battle-ready and to prevent any further losses either to the Right or to the Left.

Source: Dieter Dowe (ed.), 1980, *Protokolle der Sitzungen des Parteiausschusses der SPD 1912 bis 1921. Band II*, pp. 949–51.

5.3   *Reasons Given by Leading Social Democrat Otto Wels for the Party's Unwillingness to Return to Office after the 1920 Elections*

Report of Otto Wels, Party Chair, to the Kassel Congress of the SPD held in October 1920

Despite their victory[18] the first step of the leader of the DVP, Dr. Heinze, was to invite the SPD into the cabinet he was forming...We naturally refused to enter into this peculiar mishmash of monarchists and big capitalists...Apart from our refusal in principle to associate ourselves with a monarchist party,[19]

---

18   The DVP was very successful in the elections of 6 June 1920, increasing its share of the vote from 4.4 percent to 13.9 percent.

19   The October 1920 SPD Congress accepted an amendment by Ernst Eckstein ruling out any cooperation (at national level) with a party which (like the DVP) was not committed to the republic. The next SPD Congress, in 1921, rescinded this, voting by 290 to 67 in favour of a coalition with the DVP (Breitman 1981, pp. 78). There was strong opposition from the left of the Party to this decision, on the ground that it would deter the remnant of the USPD from returning to the fold. In fact at the 1922 Congress of the USPD Kurt Rosenfeld complained that 'the SPD prefers a grand coalition to the unification of the proletariat', although this did not prevent him from reentering the SPD later in the year (*USPD Parteitag 1922*, p. 107).

there were two grounds for this: the bourgeois parties fought their election campaign by asserting that all our misfortunes resulted exclusively from mismanagement by the Social Democrats and that socialism as such was a corrupt and destructive principle. Our reply is this: it would be an act of political stupidity ... if we were to deprive the mass of unpolitical camp-followers of the bourgeois parties of the opportunity to examine for once whether the Social Democrats are actually guilty of creating the misery of the Fatherland ... It is not Social Democracy but the war of Messrs. Westarp[20] and Stresemann that bears the guilt for bringing about the miserable situation of the food supply and the economy in general. But the Right also owed its electoral success to a hate-filled onslaught on socialism as such. Should we now sit in a government with men who not only think differently from us but characterise the core of our world view as the most terrible danger for the German people? ... We cannot sit down together with monarchists, and certainly not with anti-socialists of the stripe of the DVP. It was out of a sense of honour that we refused to enter this government, and we shall continue to stay away from this government out of a sense of honour.

Source: Sozialdemokratische Partei Deutschlands 1920, *Protokoll über die Verhandlungen des Parteitages der SPD, abgehalten in Kassel vom 10. bis 16. Oktober 1920*, pp. 35–6.

5.4   *Philipp Scheidemann Defends the Idea of a Coalition with Other Parties (September 1921)*

It goes without saying that we can only enter a government with parties which *respect* the Constitution. But does that mean we can only cooperate with parties which have *accepted* the Constitution? I say it does not. For otherwise it would be impossible to work either with the USPD or the DVP. They have both rejected the Constitution ... Before forming a government we must draw up a minimum programme. Parties which are ready to accept the programme cannot be excluded in the long run from participating in the government. A coalition government is not a community of like-minded people but a working association. Otherwise, cooperation with the Centre Party would be just as difficult as it is with other parties ... We must get used to the idea of coalition governments for a long time ... But all coalitions are transitory. What is everlasting is the unity of all the working people of Germany, and, beyond Germany, their unity over the whole world. That is the goal we are aiming at.

20   Count Kuno Westarp (1864–1945), leader of the German Conservatives before 1918. Joined the DNVP after 1918, member of the Reichstag from 1920, led the DNVP from 1926–28. Left in 1930 and founded the Conservative People's Party.

Source: Sozialdemokratische Partei Deutschlands 1921, *Protokoll über die Verhandlungen des Parteitages der Sozialdemokratischen Partei Deutschlands, abgehalten in Görlitz vom 18. bis 24. September 1921*, pp. 175–6.

5.5 *Franz Krüger*[21] *Gives Reasons Why the SPD Should Not Continue to Stay Out of Office (September 1921)*

If today some Party comrades look at the question of entering a government from the point of view that Social Democracy can only enter a government in order to put into effect certain demands, and that it can leave the government again when these prerequisites are no longer fulfilled, this was perhaps justifiable previously, when the government was completely independent of parliament. But now, when according to the republican and democratic constitution the whole power of the government derives from the people, it is no longer possible to take up this attitude ... Today Social Democracy ranks as one of the most important factors in Germany. It represents the foundation of our whole economic and state life, the working strata. It represents the part of the population which must be enlisted in cooperating with the state if we want to arrive at a healthy political situation.

Source: Sozialdemokratische Partei Deutschlands 1921, *Protokoll über die Verhandlungen des Parteitages der Sozialdemokratischen Partei Deutschlands, abgehalten in Görlitz vom 18. bis 24.September 1921*, pp. 136–7.

5.6 *The Ten Demands of the ADGB and the AfA, November 1921*

1 Twenty five percent of material assets (*Sachwerte*)[22] are to be transferred from the big limited companies to the Reich. Smaller concerns and agricultural enterprises are also to be taxed at the same level.
2 The coal mining industry to be socialised.
3 Transport enterprises to be reorganised.
4 Foreign trade is to be placed under government control.
5 Imports are to be restricted to items of basic necessity.

---

21 Franz Krüger (1887–1924), SPD, chair of the Berlin SPD branch, member of the National Assembly in 1919, member of the SPD executive 1920–24.

22 This expression has sometimes been translated with the rather mystical phrase 'real values', most notably by Gerald Feldman in his *magnum opus* on the years of inflation, *The Great Disorder* (Feldman 1993). It is important to note, however, what the supporters of this idea wanted to appropriate. Agricultural property, urban housing and commercial enterprises were listed in the original proposals presented to the Wirth cabinet on 19 May 1921 (*Kabinette Wirth, I*, 1973 pp. 7–13.)

6 Export duties are to be increased to cover foreign exchange gains completely.

7 Immediate introduction of the Emergency Capital Levy (*Reichsnotopfer*)[23]

8 Immediate collection of income taxes. Taxpayers must pay their taxes immediately.

9 A heavy tax to be imposed on profits from foreign exchange transactions.

10 Private economic monopolies are to be placed under supervision (*Kontrolle*).

Source: 'Forderungen der Gewerkschaften zur Rettung der deutschen Wortschaft', *Correspondenzblatt des ADGB*, 31: 48, 26 November 1921, p. 679.

5.7   Resolution on the Campaign for a Tax on Property, Adopted by the CC of the KPD, 17 November 1921

1 All previous tax struggles led by the working class have remained within the framework of the bourgeois state and the bourgeois economy. This was the case ... as long as the foundations of the capitalist economy remained intact ... 'Tax reform' at such times is a favourite remedy of bourgeois and particularly petit-bourgeois reform quackery.

2 Nevertheless, at times when the bourgeois state is affected by revolutionary convulsions taxes can be used by the working class and the petty bourgeoisie as the instruments of an attack on the foundations of the capitalist economy, on private property.

3 In present-day Germany ... the tax struggle can be used as a powerful weapon of attack on capitalist property, bringing together the working class and at least some sections of the petty bourgeoisie. But this is only the case when the taxes swell up to colossal dimensions ... that is to say when they turn into a form of confiscation of capitalist property and income on a grand scale.

4 This confiscation of capitalist income and property can only be achieved to a very limited extent through the method of monetary taxation. The more valueless paper money becomes, the more illusory is the hope of monetary taxation. Here there is only one effective method: the state confiscates not monetary values, scraps of paper, but real material assets. It confiscates in kind, by making itself the co-proprietor of capitalist enterprises and levying its share of the proceeds directly at the point of production.

---

23   This does not refer to the introduction of the Emergency Capital Levy, as this had already been introduced in December 1919, but to the collection of the second tranche of the Levy, which was currently a subject of dispute between the DVP (which opposed it) and the other coalition parties. See Winkler 1985, p. 455.

5 It is clear that the immense burden of state indebtedness (war loans etc.) must be lifted from the economy. The simplest way to do this is by abolishing interest payments on internal debts. Only the advance of the revolution in Central and Western Europe can lighten the burden of the reparation debt.

6 The 'requisitioning of values in gold', i.e. the confiscation of capitalist property and income at the point of production, can only be carried through by a determined offensive on the part of the working class. This offensive must develop out of the defence the workers are putting up against the immense new burdens that threaten them. The 'requisitioning of values in gold' is thought of by the USPD and the SPD as a means of calming down the workers. We communists have the task of thwarting this deception.

[7 is omitted]

8 In formal terms, the requisitioning of values in gold constitutes 'state capitalism'. But it is a state capitalism of a special type: the state is used as a machine to confiscate capital, to take the burden from the workers, and to begin the central regulation of production...The control of the enterprises taken over by the state must lie with the Factory Councils...The state bureaucracy will therefore not administer these concerns.

9 These measures are not state capitalism in the sense advocated by Hilferding or Scheidemann.

10 The economic history of Germany since the [November] revolution is a story of the systematic dismantling of state intervention in the private capitalist economy and the systematic construction of giant private capitalist concerns, which under the direction of Hugo Stinnes...have become the rulers of the state...The struggle over taxes ultimately crystallises around the question of whether Stinnes gets the state into his hands and through the state the masses, or the state, through the masses, seizes hold of Stinnes and similar people.

11 In taking up the struggle for the requisitioning of values in gold, the KPD invites the USPD, the SPD and the trade unions to join in and wage it together with us. The requisitioning of values in gold is not in itself a communist demand. It is, however, an essential step towards lightening the burdens of the working masses. it is a demand put forward by the USPD and the SPD themselves...We Communists have taken up this demand. We shall mobilise the broadest masses for it, side-by-side with the USPD and SPD leaders if they stick to their demand; in opposition to them, but with the masses, if they leave them in the lurch by abandoning it.

Source: *Die Internationale, III*, 14, November 1921, pp. 514–17.

Note: The acceptance of the London Ultimatum of May 1921 obliged the government of the Centre Party leader Joseph Wirth[24] (which included the leaders of the SPD) to prepare a further fiscal reform, modifying the system set up by Erzberger[25] in 1919, so as to make the existing taxes more productive, and thus provide the wherewithal for the payment of reparations. But in what form was the money to be extracted from the population? The Social Democrats called for the requisitioning of material assets (*Sachwerte*), since these held their value, as opposed to monetary wealth which was constantly depreciating. The right-wing parties condemned this as 'creeping nationalisation', advocating instead an increase in indirect taxation, which would of course hit the poor disproportionately. Wirth's proposed tax programme of 6 June 1921 went some way to satisfying the Social Democrats, but met with tremendous opposition from the Right and from the liberal DDP which was also part of the coalition. Hence in August the government gave way to the Right and laid heavy taxes on consumption goods instead of taxing property. The property tax and a capital gains tax remained in force, but in a watered-down form.

The subsequent months saw a fierce parliamentary conflict over these proposals, and the KPD saw this as a suitable opportunity for 'United Front' agitation. By issuing these demands the Party was in fact taking up proposals (the 'Ten Demands') that had just been decided on by the ADGB and the AfA (5.6) and taking them a step further. The ADGB had called for the confiscation of 25 percent of material assets, and the KPD raised this to 51 percent.[26] The SPD was still in government at this stage, and it agreed on 9 March 1922 to a compromise by which a forced loan of a milliard (1,000,000,000) gold marks would be imposed on property, on a sliding scale from one percent to 10 percent. The property tax itself was now abandoned The capital gains tax was not intended to come into force until December 1925 and it was to be limited to gains made over the preceding three years. The forced loan was deprived of any impact by the establishment of a fixed rate of 1 to 70 for the conversion of gold into paper marks. This rate very quickly became unrealistic owing to the rapid inflation of the next two years.

---

24   Joseph Wirth (1879–1956), leader of the Centre Party and Chancellor of coalition governments including the SPD between May 1921 and November 1922.

25   Matthias Erzberger (1875–1921), leader of the Centre Party, Finance Minister in the Bauer cabinet, 1919–20. Murdered in 1921.

26   See Doc.5.6. The ADGB decided on these demands on 15 November (Broué 2006, p. 578 n. 79).

5.8   *Resolution Proposed at the 1922 Congress of the Free Trade Unions*
        (ADGB) Against Collaboration with the Employers and in Favour of
        Factory and Workers' Councils

In the ruling social order, capital has at its disposal both political and economic power, on the basis of its ownership of the means of production. This power can only be overcome by conducting the class struggle in both the political and the economic spheres. There can therefore be no community of interests between capital and labour, and to attempt to hide one's class consciousness is to hand an asset to the opponent. It is an illusion to assume that the true interests of the proletariat could be promoted by building a community of interest between capital and labour.

The proletariat needs a thorough training in economic questions in order to conduct the struggle successfully. It must gain this knowledge independently and it cannot receive it by participating in Working Associations (*Arbeitsgemeinschaften*) with the class opponent. In these associations, the employers by no means put forward what is in the interests of the national economy but aim purely at presenting the industrial situation in the way most favourable to maximising their profits and gaining an advantage in the competitive struggle among capitalists.

The whole history of the class struggle teaches us that a ruling society has never voluntarily and gradually given up its position, leaving the field of battle to the opponent.

The Eleventh German Trades' Union Congress therefore rejects the Working Associations with the employers. The only effective instruments for the transformation of the economy are organs composed of the representatives of the exploited class itself. In the revolution [of November 1918] the German proletariat demanded that its organs should be the Workers' and Factory Councils, which must by their very nature be in conscious opposition to the ruling order.

Recognising this, the Congress demands that on the basis of the Factory Councils ... independent Workers' Councils be formed for each district, to be associated at the centre through a Workers' Council for the whole Reich.

Josef Simon,[27] Nuremberg, for the shoemakers' union
Robert Dissmann,[28] Stuttgart, for the metalworkers' union

---

27   Joseph Simon (1865–1949), USPD, SPD after 1922, chair of the Shoemakers' Union, member of the Reichstag 1920–33.
28   Robert Dissmann (1878–1926), USPD, SPD from 1922, chair of DMV (Metalworkers' Union) from 1919.

Source: Allgemeiner Deutscher Gewerkschaftsbund 1922, *Protokoll der Verhandlungen des elften kongresses der Gewerkschaften Deutschlands, Leipzig, 19–24 June 1922*, p. 485.

Note: This resolution was subsequently withdrawn in favour of one calling simply for the ADGB to leave the Central Working Association (*Zentralarbeitsgemeinschaft*) set up in 1918. This was adopted by 345 votes to 327. The ADGB leadership, however, refused to accept it, indicating that it would be regarded as a vote of no confidence in them. The Congress thereupon changed its mind and voted for the official resolution retaining the connection with the employers. The Free Trade Unions in fact stayed in the Central Working Association until January 1924.

5.9   *Robert Schmidt[29] (SPD) Advocates Requisitioning Material Assets as a Step Towards Socialism*

The requisitioning of material assets is an intermediary step towards socialism. Material assets (*Sachwerte*) are not devalued by the fall in the value of Germany's currency, and the state would be in a different position if it had secured a share in the means of production immediately after the revolution. The industrial firms have developed in recent years into gigantic concerns and they have attained immense economic and political power. I therefore consider the demand made by the SPD party group in parliament[30] ... to be entirely justified. The transfer of a portion of the wealth of the owners of material goods to the whole community would in no way have disturbed or hindered production. It also has nothing whatsoever to do with the fantastic ideas of the Russian communists. We have kept our feet planted firmly on the ground.

Source: Sozialdemokratischen Parteitags in Augsburg 1922, *Protokoll des Sozialdemokratischen Parteitags in Augsburg, Gera und Nürnberg 1922*, pp. 24–5.

5.10   *Robert Dissmann's Resolution of June 1924 on the Need for the SPD to Conduct an Uncompromising Opposition to the Government*

In the last few years the policy of the VSPD[31] has been directed towards extending and securing the Republic, to maintaining the territorial integrity of the

---

29   Robert Schmidt (1864–1943), SPD, Minister of Food 1919, Economics Minister 1919–1920, 1921–22, 1929–30, Minister of Reconstruction 1923.

30   Schmidt refers here to the proposal already made in June 1921 by the Social Democrats in the Wirth cabinet and abandoned in August 1921 in the face of strong opposition from the political right. See above, 5.7.

31   VSPD: United Social Democratic Party. The SPD adopted this title after the remnant of the USPD rejoined it in 1922.

parts of the Reich still left to us after the peace treaty by agreeing to the payment of reparations, and finally to sharing out the burdens of the war in a fair
manner within Germany. But these goals have by and large not been attained.

In the economic sphere the German bourgeoisie has made the payment
of reparations impossible by deliberately ruining the currency, and instead of
bearing the burdens it was morally obliged to shoulder after the war had been
lost it engaged in a gigantic process of self-enrichment achieved through the
impoverishment and expropriation of the *Mittelstand*, the state officials, the
salaried employees and the workers.

In foreign affairs this policy by the bourgeoisie led to the invasion of the
Ruhr. It endangered the gradual dismantling of the occupation of Germany
provided for in the Peace Treaty and it resulted in an extension of that occupation and an increase in the burdens deriving from it.

The internal unity of the Reich has been seriously undermined; the Republic
is threatened by armed bands, and a reactionary administration is promoting
all these dangers to the Reich and preventing the peaceful reconstruction of
the state; a vicious system of justice is making a laughing-stock of the law and
the rights guaranteed by law.

Experience has shown that all these dangers were successfully warded off as
long as the working class was able to defend its interests with its own strength.
When the working class started to substitute for the energetic prosecution of
its own interests a concern for wrongly understood general interests, the above
consequences came to the fore, both at home and abroad. The bourgeoisie has
proved that it conducts the fight against internal enemies with no less brutality
in the republican form of the state than in any other, and that therefore Social
Democracy's responsibility for this state can go no further than the extent to
which the working class actually has power in the state.

The VSPD's policy so far has involved coalitions with more or less democratic
sections of the bourgeoisie. It has thereby neither succeeded in banishing the
above internal and external dangers nor in retaining for the working class as
a class the power it needs so as to protect its own interests. The criminal economic policy of the bourgeoisie has seriously endangered the existence of the
trade unions and the cooperatives, the social security and protection of labour,
and the eight-hour day. Reliance on the bourgeoisie in the political sphere has
led to a reduction in our influence among the working class, as shown in the
recent elections to the Reichstag.

The VSPD, as the Party of the working people, must win back this influence,
and the Party Congress therefore calls on the Party and its organs, in parliament as well as the press, in practical politics as well as in agitation, to let itself
be guided by the idea of an irreconcilable class struggle between the bourgeoisie and the proletariat. This struggle must be conducted shoulder to shoulder with all working people who honestly serve the cause of the proletariat in

town and country, in the knowledge that only a party which brings the masses together for this struggle and fills them with confidence is in a position to save the people and the Reich from the present emergencies in home and foreign affairs and bring about the final work of emancipation which is socialism.

Source: Sozialdemokratischer Parteitag 1924, 'Resolution 243 (Dissmann and Comrades)', p. 210.

Note: Dissmann spoke in support of this resolution at the Congress. In his speech he distinguished between two views of coalition with non-socialists. A coalition, he said, could either be seen as a necessary evil, a temporary measure, in which case the highest possible price could be demanded for entry, in the interests of the proletariat. Or it could be the kind of coalition 'where you always want to be in the government and thereby take over responsibility for the state and constantly have to take heed of the bourgeois coalition parties'. He clearly did not favour this second view of coalition. It had led the Party in the wrong direction, involving it in a deal which sabotaged the policy of fulfilment and shifted the burdens onto the shoulders of the workers. This criticism would apply most clearly to the SPD's participation in the cabinets led by Josef Wirth between May 1921 and November 1922 and the Stresemann cabinets of August to October and October to November 1923. The Dissmann resolution was rejected by the majority of the delegates, who voted instead for the following resolution by the former Chancellor Hermann Müller. The voting figures (262 to 105) indicate however the considerable strength of the left-wing opposition within the SPD at this time.

5.11   *Hermann Müller's Resolution on the Continuing Need for Coalition Agreements*

Coalition policy is not a question of principle but of tactics. Since the [November] revolution the multi-party system has frequently compelled Social Democracy to participate in governments jointly with bourgeois parties both in the Reich and the States.

The decisive reasons for this lay firstly in foreign policy and secondly in home affairs. In foreign policy the interests of the working class required the pacification of Europe. In internal policy they required that the republic be secured against the onslaught of the reactionaries.

Since the defeat of Germany in the War, it has only been possible to pursue a successful foreign policy on a republican basis. At the same time, the Republic is the given foundation for the struggle for the final goal, which is socialism. The objective of participation in the government must be to strengthen democracy and imbue the bourgeois republic with a social content: Social Democracy should therefore only enter a coalition after weighing up all its advantages and disadvantages for the less well-off members of society, so as to make sure that the working class does not have to make one-sided sacrifices.

Source: Sozialdemokratischer Parteitag 1924, *Protokoll mit dem Bericht der Frauenkonferenz*, pp. 204–5.

5.12   *Theodore Leipart Advocates a More Political Standpoint for the Trade Unions in 1925*

In view of this development [the increased strength and boldness of the reactionaries] the trade unions are less and less able to remain passive in dealing with political elections. For this reason, the vital interests of the trade unions, which in this case are identical with the vital interests of the German working class, have in recent years compelled the Federal Executive and the Federal Committee to take up a positive stance *in regard to the political elections* and to support the election of Social Democratic candidates. We have made this decision ... because we are convinced that of all political parties the SPD is the only one that supports the true interests of working people ... The republican form of state is more secure and well-established in Germany now than it was three years ago. The trade unions banded together in our Confederation [the ADGB] are some of its most emphatic supporters and defenders ... I shall not fail to add that the trade unions and the German working class are not just concerned with the form of the state but will struggle to fill it with the necessary social content.

Source: Kongreß der Gewerkschaften Deutschlands 1925, *Protokoll der Verhandlungen des 12.Kongresses der Gewerkschaften Deutschlands, abgehalten in Breslau vom 31.August bis 4.September 1925*, p. 111.

5.13   *Resolution Calling on the SPD Parliamentary Group to Pursue a Policy of Determined Opposition to the Bourgeois Parties (September 1925)*

The developments of recent months have shown that as the situation of the German Republic becomes increasingly stable both at home and abroad, the bourgeois parties are starting to show an increasing lack of restraint in promoting the interests of the classes they represent. This self-interested policy of the bourgeois parties is revealed most sharply in the areas of fiscal and tariff policy. The Centre Party, as well as the Democrats at decisive points, have restored the solidarity of interests that unites the bourgeoisie. The Centre, in particular, has again openly become the stirrup-holder of the reaction in all questions of internal and foreign policy. Isolated objections from within the ranks of these parties change nothing in this basic fact. It thus appears that the proletariat and the Social Democratic Party have to rely on themselves and their own strength in all vital matters, and that all the bourgeois parties will only enter and maintain alliances as long as they themselves can gain an advantage from them.

Under these circumstances, the Party Congress calls on the SPD parliamentary group to represent the interests of the proletariat in all future struggles without any consideration for the bourgeois parties, in such a way that the proletarian supporters of those parties themselves recognise in the SPD the representative of their interests and thereby increase the size of the great army of class-conscious proletarians.

Source: Sozialdemokratischer Parteitag in Heidelberg 1925, *Protokoll mit dem Bericht der Frauenkonferenz*, pp. 316–17.

Note: This proposal by the left of the SPD, represented by Paul Levi, Max Seydewitz[32] and others, associated with the journal *Sozialistische Politik und Wirtschaft*, was defeated by 285 votes to 81.

5.14   *The Joint SPD-KPD Proposal for the Expropriation of the Former German Princes, 28 April 1926*

On the basis of Article 153 of the German Constitution it is determined that:

Article I

The whole of the property of the princes who ruled in parts of the German Empire until the overthrow of that state in 1918, as well as the whole of the property of the princely houses, their families and their dependents, is to be confiscated without compensation for the benefit of the community.

The expropriated property will become the property of the State (*Land*) in which the princely house in question ruled until its removal or abdication.

Article II

The expropriated property will be utilised for the benefit of:

a) the unemployed;
b) the war-wounded and the dependants of those killed in the War;

---

32   Max Seydewitz (1892–1986), SPD, leader of left wing of SPD after Levi's death in 1930, and editor of the journal *Der Klassenkampf*, member of the Reichstag 1924–32, joint chair of the SAP 1931–33.

c) state pensioners;

d) the needy victims of the inflation;

e) agricultural workers, tenants and small farmers, through the provision of settlement land on the rural possessions that have been expropriated

The castles, manor houses and other buildings expropriated will be used for general purposes of welfare, culture and education, and in particular for the establishment of convalescence and care homes for the war-wounded and surviving dependants, and state pensioners, as well as for children's homes and educational establishments.

Article III

All dispositions brought into effect after 1 November 1918 in relation to the property expropriated by this law, whether by court judgment, arbitration, contract or in any other manner, are hereby declared null and void.

Article IV

Regulations for the implementation of this law will be laid down by a decree which is to be issued within three months of the official confirmation of the result of the referendum. This law must in particular determine more precisely the way in which Article II of this law, concerning the utilisation of the expropriated princely property, is to be applied by the individual States.

Signed: Otto Wels (SPD)

Ernst Thälmann (Central Committee of the KPD)

Dr. Kuczynski[33] (Commission for the Expropriation of the Princes)

Source: *Verhandlungen des Reichstags*, vol. 408, nr. 2229; reprinted in Sozialistische Einheitspartei Deutschlands Zentralkomitee 1975, *Dokumente und Materialien zur Geschichte der deutschen Arbeiterbewegung*, Vol. VIII, pp. 306–7.

Note: The campaign for the expropriation of the former princes was begun by the KPD with its proposal of 25 November 1925 for the confiscation of their property. The Party then issued an Open Letter asking the SPD to join it in calling

---

33 René Robert Kuczynski (1876–1947), statistician, chair of the German League for Human Rights, set up the Commission for Expropriation of the Former Princes in 1925, withdrew from political life in 1926 and worked after that on statistical research projects in the USA.

for a plebiscite on the issue.[34] The SPD leaders considered that this would be
a waste of time and effort, since a majority of the electorate would never support it, but the idea was very attractive to rank-and-file Social Democrats, and
it was the fear of losing their supporters to the KPD that led them to join the
campaign, despite their doubts.[35] The result was perhaps the most successful
'united front' campaign ever waged by the KPD. The two big parties of the Left
were joined by non-socialist pacifists such as Helene Stöcker[36] and Ludwig
Quidde,[37] the physicist Albert Einstein, the theatre critic Alfred Kerr and many
other prominent Weimar intellectuals. The plebiscite (*Volksbegehren*) took
place in March 1926 and was seen as a great success: with 12.5 million supporters it outstripped by two million the number of votes the two parties of the
Left might have expected to receive by themselves. But a further hurdle had
to be passed: according to Article 73 of the Weimar Constitution, to succeed,
the plebiscite had to be followed by a referendum (*Volksentscheid*) in which
more than half the electorate voted in favour. With 16.7 million votes in favour,
the referendum of June 1926 failed to reach the 20 million figure required, and
the campaign thus ended in failure.

5.15   Paul Levi's Analysis of the Bourgeois Bloc (Bürgerblock) Government, January 1927

After long endeavours it has finally come to pass, and one can only say: what
a good thing! We do not say this because we think: the worse, the better. Not
at all. Most of the disagreements we had with tactical decisions of the Party or
the parliamentary *Fraktion* in recent years were about the most effective way
of keeping the German Nationalists out of the government for the foreseeable
future.

We believe that the foundation of all parliamentary power lies in extra-
parliamentary facts; we believed that at the time of the Dawes Pact in 1924,
or the Locarno Treaty in 1925 it would have been possible to create extra-
parliamentary facts by welding together the masses of electors and relying on
the increased strength of the SPD's influence and reputation ... but the fact is
that extraparliamentary facts were *not* created of sufficient strength to allow an
authoritative stand in parliament against a 'bourgeois bloc', i.e. a combination

34   The Open Letter of 2 December 1925 is printed in Sozialistische Einheitspartei Deutsch-
      lands Zentralkomitee 1975, p. 281.
35   See in detail Schüren 1978, pp. 75–82.
36   Helene Stöcker (1869–1943), pacifist and sexual reformer, chair of the International
      Association for the Protection of Motherhood and Sexual Reform.
37   Ludwig Quidde (1858–1941), DDP member, chair of the German Peace Association.

of the whole bourgeoisie up to and including the German Nationalists. But enough of the past.

To be mistaken about one's one weaknesses is far worse than merely to be weak. In my view our Party's policy in recent years has been determined by a failure to recognise that the real political power of the proletariat is dwindling. If the dwindling of our forces – it doesn't matter whether this happened with or without mistakes on our part – weakens us in parliament, we must conduct our policies with the aim of recovering our strength. But the parliamentary party seemed to be dominated by the idea that one could stop the decline by holding on to parliamentary positions...

If we now see it as a piece of good fortune that the 'bourgeois bloc' has been formed this is not because we regard it as a splendid institution which will save the country. We see it rather as a curse, at least for the masses. But with its coming the class forces in Germany are now precisely represented in parliament and it therefore destroys any illusions we may have about our parliamentary or extra-parliamentary position.

In parliamentary terms the phantom of the 'grand coalition' now fades away, the phantom of various common interests, the phantom of the 'left wing of the Centre Party'... We were not believed when we repeatedly pointed to the impossible twaddle purveyed by such a person as Wirth, or by the 'Republicans' in general, who said we were all brothers under the Black-Red-Gold flag and who knew nothing of any conflict between capital and labour... Now the Centre Party is again black, and reactionary as it always was: much of our Party's progress has rested on advertising the true nature of the Centre Party. The phantom of 'extra-parliamentary facts' has also vanished. Many of our friends failed to understand the low opinion we had of the *Reichsbanner*. We would be the last to deny the value of such organisations. But the *Reichsbanner* was the incarnation of the idea of the Grand Coalition. It this was a will o' the wisp, then so too was the *Reichsbanner*. An organisation is good if it is proletarian, but not when its leadership stands with the other side when things get serious.

We are full of confidence in the future, not because we see the 'bourgeois bloc' as a victory for the revolution, but because it demonstrates the defeat of the revolution, brings us face to face with the victory of the bourgeoisie, and thereby guarantees a better future, a revolutionary future. For now nothing more stands between the working class and its historic task: no more pieces of paper, no more illusions.

Source: Paul Levi 1927, 'Der Bürgerblock', *Sozialistische Politik und Wirtschaft*, 28 January 1927.

5.16 *Siegfried Aufhäuser's Resolution of 1927 Calling for Opposition Instead of Coalition*

The formation of a government by the 'bourgeois bloc' reveals the sharpening of class antagonisms in the German Republic. Previous attempts to further the interests of the working class in the Republic by a coalition with bourgeois parties have been unsuccessful.

The task of Social Democracy in the German Republic is to represent the class interests of the proletariat vis-à-vis the class rule of capitalism, and to fight for social demands and socialism. In comparison with this task, the fight to maintain the Republic, which the bourgeoisie is prepared to tolerate, is of less significance. The fighting front in the German Republic should no longer be formed under the slogan of 'Republicanism versus Monarchism' but rather 'socialism versus capitalism'.

In view of the current political constellation, the tactics of Social Democracy must be *opposition, not coalition*. The Congress resolves to conduct this opposition without worrying about the bourgeois parties, in the spirit of the proletarian class struggle, and using all appropriate parliamentary and extra-parliamentary means.

Source: Sozialdemokratischer Parteitag in Kiel 1927, *Protokoll mit dem Bericht der Frauenkonferenz*, p. 272.

Note: This was Resolution 202, put forward by Siegfried Aufhäuser, Toni Sender[38] and Comrades to the SPD's 1927 Congress. It was rejected by 255 votes to 83 after a debate. in which Rudolf Hilferding spoke against the motion (see Document 4.7) and Aufhäuser spoke in favour (see Document 4.8).

5.17 *Georg Decker's 1930 Critique of the Opponents of Coalition Politics*

If Paul Levi was right about himself, the last communist in Germany has now left the political stage.[39] He claimed that he remained a communist whereas the official communists had long since ceased to qualify for that description. But Social Democracy has taken leave of Paul Levi with deep pain, considering him as one of their own. There is no contradiction in that, either for Levi or for the Party, because communism, as he understood it, was a particular form of

---

38   Toni Sender (1888–1964), USPD, SPD from 1922, member of the Reichstag 1920–33.

39   The article was written just after Paul Levi's death in February 1930 as a result of a fatal accident, which may have been suicide.

socialist opinion which could come into force only within the great current of the socialist workers' movement...

Why does opposition arise within a party? In the case of many parties, social differences are one factor which gives rise to political difficulties. Different interests are represented within the bourgeois parties. There are different interests within Social Democracy too, but here there is differentiation within a social unity characterised by particularly strong class solidarity. Special interests are subordinated to the good of the whole movement.

But a different kind of differentiation plays no small role in the SPD: the difference between the local conditions in which the Party acts. This is not a difference of *interests* but of tasks. In industrial districts the tasks are different from those in the countryside. Newer industrial districts differ from older ones. The tasks also differ according to the *competitors* the Party faces. For a Social Democratic organisation which has the Communist Party as its sole opponent, many questions are posed differently from in areas where the organisation has to fight the Centre, the BVP or the National Socialists... Hence in Coblenz or Munich they have a very different picture of the world from that prevailing in Berlin or Chemnitz. The origins of opposition have to be investigated historically in individual cases. In Chemnitz, for example, the Independents did not split off from the Party, and there arose a particular 'Chemnitz tendency' among the Majority Socialists which is now an explicitly oppositional organisation...

But I am concerned here with the more general reasons for the emergence of opposition in Social Democracy... It emerges because views diverge on the relation between the concrete political objectives and the grand aim of the movement, the 'final goal', as people call it. That is why Eduard Bernstein's revisionist opposition arose. At that time the opposition was *from the Right*. This reformist opposition was necessary and fruitful, and it achieved its aims to a large extent. Now the foundation of opposition is the opposite: the emergence of a *radical* opposition is just as well founded on the objective conditions as was the revisionist opposition previously.

Of course, the antagonism between reformism and revisionism no longer exists in its previous form. No one would think of demanding that Social Democrats refuse to agitate for unemployment insurance because it is incompatible with capitalism and therefore to fight for it is to promote reformist illusions... Paul Levi the radical never tired of fighting for the reform of the judicial system... To stress the connection of present problems with the achievement of longer-term goals is a very important task, and this *could and should* be the function of the radical opposition. But the existing opposition does not do this, as it does not possess the necessary requirements.

These are, first, that they must be *revisionist*, not in the sense of a 'right-wing' revisionism, but in the sense of revising old theoretical conceptions and much-loved traditions. The present opposition fails completely in this respect... It holds onto certain Marxist formulas, repeated again and again, very often misunderstood, and not revised on the basis of later developments... New experiences should be recognised and brought into line with socialist objectives, so that one doesn't just ask how socialists treated this in earlier times, but what kind of socialist policies there should be in view of the new facts.

Secondly, opposition, to be fruitful, must act in all spheres with great vigour. Paul Levi did this in his own special sphere. But the present opposition does not. It fails to notice that one cannot say how politics *in general* must be conducted if one doesn't constantly offer concrete solutions. This failing, in connection with the conservative attitude I mentioned earlier, has the result that the opposition in Social Democracy tends towards political passivity, whereas what is required of Social Democracy in the present situation is the highest and most effective level of activity.

Source: Georg Decker, 'Opposition', *Die Gesellschaft. Internationale Revue für Sozialismus und Politik*, VII, 3, March 1930, pp. 196–204.

Note: Georg Decker (pseudonym of Yuri Petrovich Deneke, 1887–1964, a Menshevik exile from Russia), was an active journalist on the Right of the SPD until his emigration in 1933.

5.18   *Franz Petrich[40] on the Fateful Consequences for the SPD of their Decision to Remain in the Coalition of 1928–30*

In the March issue of this journal Comrade Decker has combined an evaluation of the work of Paul Levi with a critique of the opposition. How fortunate it would have been if he himself could have replied! We are not surprised that Decker has arrived at a completely negative judgement about the achievements of the opposition up to the present... If we want to look at the matter in its essential aspects we must look at Decker's overall attitude to the Party's policies, and in particular his views on the question of coalition. We must ask whether his sociology is so up to the minute as to justify him in drawing up

---

40   Franz Petrich (1889–1945), metalworker by profession. SPD from 1912, member of SPD district executive in Thuringia 1930–33, editor of main SPD newspaper in Thuringia 1919–33, member of the Reichstag 1932–33.

such a devastating report on the opposition. Where he is going with his socio-logical observations is unclear. Does he want to create a 'revolutionary neo-revisionism' which will bring about our theoretical salvation?

He says that the old beauty is no longer true and the new truth is not yet beautiful. What is the 'new truth'? It finds expression in the policy of coali-tion, not so much theoretically as in practice... The German Party has no theory of coalition politics. Decker reproaches the opposition with too great a dependence on quotations from Marx, and an application of misunderstood formulas. We believe, however, that these 'formulas' are applications of the Marxist method, the revolutionary method which Marx applied with tremen-dous success in the Communist Manifesto and the Eighteenth Brumaire... We can say without any overweening pride that the opposition's prognoses about the policy of coalition have been fully confirmed in the last two years... The opposition is in fundamental agreement with the best opinions of interna-tional Marxism. Otto Bauer has given the most penetrating presentation of the problem of coalition politics on the basis of the experience of the Austrian Revolution. He was the first to point out that Social Democracy can neither strive in general for a coalition, nor reject it in general. As he says: 'It depends on the concrete historical situation'. One can enter a coalition when it represents 'not an abandonment of the class struggle but its result'. It is 'the expression of a temporary power relation between the classes which are in conflict'.

But the coalition formed in the summer of 1928 did not fulfil these require-ments. It arose out of purely political considerations, and it rested on a parlia-mentary combination.The weak approach of the Social Democratic ministers towards many important questions reflected this false calculation; in order to keep the coalition in being they had to give way again and again to the pres-sure of the bourgeois coalition parties... Hilferding's activities in the Ministry of Finance demonstrated every day that he was the prisoner of finance capital, and that he existed on its charity. The moment that he became superfluous to finance capital's needs he was removed from office. The neo-revisionists have failed to make clear the basic significance of the given economic conjuncture for coalition politics. Instead they subordinated everything to foreign policy, claiming that the requirements of foreign policy made it unavoidable for Social Democracy to remain in the coalition.

Source: Petrich, 'Kritik der Opposition. Antwort an Genossen Decker', *Die Gesellschaft. Internationale Revue für Sozialismus und Politik*, VII, 5, May 1930, pp. 454–61.

5.19   *Rudolf Hilferding's Criticism of the SPD's Decision to Withdraw from the Government in 1930*

Since the revolution [of 1918], Social Democracy has been compelled to participate in the government for two reasons: to maintain democracy and the parliamentary system, and to carry out the sole foreign policy that is possible ... These are not the only reasons for being in government: taking part in the government makes it easier to put into effect the specific demands of the workers, and above all it makes it easier to ward off any harmful measures ...

It is social policy that has caused Grand Coalitions to collapse in the Reich: in 1923 it was the attack on the eight-hour day, and in 1930 it was the question of unemployment insurance. The struggle over unemployment insurance was conducted very sharply in the summer of 1929 ... Social Democracy managed to end this struggle successfully without allowing any serious damage to be inflicted on the unemployment insurance system ... but in view of the rise in unemployment and the concomitant need for additional funds, the call for reform of the system was again taken up .... Even then a solution appeared to have been found which could be accepted by both sides. It involved an increase in contributions from three-and-a-half to four percent ... But this was rejected by the DVP ... Dr. Brüning then proposed a compromise ... which in essence amounted to postponing a final decision ... The Social Democrats rejected the compromise because they thought it would lead eventually to a reduction in the level of unemployment benefit. But the decision to leave the government and allow the formation of a cabinet heavily dependent on the Right has not made the defence of unemployment benefit any easier. The SPD has gained nothing from its withdrawal from the government, precisely from the point of view of unemployment insurance. The fear that things would get worse in any case this autumn was not a sufficient reason to take such a fateful step. It is not a good idea to commit suicide out of a fear of death.

The *Fraktion's* decision must also be looked at from the broader angle of the current political situation. It is certainly true that the Republic is hardly threatened any longer with violent overthrow. That is not the danger. But the future of German parliamentarism and democracy may be endangered in a different way ... The President of the Reich [Hindenburg] has far-reaching powers ... There is no doubt that if the parliament fails to perform its most important and basic function, namely to form a government, the power of the President will grow at the expense of the parliament, and he will have to do what the parliament has failed to do ... The real danger for the future of German parliamentarism comes not from without but from within. Ajax fails through Ajax's strength. Avoiding this danger was always a decisive factor in Social Democracy's decision to take over responsibility in the most difficult and disadvantageous situations. But that was exactly how it was when the *Fraktion* took its recent decision ...

If the 'grand coalition' were to collapse, it was known that the formation of a purely parliamentary cabinet would be absolutely impossible. And in fact Brüning's cabinet came into being as an anti-parliamentary government ... My critical stance towards the policy of the SPD in this situation by no means excuses the other coalition parties ... The parties which rejected the original government proposal on unemployment insurance also bear a very great responsibility ... What is of decisive importance in all this is the position of power suddenly attained by the German nationalists, or at least the interests represented in that Party.

Source: Hilferding, 'Der Austritt aus der Regierung', *Die Gesellschaft. Internationale Revue für Sozialismus und Politik*, 1930, 1, pp. 385–91.

5.20   *Carl Mierendorff Analyses the SPD's Election Defeat of September 1930*
All the SPD's decisions are now imprinted with the fact of the defeat of 14 September 1930. It is the reason for the change in our tactics towards the Brüning government, against which we were on the offensive before that date, whereas now we are forced onto the defensive. This is the deeper reason for the complete reversal of policy on the question of the vote of no confidence and the emergency decrees. Was this defeat unavoidable? The answer, unfortunately, is no. The core problem of the SPD, the *problem of leadership*, casts a gigantic shadow over us. *It is not the ordinary soldiers who have lost the battle but their leaders.* There was mistake after mistake. Social Democracy fought the election facing the wrong way. It fought first and foremost against the Brüning government (and its policy of emergency decrees) whereas our main opponents were the National Socialists. It fought at the wrong time, because the dissolution of parliament hit Social Democracy at a moment when it was not in the least prepared for a duel with its main opponent, National Socialism. And why? Because the real danger, the National Socialist movement, was neither noticed nor properly factored in by the party leadership.

It had been clear to everyone, at the latest since the local elections in Prussia,[41] that the National Socialist movement had favourable prospects. There was no doubt that it would make further advances ... Yet Social Democracy undertook practically no systematic struggle against the National Socialists.

---

41   The NSDAP made startling advances in the local elections held on 16 November 1929 in Prussia, raising their vote in Berlin, for example, from 2.8 percent to 5.8 percent.

It failed to seize this great opportunity to present the true socialist doctrine to new voters in a fight against a pseudo-socialist movement ... This opponent made necessary completely new techniques and tactics of struggle, and these were not available ... The capital mistake here is to be sought in an *underestimation of extra-parliamentary operations.* For years the SPD had turned its face exclusively towards parliamentary processes, as if it were in a hypnotic trance ... The Fascist danger can only be banished by taking up the struggle for the destruction of the National Socialist illusion in the electorate and public opinion.

Source: Mierendorff, 'Lehren der Niederlage', *Neue Blätter für den Sozialismus* 1.11, November 1930, pp. 481–4.

5.21   *The SPD Proposes Measures to Combat Unemployment in 1931*

Social Democracy is convinced that all ways must be tried to restore to the millions of unemployed people an existence worthy of their human dignity. Again and again the SPD and the Free Trade Unions have worked out proposals which are intended to lead to the goal of re-integrating the millions of unemployed into the labour process, and making them happier, more joyful and contented. These proposals are grouped around two major objectives: first, to create political confidence in Germany and towards Germany, internally and externally; and second, to alter the economic conditions under which the process of production has to develop among a nation of 65 millions such as the Germans, so that adequate work can be available for all, and everyone shall have their share in the social product.

The terrible consequences of rationalisation must be confronted by reducing the hours of work for all employees. The economic depression must be fought by significantly reducing prices, intervening strongly against the monopoly rights of the cartels and altering commercial policy. Purchasing power must be increased by the reduction of commodity prices, which will increase sales and thereby bring the factories back into full operation. The economy will then return to its normal course of development. Social Democracy therefore most sharply rejects the idea of first reducing wages and then waiting until prices also fall, because this contradicts all economic laws and can only result in a worsening of the crisis in sales and purchasing power.

Source: Sozialdemokratische Partei Deutschlands 1931, *Das Gespenst der Arbeitslosigkeit und die Vorschläge der SPD zu ihrer Überwindung,* Heilbronn: p. 22.

5.22   *The Trade Union Movement Demands a 40-hour Week to Combat Unemployment, 1931*

Resolution of the Federal Executive of the ADGB on the Crisis in the Economy and the Forty-Hour Week, September 1931

The length and seriousness of the world economic crisis is a result of the superimposition of numerous disturbances on each other. The tension between productive capacity and purchasing power, which is customarily the critical factor in the capitalist economy, has taken on extraordinary dimensions. Added to this is a series of special factors, the effects of which have had a catastrophic impact in Germany in particular.

The development of the crisis has shown that the political organisation of the world has not attained the level necessary for the economy. The world has the choice between either reducing tensions by an honest rejection of war, i.e. by general disarmament, and thereby fulfilling the necessary condition for a world economy, or abandoning the world economic context and drawing all the unpleasant consequences which result from this abandonment.

While recognising that even if things develop favourably a full utilisation of the available productive apparatus is not to be expected very soon, the Congress emphasises the urgent need to reduce unemployment by systematically shortening the hours of work. The Congress instructs the Executive to put forward with the utmost vigour the demand for a *legally compulsory, universally valid, forty-hour working week*. The Congress declares that it is the duty of all trade-union officials and all trade-union members to support this demand with all their strength in order to lessen the national emergency of unemployment and once again to place the labour power that is lying idle at the service of the national economy.

Source: Kongress der Gewerkschaften Deutschlands, *Protokoll der Verhandlungen des 14.Kongresses der Gewerkschaften Deutschlands 31.August bis 4.September 1931*, Frankfurt, 1931, p. 21.

5.23   *The Trade Union Movement Calls for Job Creation: The 'WTB Plan' of 1931*

Theses on the Fight Against the Economic Crisis

1   The Failure of the Automatic Mechanism of Capitalist Crisis

The mechanism of the capitalist system which is alleged to have the capacity and the strength automatically to overcome economic crises is unable to function in the present crisis. This failure is primarily founded on two facts, the existence of which distinguishes the present crisis from earlier ones, namely:

a) the *total character of the crisis*, in two respects: its spatial extension over the whole world, and its simultaneous hold on all branches of the industrial and agricultural economy, as a result of which there is no healthy sector such as formed the starting point for previous recoveries of the unhealthy parts of the economy.

b) the complete national and international *destruction of the credit mechanism* at a time when, assuming the crisis ran a 'normal' course, the economic recovery would be set off by a flow of large and cheap credits into the system.

As the self-healing mechanism is no longer functioning, attempts have been made to restore the economy to health by altering price levels. This policy of universal price and cost reduction, especially wage reduction, has not only failed to alleviate the crisis, it has worsened it considerably.

In this situation it a vital necessity for the labour movement to look for means of *deliberately influencing the course of the economic cycle*...All the means and conditions of production are abundantly available both internationally and in the German economy. The policy of contraction, however, has brought the available amount of purchasing and consumption power into an ever more serious imbalance with productive capacity. *The impulse must therefore come from the consumption side.*

2   Public Works to Provide a Conjunctural Impulse

Since a growth of the power of consumption is not to be expected in the private economic sphere, additional purchasing power must be injected from outside. The most appropriate method...is the setting in motion of *large-scale public works*, the costs of which are essentially made up of wages and salaries. This additional purchasing power, if it were large enough, would push the whole economy into recovery...

Job creation must form the kernel of our action programme for dealing with the economic cycle, within the framework of the German economy. The programme of job creation, however, leads on the question of finance, involving the provision of *supplementary credit*. So far, all plans of this kind have been criticised in Germany as 'inflationary'. Current German economic policy has gone in precisely the opposite direction...

3   Credit and Currency Policy

The labour movement must set its face emphatically against any continuation of the deflationary policies pursued by the government of the *Reich*...We must demand a rapid and decisive *cessation of deflationary policies.*

[4 International Measures of Job and Credit Creation][42]

5   The Fight Against the Crisis Nationally, Within the German
           Economy

Social Democracy must develop an entirely concrete programme for fighting
the crisis within the national framework ... The measure that should occupy
the central point of the planned economic fight against the crisis is the use of
public works to employ one million unemployed people. Preference should
be given to those activities which do not put products onto the market, and
therefore do not compete with existing branches of production. Job creation
will call forth a revival of the consumer goods industry and thereby soak up
into employment a further considerable section of the unemployed. A sum
of about 2,000 million *Reichsmark* would be needed to finance these public
works ... There is no need to fear that an unlimited inflation like that of 1922–23
would result from a single currency loan of this nature, limited to a definite
amount and earmarked for the purpose of stimulating activity. The guarantee
against inflationary effects ... lies not only in these limits but in the fact that an
immense amount of productive capacity is lying idle. As a result, an increase
of production can follow behind the increase in purchasing power ... without
any difficulty.

           Conclusion

In the immediate future, the Party and the trade unions must concentrate their
activity on the fight against the crisis, in the form appropriate to awakening
the greatest degree of activity among the workers, to bringing them together
again and to securing the support of other social groups. The negative side of
our action programme must run like this: 'No more deflation, no more wage
cuts'. The positive side must have as its nucleus the following two demands:
'International reconciliation and international job creation'.

Dr. Baade,[43] F. Tarnow,[44] W. Woytinsky[45]

---

42   This section has been omitted.

43   Fritz Baade (1893–1960), SPD, economist and agricultural expert, member of the Reichstag
      1930–33.

44   Fritz Tarnow (1880–1951), trade unionist, head of the Union of Woodworkers 1921 to 1933,
      SPD, on executive of ADGB 1928 to 1933, member of the Reichstag 1928 to 1933.

45   Vladimir Woytinsky (1885–1960), economist of Russian origin, active as journalist in
      Germany from 1922, head of the ADGB's statistical department 1928–33.

Source: M. Schneider 1975, *Das Arbeitsbeschaffungsprogramm des ADGB*, pp. 225–30.

Note: The WTB Plan (the name is formed from the initial letters of the surnames of its authors, Wladimir Woytinsky, Fritz Tarnow and Fritz Baade) was laid before the ADGB Executive on 23 December 1931. It met with a broadly favourable reception, and most of its provisions were adopted by an emergency congress of the ADGB called together in April 1932 to discuss the economic crisis. The orthodox economic theorists of the SPD, however, whether Marxist or not, regarded the plan as entirely unrealistic. Hilferding in particular was strongly opposed, arguing that the plan was likely to cause inflation. There was also opposition on political grounds: the SPD leaders did not want to get into a conflict with the Brüning government.[46] The Party therefore rejected it. Only after the fall of Brüning and the disastrous elections of July 1932 did the SPD come forward with its own plan for job-creation in order to 'prevent a breach between the trade unions and party', as Tarnow put it. Hilferding continued to be fiercely opposed. 'You are merely showing that you are not Marxists', he said. By that time there was in any case no chance that such a plan could be accomplished under Weimar. The only party to welcome the WTB Plan was Hitler's NSDAP, and when the Nazis came to power they applied many of its ideas, reaping much credit among the mass of the people and laying the basis for Germany's economic recovery and expansion in the later 1930s.

---

46   Harsch 1993, p. 166.

CHAPTER 6

The Moscow Connection: The KPD and the Comintern

Introduction

The German communists' original connection with the Bolsheviks in Moscow was emotional in nature; they regarded them with admiration as having shown the way they should follow, the path of revolution. The decisions made by the KPD in its early years were not affected by financial inducements or bureaucratic ties. As Dietrich Geyer has pointed out, 'the Bolsheviks did not have to enforce their dominance over the KPD; it resulted from the unquestioned authority of the Russian Party and its leading personalities'.[1] The early KPD leaders, in particular Paul Levi, looked to the Bolsheviks, particularly Lenin and Radek, for advice and also moral support against the syndicalists and ultra-leftists within the Party who rejected parliamentary activity and considered that the German Revolution, far from having been defeated by mid-1919, was still on the upsurge. For their part, the Bolsheviks were very ready to give advice, though at that stage it was not always accepted. At the end of 1919 there was open disagreement, almost on a basis of equality, between Lenin and August Thalheimer on the way to attract the masses of workers still in the USPD towards communism. In this case, the Communist International actually accepted the German communist's view.[2] After 1921, however, the atmosphere changed in several ways. Moscow began to send instructions rather than advice to the KPD, and the Russian Bolsheviks tended to adopt a single political line, which had to be implemented by the Party, rather than, as previously, sending individual pieces of advice which might vary from person to person.

The emotional bond with the Bolsheviks remained strong throughout the Weimar Republic, but other forms of connection came to be more decisive. There was naturally a degree of financial dependence (6.4), although this was not as complete as has sometimes been suggested, because considerable amounts of money were raised from party members. Perhaps more significant was the bureaucratic connection, which began with the setting up of the Executive Committee of the Communist International (ECCI), the body responsible for enforcing the directives of the headquarters of the Communist

---

1   Geyer 1976, p. 17.
2   Broué 2005, p. 348.

International in Moscow. In theory the ECCI represented the whole world-wide communist movement, but in practice the dominant position was held by the Russian Communist Party (6.1). As time went on, the ECCI intervened more and more in the affairs of the German Party (as indeed those of all the other communist parties), and its interventions covered not just policy but personnel. This increase in centralised control from Moscow is evident in several of the documents printed here. It would be fair to say that after about 1928 the KPD's general policy in the most important strategic and tactical questions was determined outside Germany. No initiative could be taken by the Party without the agreement of the ECCI, and the ECCI's line was determined by the Russian delegation. This was true both positively, in the case of the decision to outbid the German nationalism of the Nazis which resulted in the August 1930 Programme, and negatively, in the case of Stalin's intervention to deter the KPD leaders from moving towards some degree of cooperation with the Social Democrats in the summer of 1931.

The Party's basic objectives also changed in the later period. Until roughly 1924 the main aim of the KPD was to achieve a socialist revolution in Germany. This remained the objective even after it was clear that the 'German October' of 1923 had failed. The immediate reaction to failure was to find scapegoats, within the Party, certainly, but also outside. The Social Democrats, always viewed with suspicion, now started to be described as 'Fascists'. 'Social Democracy is objectively the moderate wing of Fascism', wrote Stalin in September 1924. 'Fascism and Social Democracy are not antipodes, they are twins'. He also appeared to maintain that the German Revolution was not over: 'It is false to say that the decisive battles have already occurred, that the proletariat has suffered a defeat and that the revolution has been postponed for an indefinite period. The decisive battles in the West still lie ahead'.[3] Trotsky, as so often, found an appropriate analogy for this attitude: 'On descending the stairs a different type of movement is required from when ascending; but in 1924 those in charge of the Comintern kept on repeating that the stairs led upwards. They maintained the course towards armed insurrection verbally after the revolution had already turned its back on us'.[4]

In 1925, however, it had to be conceded by the Comintern that the revolutionary period had ended. The Party's aims from now on were to stay in existence and recruit more supporters, and, more importantly, to defend the only socialist revolution, the one that had taken place in the Soviet Union, in other words to defend the Soviet Union and promote its foreign policy. As Stalin put

3   Stalin 1953, pp. 294–5.
4   Trotsky 1996, pp. 131–2.

it in 1925, the Party's task was 'to support the Soviet regime and frustrate the interventionist machinations of imperialism against the Soviet Union, bearing in mind that to preserve and strengthen the Soviet Union means to accelerate the victory of the working class over the world bourgeoisie'.[5] The KPD therefore naturally supported all Soviet diplomatic initiatives, including moves towards an alliance between the Soviet Union and the bourgeois German state, a state the Party was committed to resisting. This sometimes had contradictory results. The Party naturally condemned German militarism, but in December 1926 the SPD politician Philipp Scheidemann exposed the secret military cooperation between Germany and the Soviet Union, whereby the Reichswehr was able to develop prohibited weapons on Soviet territory. The KPD rejected his accusations with indignation. There could be no anti-militarist campaign by the Party on *this* subject (although this didn't stop the dissident left communists who had recently been expelled from raising the question in the Reichstag).

Defence of the Soviet Union also meant taking seriously the threat of intervention by capitalist powers, which the Russian leaders regarded as genuine. From 1927 onwards this was a matter of particular concern. Stalin told the 15th Party Congress of the AUCP (B), held in December 1927, that the leaders of Social Democracy were now 'actively' preparing a war of intervention against the Soviet Union, and that they were the most dangerous of the political opponents of communism.[6] The Comintern's response to the alleged threat was to adopt the 'class against class' policy, which meant abandoning any possible united front with the Social Democrats, and in fact treating them as the main enemy of communism. The KPD thus reverted to the terminology of 1924, and the Social Democrats were now routinely referred to as 'Social Fascists'. A year later after it had been introduced, this line was made more acceptable to communists on the spot in Germany by the sanguinary events of the 1st to 3rd of May 1929 in Berlin, when a communist decision to hold a May Day demonstration which had been banned by the Prussian government led to clashes between demonstrators and the police, who were responsible to the Social Democratic police chief of Berlin, Karl Zörgiebel. After three days there were 33 dead and 198 severely wounded demonstrators (and one accidental police casualty).[7] In Moscow the demonstration was regarded as part of the campaign against the danger of capitalist intervention against the Soviet Union; but the response of the police was seen as proof that the SPD leaders were

---

5   Stalin 1954, pp. 57–8.

6   Wieszt 1976, p. 23.

7   There are many detailed accounts of these events and their background. Two useful brief discussions are Rosenhaft 1983, pp. 33–40 and Bowlby 1986, pp. 137–58.

closely tied to the capitalist state. This view was shared by many on the Left in Germany, and it made the 'Social Fascist' line more convincing than it would have been otherwise.

The SPD continued to be treated as a 'Social Fascist' party by the KPD for the remainder of the Weimar Republic, even after March 1930 when it lost power nationally. None of the KPD leaders showed any sign of disagreeing with this view. There were several reasons for this. In part it was a reflection of the lack of independence of the Party leaders who had now reached the top after several years of factional conflict in the course of which both left and right 'deviationists' had been forced out. Clara Zetkin voiced her disagreement in private, in a letter of 19 June 1929 to Piatnitsky.[8] But she stayed a member, submitting in a disciplined fashion to the decisions arrived at by the Party majority. In part it was a genuinely held opinion that the Social Democratic government was pursuing a pro-Western foreign policy orientation which would damage the Soviet Union. In other words, there were people who accepted the arguments of Stalin and his supporters. The private utterances of KPD leaders, as presented by Bert Hoppe, did not differ from their public position. It is in any case difficult to find a purely private opinion at this time, on this subject.

Where there was disagreement in the early 1930s was over the attitude to be taken to ordinary Social Democratic workers. At first the view taken was that they too were Social Fascists, but in April 1930 the ECCI introduced what Stefan Hoppe has called 'a bit of fine tuning'.[9] A distinction was made between 'the Social Fascist bureaucracy and the upper stratum of skilled workers, on the one hand, and the broad working-class masses (including a significant section of skilled workers, pushed along the road of struggle against the bourgeoisie by the impact of capitalist rationalisation) who were still under Social Democratic influence' but could be prised away from this.[10] At first there was some apparent justification for the 'Social Fascist' line, owing to the SPD's policy of tolerating the Brüning government, which did not rest on a parliamentary majority, but even after Brüning's replacement in 1932 by von Papen, and the SPD's decision to abandon toleration and go into opposition, the KPD continued to see the Social Democrats as the main enemy, rather than the National Socialists. The Comintern did make certain slight modifications, allowing

---

8   'The policy of the present CC is harmful and dangerous. It stands in sharpest contradiction to the principles of communist policy established under Lenin's leadership'. (Reuter 2003, p. 152.)

9   Hoppe 2007, p. 159.

10   Confidential letter of 26 April 1930 from the Political Secretariat of the ECCI to the CC of the KPD (Gintsberg 1994, p. 154).

the Party to move tentatively towards recognising the true extent of the Nazi danger (6.11, 6.12). This culminated in the appeal 'To All German Workers' of 26 April 1932 by which the KPD proclaimed its readiness to 'fight together with any workers' organisation which genuinely wants to conduct a struggle against cuts in wages and benefits' and to construct 'a united fighting front' against 'the capitalist thieves and the ever-increasing impudence of the Fascist gangs', and a month later the Party called for the setting up of 'unity committees of Anti-Fascist Action',[11] but the view taken in Moscow, by Stalin first and foremost, but also by men such as Manuilsky and Piatnitsky, who were in charge of Comintern policy, was that the main attack should continue to be directed against Social Democracy. It is hardly necessary to add that the KPD, as a highly disciplined member of the Communist International, was not likely to contest this evaluation by the men in Moscow. The fear of being counted as a deviationist provided a strong incentive to following instructions from the centre of the communist movement.[12] Ernst Thälmann, the Party leader, may possibly have had private doubts right at the end. He wrote a letter to Knorin[13] in which he outlined the Party's current work in the Anti-Fascist Action 'and the anti-Versailles campaign' without once using the expression 'Social Fascism'.[14] But the public rhetoric did not change.

When Papen mounted his coup against the Social Democratic government in Prussia (20 July 1932) the KPD called for a general strike in protest. While not actually condemning this, the Comintern leaders were very careful to limit its scope: 'We do not consider it necessary to take all measures to organise this strike' and 'We advise the party not to allow itself to be provoked into armed conflicts', and 'not to call demonstrations in the Berlin area', while one of the strike's aims was 'to strengthen still more the unmasking of the SPD, on the shoulders of which the Fascists have come to power'. This letter was signed by Kaganovich and Molotov and confirmed by Stalin.[15] To the very end, the Comintern seriously underestimated Hitler and the Nazis. Moreover, Stalin did not consider that a Nazi seizure of power in Germany would increase the threat to the Soviet Union: he had been assured by Kaganovich in 1932 that

11   Winkler 1987, pp. 554–9.
12   Hoppe 2007, p. 303.
13   Wilhelm Knorin (1890–1939), Latvian Bolshevik. Held various important positions in the Comintern apparatus, including head of the Central European Secretariat, 1929–35, and member of the ECCI's Political Secretariat, 1931–35.
14   Thälmann to Knorin, 27 November 1932 (Gintsberg 1994, p. 166).
15   Khlevniuk et al. (eds.) 2001, p. 237.

'a leading National Socialist' had told him that Germany would never attack the Soviet Union.[16]

Documents

6.1   *Rudolf Hilferding's Arguments Against Joining the Communist International, at the USPD Congress of October 1920*

That is what is typical of them: they believe in Moscow that these struggles [such as the one in Italy] can be decided from there [Moscow] on the basis of some higher insight than is possessed by the comrades who are themselves active in those countries. In our view, this is quite impossible, because we are naturally of the opinion that only the proletariat of the country in question can decide on the individual phases and stages of its struggle ... The actual meaning of the Organisational Statutes of the Communist International is this: the European working-class movement, just like the movement in the East, is to be transformed from an end in itself and a genuinely independent and autonomous movement of Western European workers into an instrument of the power politics of the Moscow Executive Committee [the ECCI]. And the central committee of the Executive is nothing other than the central committee of the Russian Communist Party (loud shouts of dissent from the Left) ... Nothing you tell us about the representatives of other countries [on the ECCI] can deceive us for one moment about the fact that these so-called representatives are in reality very closely dependent on the Russian communists, and they would not have become representatives if they were not dependent on them and if they did not continue to be so. We can see what the reaction is to every independent expression of opinion by representatives of other parties: when the representatives of Sweden and Italy make opposition they are told to change their views or suffer a split in their party. We cannot adopt these conditions [the conditions of admission to the Communist International] because we must maintain the independence of our movement, because, to adapt Rosa Luxemburg's phrase, we do not want to hand over the conductor's baton to any party whatsoever, however closely allied with us it may be ... The real content of the provisions on organisation [in the Organisational Statutes of the Communist International] is that we are no longer to be permitted to work out our own policy, that we are no longer to be allowed to establish what we want to do or to evaluate the situations we alone can best evaluate. We can evaluate these situations best, not because we are cleverer or more far-sighted,

---

16   Hoppe 2007, p. 315.

but simply because only he who is fighting on the field of battle is able to gain a view over it.

Source: Unabhängige Sozialdemokratische Partei 1920, *Protokoll über die Verhandlungen des ausserordentlichen parteitages in Halle, 12–17 Oktober 1920,* pp. 188, 197–8.

6.2   Report to the Zentrale *of the VKPD from Curt Geyer[17] on His Experiences in Moscow as German Delegate to ECCI, February 1921*

At the 21 February session of the 'narrower bureau of the [Executive Committee of the] Communist International' Zinoviev said this; 'Even without the Italian question we are faced with a serious crisis in the German party. One must ask whether the synthesis which created the Party is actually healthy'.

In this session the representative of the VKPD [Geyer] saw himself forced into the role, not of a colleague with equal voting rights, but the defender of a section under accusation. What were the main points of this accusation? (1) Lack of activity. The members of the ECCI differed in their degree of understanding of our situation – Radek saw the true state of the struggle, Guralsky[18] did not – but they all found the tempo too slow. (2) The attitude of the VKPD *Zentrale* to the KAPD. The ECCI members viewed the KAPD as the scourge of the VKPD, they saw it as the critic who was *right* about the tempo and politics of the VKPD, and the active, driving element of the revolution. The KAPD was not attacked for putschism; the ECCI advised the VKPD to form joint committees with it . . . The conclusion was that the ECCI found the tactics of the KAPD more sympathetic, whereas it saw vacillating and opportunist elements in the VKPD's tactics. It was, however, clear that the ECCI had no definite tactical line of its own. The 'Open Letter'[19] was hotly disputed. Radek stood alone in his defence of it. All the rest saw it as a regrettable deviation towards opportunist tendencies and a factor in the Party's passivity . . . Guralsky's main idea was that the sharpest possible direct action should be undertaken, sparked off by a provocation of the proletariat by the *Orgesch,* which in turn was to be provoked by the Party at the proper moment. The *Orgesch* provocation would bring the class itself into action. Guralsky referred to the experience of the Kapp putsch in justification of this idea. Radek disagreed. This is what he said in the plenary

---

17   Curt Geyer (1891–1967), USPD 1917, chair of Leipzig Workers' and Soldiers' Council 1918, KPD 1920, KAG 1921, SPD 1922. Member of the Reichstag.

18   August Kleine is referred to here by another of his aliases, Samuel Guralsky.

19   For the Open Letter from the VKPD to other organisations, calling for united action, see above, 4.5.

session [on 22 February 1921]: 'Bukharin has the recipe for revolutionary action in Germany, but I hope he never gets the chance to apply it ... If we now strike out in a partial action and the *Orgesch* attacks us, we shall be defeated, and neither the Majority Socialists nor the Independents will fight for us'.

Since there was no clear view on tactics, and the ECCI leadership did not want to admit its desire to adopt new tactics, they discussed the *Levi problem* ... Someone launched the idea of isolating the 'right wing' (Levi) and co-opting the 'left wing' (Ernst Meyer,[20] Paul Frölich[21] and Ernst Friesland) while retaining the 'healthy centre' of the Party (Heinrich Brandler, Clara Zetkin) ... The next day a plenary session of the ECCI began ... The question of the 'Open Letter' was not clarified there because comrade Radek threw the authority of Lenin into the scales against Zinoviev, Bukharin and Béla Kun ... Hence Zinoviev declared that these questions of tactics *would be left open as questions for discussion*. The lack of an unambiguous position was apparent in all the other questions as well ... The ECCI is not a politically effective body. The 'narrower bureau' was supposed to work out a letter to the *Zentrale* on the trade union question – but it did not ... No instructions were given to the prominent ECCI representatives[22] who were sent to Germany on the tactics to be jointly pursued by the VKPD and the KAPD. I simply do not know whether the two representatives received concrete tactical instructions ... or whether they had a free hand to act according to their inclinations, which in both cases are left communist in nature.

Source: *Archiv der sozialen Demokratie der Friedrich-Ebert-Stiftung, Bonn. Nachlass Paul Levi*, 159/14, Report from Curt Geyer to the *Zentrale*, 21–22 April 1921.

6.3   *Letters from Karl Radek to the* Zentrale *of the VKPD Concerning the March Action of 1921*

a) Max [Radek] to Brandler, Thalheimer, Frölich, Meyer, Böttcher, and Felix [Wolff],[23] 14 March 1921

---

20   Ernst Meyer (1887–1930), member of Spartacus League 1916–18, member of KPD *Zentrale* 1919–20, 1921–23 member of Political Bureau 1927–29, led the KPD 1921–22, subsequently regarded as a member of the 'Centre Group' in the Party until his death.

21   Paul Frölich (1884–1953), Bremen Left Radical, member of KPD *Zentrale* 1919–24, rightist after 1924, joined KPO in 1929 and the SAP in 1932.

22   This refers to Felix Wolff and Béla Kun.

23   Felix Wolff was one of the party names of Werner Rakov (1893–1937), also known as Nicolas Krebs, who was the son of a German worker in Russia. He became a Bolshevik in

Dear Comrades,

The situation in Russia is difficult. Spring and summer will be very difficult. Help from abroad to raise confidence here is very necessary... The situation in your Party is clear to me. Levi is trying to create a faction under the slogan: mass party or sect? This is a swindle, since he himself is destroying the Party by his policy, whereas we can bring in fresh mass support by activating our policy. No one here is thinking of a mechanical split, or any kind of split at all in Germany. What is needed is to bring out the points at issue clearly, to make the left wing intellectually dominant. Levi will soon be bankrupt. But we must do all we can to prevent Däumig and Zetkin from joining him in his bankruptcy.

Everything is dependent on the world political situation. If the chasm between the entente and Germany widens, if perhaps it reaches the point of war with Poland, we shall find some way to intervene. You must do all you can to mobilise the Party, precisely because these possibilities exist. One cannot shoot an action out of the barrel of a pistol, as it were. If you do not do everything you can to bring home to the communist masses the feeling that action is needed, by constantly urging them to take action, you will have failed again at a great moment... Think less of 'radical' formulae than of the deed. Think of setting the masses in motion. If war does come, do not think of peace, or merely of protest, but of getting hold of weapons. I am writing all this hastily, at the Party Congress.[24] Greetings.

b) Radek to the *Zentrale*, 1 April 1921

Dear Friends,

At the moment I only have radio reports of the situation. It is hard to decide on the basis of these reports whether the present movement is a spontaneous action or one begun by the Party... I assume that it is a party action. I fear you have made your move a few weeks too early. I fear that it was a tactical error not to have waited until a conflict broke out between Germany and Poland... In whatever way the action ends, I believe it will bring the Party forward. If we are defeated, the differences within the Party will be brought back to the correct basis. Levi... will doubtless raise the accusation of putschism, and whole uproar will be revealed for what it is: the start of the clear crystallisation of the

---

1917, and in 1919 entered the Comintern apparatus. He was sent to Germany in February 1921 along with Béla Kun and continued to represent the ECCI there until his expulsion by the German authorities in 1922. He was expelled from the KPD and the Comintern in 1933 and executed in 1937.

24 The Tenth Party Congress of the RCP(b), held between 8 and 16 March 1921.

right-wing faction. Watch out! Brass[25] and Koenen[26] are here. On Saturday we shall have an official session with their participation.[27] Brass will demand from us a declaration as to whether we are working towards a split in the German Party, as Rákosi[28] is alleged to have said ... We shall point out that the twenty-one conditions [of admission to the Communist International] have not been fulfilled. We shall mention by name the elements who are hindering the Party's development into a genuinely revolutionary party, and express the conviction that the German workers ... will be capable of rendering those elements harmless. Party differences should not be fought out in conventicles but *openly*, in meetings of the Party leadership and the press ... Geyer is a milksop. Geyer and Brass are in alliance. I shall ask Geyer whether he is representing the *Zentrale* in Moscow or just the 'five'.[29]

Note: Radek's letters to the KPD leadership display the ambiguity of his attitude. He was one of the originators of the 'united front' policy put forward in the Open Letter of 8 January 1921, and he rejected the theory of the 'revolutionary offensive' at a session of the ECCI on 21 February 1921, but in his letter of 14 March, above, he strongly implies that immediate action by the masses is needed, involving the use of weapons.[30]

Source: *Nachlass Paul Levi*, 55/3 (for Radek's letter of 14 March 1921), 55/2 (for Radek's letter of 1 April 1921).

---

25 Otto Brass (1875–1950), chair of the Remscheid Workers' and Soldiers' Council in 1918, member of the SPD, then the USPD, joined the KPD in 1920, expelled with the Friesland group in January 1922, and joined the KAG, the group set up by Paul Levi. See below, note 30.

26 Wilhelm Koenen (1886–1963), SPD member, then USPD party executive, led USPD Left into KPD 1920, member of the KPD *Zentrale* 1920–24, member of the Centre group from 1924, CC 1929–31, emigration 1933.

27 This was the 3/4 April 1921 Plenary Session of the ECCI in Moscow, at which Radek accused the 'right wing' of the VKPD of sabotaging the March Action, and 'adopted an attitude which tended towards putschism' according to Geyer (report of 21/22 April 1921, *Nachlass Paul Levi*, 159/14).

28 Mátyás Rákosi (1892–1971), Hungarian communist, People's Commissar in the Hungarian Soviet Republic of 1919, later performed various functions in the Comintern apparatus, headed the Hungarian Communist Party 1945–56.

29 The five: the members of the *Zentrale* who resigned on 22 February 1921 in protest against the methods used by the ECCI to force a split in the Italian Socialist Party (Paul Levi, Ernst Däumig, Otto Brass, Clara Zetkin and Adolph Hoffmann).

30 See in detail Fayet 2004, pp. 374–80.

6.4 Ernst Friesland Criticises the Attitude of the Comintern to the KPD, December 1921

The ECCI and the RGI[31] kept on sending us manifestos, containing in particular attacks on Amsterdam... We said the German workers had had enough of manifestos and would prefer there to be less abuse of other working-class parties and more objective discussion of matters of interest... Our attitude was not based on hostility to the Executive [of the Comintern]. We thought it obvious, however, that, as the German Party, we were not only justified in proceeding, but obliged to proceed, on the basis of conditions in Germany, within the framework of the present political situation... This attitude on the part of the KPD *Zentrale*, for which the General Secretary of the Party, Comrade Friesland, was considered personally responsible, called forth estrangement among some members of the Executive.

During the ZA[32] session [of 16/17 November 1921] Eberlein proposed that Friesland be replaced by Pieck[33]... At that time, the proposal was rejected. There is no doubt that certain members of the ECCI[34] have directly or indirectly exerted an influence on personal relations in the German *Zentrale*, and this has inflicted serious damage on the German Party and the International itself. It is clear that with such influence being exerted on the Communist Party by an ECCI member it will be impossible to find any statesmanlike person prepared to direct the Party's policy. The danger is that instead of this the only people available will be comrades who are ready to respond to every nod and wink, even when this does not suit the needs of the Party... The comrades concerned in the March Action should admit that they made a mistake, and

---

31 RGI: Red Trade-Union International (*Rote Gewerkschaftsinternationale*). This organisation was founded in Moscow in July 1921 as the trade-union counterpart to the Comintern. Known in English either as RILU (Red International of Labour Unions) or Profintern (from its Russian title). See in detail Tosstorff 2004.

32 ZA: *Zentralausschuss* (Central Committee). This body consisted of the members of the *Zentrale* plus representatives of the Party's regional branches. It met periodically for the purpose of exercising supervision over the activities of the *Zentrale*. It was replaced in 1925 by the differently structured *Zentralkomitee*. See below, chapter 11.

33 Wilhelm Pieck (1876–1960), founder member of the Spartacus League 1916, KPD *Zentrale* 1919, 1920–24, member of the KPD Political Bureau from 1929, member of the ECCI from 1928.

34 This comment refers first and foremost to Radek, who possessed a private channel of communication with the German Party in the person of, first, Felix Wolff (from February 1921 until his expulsion from Germany in 1922) then August Kleine (Guralsky).

draw the obvious consequences.[35] This is particularly important now as the new policy of *not* pushing workers into struggles against their will is beginning to bring us the confidence of broad strata of the proletariat. If the Party continues its policy, without looking left or right, it will without doubt have taken the KAG[36] back into its ranks within two to three months. If the KAG's demands are justified, they must be conceded...

It is a vital necessity for our Party's further development that it should become financially independent. In the long run, the Party cannot exist if it has to be maintained with foreign money. Only a communist movement supported and maintained by the working class itself can have any significance or strength. The excessive application of organisational instruments by the *Zentrale* is liable to spread a dangerously bureaucratic attitude instead of an independent outlook in some party organs. A glance at our party press is enough to confirm this statement. The same thing can be said of the ECCI ... The ECCI cannot replace the Central Committees of the various national parties. On the contrary, the Communist International can only attain a strong position if its member parties themselves have the chance to evaluate their experiences. In the atmosphere created by the exertion of personal influence over individual members of the *Zentrale*, and by the flow of unofficial correspondence [with Moscow], it is impossible to build up responsible party centres capable of winning the confidence of the working masses of their country...

[There follow complaints about Radek's letters from Moscow and about the way the ZA was being manipulated as a weapon against the *Zentrale*.]

The ECCI must unconditionally provide real, not paper, guarantees against a continuation of this kind of influence ... Centralisation by the Communist International must not consist in a schematic application of one country's experience to other countries... The communist parties of each individual nation must have freedom of manoeuvre to develop their tactics. Without this, they will turn into sects which have no political influence and are incapable of action... The Party should cooperate with other workers' organisations, not

---

35   This is directed mainly against Hugo Eberlein, who was regarded as the KPD leader most compromised by his actions during March 1921 as head of the Party's military apparatus. He did in fact retreat temporarily to Moscow, though he remained a member of the KPD leadership until 1928.

36   *Kommunistische Arbeitsgemeinschaft* (Communist Working Group). This was set up by Paul Levi and other expelled communists in September 1921. The group was not intended to become a political party but to work for a reformed and independent KPD. When this was found to be impossible the group joined the USPD. For its programme, see below, Chapter 12.

attempt to expose them as traitors. It is wrong to attack the KAG: they still believe in the revolution and in the building of a big communist party ... If the *Zentrale* rejects the demands of the KAG, the left wing will again win the upper hand in the Party and it will be destroyed.

Note: The apparent issue at stake in this dispute between Ernst Friesland, at that time the leader of the Party, and his opponents, was the attitude the Party should take up towards the KAG, the group set up by the expelled former leader, Paul Levi. The KAG explicitly rejected any idea of leaving the KPD. Its aim however was to persuade the KPD to become more independent. Thus the real issue was in fact relations with the Executive Committee of the Communist International, hence with Moscow. Loyalty to the International was the decisive factor when the Political Bureau voted on 12 December 1921 by five votes to three to remove Friesland as General Secretary of the Party.[37]

Source: Friesland, *Zur Krise unserer Partei*, Berlin, 1921, pp. 1–14.

6.5 Grigorii Zinoviev's Letter of 18 July 1922 to the KPD Leadership About the Berlin Agreement for Joint Action

A Confidential Letter to the German Party

I turn now to the attitude of the Party. We have as far as possible followed the course of events in Germany. We have read your reports very attentively and thank you for their thoroughness. The tactics you pursued in the first few days [after the murder of Walter Rathenau] seem to all of us to have been feeble, to judge from the way they are expressed in *Die Rote Fahne*. One should not have cried 'Republic! Republic!' in the kind of situation that existed then. One should rather have put before the eyes of the masses the fact that present-day Germany is a republic without republicans. One ought at this moment of agitation to have demonstrated to the broad working masses, who are not so much interested in the republic as in their economic interests, that the bourgeois republic is not only no guarantee that the class interests of the proletariat will be protected, it is in the given situation exactly the reverse, it is the best form for the oppression of the toiling masses. One ought not to play one single note in harmony with the SPD and the USPD. The united front should never, never, never exclude the independence of our agitation. That independence is a *conditio sine qua non* for the united front. We are prepared to negotiate with the SPD and USPD people, but not as poor relations. We negotiate as an

---

37   See Broué 2005, p. 573.

independent force, with a face of its own, which it always keeps, and opinions of its own, which it tells the masses from A to Z.

Source: Kommunistische Internationale 1922, *Protokoll des IV. Kongresses der Kommunistischen Internationale, Petrograd-Moskau, vom 5.November bis 5. Dezember 1922*, p. 198.

Note: When, at the Fourth Comintern Congress, Zinoviev revealed the existence of this letter, there was some disagreement as to whether or not it constituted an official communication from the ECCI. In form it was a private letter from Zinoviev, and thus a typical example of the Comintern's way of bypassing its own official machinery. Was it to be treated as an official instruction? If so it had to be obeyed. Or was it an underhand intrigue aimed at strengthening the ultra-left opposition to the then leader of the KPD, Ernst Meyer? The latter interpretation is made highly plausible by a passage from Meyer's letter of 24 July 1922 to his wife, Rosa Meyer-Leviné, in which he describes the miserable defeat suffered by August Kleine (Samuel Guralsky), the ECCI's representative, at a recent session of the ZA, and adds, 'the main impulse to Kleine's behaviour [in siding with the ultra-left] was provided by a stupid letter from Zinoviev to us, in which he advocated independent action by the KPD, at least a 24-hour protest strike.'[38]

6.6 *Heinrich Brandler on His Discussions with the Leaders of the Comintern During the Summer of 1923*

I was in the Soviet Union ... from the middle of April until the middle of May 1923, at the session of the ECCI at which we were compelled to include Ernst Thälmann and Ruth Fischer in the *Zentrale*. It was at this meeting that Trotsky discovered in the shape of Thälmann the 'proletarian gold' that was needed to provide a counterweight in the *Zentrale* to my 'Social-Democratic tendencies'. That provided extra support for Zinoviev's faction in the KPD. Stalin intervened too, winning to his side Maslow, who had been retained in Moscow at Lenin's suggestion. I was against this method, but I went along with it, just as I submitted to discipline in the session from the middle of August to the end of September. This second session was the one in which the plan of action for the revolution was decided ... Radek introduced the April meeting, and Trotsky introduced the one in September ... Neither in Moscow, nor during Radek's and Piatakov's stay in Germany, did we learn anything of the Russian factional struggles. That is hard to believe, but it is a fact. Only in December 1923 did

---

38   Weber 1968, p. 186.

we learn of these conflicts, after Zinoviev's letter accusing me of treachery to the revolution ... [A month later, on 21 January 1924 the Presidium of the ECCI passed a resolution on 'The Lessons of the German Events'.] Neither Thalheimer nor myself accepted it. As late as the Fifth Congress[39] I declared that I would strive for it to be revised. This revision could not take place, because the question of the German October was entangled with the factional struggle in the Soviet Union. And that is how the KPD was ruined ...

I did not oppose the preparations for the uprising of 1923. I simply did not view the situation as acutely revolutionary yet, reckoning rather with a further sharpening. But in this affair I considered Trotsky, Zinoviev and other Russians to be more competent – mistakenly. I strongly objected to the attempt to hasten the revolutionary crisis by including communists in the Saxon and Thuringian governments – allegedly in order to procure weapons. I knew, and I said so in Moscow, that the police in Saxony and Thuringia did not have any stores of weapons ... I declared further that the entry of the communists into the government would not breathe new life into the mass actions, but rather weaken them; for now the masses would expect the government to do what they could only do themselves. I did not understand why a fixed date was to be set for the revolution, and I said that for this purpose they would have to send us someone with expert knowledge ... In secret discussions I was offered not only deliveries of weapons, but also eventual military assistance in East Prussia ... Our friends demanded [in 1924] that we [Brandler and Thalheimer] should refuse to submit to the order [from the ECCI] exiling us to Moscow and take up the fight at home, and be prepared even to split the Party. I rejected this idea because [among other things] the KPD was financed by the Comintern, which enabled it to issue twenty-seven newspapers and pay two hundred functionaries. Even if ... we were to win over half the membership, we would not be able to publish as many as four newspapers or pay a dozen functionaries from our own resources.

Source: 'Letter from Heinrich Brandler to Isaac Deutscher', in 'The Brandler-Deutscher Correspondence', *New Left Review*, 105, pp. 72–7.

6.7 *The ECCI's Confidential Letter to the KPD* Zentrale, *Sent in Late November or Early December 1923*

Your over-estimation of the level of political and technical preparation led unavoidably to the political error you made. We in Moscow regarded the entry

---

39   The Fifth Congress of the Communist International, which was held between 17 June and 8 July 1924.

of the communists into the Saxon government only as a military-strategic manoeuvre. You turned it into a political bloc with 'left' Social Democracy which tied your hands. We saw the matter in this way, that entry into the Saxon government would signify the conquest of an area of concentration from which we could develop the strength of our armies. You turned participation in the Saxon ministry into a banal parliamentary combination with the Social Democrats. The result was our political defeat. And what is even worse, something very reminiscent of a comedy occurred. We can tolerate a defeat in a struggle, but when a revolutionary gets into a well-nigh ridiculous situation on the eve of an uprising, that is worse than a defeat. In the whole of the Reich the Party entirely failed to conduct a policy which could and must form the introduction to the decisive struggle. Not one single decisive revolutionary step was taken. You did not even talk a relatively clear communist language. There was no serious step to further the arming of the working class in Saxony, no serious practical measures were taken to create Councils there. Instead of this we had a 'gesture' by Böttcher, who declared that he would not leave the building of his ministry until he was forcibly removed (on 29 October 1923). No, comrades, that is not the way one prepares a revolution.

Source: Zinoviev quoted this letter in his speech to the 13th Party Conference of the RCP (b) 16–18 January 1924, also published in German in *Internationale Pressekorrespondenz*, 4: 16, 4 February 1924, p. 169.

Note: This unfair and unjust attack on the Brandler *Zentrale* in the immediate aftermath of the October defeat was dictated by Zinoviev's need to preserve his position as head of the ECCI and to dissociate himself from errors for which he was equally responsible. The fact that this distorted account was not contradicted (even by Trotsky) at the 13th. Party Conference throws light on the subordination of the KPD to the Comintern. The ECCI never made a mistake, it was thought; if mistakes were made, it was the fault of the individual communist parties.

6.8   *Zinoviev's Letter of 31 March 1924 to Ruth Fischer and Arkady Maslow*
To Comrades Arkady Maslow and Ruth Fischer

Dear Comrades,

An attitude seems to have arisen among you to the effect that we have given way to the complaints of the 'Centre Group', and that we are hesitating as to whether we ought to share with you the responsibility for the new leadership of the KPD, as if we are not placing the necessary confidence in you, or as if we are wrapping ourselves up in the gowns of infallible schoolmasters, subjecting their new pupils to a strict examination. All that is nonsense. In reality we are completely ready to bear along with you the full responsibility for the course of events in the KPD if a Left majority is available and ready to give full support to the coming Left *Zentrale*... If, despite this, we are disturbed, this is to be ascribed to a number of serious facts.

The trade-union question is decisive. If either of you thinks he or she can rapidly invent a 'new type' of proletarian mass organisation, then he or she is committing a very big mistake. The trade unions are not an invention [but] the historically given form of proletarian mass organisation for the length of a whole epoch... One should not allow oneself to be influenced on this point by KAPD attitudes, because that would signify the *ruin of the Party*.

Consider this: if one gives way to the 'new tactics' in the trade union question,[40] if one appeals in questions of organisation to the tradition of Rosa Luxemburg, which is in this respect Menshevik,[41] if one adopts resolutions against the united front tactic as such, if one adopts an incorrect tone towards Soviet Russia (cf. *Der Rote Kurier*),[42] if one speculates on a so-called 'crisis in the Communist International', where does one then differ from the KAPD?

Do not comfort yourselves by saying that the ultra 'left' does not represent a serious force at present... The present German situation objectively contains the danger referred to by Lenin as 'Left Liquidationism'. If you do not decide openly to oppose this left liquidationism you will yourselves become prisoners of it. You have reported very thoroughly on the petty machinations of one or the other member of the 'Centre Group'. But all that is stuff and nonsense compared with the question of whether you are going to make ideological concessions to left liquidationism. If you do, we shall be obliged to enter into open polemics against you and struggle against you. If not, we shall not differ from you...

Your opponents, such as Radek and company, are doubtless speculating on your committing some serious errors [at the forthcoming Party Congress of the KPD] in order to take their revenge above all before the public opinion of the Russian communists. We on the other hand are convinced that our delegation

---

40 By 'new tactics', Zinoviev means the Left's decision to set up industrial unions which were independent of the existing trade unions, and to call upon communists to leave the latter and join the former.

41 A reference to articles in RF on 21 and 25 March 1924 in support of Rosa Luxemburg's views on organisational questions by one of the leading 'ultra-leftists', Arthur Rosenberg, and his young Berlin supporter Samosch Muschinski, of whom little is known except that he was of Russian origin.

42 This newspaper was the Leipzig organ of the KPD. It was under the control of the ultra-left at this time.

[the ECCI delegation to the KPD Party Congress] will succeed in arriving at an agreement with you on all the most important questions.

Moscow, 31 March 1924   G. Zinoviev

P.S. I am not quite clear as to how far Rosenberg and Scholem will stick to their 'ultra-left' errors. We hope they do not. For in that case comradely cooperation with them would be entirely impossible.

Source: *Bundesarchiv, Koblenz*, R 43 /2671, L 483182–4. Printed in H. Weber (ed.) 1968, 'Dokumentation zu den Beziehungen zwischen der KPD und der KI', VJFZ, 16, pp. 190–1.

Note: This letter from Zinoviev to the two main leaders of the left current in the KPD in 1924 is an interesting example of the attempt to split the Left, or at least capitalise on the divisions within it before it had even taken control of the Party. Even more remarkably, Zinoviev and Bukharin also sent a joint letter to Thälmann and Schlecht letting them know about the letter to Fischer and Maslow, but they did not inform Fischer and Maslow about this second letter. Clearly Thälmann was already a favoured candidate for the future leadership, even at this early date, partly because, as Brandler implied (see above, 6.6) he had the advantage of being a proletarian rather than an intellectual of bourgeois origin.

6.9   *Open Letter from the ECCI to all Organisations and Members of the KPD, August 1925*

Dear Party Comrades,

    During the last session of the Enlarged Executive – March to April 1925 – and shortly after that, we had a thorough discussion with the KPD's delegates about the areas in which in our opinion the greatest deficiencies in party work have come to light. The most important problem – then and now – is how to increase our Party's *attractiveness*, the problem of winning over the masses, and in particular the masses of Social Democratic workers. Our general political line has been determined from this point of view, and we have looked at the other questions from this angle as well. The following tasks arise in this connection: work in the *trade unions; methods of convincing* the Social Democratic workers (questions of propaganda, 'adopting a different tone' etc.); *the normalisation of party life* (intra-party democracy, utilising the former Opposition, freedom of discussion, submitting party functionaries to re-election, the drawing in of new leading forces) ... and the liquidation of the hidden struggle against the Communist International (liquidation of the practice of sending so-called independent emissaries to other parties, honest implementation of the real Bolshevik line).

The three most important problem areas discussed in the negotiations [between the ECCI and the delegates of the KPD before the Tenth Party Congress] were:

Firstly: *Right deviations.* The ECCI pointed out that a number of right deviations were present within the Fischer-Maslow leading group, such as an excessively parliamentary attitude. Secondly: the trade-union question. It was resolved that a real change of approach had to be made in the trade-union question, and that a strong, viable trade-union section should be demonstratively elected at the Party Congress, or that the Party's new *Zentrale* should be given instructions to do this afterwards. Thirdly: new leading forces. The representatives of the ECCI insisted that new leading forces be elected to the *Zentrale*, in particular comrades experienced in trade-union work, including some oppositional comrades. The purpose of this was not to drag the work 'to the right', as has been asserted with deliberate untruthfulness, but to provide a means of entry for vacillating members of the Party...The ECCI repeated its advice on the composition of the *Zentrale* on *three* subsequent occasions. At the Party Congress, Comrade Ruth Fischer's group not only sabotaged the decisions but treated the ECCI delegation in such a manner that the latter was forced to make a declaration about this. At the end of the Congress an offer of alliance by the Scholem-Rosenberg group against the Executive was tacitly accepted. This was an unprincipled act, since the Congress had been conducted *politically* in a spirit of struggle against the ultra-left...

All this produced a severe crisis. The *first* delegation which came to us [from the KPD] with instructions to demand that the ECCI delegation be disavowed had to admit, after a stormy discussion, that the Executive was in the right...In the meantime, it was decided to have a broader group of representatives sent. Comrade Fischer delayed their arrival with all possible means. The second delegation split up into two groups. Comrade Fischer initially fought against the ECCI's criticisms, but after long discussions...she too gave a declaration in which she recognised their correctness...

[After sections on 'The General Situation' and a critique of 'The Trade Union Work of the Leading Group in the Party' the document proceeds:]

3   The Party's Relationship with the Communist International
Ever broader layers of the [German] working class are driving towards joining up with the victorious working class of the Soviet Union. This process is reflected in our own [party] ranks in a permeation with Leninism, an assimilation of

the experiences of the Bolsheviks. Conversely, the vacillations and betrayals of certain groups of workers influenced by the hue and cry mounted by the bourgeoisie against Moscow find their ultimate reflection in the 'anti-Muscovite' tendencies within our party, tendencies which are directed against the Soviet Union, the Russian Communist Party and the Comintern.

This danger is the more serious in the KPD in that *all* its present tendencies and shades of opinion, without exception, are still strongly influenced by Social Democratic, 'Western European' traditions.

Every deviation from communist politics so far in Germany has started off with an attack on Soviet Russia, the Russian Communist Party or the Comintern. Seven years of experience of the German Revolution teaches us that *all* deviations of this kind, irrespective of whether they were under a right or a 'left' mask, either developed directly into Social Democracy or entered in practice into an alliance with it. This is true of the KAPD, Levi, Friesland, some of the Brandlerites, the Schumacher[43] group and so on.

The change in the political situation, the definitive move by the German bourgeoisie towards a Western orientation, and the anti-Russian agitation of Social Democracy, which is now at its height, all make the danger of anti-Bolshevik deviations in the KPD greater and more acute than ever before.

The ultra-left Scholem-Rosenberg-Katz group, which accuses the Comintern and its most important parties of 'opportunism', not only has nothing in common with Leninism but has assumed an explicitly anti-Bolshevik character in its attitude to the problems of the German Revolution.

But dangerous and essentially Social-Democratic deviations of this kind exist not only in the officially ultra-left group but also among the leading personalities of the Maslow-Ruth Fischer group. The writings of Comrade Maslow cannot be evaluated as a contribution to the serious, conscientious theoretical education of the Party in the spirit of Leninism. In particular, his latest literary works constitute a hidden and extremely dangerous attack on the foundations of Leninism and the whole policy of the Comintern in the present period ... Behind the mask of a struggle against Trotskyism and the renegade [Paul] Levi, Maslow attacks Lenin, claiming that he 'misconceived the true character of the KPD' [in 1921]. Under the mantle of a struggle against

---

43   Wilhelm Schumacher (born in 1880), 1910 SPD, 1917 USPD, 1919 KPD, trade unionist and
        ultra-leftist. He split the Berlin Clothing Workers' Union in 1924 by founding a separate,
        communist-run trade union, and he continued to advocate a policy of splitting the trade
        unions, even at the Fifth Comintern Congress, to which he was a delegate. Condemned by
        as a deviationist for this, he was expelled from the KPD in September 1924, along with two
        other leaders of separate communist trade unions.

'Western European' deviations from communism, Maslow propagates a 'Western European communism' of the worst kind. It is no accident that precisely now, in 1925, Comrade Maslow makes the Third World Congress [of the Comintern] the target of his attack. The Third World Congress embodies *that concrete element* in the development of Leninism which is of the greatest immediate practical significance for all communist parties in the present situation, and first and foremost for the German Party... The Third Congress worked out the concrete policy of the communist parties in the present period of transition between two revolutions. It placed the slogan 'To the masses' in the centre of our policy, that is to say it set the course towards the winning over of the immense majority of the working class. It thereby established the starting-point for the Bolshevik tactic of the *united front*, which forms the *axis* of our present policy.

Anyone who denies this very important turning point in our tactics – as Comrade Maslow has done – anyone who discredits it as a 'right turn' or derides it as a concession to Trotskyism thereby attacks the foundations of the Comintern... The attitude of the group of Comrade Maslow to the Comintern has been incorrect and un-Bolshevik since the Third World Congress... In the course of the last year, and despite the objections of the Executive, Comrade Ruth Fischer has repeatedly sent out emissaries to various sections of the Comintern with the 'mission' of altering the tactics of the Executive by factional means... These [anti-Bolshevik] tendencies found a particularly sharp expression at the latest Party Congress of the KPD. All the Executive's proposals on the trade union question and the question of the composition of the *Zentrale* were rejected, despite the promises given beforehand. There was no reference at the Congress to the promised demonstrative turn in our trade union policy, apart from in Comrade Thälmann's speech. The whole German Party, above all the best comrades of the German Left in all the organisations and districts of the Party, has the duty to exert all its strength to break with the un-Bolshevik system promoted by the Maslow-Fischer group in relations between the Party and the Comintern. There must be a definitive break with the system of 'double book-keeping' employed for a whole year towards the Comintern by those comrades. Instead of honestly carrying out the correct line of the Comintern this group pursued continuous delaying tactics, telling their own Party's members about an alleged 'rightward pressure' coming from the Executive, and telling the Executive about an alleged 'pull towards the ultra-left' coming from members of the Party itself.

The experiences of the period of struggle since the Frankfurt Party Congress [of 1924] have demonstrated to every single German communist that the Comintern was absolutely right as against the Maslow-Fischer group on *all* disputed questions. It was right about the united front tactic and the trade-union question. It was also right about the presidential elections, and right too in its warnings – ignored for a year – about the ultra-left danger in the Party. We are firmly convinced that the communist workers of Germany will recognise very quickly that the Comintern is absolutely right about the present issues, whereas the Maslow-Ruth Fischer group is absolutely wrong.

Source: *Die Rote Fahne*, 1 September 1925; *Inprekorr*, No. 128, 4 Sept. 1925, pp. 1863–70.

Note: The 'Open Letter' was secretly adopted in Moscow by the Presidium of the ECCI in the middle of August 1925. It reflected the fury of both Zinoviev and Bukharin at the disobedience of the Fischer-Maslow leadership of the KPD. The German communist leaders at first tried to defend themselves against the Russians' attacks, but soon gave way, and eventually the open letter was signed by every member of the German delegation. It was greeted with astonishment in Germany, as no one outside the inner circle had any idea that there was a conflict between the Comintern and the KPD leadership.[44]

6.10   The Secret Agreement of 29 February 1928 Made at a Joint Session of KPD and Soviet Communist Party Delegates

The joint session of the delegates of the KPD and the AUCP (B) hereby resolves:

1) that the right danger in the working-class movement in Germany, the expression of which is the SPD, represents the main danger
2) that this situation makes it necessary to direct the attention of party members more strongly towards the struggle against the right danger in the Party (including Trotskyism)
3) that overcoming the ultra-left danger constitutes one of the necessary prerequisites for a successful struggle against the right danger within the Party, as also in the working-class movement in general
4) that this standpoint rules out any toleration of the carriers of the right danger within the Party and that a genuine concentration of revolutionary forces in the Party can only be achieved, and must be achieved, on the basis of this line
5) it follows from the above that

---

44   Weber 1969, vol. 1, p. 126.

a) the selection of Party workers for leading functions in all areas of party work, inside and outside the Reichstag, must be subordinated to the requirements of this line;

b) the immediate reorganisation of the trade union section in accordance with the policy of the CC of the KPD is necessary

c) it would be inappropriate to put forward comrades Brandler and Thalheimer as candidates for the Reichstag

6) attention must be directed to the application of objective criticisms to shortcomings in party work, to the improvement of the practical work of the CC of the KPD, and to raising the level of work by selecting new forces and drawing them into the work in leading roles.

Moscow, 29 February 1928

Signed:

Thälmann, Ewert, Remmele, Dengel, Gerhart, H. Neumann, C. Blenkle
Bukharin, Stalin, Tomsky, Molotov, Lozovsky, A. Mikoyan, Pyatnitsky

Source: *Vierteljahreshefte für Zeitgeschichte*, 16, No. 2, April 1968, pp. 207–8.

Note: As required by the agreement, clauses 5b and 5c were immediately applied. There was a thorough purge of the Party's trade union section, starting at the top with the sacking of Jakob Walcher,[45] its director. Brandler and Thalheimer were not put forward as KPD candidates for the Reichstag. The other changes occurred more gradually over the year.

6.11 Instructions from the Secretariat to the District Leaderships (15 November 1930)

Fascism remains the main enemy of the Party in the class struggle, Social Democracy remains the main enemy within the proletariat. It must be stressed that the Party as a whole has not in its activity met the tremendous demands which are posed by the present situation. Any tendency either to rest in a self-satisfied way on the laurels of the 14 September [elections] or to accept Fascist dictatorship fatalistically as an unavoidable fact must be resisted unconditionally. Recruitment work for the Party and the press, at present completely inadequate, must immediately be raised to the highest level.

The most important task now is to open heavy ideological and political fire on German Fascism, above all on the National Socialist movement. The Nazis

---

45 Jakob Walcher (1887–1970), Spartacist, founder-member of the KPD, member of the *Zentrale* 1919–23, in charge of trade-union work until 1928. Expelled from the Party for rightist deviations in 1928. Member of the KPO 1928–32. Joined the SAP in 1932.

should be given no time to regroup their forces, to catch their breath, to accustom themselves to their new tasks as a future government party. What we lack is not so much 'new slogans' as rather exposure of the Nazis using concrete facts, using all the betrayals of the national and social interests of the working people that they commit every day inside and outside parliament ...

It is particularly important in the fight against the National Socialists to make use of all the arguments of international policy which make our campaign easier. Particular attention must be paid to the decline of Italian Fascism, to the economic crisis, the wage cuts and the unemployment in Mussolini's 'Third Reich'. At the same time we must conduct an effective, resounding mass propaganda campaign for the Soviet Union and the successes of socialism ...

Social Democracy has made considerable progress on the path of betrayal. The appointment of Severing and Grzesinski[46] is the public expression of firm agreements reached secretly between Brüning and the Party leadership of the SPD. Social Fascism in Germany has thus reached a new level of development, the highest so far. The Social Democratic leadership has removed every hesitation in its own ranks, every inclination to toy with the idea of opposing the establishment of Fascist dictatorship in Germany. It is firmly resolved to cooperate actively in the establishment of Fascist dictatorship. It regards it as its special 'historic mission' to employ the Severing-Grzesinski police apparatus with ruthless energy and harshness against the revolutionary proletariat, against the starving unemployed, against the striking masses of workers, against the Communist Party, against all revolutionary mass organisations. The prohibition of *Die Rote Fahne*, the central organ of our Party, the police surveillance of all communist demonstrations, the open, Fascist, breach of all the 'freedoms' guaranteed in the Weimar constitution, are intended to be the starting signal for the prohibition of demonstrations in Berlin and all over Prussia, the provocation of bloody clashes, and – sooner or later – the banning, the violent suppression, of the Communist Party.

The three great links in the chain of proletarian revolution are:

1 Ideological, political and militant mass struggle against Fascism
2 The unleashing of economic struggles in all industries and regions of Germany
3 The strongest possible promotion of the fight of the unemployed, firm leadership of the unemployed movement, the organisation of the unemployed under the banner of the RGO, and a close fighting alliance between the unemployed and the factory workers.

---

46   Albert Grzesinski (1879–1947), SPD, member of the Prussian Diet 1921–33, Berlin Police Chief 1925–26 and 1930–33. Prussian Minister of the Interior 1926–30.

All three tasks have as their prerequisite the unmasking of Social Democracy, particularly its sham radical 'left wing', leading to the liquidation of the reformists' mass influence and the destruction of Social Democracy as a party.

Source: Hermann Weber and Johann Wachtler (eds.), 1981, *Die Generallinie. Rundschreiben des Zentralkomitees der KPD an die Bezirke 1929–1933*, no. 31, 15.11.1930, 'Anweisungen des Sekretariats an die Bezirksleitungen', pp. 236–40 (extracts).

Note: These instructions show that after the elections of September 1930 there was a degree of recognition of the Nazi danger within the KPD leadership, but it had always to be balanced with the need to destroy Social Democracy, as the party of 'Social Fascism'. The KPD leaders thought that Brüning's 1 December 1930 presidential decree issued under Article 48, which reduced state employee's salaries and increased taxes on consumer goods proved that a 'Fascist dictatorship' had already been established in Germany. The view in Moscow was different (Stalin described the draft resolution as 'worthless'), and after a 'stubborn fight' by the KPD leaders, they had to give way and agree that Fascism had not yet come to Germany, although it was 'ripening'. It is not clear why Stalin took up this rather sensible position. It may have been for foreign policy reasons, because relations with Brüning's government were better than they had been with the previous SPD government, or it may have been because he didn't want the KPD to give the impression that the fight against Fascism had already been lost.[47]

6.12 Resolution by the Political Secretariat of the ECCI on the Referendum in Germany (*Moscow, 16 September 1931, Secret*)

The Communist Party has succeeded in convincing significant masses of Social Democrats and reformist trade unionists of the counter-revolutionary character of the policy of the 'lesser evil'. The KPD's ultimatum, and Severing's reply, have shown to the workers, including the Social Democratic workers, that Social Democracy is a direct ally of monopoly capital and its policy of plundering the working masses, and is directly responsible for starvation, poverty and unemployment... Without isolating Social Democracy there cannot be a victorious struggle against Fascism and the capitalist offensive. The united front of Hugenberg-Severing-Seydewitz-Brandler has taught us this. The shameful collapse of Social Fascism's endeavours to use its most 'leftish' detachments in a provocative and demagogic exploitation of the 'democratic' illusions of the masses against the Communist Party has forced it to go over to open police

---

47 See the discussion in Hoppe 2007, p. 190.

violence, to deprive the masses of workers of their 'democratic liberties' and thereby to expose its actual *bloc* with the Fascists. The 'left' Social Democrats have been forced to reveal themselves openly as a buffer between the KPD and the mass of Social Democratic workers, and the Brandlerist and Trotskyist renegades have openly revealed themselves as a direct agency of Social Fascism.

The significance of the referendum consists in this, that despite the conditions of harsh police terror in which it took place, despite the banning of the communist press and the outlawing of revolutionary meetings and demonstrations, the Communist Party succeeded in a short space of time in mobilising its forces, displaying by that very fact its high degree of manoeuvrability. At the same time, the referendum campaign once again revealed the fundamental weakness of the KPD at the present stage: the position of the Party in the factories seriously lags behind its general growth. This finds expression in a series of cases in its highly inadequate resistance in the factories to the poisonous and demagogic attacks of the Social Democrats. Agitational work, which started very late, as a result of the overall tardiness of the KPD's campaign for the referendum, was not supported by a sufficiently strong organisational system in the factories... The decisive significance of the referendum campaign consisted not in the voting itself but in the extra-parliamentary organisation of the masses of the German proletariat for a decisive resistance against the preparations of the German bourgeoisie, with the aid of Social Democracy, for a 'grand plan' of an offensive against working people's standard of living under the flag of 'self-help'.

Endeavouring to create the conditions for an open and unhindered cooperation with the German bourgeoisie in the task of implementing the 'grand plan' of a capitalist exit from the crisis, Social Democracy is the main striking-force in all the bourgeoisie's attempts to force the Communist Party into illegality, fearing that it will expose it before the broad masses of workers.

Source: Komolova (ed.), 1999, 'Rezoliutsiia Politsekretariata IKKI o referendume v Germanii' in *Komintern protiv Fashizma, Dokumenty* Moscow, *Nauka* No. 70, pp. 273–4.

6.13   *The KPD's Guidelines for its Anti-Fascist Action (26 May 1932)*

The events in the Prussian Diet[48] must be utilised, in line with the Central Committee's call for Anti-Fascist Action,[49] to create the greatest possible

---

48   On the 24th and 25th of May 1932 the newly elected NSDAP deputies in the Prussian Diet attacked the KPD's main speaker, Wilhelm Pieck, who was defended by his colleagues. There were violent physical clashes, which resulted in the suspension of the session.

49   The CC of the KPD proclaimed its 'Anti-Fascist Action' on the same day, 26 May.

reinforcement of the mass struggle against Fascism and the formation of a broad united front movement, which we are calling into existence under the overall slogan of 'Anti-Fascist Action'. In this connection it is of decisive importance that we present ourselves boldly and self-confidently to the masses, concentrate everything on the unified mass struggle and fight against moods of depression or individualistic putschism. The following are the most important political points to bear in mind in the campaign, which must start immediately:

1 The Fascist threat to the German working class has entered an acute stage, when any loss of tempo in regard to the defensive action of the working class could bring about fateful consequences. Only the immediate introduction of militant actions by the broad masses can prevent the participation of *Hitler* Fascism in the government, which would signify a very dangerous step on the way to Fascist dictatorship in Germany.

2 The events in the Diet have again made clear to the masses the role of the Nazis as the active terror organisation of finance capital, the goal of which is open Fascist dictatorship. The attack in the Diet serves to mask their anti-working class role, it signifies an attempt to divert the masses of their supporters and the revolutionary proletariat towards individual terror or to create moods of depression in the proletariat. The attack arises from their powerless fury over the way the communists have exposed them politically (exposing their avoidance of discussion of the demands of the unemployed, Versailles, etc.).

3 The cowardly, denunciatory and hypocritical role of the SPD *Fraktion*, which is attempting to absolve the Nazis and lay blame on the KPD, is a continuation of the Braun-Severing policy of doing the dirty work for Fascism, and it again characterises the role of the leaders of the SPD and the ADGB in serving the capitalist system and Fascism. Its present attitude already clearly shows what role it will play in the coming struggles of the German working class against Fascism.

[4,5]

6 The 'Anti-Fascist Action' does not signify even the slightest lessening of the struggle against Social Fascism, or the slightest concession to the method of bargaining between leaders. It is not a united front from above, but the organisation of a broad mass movement from below. The 'Anti-Fascist Action' must be organised as a mass movement through the collective decision to join of all the workers in a factory or a department, or local trade-union organisations and mass organisations of other kinds such as oppositional groups of the *Reichsbanner*, the SPD or the SAP. Collective decisions of this kind must never take place through agreements between leaders or in return for political concessions, but on the basis of revolutionary mass mobilisation from below.

7 What is decisive is the immediate introduction of fighting measures of 'Anti-Fascist Action', the organisation of red mass self-protection in the factories, at the unemployment exchanges and in working-class districts. The taking up of mass work, starting from the factory, in the rural districts, and among certain middle-class strata, the creation of a broad and active mass mood of hatred and the will to fight against bloody *Hitler* Fascism. Such an offensive anti-Fascist mass mood is the best way of bringing to a halt the wave of Fascist chauvinism.

[A number of concrete measures for the Party's districts to take are then outlined.]

Berlin, 26 May 1932   Central Committee of the KPD

Source: Weber, H. and Wachtler (eds.), 1981, 'Rundtelefonat des ZK zur Antifascistische Aktion' in *Die Generallinie. Runschreiben des Zentralkomitees der KPD an die Bezirke 1929–1933*, 26.5.1932:, doc.64, pp. 489–91 (extracts).

CHAPTER 7

Socialism and Foreign Policy

Introduction

Immediately after coming to power in November 1918, the Council of People's Representatives accepted the policy recommendations of the officials they had inherited from the previous era, the SPD members wholeheartedly, the USPD with some reservations. The People's Representatives wanted to secure an agreed peace with the West, and engage in active hostility against Soviet Russia in the East. As Ulrich Brockdorff-Rantzau,[1] the new German Foreign Minister, pointed out in February 1919: 'We are in fact in a state of war with Russia'. Hugo Haase, speaking for the USPD, claimed later that the government of which he was a member had followed a socialist foreign policy, but there appears to be no trace of this. Continuity with the previous regime was demonstrated both in the cautious and conciliatory approach taken to the armed forces (for which see Chapter Eight) and in the setting of foreign policy objectives (7.4). But a sense of the reality of military defeat and the impossibility of resisting the demands of the victorious Entente Powers compelled the Social Democrats to modify their position on this. Philipp Scheidemann resigned rather than sign the Versailles Treaty; but his successor as Chancellor, Gustav Bauer, was also a member of the SPD and he did sign it.

In subsequent years the SPD pursued a pro-Western orientation in foreign policy, although this did not rule out the objective of revising the Versailles Treaty, which they had in common with most of German opinion. The way to revise Versailles, the SPD said, was through peaceful negotiations with the West, while maintaining friendly relations with all the powers. This meant that they opposed any attempt to forge a separate alliance against Versailles with Soviet Russia. As Hermann Müller put it in 1921 'We are placing our hopes on the revision of the treaty, not on intrigues' (7.8). The KPD, in contrast, naturally favoured a Soviet alliance, as did the extreme right (for different reasons).

The Franco-Belgian occupation of the Ruhr in January 1923 caused considerable indignation among most, perhaps all, Germans. 'A cry of indignation rose up from the whole German nation', wrote Otto Braun, 'and it had a strong impact on me as well, although I was always accustomed to judging political

---

1 Ulrich Graf von Brockdorff-Rantzau (1869–1928), German Foreign Minister 1918–19, Ambassador to Moscow 1922–28.

events with calm sobriety'.[2] The SPD was out of office at the time, but the Cuno government was keen to involve the Party, and the trade unions, in its policy of passive resistance to the occupiers. The left of the SPD was hesitant about joining hands with the nationalist Right in this way, but by mid-January the Party leaders had won the day and the SPD decided in favour. Breitscheid went so far as to describe the passive resistance as a 'proletarian class struggle', adding that 'the French policy of violence would be defeated by the non-violence of the working class'.[3] The KPD saw the foreign policy crisis as a political opportunity. It was considered that the rising German nationalist agitation could somehow be converted into a revolution against the bourgeois republic, or at least that nationalist revolutionaries (including the Nazis) could be turned into communists by appealing to the common foreign policy interests of Germany and the Soviet Union in destroying the hated Versailles Treaty. The Bolsheviks also shared this view. Karl Radek, with his equally strong Russian and German connections, was the ideal person to put the idea forward (7.10). He later explained the 'Schlageter line' succinctly in an article in the Party newspaper: 'It would be ridiculous to think that Fascism could be defeated solely by the force of arms. One must fight against it politically ... by showing the petty-bourgeois masses the true road of struggle for their own interests. They are fighting against Germany's enslavement by the Versailles Treaty'. But the KPD is fighting for the same thing, he added. Hence 'the German communists are obliged to do all they can to convince the petty-bourgeois Fascist elements that communism is not the enemy but a shining star pointing the way to victory'.[4] If 'victory' had been achieved in 1923, however, it would have been either a communist victory over Fascism, or a Fascist victory over communism, not a joint victory by both sides. There seems, however, to have been no opposition within the KPD to Radek's idea, although Hermann Remmele did note the irony of engaging in friendly negotiations with people who 'murdered Karl Liebknecht and Rosa Luxemburg'.[5] This curious episode in communist history did not last long, but it had a certain significance, first in that it paralleled the continuing secret Soviet-German collaboration in undermining the military provisions of the Versailles Treaty, and second in that it pointed the way to the return to a 'national populist' line by the KPD in 1930.

After the storms of the French occupation of the Ruhr and the hyperinflation had died down, the SPD consistently supported the policy of Gustav Stresemann, now a permanent fixture as Germany's Foreign Minister (until

2   Braun 1949, p. 122.
3   Feucht 1998, p. 253.
4   *Die Rote Fahne* 1923, 27 July 1923.
5   Speaking on 12 August 1923 in Stuttgart (Weber 1969, vol. 1, p. 49, n. 105.)

his death in 1929). Stresemann aimed to achieve a reconciliation with the Western powers, and, by accepting that Germany had to pay reparations, to persuade them gradually to remove or alleviate the more onerous aspects of the Versailles Treaty, such as the continued occupation of the Rhineland and the severe restrictions on German armaments. In the long run, this policy was extremely successful. The Western powers evacuated the Rhineland, and the Military Control Commission, the body which had attempted to check up on the status of German re-armament throughout the 1920s, was withdrawn in January 1927. Under the Young Plan of 1929, strongly supported by the SPD, Germany recovered her full sovereignty. The next step was to get rid of the reparations payments altogether. This was Brüning's main foreign policy aim after 1930, and he achieved this, thanks to the economic and financial crisis of the early 1930s. In June 1931 reparations payments were suspended for a year, under the 'Hoover Moratorium'. But this was not enough. The weaker Germany's financial position, the stronger Brüning felt. By January 1932 he felt strong enough to tell the British ambassador that Germany would never pay any more reparations. The SPD leaders, who still supported the government at that stage, were uneasy about this confrontational approach, preferring, as Breitscheid said in December 1931, to leave open the possibility of paying reparations in the future, in order to keep on good terms with the French socialists, and to distinguish SPD policy from that of the German nationalists. Leipart, the head of the Free Trade Unions, in contrast, demanded the immediate abolition of all reparations payments and war debts, claiming that Germany 'had already made all the reparation that needed to be made',[6] then in June 1932 at the Lausanne Conference they were finally abandoned. By that time, however, the SPD's views of foreign policy had ceased to be relevant, as Brüning had been replaced by von Papen and the Party had moved from toleration to opposition.

Documents

7.1   *Philipp Scheidemann's Speech of 12 May 1919 Against the Versailles Treaty*
When I see in your ranks the representatives of all the German tribes (*Stämme*) and lands sitting side by side ... and, sitting side by side with the deputies of the lands that are not under threat, the men (*Männer*) from the threatened lands and provinces who will sit here for the last time as Germans among Germans if our opponents have their way, I am united with you in the seriousness and

---

6   Winkler 1987, p. 464.

sacredness of this moment, over which one single commandment should be written: we belong together (Cries of: Bravo!)...We are one flesh and one blood, and he who tries to divide us cuts with a murderous knife into the living body of the German people...We are not pursuing nationalist chimeras here: no questions of prestige and no thirst for power have any part in our deliberations...The basis of our discussions is as follows: this thick book (pointing to the document containing the Versailles peace conditions) with which a great people is to be forced through blackmail and extortion into agreeing to enslavement and accepting the position of helots cannot be allowed to lay down the law for the future...Without ships, without cables, without colonies, without foreign investments, without the right to collaborate in setting the prices of the goods to be delivered by us as tribute – I ask you, who can, as an honourable person, I will not say as a German, who, as an honourable man of his word, could accept such conditions? What hand would not wither which laid itself and us in these chains?

We have made counter-proposals and we shall make still more. In the view of the government of the Reich, this treaty is *unacceptable* (Long, wild applause)...This treaty is so unacceptable that I still cannot believe that the whole world could tolerate it...Away with this murderous plan!

Brothers in German Austria, who in the darkest hour have not forgotten the road to the total union of the German people, we thank you and hold fast to you!...A united people can do much, especially when it protests not only for itself but for the community of all nations against the perpetuation of hatred, as we do today...We know that the coming peace will be a hard one for us, and we will bear it honourably...but only if it is a peace treaty that can be kept, a treaty that leaves us in existence...We are no longer fighting, we desire peace. A curse on those who started the War! But a triple curse on those who delay a genuine peace even for a day!

Source: Nationalversammlung 1919, *Stenographische Berichte über die Verhandlungen der Verfassunggebenden Deutschen Nationalversammlung*, vol. 327, 38th. Sitting, 12, pp. 1082–6.

Note: Scheidemann's feelings were shared by almost the whole of the National Assembly. The only sign of dissent to the picture of complete national unity from right to left came from the USPD (the KPD was not represented in the Assembly, but see 7.2 for its position). For the USPD, Hugo Haase began like everyone else by pointing to the injustice of the peace conditions, but he also warned against 'stupid and senseless acts arising from anger over the peace', and he claimed that there was an inherent contradiction in a government which called upon the people to stand by it while filling up the prisons with its political opponents, and 'turning the peaceful city of Leipzig into an armed camp'.[7] But on the specific issue of Germany's refusal to sign the peace treaty Haase too was unable to bring himself to oppose the majority view. Even so, despite this unanimity, Germany still had to accept the Versailles Treaty. Hermann Müller, on behalf of the SPD leadership, appealed on 21 June 1919 for a unanimous vote by his Party in favour of the Treaty. Scheidemann himself publicly withdrew his violent remarks about the treaty some months later.[8]

7.2   *'Guidelines on the Peace', Issued by the KPD* Zentrale, *19 May 1919*

I

The peace conditions of the Entente ... are the reflection of the internal and external political and economic situation of Germany after four-and-a-half years of a lost imperialist war and seven months of the political restoration of the imperialist classes by a government of apparent revolution and real counter-revolution ...

II

The political result [of the rule of the government of Ebert and Scheidemann] is the recreation of militarism in the barbaric form of the mercenary army ... They have restored in a new form the mode of domination which existed before the War: the military state.

Imperialist and nationalist tendencies are again operating at full strength. The phraseology has changed – but the essence remains the same. The tactical methods are: to play off moderate American imperialism against the French and English variety, and to use all the internal conflicts of the victorious imperialist powers as a new springboard for an imperialist foreign policy ... Here are the results of this period in foreign policy: the breaking off of relations with Soviet Russia, war against Soviet Russia,[9] war against Poland,[10] the unsuccessful

---

7   Heilfron 1919/20, vol. 4, 39th. Sitting, 12 June 1919, pp. 2696 and 2698.

8   In a speech on 7 October 1919, printed in *Verfassunggebende Nationalversammlung* 1919, p. 2886.

9   This refers to the activities of Reichswehr units led by General von der Goltz in the Baltic lands during 1919.

10   German troops had recently become involved in a military conflict with Polish units in Upper Silesia.

attempt to annex German Austria.[11] In summary: complete isolation in foreign policy.

III

With its peace conditions, the Entente is repressing German neo-imperialism; but at the same time it is trying to repress the coming proletarian revolution. The peace conditions will destroy the military power of German imperialism, but at the same time they will deliver a defenceless proletariat into the hands of the bourgeoisie at home and abroad. The handing over of the criminal generals and politicians of Germany to the Entente's military courts frees the German working class from them, but only in order to whip up chauvinism among the Entente masses. The high level of the tribute burden [the reparation payments imposed by the Treaty of Versailles] and its unlimited nature delivers over Germany's working class and the petit-bourgeoisie to annihilation, along with the bourgeoisie.

The handing over of the Saar district and Upper Silesia and the occupation of the left bank of the Rhine will condemn Germany's industrial production to collapse. The peace conditions of Versailles are distinguished from those of Brest-Litovsk by their refined and systematic nature; those of Brest-Litovsk were just as brutal, but crude. The Versailles conditions are equivalent to those of Brest-Litovsk in their unrestrained and blind instinct for imperialist plunder. Their madness is methodical, whereas Brest-Litovsk was madness without method.

IV

Under the rule of bankrupt German imperialism, the acceptance of the peace conditions ... would be as catastrophic as their rejection. To sign them would be to lead the country to economic collapse and poverty without an end in sight ... Not to sign them would equally abandon the country to deadly exploitation by Entente capital, but in this case made more severe by a military occupation, by foreign domination ... Military resistance is hindered by the fact of the rule of the counter-revolution and of capitalism.

The proletariat is not prepared to fight for the maintenance of its chains. This fact also rules out a military alliance with Soviet Russia and Hungary.[12]

---

11   Ebert called in February 1919 for the unification of Austria with Germany (the so-called *Anschluss*) but this was ruled out at Versailles. The German and Austrian Social Democrats supported the idea, the KPD opposed it at this stage.

12   The KPD thus did not call at this time for an alliance of Soviet Russia with *bourgeois* Germany against the Versailles Treaty. In their view, only the overthrow of the German bourgeoisie could make such an alliance possible.

VI

The only possible, and unavoidable, way out is the overthrow of bourgeois rule. the setting up of the proletarian dictatorship in the shape of the pure Council System, socialist production in industry and agriculture, and hence joining up with the world revolution.

X

The decision on acceptance or rejection of the peace conditions by the government of Councils will depend on the concrete situation.

XI

The KPD therefore rejects the acceptance or the rejection of the peace conditions by the Ebert government as being equally disastrous for the proletariat.

Source: *Die Internationale*, I, 1919, 2/3, pp. 28–32.

7.3 Eduard Bernstein's Speech on the Need to Accept the Versailles Treaty, June 1919

Comrades, the reason why the SPD has lost the great trust, indeed the great love, it enjoyed previously in the International, is well known[13] ... Backward glimpses cannot entirely be avoided, although we all want to go forward.

What we see before us is the result of four-and-a-half years of war, conducted with the means the Party has itself in part condemned ... For me the fourth of August, 1914 was the blackest day of my life. In my view our attitude then was a misfortune for our people, and a misfortune for civilisation. If we had said no to the War, the German people would not have suffered more than they did. But millions fewer would have been killed and crippled in the War.

The peace conditions the Allies have imposed on us are harsh, very harsh, and in part ... *simply impossible*. But Scheidemann too has recognised this: we also recognise the need for a great part of the Treaty. Nine tenths of the conditions are necessary and unavoidable.[14] Dear Comrades! If you disagree, you disavow the German government itself, which has conceded nine-tenths of the conditions. Do not forget one thing: France has been hit harder by the effects of this war than Germany. Any expert can tell you that ... Wels talks as if there were no one but imperialists over there.[15] I should like to warn you against

---

13   The 'obvious reason' is the SPD's continuing support for the German war effort throughout the First World War.

14   The minutes add at this point: 'persistent loud opposition and great turbulence in the hall'.

15   In his official report as the chair of the SPD (see 7.4).

throwing the word 'imperialism' around to such an extent that it loses all its meaning. There are certainly some imperialists over there . . . but if we want to grasp the situation correctly we must bear in mind that there are other parties over there too, great classes not infected by that poison. Patriotism is in itself not something to be rejected, and our attitude, and mine too, is truly not dictated by a lack of patriotic feeling. The demands made of Germany, which are in part very harsh, have in most cases nothing to do with imperialism.

Let us have no intrigues! No secret agents should be sent into other countries! No plots should be hatched! . . . We must make a clean break with this system. We want the policy of the German republic to be honest and upright . . . As a socialist party, a party of the International, we want mutual assistance and aid from other socialist parties. We want to finish with all the plundering of the old diplomacy, the old system. Our foreign policy must be one of unreserved internationalism. That will be the best policy for our people, the best policy for Europe, and the best policy for the whole civilised world.

A regrettable linguistic custom has been retained from the time of cabinet diplomacy: one speaks of countries as of persons, and if one speaks of one's own country one say 'we'. But a country is made up of parties, classes, strata of the most varied kind. If I say 'the German government of that time was guilty', I do not mean 'the people of Germany were guilty', least of all the German working class. When it is said that I stand alone in Germany with my opinions . . . I am man enough to stand alone. I only regret, in the interests of the Party as a whole, that I am almost isolated here.

Source: Sozialdemokratische Partei Deutschlands 1919, *Protokoll über die Verhandlungen des Parteitages der SPD in Weimar*, pp. 241–9, 280.

Note: Bernstein's views were rejected almost unanimously by the Congress. His sole defender was Gustav Hoch.[16] His resolution, no. 242, was struck out and replaced with Resolution 244, introduced by Braun, Löbe and Wels, in which 'indignation' was expressed over the 'unreasonable demands' of the Entente and the 'imposition of a dictated peace'. The peace conditions were declared 'incompatible with the basis of Wilson's peace conditions' and the International was called upon 'to protest against the most unheard of dictated peace in modern history'.

---

16   *Protokoll* 1919, pp. 253–81.

7.4 *Report of the MSPD Party Leadership, Delivered by Otto Wels on*
10 June 1919

In the past few weeks we have lived through the worst period of our history. The past weighs on us heavily and gloomily and the future looks even bleaker. We no longer determine our own fate. On the contrary, it lies in the hands of the victorious imperialism of the Western powers. They are continuing their fight against the German people because our struggle for a better peace is at the same time a struggle for socialism and against any kind of imperialism. The bitterness of our opponents against us is explained by the fact that Germany is the country where the ideals of socialism will have to be realised. We are counting on the support of our like-minded comrades in the West. They must support us, because our struggle for peace is also a struggle for international socialism.... In the days of the collapse the German people had only one hope: German Social Democracy. Our war policy was from the very beginning a peace policy. It won us the confidence of the whole German people, far beyond the circles and strata which supported Social Democracy during the war out of political conviction. It is therefore incomprehensible that resolutions like the one from Jena, Number 183, are brought before this Party Congress.[17] Our success in the elections of 19 January has proved the correctness of our policy during the War. If anyone wanted to question its correctness he would only have to have a look at the past to become convinced he was mistaken.

Source: Sozialdemokratische Partei Deutschlands 1919, *Protokoll über die Verhandlungen des Parteitages der SPD, abgehalten in Weimar, vom 10. bis 15. Juni 1919*, Berlin, 1919, pp. 140–1.

7.5 *Adolf Braun's 1919 Speech on the Relation between Nationalism*
and Socialism

It is definitely no longer necessary to discuss the fourth of August 1914, because a new foundation for the Party's work has been found in the November days of 1918...I am delighted by the national tone taken by comrade Wels.[18] We must decisively and vigorously put forward the national standpoint which is anchored in our international conception. The wave of nationalism from the

---

17   Resolution 183 declared: 'The ruling circles in Germany not only bore their share of guilt for the outbreak of the war, but also were working secretly towards it with the aim of fulfilling their imperialist plans, and they continued this policy throughout the whole of the War. The Party Congress therefore regrets the attitude of the parliamentary party during the war as being in the interest neither of the working class nor of the German people'.

18   See 7.4.

Wilhelmine epoch, the nationalism of the Pan-German and National Liberal imperialists and capitalists, should be dashed to pieces on the rock of our nationalism. Our nationalism does not stand in contradiction to internationalism. This context must be emphasised precisely on the expected eve of a dictated peace...Let us say no more of the causes of the war of 1914. These discussions do not strengthen the Party and they do not make the unification we want [with the USPD] any easier.

Source: Sozialdemokratische Partei Deutschlands 1919, *Protokoll über die Verhandlungen des Parteitages der SPD, abgehalten in Weimar, vom 10. bis 15. Juni 1919*, p. 189.

7.6 *Max Cohen's Plea for Reconciliation with France, Delivered at the 1920 Congress of the SPD*

If we want to achieve any amelioration of the Versailles Treaty we can only do this through an understanding with France. And if France sees that Germany...is ready to go to the limit of what is possible, and, further, if she sees that the great mass of the German people are absolutely opposed to the policy of *revanche*, I am convinced that we shall not only soften the harsh and impractical provisions of the Versailles Treaty but get into a tolerable and constantly improving relationship with our French neighbours. (Interjection: Occupied territory!)

Yes, certainly, things are bad in the occupied territory, and everyone will regret the excesses that take place there, but what happens there is not a specifically French phenomenon. That kind of thing happens everywhere where a country is occupied by foreign troops. And if one looks at the documents on the occupation of France by Germany in 1871 I do not think that any great difference will be perceived. What is important is this: we must make up our minds to stop hoping for help from England. We should not accept any rapprochement with England that is achieved at the cost of a potential understanding with France.

Source: Sozialdemokratische Partei Deutschlands 1920, *Protokoll über die Verhandlungen des Parteitages der SPD, abgehalten in Kassel vom 10. bis 16. Oktober 1920*, pp. 57–8

Note: Cohen's speech was received with indignation (especially his views on the question of Germany's occupied territory). The chair of the Congress, Philipp Scheidemann, summed up the debate by saying that he hoped the whole of Germany did not contain another comrade with Max Cohen's views (p. 70).

7.7   *Karl Franz*[19] *in 1921 on the Need to Defend German National Territory in Upper Silesia*

For us Upper Silesians the question of whether we form a government with the DVP is at the moment fairly irrelevant. At the moment we are happy with any government which manages to keep Upper Silesia as a component part of the German Reich. (Cries of: Bravo!) We live with the danger that we shall be sundered from the Upper Silesian cultural community and thereby thrown back at least one hundred years in our development. We therefore have the most urgent interest ... in preventing this misfortune from befalling the working class of Upper Silesia.

But precisely where the parties of so-called order claim to be helping us, they are failing, and instead bringing about an increase in our misfortunes. The excesses of the Free Corps in Upper Silesia have brought great misery to the Upper Silesian population. These troops were less interested in liberating Upper Silesia from Polish terror than in marching on Berlin to overthrow the government there.[20] In our view the government has not been sufficiently energetic in combating this Free Corps nuisance.

Source: Sozialdemokratische Partei Deutschlands 1921, *Protokoll über die Verhandlungen des Parteitages der SPD, abgehalten in Görlitz, vom 18. bis 24. September 1921*, p. 193.

7.8   *Hermann Müller on the Way to Revise the Versailles Treaty, 1921*

We must demand that this League of Nations be de-politicised ... When the doors of the League are open to us, we shall be ready to cooperate in improving it. The success of this work will depend on the trust we can win in the world as Germans. We are placing our hopes on the revision of the treaty, not on intrigues. We do not want to pursue a policy of alliances with individual nations, but to cooperate with every nation which is willing to work together with us for the peace of the world ... We can only win the confidence of a previously hostile world through a policy of peace, which removes the idols of a bloody past from our domestic altars once and for all ... We shall not achieve a just and lasting peace through protests and declamations. The only way to achieve it is through fulfilling the peace treaty in so far as this lies within our power.

---

19   Karl Franz was the SPD deputy for the district of Kattowitz (Polish name: Katowice) in Upper Silesia.

20   Free Corps units from Upper Silesia took part in the Kapp putsch of March 1920.

Source: Sozialdemokratische Partei Deutschlands 1921, *Protokoll über die Verhandlungen des Parteitages der SPD abgehalten in Görlitz, vom 18. bis 24. September 1921*, pp. 280–1.

7.9   *Hermann Müller on the French and Belgian Invasion of the Ruhr, January 1923*

The German working class has always been unanimous on the fact that it has nothing good to expect from any militarism, hence not from French militarism either ... Poincaré wants the Rhine. Till now he has not yet achieved his desire. Nor will he do so in the future. Not just because the German workers of the Ruhr and the Rhineland love their country with the same burning love that Jaurès, the assassinated leader, felt towards his French fatherland, but also because the German workers will reject a capitalism which makes its entrance accompanied by tanks and resting on the strength of bayonets, and puts forced labour for the foreign conqueror before the needs of the fatherland.

Source: Allemagne Verfassunggebende Nationalversammlung 1928, *Verhandlungen des Reichstags. Stenographische Berichte*, Vol. 357, p. 9424, Session 286, 13 January 1923.

Note: The SPD was thus part of the almost universal German reaction to the Franco-Belgian occupation of the Ruhr in 1923. Müller's remarks were rather on the moderate side. One can compare him with Ebert, calling on the German people in February 1923 'to conduct a People's War against the occupying forces', or Severing, who told Gessler[21] in April 1923 that 'he would gladly welcome any measure that might add to the instruments of power the Reich has against an external enemy'.[22]

7.10   *Karl Radek's 'Schlageter Speech', 20 June 1923*

We have listened to Comrade Zetkin's incisive and wide-ranging speech on international Fascism – that hammer which is intended to fall with destructive force on the head of the proletariat but will strike first and foremost at the very petit-bourgeois strata who are swinging it in the interests of big capital. There is no way in which I can either extend or supplement her speech.

---

21   Otto Gessler (1875–1955), DDP, Minister for Reconstruction 1919–20, Minister of Defence 1920–28. Member of the Reichstag 1920–24. Resigned from DDP 1927.

22   Rüdiger Bergien, 'The Consensus on Defense and Weimar Prussia's Civil Service', *Central European History*, 41, 2, June 2008, p. 185.

I could not even follow it well, as I kept recalling to my mind the dead body of the German Fascist, our class enemy, who was condemned to death and shot by the executioners of French imperialism, that powerful organisation of another section of our class enemies ... During the whole of Comrade Zetkin's speech on the contradictions of Fascism the name, and the tragic fate, of Schlageter,[23] was whirling round in my brain. Let us think of him now, when we are in the process of determining our political attitude to Fascism. The fate of this martyr of German nationalism should not be ignored or brushed aside with a deprecatory phrase ... Schlageter, courageous soldier of the counter-revolution, deserves an honourable and manly evaluation from us, the soldiers of the revolution ... If those groups of German Fascists who genuinely want to serve the German people do not understand the meaning of Schlageter's fate, then Schlageter has fallen to no purpose, and these are the words they should inscribe on his gravestone: 'His journey led to nothingness'. Schlageter fought in the *Freikorps* unit that stormed Riga. We do not know if this young officer understood the meaning of his action ... Against whom are the German *völkische*[24] fighting? Are they fighting against Entente capital or the Russian people? With whom do they want to make an alliance? With the Russian workers and peasants, in order to shake off, together with them, the yoke of Entente capital? Or with Entente capital, in order to enslave the German people?

Schlageter is dead. He cannot answer the question. At his grave his comrades vowed to continue his struggle. They must answer: against whom, at whose side, are you fighting? The path Schlageter chose, risking death, speaks in his favour. It tells us that he was convinced he served the German people. But Schlageter thought he served the German people best by helping to assert the domination of the classes which have led the German people up till now and brought immense misfortune to them.

We ask the honourable, patriotic masses who want to fight against the French imperialist invasion: how do you want to fight? On whom do you want to lean for support? ... One cannot conduct war at the front when the hinterland is in revolt. When Gneisenau and Scharnhorst, after Jena, pondered the question of how the German people was to be brought out of its humiliating position, they answered: only by making the peasants free ... In considering the fate of the German nation at the beginning of the present century, the German working class occupies the same position as the German peasantry

---

23   Albert Leo Schlageter (1894–1923), German army officer, member of the Free Corps, fought against French troops in 1923, sentenced to death for this.

24   A general term for those on the extreme nationalist Right. English translations have varied between 'racists', 'racialists' and 'folkists'.

did at the beginning of the previous century. One can only free Germany from the bonds of slavery together with the working class, not against it!

Only when the German cause is the cause of the German people, only when the German cause means the struggle for the rights of the German people, will that cause find active friends to aid it...If Germany is to be capable of fighting, it must present a united front of working people, the workers by hand and brain must unite to form an iron phalanx...United together to form a victorious, working nation, Germany will be in a position to discover gigantic sources of energy and resistance which will overcome every obstacle. By making the cause of the people the cause of the nation, you will make the cause of the nation the cause of the people. This is what the KPD and the Communist International have to say at the grave of Schlageter. We have nothing to conceal, for only the entire truth is capable of opening the path to the suffering and distracted national masses of Germany who are groping in the dark. The KPD must say openly to the nationalist petit-bourgeois masses: anyone who seeks to enslave the German people, to pitchfork it into adventures, in the service of the profiteers and speculators, the coal and iron barons, will come up against the resistance of the German communist workers. They will answer force with force. He who, through lack of understanding, joins forces with the mercenaries of capital, will be fought with all means available to us. But we believe that the great majority of the nationally-inclined masses belong not in the camp of capital but that of labour. We want to find the way to these masses, we shall find the way. We shall do everything to ensure that men like Schlageter, who were ready to go to the grave for a common cause, journey not into nothingness but into a better future for the whole of mankind, that their blood is shed not for the profits of the coal and iron barons but for the cause of the great German working people, which is a part of the family of nations fighting for their liberation. The KPD will tell this truth to the broadest masses of the German people, for it is not only the Party of the industrial workers' struggle for their daily bread but the Party of the proletarians fighting for their liberation, a liberation which is identical with the freedom of the whole people, the freedom of all that toils and suffers in Germany. Schlageter himself can no longer hear us. But we are sure that hundreds of other Schlageters will hear and understand this truth.

Source: Communist International 1923, *Protokoll der Konferenz der Erweiterten Exekutive der Kommunistischen Internationale, Moskau 12–23 Juni 1923*, pp. 240–5, reprinted in *Die Rote Fahne*, No. 144, Tuesday 26 June 1923.

7.11 *'Down with the Government of National Shame and Treachery':*
Proclamation of 29 May 1923 by the KPD Zentrale

To the German proletariat

To all working sections of the German people

The press organs of big capital are vying with each other to spread the wildest intentional falsehoods, with the aim of creating among the mass of the population the fixed conviction that the working class of the Ruhr, led by the communist party, has broken the ranks of the resistance against French imperialism and opened the front for the French imperialist enemy to enter. There is talk of mob rule, of frenzied murder and mayhem. After public opinion had been whipped up for a week with these lying reports, the representative of the German government, Dr. Lutterbeck,[25] turned to *the French general staff*, asking the murderers of the workers of Essen, the executioners of Schlageter, to give the German republican government permission to use its own machine-guns to shoot down German workers, its own fellow nationals.

All the atrocity-stories about mob rule in the Ruhr district are shameless lies, all the reports about the opening of the Ruhr front by the workers are untrue. The truth is the opposite: the German bourgeoisie is dismantling the resistance front on the Ruhr: *it is preparing a capitulation... at the expense of the masses* and in order to conceal these facts it is seeking to provoke a bloodbath in the Ruhr, which would give it the opportunity of saying 'We cannot fight on two fronts at once, so I am capitulating before the foreign enemy'.

The Ruhr workers struck because prices had risen 100 percent since February and they had had no wage increase. A fight developed with the bandit organisations maintained by heavy industry; the fight was exploited by unorganised, starving elements for the purpose of plunder. German and French provocateurs undoubtedly played a part in this. But from the moment that the organised working class took over the security service not a hair of anyone's head was touched.

There is no rising in the Ruhr, there are no communist disturbances, the starving workers are on strike there, and they are maintaining exemplary order in their struggle.

This struggle could be ended tomorrow if the heavy industrialists gave the workers the small concession they required, but these gentlemen do not want to do that, not only because they tremble over every *pfennig* of expenditure

---

25   Dr. Lutterbeck, the Deputy District President of Düsseldorf, wrote to the French general in command there on 26 May asking him to authorise German police to enter the occupied zone and restore order (Broué 2005, p. 708).

despite growing fat on government money, but because they *desire an uprising*, they want the muskets to shoot and the sabres to cut, and they want to be able to cry 'We are forced to capitulate'.

The Cuno government is bankrupt. It arose out of the desire of the German bourgeoisie to win a reduction of the reparation demands from French imperialism, and it has shown itself incapable of defending the interests of the German people against the shameless avarice of the heavy industrialists.

This government, which has done nothing but put out nationalist propaganda since the first days of the struggle in the Ruhr, is now *openly begging* the French general staff for permission to shoot down German workers. This is the question we ask of German Social Democracy, of the ADGB: what do you, the representatives of the majority of the German working class, propose to do to make the bloodbath in the Ruhr impossible?

We ask the nationally-minded petit-bourgeois masses, the mass of German officials and intellectuals, what do you propose to do against a government which dares to turn to the French generals, as shamelessly as a public prostitute, with the request to be allowed to slaughter fellow Germans? We are convinced that the great majority of the nationalist masses are honourable and sincerely convinced human beings who have been led astray and do not understand that the Entente is not their only enemy, and we call on these elements: will you at last open your eyes, will you not see that you are the instruments of the most rapacious plunderers of the German people? Will you not help to free the German people from these parasites, so as to make it capable of fighting against the government of this band of racketeers which is handing Germany over to French capital to keep itself in power and obtain permission to shoot German workers?

We do not know what the Social Democrats, or the ADGB, or the petit-bourgeois nationalist masses will say, but do know what every honourable German worker must say:

Down with the government of national shame and treachery!

Down with a government which turns to the executioners of the Entente to ask for permission to shoot at German workers!

Down with a government which wants to hand over the railways to private capitalists!

Down with a government which lets workers, craftsmen and small officials starve while it fattens up the capitalists!

Up with the united front of all working people, workers by hand and brain in town and country!

Up with a government of working people, enjoying the trust of the masses abroad, and in a position either to secure peace, even at the cost of sacrifices, or to organise the resistance of the German people if French imperialism refuses to agree to a peace!

To prison with the government's representative, Dr. Lutterbeck! Let him be brought before a People's Court, charged with treason!

Let those who gave him the order to present the shameful request to the French generals also face a People's Court!

Workers of the whole German Reich! Say what you think of this government in gigantic meetings and demonstrations!

Arm to support the workers of the Ruhr! Arm to fight against the burdens the big capitalist capitulators are proposing to lay upon you!

KPD *Zentrale Reich*
Committee of German Factory Councils

Source: *Die Rote Fahne*, 29 May 1923.

7.12   *International Policy Document Adopted by the SPD in 1925*

As a member of the Labour and Socialist International, the SPD fights in joint actions with the workers of all countries against imperialist and Fascist aggression and to make socialism a reality.

It opposes with all its strength any worsening of antagonisms between the peoples of the world and any threat to peace.

It demands that international conflicts be settled peacefully and that they be submitted to obligatory courts of arbitration.

It upholds the right of self-determination and the right of minorities to democratic and national self-government.

It opposes the exploitation of the colonial peoples and the violent destruction of their economies and their culture.

It demands international disarmament.

It advocates the establishment of European economic unity, which has become urgent for economic reasons, and the creation of a United States of Europe, in order to attain a solidarity of interest between the people of the whole continent.

It demands the democratisation of the League of Nations and its conversion into an effective instrument of peace policy.

Source: Sozialdemokratischer Parteitag in Heidelberg 1925, *Protokoll mit dem Bericht der Frauenkonferenz*, p. 10.

7.13   *Speech by Otto Wels in Favour of the SPD Parliamentary Party's*
        Motion in the Reichstag Demanding the Cessation of Work on
        Armoured Cruiser A, 15 November 1928

The SPD *Fraktion* has proposed that all work should cease on Armoured Cruiser A. The reason why we have made this proposal is based in the final analysis on the wishes of the German electorate expressed clearly and unambiguously on 20 May.[26] We are not fighting *against* the Reichswehr but in order to make it a reliable instrument of the Republic. We are by no means unaware that the Reichswehr must have an arm extended over the ocean.

But for us the highest commandment of all is the demand for the strictest economy and fitness for purpose. We have no right to waste the laboriously collected tax income of the Reich in this manner. It has been pointed out that that the Armoured Cruiser is necessary in order to prevent a blockade of our coast. I would ask, however: who is the opponent whose blockade we are trying to prevent? We cannot stop the Great Powers from blockading with armoured cruisers, and we can stop the smaller countries even without armoured cruisers. Russia is probably meant here: but the Russians could blockade our Baltic coast if they needed to. They would be careful not to do this, however, because it would be senseless to blockade one part of the country and leave the other part untouched. The freedom of passage to East Prussia has also been mentioned. Allow me to remark that this is an agitational slogan of the most absurd kind. For if they are talking about Poland, it should not be forgotten that Poland has plenty of aeroplanes and some submarines, which we lack, and the armoured cruiser would be completely defenceless against them.

Source: Allemagne Verfassunggebende Nationalversammlung 1928, *Verhandlungen des Reichstags* Bd. 423, p. 325.

Note: The cabinet presided over by Hermann Müller of the SPD voted to start building an armoured cruiser on 10 August 1928, although the SPD had campaigned against this before the 1928 elections to the Reichstag. They accepted the armoured cruiser unwillingly, in order to keep the bourgeois parties in the coalition. The majority of the Party was opposed to this, and on 15 August 1928 the Party Committee expressed its 'regret that the SPD ministers had voted for the Armoured Cruiser without consulting either the Parliamentary Party

---

26   At the elections of 20 May 1928 the SPD gained a considerable increase in votes and its parliamentary representation went up from 131 to 153, a result which Wels ascribes here in part to the agitation against the building of Armoured Cruiser A.

or the Party Committee'.[27] The SPD *Fraktion* introduced its resolution demanding the cessation of work on the armoured cruiser on 15 November and it insisted that its own cabinet ministers vote in favour of the motion, which condemned their own policy, as a matter of party discipline. They did so.

7.14 Hermann Müller (SPD Chancellor of Germany) Addresses the General Assembly of the League of Nations on 7 September 1928 on Disarmament

The League of Nations has been actively considering this aspect of the peace problem over the past year [i.e. the need to prevent war] but the same cannot be said of the other aspect of the problem, namely, the need to get rid of armaments. I make no bones about saying that I am seriously concerned about the state of the disarmament question. We are faced with the undeniable fact that the long discussions here in Geneva in regard to disarmament so far not led to any positive results of any kind.

The Assembly cannot be content today simply to say that there is still ground for optimism. In my view its most urgent duty is to adopt a resolution which can transform hope into reality … It is obvious that a country like Germany, which has been completely disarmed, finds the failure of the discussions about disarmament particularly painful. Look at the situation: one nation has achieved something quite extraordinary by completely disarming itself.[28] It sees that, despite this, it is at the slightest opportunity deluged with the gravest insinuations and reproaches by certain voices from abroad, and if at all possible it is presented as the enemy of world peace. And at the same time it perceives that other countries continue to expand their military resources without incurring any criticism.

Germany's disarmament must no longer exist as a unilateral act done by the victors of the World War, using the power they possessed. The contractual promise that Germany's disarmament would be followed by general disarmament must finally be fulfilled. The article of the statutes of the League of Nations which makes this promise a fundamental principle must finally be put into effect. Whether this involves complete disarmament or simply a reduction of armaments is not important. It simply must not come to pass that the great step forward which began with the setting up of the League of Nations turns into a retreat, which will certainly bring us to a level of international life

---

27 *Deutscher Geschichtskalender* 1928, p. 300.

28 As head of the German government, and a well-informed politician, Müller would have been well aware that Germany was not 'completely disarmed' and that covert rearmament had been proceeding for years.

inferior to what existed previously, because, once lost, confidence can hardly ever be restored. I cannot admit the objection that a problem of this scale cannot be solved in a short space of time. After all, those who lost the World War were asked to disarm immediately.

The ordinary person thinks in simple terms, and therefore thinks correctly. He reads that some governments have solemnly bound themselves to maintain peace,[29] yet he sees on the other hand that those governments are holding on to their old power positions and seeking to extend them. So it is not surprising when he finally begins to realise the two-faced character of international politics.

I must emphasise that Germany has never attempted to make any impossible demands. From the outset she agreed that this problem should be solved step by step. The conditions necessary for accomplishing the first stage do in fact exist ... That first stage can and must include an appreciable reduction of the present standards of armament, a reduction which would extend to armaments of all classes – military, naval and air – and would also provide for full and complete publicity in regard to all categories of armaments. I would therefore urge the Assembly to adopt a definite decision with regard to the convening of a first disarmament conference.

Source: *Schulthess' Europäischer Geschichtskalender. Neue Folge.* Vol. 44, 1928, Munich: Beck, 1929, pp. 452–56.

Note: The French Foreign Minister Aristide Briand[30] replied to Müller's speech a few days later, contradicting his claims about German disarmament. The Disarmament Conference which he was hoping for finally convened in February 1932, but under very different circumstances. By then the SPD was out of office, but it supported the Brüning government's demand for equality of status for Germany. The conference adjourned in July 1932 without achieving anything, and Germany withdrew its delegates from Geneva. This was effective, and in December 1932 it was agreed that Germany should enjoy 'equality of rights'.

---

29   A reference to the Kellogg-Briand Pact to renounce war as an instrument of national policy, signed on 27 August 1928 by the USA and many other governments, including the German government.

30   Aristide Briand (1862–1932), French politician and socialist leader, often in office as Prime Minister and in other posts. Foreign minister 1925–32.

7.15   *Wilhelm Keil (SPD) Advocates Keeping Contact with 'Healthy National Consciousness' in a Speech Made in August 1930*

If we want to be a real power factor, we must not isolate ourselves from the strata we describe as 'bourgeois', we should not surround ourselves with a Chinese wall. Above all, we should not come into conflict with the healthy national consciousness of those sections of the people by taking up a stubbornly anti-militarist attitude. We all hate war, certainly. But we also know how we as a disarmed and defeated nation have been treated. The mood of the young, active generation expresses the reaction against this mistreatment. We are rejected as a party because this mood does not find the strong echo among us that might be expected. We have no intention of entering into a competition with the extreme nationalists, but we ought not to lose contact with the healthy common sense of the masses . . . We cannot stick to platonic phrases about 'equality of rights' but must point out that the condition of inequality in which disarmed Germany is kept in tutelage by highly-armed states is incompatible with German sovereignty and cannot be tolerated any longer . . . If the impending disarmament conference cannot achieve any change in this situation, Germany herself must of course take into her own hands the right to build up her army according to her own requirements. How that is to happen is a matter which concerns Germany alone . . . Since 1918 we Social Democrats have in practice pursued a national policy. We were the ones who held the Reich together. But we have shied away from speaking in the national language our people understand . . . Let our words match out deeds! Let us commit ourselves to the unrestricted sovereignty of the German nation, in the field of military policy as much as anywhere else.

Source: Keil 1948, *Erlebnisse eines Sozialdemokraten*, vol.2, Stuttgart: Deutsche Verlagsanstalt. pp. 458–9.

Note: This was a speech to the SPD Parliamentary Party, published 18 years afterwards by Keil in his autobiography.

CHAPTER 8

The Search for Democracy in the Armed Forces

Introduction

The original socialist objective of a democratic people's army, which dated back at least to the 1848 Revolution, with its slogan calling for the 'universal arming of the people', was brought to fruition in an ironical way by the mass conscription of the First World War; the difference being that this was not the 'army of the people' but the 'army of William II'. As Paul Levi commented later, 'thus the solid pre-war military demand of Social Democracy was, but instead of coming from below it was imposed from the top down'.[1] Before 1918 the Reichstag was not permitted to interfere in military matters, which were a royal prerogative. Moreover, the classic socialist approach was purely negative. It was expressed in the saying: 'Not a man, not a penny, for this system'. It is true that the SPD had been taken into partnership with the Imperial government to some extent during the War, but this did not apply to the armed forces, where what was required was simply obedience. For these reasons, when the SPD inherited power after the November Revolution it had no experience of dealing with military affairs and no positive military policy. Wolfgang Sauer remarked that the top Social Democratic functionaries 'had a level of knowledge of technical military matters one can only characterise as ignorance'.[2] This continued to be the case even under the Republic: successive emergencies led to a series of hand-to-mouth experiments but no plans were made to reorganise the military in a democratic fashion (although lip-service continued to be paid to the idea). The problem was worsened by the provisions of the Versailles Treaty, which limited the army to 100,000 men and the navy to 15,000, and provided for a twelve-year period of military service. As Wels pointed out in June 1919, 'the demand for a People's Army cannot be met because the Entente insists on a professional army'.[3] The result was that the officer corps became more exclusive than it had been in the period before and during the war, when the shortage of suitable officer material had led the military authorities to relax the social requirements which made it the preserve of the sons of Prussian aristocrats.

---

1 Levi 1929, p. 43.
2 Writing in Bracher 1978, p. 211.
3 *Protokoll* 1919, p. 156.

Germany was obliged by the November 1918 armistice to bring back more than three million soldiers from the Western Front within three weeks. That is why Ebert made his telephone call to General Groener[4] on 8 November 1918 requesting military assistance and why the Council of People's Representatives entrusted the officers of the old imperial army with the job of bringing the troops back; they were the only people with the necessary experience, and the Social Democratic leaders did not think the Soldiers' Councils which had sprung up rapidly in the early days of November would be able to perform the task. In this situation the abolition of the Supreme Command of the Army (OHL) would simply have led to chaos, they thought. In return for this decision, the OHL agreed to provide 150,000 reliable troops to maintain order within the country and by implication to suppress any leftist rising.[5] This was one motive for the Social Democratic approach. There were also other motives, not less important. The Social Democrats wanted to protect German territory against the external enemies of the Reich, and to make sure the population had enough to eat. 'The central problem of the German Revolution', it has been claimed, 'was the food crisis'.[6] All these motives underlined the urgency of finding a reliable military force to restore order. The Spartacists were right to charge that the main aim of the new army was to put down the Revolution, but wrong to treat as spurious the argument put forward by Ebert and his colleagues that the army was also needed for 'defence against Polish imperialism'.[7] They really did fear a Polish invasion. The Spartacists' argument that the food crisis could be solved by imports from Soviet Russia was also unconvincing. In any case they had very little support among ordinary soldiers.

There was some opposition to the SPD's military policies from the Soldiers' Councils which emerged from the November Revolution. But it is important not to exaggerate their radicalism.[8] They did not want to establish an independent army, they simply wanted the military commanders of the traditional army to accept their subordination to the civil power, and they wanted a more democratic approach within the army.[9] The First Congress of Workers' and

---

4   Wilhelm Groener (1867–1939), First Quartermaster General of the OHL, 1918–1919. Non-party Minister of Transport 1920–23. Reichswehr Minister 1928–32. Minister of the Interior 1931–32.

5   Büttner 2008, pp. 44–5.

6   Haupts 1976, p. 227.

7   Call for volunteers issued by the Council of People's Representatives, 7 January 1919 (Sozialistische Einheitspartei Deutschlands Zentralkomitee 1958, p. 18).

8   The moderation of the Soldiers' Councils of 1918 has been underlined by Ulrich Kluge (Kluge 1975, pp. 160–97).

9   Kluge 1985, p. 22.

Soldiers' Councils adopted the 'Hamburg Points' (8.4) which sought to secure this. The former officers would not be removed; but they would have to stand for re-election. They would not be allowed to swagger around when off duty. There would be a number of symbolic changes such as the removal of military decorations. It seems these alterations were already in effect in Hamburg.[10] The implementation of the Hamburg Points 'would not have produced basic changes within the army' (Kluge).[11] The High Command, however, thought differently. It was entirely opposed to the Hamburg Points; in fact Hindenburg and Groener sent a telegram threatening their immediate resignation.[12] The Council of People's Representatives went along with the High Command's refusal. The existing structure of the army was retained.[13] On 19 January 1919 the Hamburg Points were declared to be mere 'guidelines', to be observed by the army at home and not outside the country. The power of command remained in the hands of the military. The Second Congress of Workers' and Soldiers' Councils complained about this (11 April 1919) but could do nothing. In any case, the 'Law on the Formation of a Provisional Reichswehr'[14] issued on 6 March 1919 (8.5) provided for the dissolution of the old army and the establishment of a new army without Soldiers' Councils. By June 1919 they had vanished from the scene. The SPD drew the logical conclusion from this when in 1921 it deleted the traditional call for the regular army to be replaced by a citizen army from its new party programme. The Provisional Reichswehr was replaced in March 1921 by the small permanent volunteer Reichswehr permitted by the Versailles Treaty. Pre-war traditions were preserved in the new army, and the numerical limitations imposed by Versailles made it possible to keep doubtful social democratic or liberal elements out of the officer corps. The private soldiers were themselves usually former members of the Freicorps units which had been set up in many places after November 1918 by supporters of the old order and played an important part in suppressing the revolutionary disturbances of 1918–1919.[15] In any case, membership of political associations and participation in political meetings was strictly forbidden to ordinary soldiers by the Defence Law of March 1921.[16]

---

10   Büttner 1985, p. 42.
11   Kluge 1985, p. 148.
12   Miller 1978, p. 184.
13   Kluge 1975, p. 142.
14   *Reichswehr*: this term covers both the army and the navy, and is therefore used as a shorthand expression for the armed forces in general.
15   Craig 1964, pp. 362–3.
16   Paragraph 36 of the Defence Law of 23 March 1921 (Huber 1966, p. 178).

There remained the question of civilian control. The Reichswehr, to use an often-quoted phrase, was a 'state within the state'. The SPD Minister of Defence, Gustav Noske, who had efficiently organised the military suppression of the proletarian uprisings of January and March 1919, was unable to prevent the Kapp-Lüttwitz putsch of March 1920 against the Republic, and one result of the successful mass resistance against Kapp was Noske's forced resignation. At this point, the Social Democrats had an opportunity to democratise the army, but they failed to take any energetic steps in this direction. In fact they voluntarily abandoned the Ministry of Defence, although Scheidemann advised the appointment of his party colleague Albert Grzesinski to the post.[17] Hence Noske's replacement was a right-wing member of the DDP, Otto Gessler,[18] while General Walter Reinhardt, 'the only general who was prepared to defend the republic by force of arms',[19] was replaced as chief of the army command by General von Seeckt, who had refused to oppose Kapp, and who aimed to rebuild the army on traditional lines. Ebert supported Seeckt in this, as he regarded the old officer corps as 'technically indispensable'.[20] There was no room for Social Democrats in the new army. During the Gessler years 'every vestige of socialist ideas was carefully weeded out of the Reichswehr, and every connection between the soldiers and organised labour was severed'.[21] In cordial cooperation with Gessler, Seeckt was able to exclude the civilian politicians from exercising the control over the military provided for in the 1919 constitution[22] and essentially to conduct an independent foreign policy, as Philipp Scheidemann complained in 1926 (8.7).

Seeckt left office in October 1926, and his successors steered a different course. The Reichswehr abandoned its attitude of aloofness from the civilian politicians and started to pursue 'a military and armaments policy in alliance with the government, rather than independently of it'.[23] The line now taken by the army was that the whole population must be militarily prepared for defence, and the working class could not be left out of this plan; hence cooperation with the civilian politicians, and this included the SPD leaders, was seen as essential. Actually, this change in attitude was not really advantageous

---

17   Kastning 1970, p. 31.
18   Otto Gessler (1875–1955), DDP until 1927, member of the Reichstag 1924–32, Minister of Defence 1920–1928.
19   Carsten 1966, p. 92.
20   Wolfgang Sauer, writing in Bracher 1978, chapter 9, p. 220, n. 55.
21   Rosenberg 1936, p. 146.
22   Schmädeke 1966, pp. 117–83.
23   Kolb 2005, p. 174; and in more detail Geyer 1980 and Vogelsang 1962, pp. 409–13.

to Social Democracy, as the leaders of the Reichswehr now insisted on having a government in power which would cooperate with its ambitious military plans. Hence the SPD government of Hermann Müller was forced in 1928
to agree to continue the previous government's project of building a pocket
battleship (*Panzerkreuzer A*) in order to keep the coalition in being. But it was
clear that the SPD was unwilling to give wholehearted support to the Right's
programme of getting rid of the Versailles Treaty restrictions and re-arming
Germany. The Party agreed at a cabinet meeting on 18 October 1928 to draw a
veil over the Reichswehr's previous secret re-arming activities, but insisted on
budgetary control of future expenditure of this kind. This led the most influential generals in the Reichswehr, Groener and Schleicher, to see the Müller
government as an obstacle to further progress in this direction. They much preferred the presidential government of Heinrich Brüning, which took office in
March 1930.[24] Re-armament and military re-organisation continued throughout the next three years, under Brüning and his successors, who were prepared,
in the national interest, to ignore the constraints on expenditure called for by
the Ministry of Finance in a time of economic crisis.[25]

Meanwhile, the SPD had finally got round to adopting a defence policy, at its
1929 Congress (8.8). This called for effective parliamentary supervision of military matters, and a certain degree of democratisation of the armed forces. The
more radical proposals from the left of the Party (8.9) were rejected. There was
in any case no possibility that the Reichswehr would accept the Party's proposals, even in their watered-down form, and a few months later it was removed
from office, never to return during the Weimar period.

Documents

8.1   *Telegram from the Council of People's Representatives to the German High Command, 12 November 1918*

The people's government is imbued with the desire that every one of our soldiers should return home in the shortest possible time, after their indescrib-
able suffering and their unheard-of privations. This goal, however, can only
be attained if demobilisation proceeds according to an orderly plan. If individual detachments unilaterally flood back, they will severely endanger themselves, their comrades and their country. The inevitable result of this would
be chaos, starvation and misery. The people's government expects the strictest

---

24   Wolfgang Sauer, writing in Bracher 1978, chapter 9, pp. 244–6; Carsten 1966, pp. 304–8.
25   Geyer 1981, pp. 118–19.

self-denial from you, in order to prevent immeasurable harm from being done. We request the High Command to bring the above declaration to the notice of the army in the field, and to lay down the following rules:

1) The relationship between officer and private soldier is to be based on mutual trust. The prerequisites for this are the voluntary subordination of the private soldier to the officer and the comradely treatment of the private soldier by his superior.
2) The officers continue to be in command. Unconditional obedience in the service is of decisive importance for a successful return to German soil. Military discipline and order in the army must therefore be maintained in all circumstances.
3) The Soldiers' Councils have an advisory voice in maintaining confidence between officers and men in questions of food supply, leave of absence and the imposition of disciplinary punishments. Their highest duty is to work to prevent disorder and mutiny.
4) Equal quantities of food for officers, clerical staff and men.
5) Equal advances on pay. Equal active duty supplements for officers and men. Weapons must only be used against fellow Germans in self-defence or to prevent plundering.

Signed: Ebert, Haase, Scheidemann, Dittmann Landsberg, Barth

Source: Vorwärts 1918, *Vorwärts*, 13 November 1918, New York.

Note: This telegram, signed by all six People's Representatives, shows their intention of working in co-operation with the old military establishment from the outset. Their main concern was clearly the maintenance of order and discipline. The instructions given were welcome to the High Command, but not strictly necessary. The text of the telegram was drafted by Hindenburg himself, and agreed to by Scheidemann, acting for the government. The People's Representatives' hands were thus tied from the beginning, and the failure of subsequent attempts at democratisation and de-militarisation was predictable.

8.2   *Proclamation by the Berlin Executive Council, Calling for the Setting Up of a Red Guard, 12 November 1918*
Workers and Party Comrades in Greater Berlin! The Revolution needs to be secured! You have destroyed the old citadel of oppression with your courage, now help to give a solid basis to the achievements of the Revolution.

We need your help! 2,000 politically-organised comrades and workers with a socialist background and military training must take over the task of protecting the Revolution. Put yourselves at our disposal. You will receive weapons and always be accountable to the Executive Council of the Workers' and Soldiers' Council. Measures will be taken to pay and feed you.

Comrades! Workers! Your liberty is at stake. Come along and present yourselves at Trade Union House on Wednesday the 13th of November. You will require proof of membership of one of the two Social Democratic parties and of a trade union, as well as military training.

The Executive Council of the Workers' and Soldiers' Council.
Richard Müller
Molkenbuhr[26]

Source: G.A. Ritter and S. Miller, S (eds.), 1975, *Die deutsche Revolution 1918–1919. Dokumente* 2nd ed., Hamburg: Hoffman und Campe Verlag, Doc. IV.16, p. 113.

Note: The Berlin Executive Council decided the next day not to continue with the formation of a Red Guard, under pressure from the SPD-influenced Soldiers' Councils, who saw it as a possible rival. A Republican Guard was founded instead by Otto Wels on 17 November 1918.

8.3   *Law Providing for the Establishment of a Voluntary People's Militia, 12 December 1918*

1 A Voluntary People's Militia (*Volkswehr*) is to be set up to maintain public order and security.

2 The Council of People's Representatives alone will grant authorisation to establish the detachments of this force and it will also determine the number and strength of the detachments.

3 The People's Militia is responsible only to the Council of People's Representatives. Its members will take a solemn oath to the socialist and democratic republic.

4 Only volunteers will be accepted into the People's Militia. It will be independent of the army. Its judicial and disciplinary system remains to be settled.

---

26   Hermann Molkenbuhr (1851–1927), SPD, member of the executive from 1904–27, member of the Reichstag.

5 The volunteers will elect their own leaders, in a ratio of approximately 100 volunteers to one leader and three platoon commanders; several groups of 100 will together form a battalion, and will elect the head of the battalion and his staff. A Council of Representatives consisting of five volunteers will be attached to him in an advisory capacity.

6 Every volunteer is obliged while on duty to obey the leaders he himself has elected.

7 The requirements for the acceptance of a volunteer are: a) a minimum age of 24 years, as a rule b) physical strength c) long and impeccable service at the front.

The Council of People's Representatives

Ebert. Haase.

Source: Deutsches Reich 1918a, *Reichsgesetzblatt*, Berlin: Verlag. d. Gesetzsammlungsamts 1918, p. 1424.

Note: This proclamation was a concession to the strong sentiment in the Soldiers' Councils in favour of a militia in place of the old army. The Supreme Command was naturally opposed to the whole idea. Very little progress was made towards the formation of this force, and one of the demands included in the Seven Hamburg Points (8.4) was that the process be speeded up. Eventually a force of 600 men was established, which was dwarfed by the tremendous growth in Freikorps units. Some militia units emerged in Saxony, but they were suppressed in May 1919 by the Reichswehr.[27]

8.4   *The Seven Hamburg Points, Adopted 18 December 1918 by the First Congress of Workers' and Soldiers' Councils*

1 The power of command over the army and the navy is to be exercised by the People's Representatives, under the control of the Executive Council.

2 As a symbol of the destruction of militarism and the ending of the system of blind obedience, all insignia of rank are to be abolished, and the bearing of arms when off duty is to be prohibited.

3 The Soldiers' Councils are responsible for the reliability of the troop detachments and the maintenance of discipline. The Congress of Workers' and Soldiers' Councils is convinced that troops responsible to the Soldiers' Councils they themselves have elected, and to their superior officers ('leaders')

---

27   Kluge 1975, pp. 325–47.

will display on duty the obedience unconditionally required for the achievement of the aims of the socialist revolution. When the troops are off duty, the
quality of being a 'superior officer' ceases to exist.

4 The removal of existing shoulder decorations, officers' stripes, cockades,
epaulettes and side-arms is exclusively a matter for the Soldiers' Councils
and not individual persons. Excesses harm the prestige of the Revolution
and are inappropriate at a time when our troops are returning home. The
Congress demands the removal of all military medals and insignia of rank and
nobility.

5 The soldiers themselves are to elect their leaders. Former officers may be
re-elected, where they have enjoyed the confidence of the majority of the men
of their detachment.

6 Officers of the military administration and officials holding the rank of officer are to be left in their positions in the interests of demobilisation if they
declare that they will undertake nothing against the Revolution.

7 The standing army is to be abolished, and the formation of a People's Militia
(*Volkswehr*) is to be speeded up.

Source: R. Müller, *Geschichte der deutschen Revolution*, vol. 2, Vienna, 1925,
p. 211.

Note: These seven points summarised the main demands of the rank and file
of the army and the navy during the November Revolution. The dream of a
'People's Army', dear to all democrats since the 1848 Revolution seemed about
to be realised. Yet the resolution of 18 December was also marked by a concern
for symbols rather than real issues of power, and the attitude taken to those
formerly in charge of the armed forces was ambiguous. In any case, the Seven
Hamburg Points could not be put into effect because the High Command
threatened to resign if this happened, and the SPD People's Representatives
were not unhappy to give way to this threat. The failure to implement this resolution was one of the main reasons for the resignation of the USPD members
from the government on 28 December 1918 (2.10). The decree on 'the power of
command and the position of the Soldiers' Councils' which was finally issued
on 19 January 1919 appeared to be a compromise between the views of the High
Command and the Hamburg Points, in that it preserved the Soldiers' Councils,
with a much restricted area of competence, but in practice the High Command
got its way, as the power of command was restored to the officers.

8.5   *Law for the Establishment of a Provisional Reichswehr, 6 March 1919*

The Constituent German National Assembly, in agreement with the
Commission of the States, has adopted the following law:

1 The Reich President is empowered to dissolve the existing army and to establish a provisional Reichswehr, which is to protect the borders of the Reich until the establishment of a new Defence Force (*Wehrmacht*), to be created by legislation, to put into effect the instructions of the Reich government and to maintain law and order within the Reich.

2 The Reichswehr is to be formed on a democratic basis by bringing together all the volunteer units that already exist and by the recruitment of further volunteers. People's Defence Units (*Volkswehren*) and similar associations can be attached to it. Officers and NCOs of all kinds and the office personnel of the existing army as well as its institutions and commanders can be included in the Reichswehr. The path to promotion to the rank of officer is to be opened to experienced NCOs and privates. Officers and NCOs who enter the Reichswehr are to be considered first when recruitment takes place to the future Defence Force.

3 Members of the Reichswehr are to be considered members of the army while they belong to it for the purpose of legal requirements, in particular for the supply of provisions.

[4: special provisions for Bavaria and Württemberg]

5 This law enters into force immediately but ceases to be effective from 31 March 1920.

Weimar, 6 March 1919

The President	The Reichswehr Minister	The War Minister
Ebert	Noske	Reinhardt

Source: Deutsches Reich 1919, *Reichsgesetzblatt*, No. 57, Berlin: Verlag. d. Gesetzsammlungsamts. p. 295.

Note: Detailed provisions for the implementation of this law were issued at the same time. The power of command was transferred to the Ministry of Defence and the Prussian War Ministry; commanders were to be responsible solely to their superiors; the role of elected representatives was reduced to cooperating in matters of food supply, the granting of leave and dealing with grievances in the prescribed manner. Officers were to be appointed and dismissed solely by the Reich President on the advice of the Minister of Defence.

8.6   Gustav Noske (SPD Minister of Defence) Defends his Decision to Use
         Career Officers to Restore Order in Germany after 1918

When I was Minister of Defence I had to do the opposite of what I thought was right. In the completely ruinous conditions in Germany at the end of 1918 and the beginning of 1919 the formation of a People's Army was impossible. A large section of the people did not want to have anything to do with military armaments after the long war. Another section demanded a Red Army following the Russian example, with elected officers. I had to work hard at Kiel to prevent the formation of red troop detachments. The Republican People's Militia in Berlin … was an army of bad citizens, composed of men who did not want to take off their uniforms yet because they could not find work. The only elements that could be used for forming the nucleus of a new army were career soldiers, non-commissioned officers and officers … who were as yet unable to make the transition to civilian professions. In addition there were men who remained with the army out of their warm affection for the fatherland. The volunteer units (*Freikorps*) arose from this basis. The first call for the setting up of volunteer units was made in order to protect the threatened Eastern regions of the country from being overrun by Bolshevik troops. The troop units formed under my responsibility have done a great service in restoring order in Germany. None of the leaders who later boasted of being saviours of their country could have achieved anything in 1919 if they had not been covered by me for this.

Source: G. Noske 1947, *Aufstieg und Niedergang der deutschen Sozialdemokratie*, Zürich, p. 114.

Note: Noske's assertions about the inadequacies of the Republican People's Militia are contradicted by other sources. There were two reliable Social Democratic volunteer regiments in Berlin in January 1919, according to Heinrich Winkler. They were set up by Erich Kuttner, an editor at the SPD newspaper Vorwärts and Albert Baumeister, a socialist publisher.[28] Noske chose not to use them to restore order. He relied instead on the available Freikorps units.

8.7   A Communist View of Military Questions (Paul Levi's speech of
         April 1920)

France fears the armed force which still exists in Germany. And rightly so. For even if German militarism is weaker now than during the war, if is more

---

28   Winkler 1985, p. 123.

irresponsible and immoral, and desperadoes are as dangerous externally as they are internally.

England and America, on the other hand, see German armed strength as a guarantee against Bolshevism. France therefore cooperates with what is called the 'German Revolution', the USPD etc., England cooperates with Kapp-Lüttwitz. France will naturally do her utmost to conjure away the danger of being deprived of the fruits of victory, and has therefore already gone over to undertaking *unilateral* actions against German militarism ... France sees the present moment as the last opportunity to carry through the disarming of German militarism. That was the occasion for the Kapp putsch. But the Kapp putsch was also a logical development from the error made by the German Revolution in its earliest days. The error of November 1918 was the belief that you could change a system by changing persons.

The reawakened military force, which was created expressly as a 'white guard' by the bourgeoisie, is being used to run the state in Germany. From April 1919 to December 1919 a state of siege was in operation. Then, after a mere three weeks, on 13 January 1920, they again brought back the state of siege. The Kapp putsch was the direct result of the 'Noske system' of relying on machine guns to stay in power: in the long run they will have to capitulate to these helpers. So the question raised by 13 March 1920 is the same as that raised by 9 November 1918: can the *sole* support of the capitalist system in Germany, militarism, remain in power? In November 1918 the Berlin Executive Council called for the formation of a Red Army, but they failed in their attempt to achieve this. Then the bourgeoisie created its Free Corps. How was this new military force recruited? The officers were the same as before. The private soldiers were a new stratum: no longer the proletarians of town and country but the great masses economically and morally pulverised by the war. They are the products of the decay of the lowest strata of the old society, the 'lumpenproletarians'. I do not use this word as a term of abuse, but purely sociologically.

If the weapons stay in the hands of the stratum that holds them now they will be at the disposal of any reactionary coup that is made. For this stratum has no social roots. The weapons belong in the hands of the stratum on which the whole structure rests: the proletarians in the factories. In November 1918 the German Revolution evaded this vital question, but now it will have to be decided one way or the other. The situation is much clearer now than it was in 1918. Now there is a conscious and energetic bourgeois group on one side, and the proletariat on the other. Whether we Communists as a Party have got larger or smaller is of no consequence here ... The movement of 13 March 1920 is one of the most inspiring and significant of the German Revolution, certainly more inspiring than that of 9 November 1918 ... The flames of insurrection have jumped over with volcanic strength to circles which were until then entirely foreign to the Revolution, and the kernel is today larger and more solid than it was in November 1918.

Source: *Bericht über den 4. Parteitag der Kommunistischen Partei Deutschlands (Spartakusbund) am 14. und 15. April 1920*, Berlin: Berliner Buch und Kunstdruckerei, n.d, pp. 15–19.

8.8   *Philipp Scheidemann's Speech of 16 December 1926 Attacking the Role of the Reichswehr as a 'State within the State'*

Serious concern for our country has led us to investigate the politics of the Reichswehr... An armed force, vital sections of which conduct their own policy, a policy diametrically opposed to democracy and peace (Oho! from the extreme Right, enthusiastic applause from the Social Democrats) cannot be retained in its present condition... The Reichswehr has developed increasingly into a state within the state, a state which follows its own laws and pursues its own policies. I shall prove this to you with facts... These facts will not come as a surprise to people abroad. The whole world knows very well what is happening here... The nation which is least well-informed about the Reichswehr is the German nation.

I have three main complaints to bring forward. First, the great expense of financing the Reichswehr; second the relationship of the Reichswehr to radical right organisations; third those activities by the Reichswehr which are liable to create very great difficulties for our foreign policy. The factual reports in the Manchester Guardian about the connections between the Reichswehr and Russia, the construction of aeroplanes there, the manufacture of gas weapons and bombs... compel us to make certain occurrences impossible under all future circumstances... I shall give some examples. It is reported reliably from Stettin[29] that three transport ships arrived in September and October of this year from Leningrad... From 1923 until 1926 an organisation called GEFU existed, with the function of setting up a factory in Russia to make gas grenades. It has now been replaced by a similar organisation called the WiKo.[30]

As long as the ship of state sails calmly on we don't need to worry... But who knows what will happen when the weather changes? And if troubled times come, an armed force which is hostile to the democratic republic will

---

29   Now Szczecin in Poland.

30   GEFU (*Gesellschaft zur Förderung Gewerblicher Unternehmungen*) = Company for the Promotion of Commercial Enterprises. WiKo (*Wirtschaftskontor G.m.b.H*) = Commercial Office Ltd. See Carsten 1966, p. 233.

of course pose a tremendous danger. The republic needs an armed force on which it can rely in all circumstances ... We demand a root and branch reform of the Reichswehr. We want a Reichswehr which does not fraternise only with one part of the nation ... The degree of secret re-armament is naturally exaggerated abroad. Germany, in its disarmed condition, cannot conduct a war, and this fact is not altered by secret re-armament. But secret re-armament irresponsibly damages our foreign policy.

The opponents of disarmament outside Germany constantly point to the fact that Germany has not implemented her own disarmament in reality, only in appearance. The worst danger, however, is the growth of wildly unrealistic opinions among the people who secretly play with forbidden weapons. The conclusion of the agreements aimed at securing Germany a secret supply of munitions was a mistake even in 1919. The continued implementation of these agreements after Locarno and the entry of Germany into the League of Nations would be something much worse. We demand binding guarantees that this will cease. An end to this dishonesty! No more Soviet munitions for Germany, or Soviet weapons!

Source: Deutsches Reich 1927, *Verhandlungen des Reichstags. Stenographische Berichte Bd. 391*, 3 November 1926–4 Februar 1927, pp. 8577–85.

Note: This speech had a tremendous impact at the time. It was 'like a bomb going off', the SPD newspaper *Vorwärts* reported. The Right and the communists noisily opposed Scheidemann's views; even the liberals and the Centre Party were alienated. The SPD 'stood alone'. Whereas the day before there were serious discussions about the Party's inclusion in a coalition cabinet, this was out of the question afterwards. Cooperation with the SPD, General Reinhardt remarked had become 'difficult, if not impossible'.[31] In the longer term, Scheidemann's speech made very little difference. The SPD won the parliamentary vote of no confidence in the cabinet of Wilhelm Marx, but he simply formed a new one, this time including the monarchist DNVP. The Reichswehr continued to go its own way, clandestine re-armament continued, as did secret cooperation with the Soviet Union.[32] It has recently been claimed that there was 'common ground' between the civilians, including some leading Social Democrats,[33] and the military on the need to evade the provisions of

---

31   Carsten 1966, p. 256.
32   Gorlow et al. 1996, pp. 139–40.
33   The influential SPD Minister of the Interior in Prussia Carl Severing thought Scheidemann was wrong to go public about illegal re-armament (Severing 1950, p. 103).

the Versailles Treaty.[34] Whether that is so or not, Scheidemann's public denunciation of Germany's illegal rearmament angered all parties to the right (and to the left!) of the SPD, who saw the army's evasion of the provisions of the Versailles Treaty as perfectly legitimate, while they regarded this kind of whistle-blowing as treasonable.

8.9   SPD Principles of Defence Policy, Adopted in May 1929
I
The SPD rejects war as an instrument of policy. It calls for the peaceful settlement of all international conflicts by obligatory courts of arbitration, and for the democratisation of the League of Nations and its development into an effective instrument of peace. It is determined, in line with the decisions of the Brussels Congress of the Labour and Socialist International held in August 1928, to exert the strongest pressure, even with revolutionary means, against any government which refuses to submit to the decision of a court of arbitration and which takes steps towards war.[35]

II
As a member of the Labour and Socialist International, the SPD fights for complete disarmament through international agreements. Disarmament will only serve the cause of peace when it is not a one-sided obligation imposed by the victors on those defeated in the World War. A lasting peace can only be achieved between nations which enjoy equal rights.

The historic mission of being the pioneer of international disarmament has fallen to the German Republic. It can only fulfil this mission when it does not exceed the one-sided limits to its armaments that have been imposed on it, and when it does not attempt to evade or breach them, thereby giving other Powers a reason or a pretext for rejecting international disarmament agreements and increasing their armaments still further.

The SPD does not accept that the German Republic has an obligation to rearm right up to the limits imposed upon it without regard to the political or military usefulness of those armaments. It calls for the systematic voluntary dismantling of Germany's military armaments, while bearing in mind the country's political, economic, social and financial situation.

---

34   Bergien 2008, p. 180.

35   This was part of the Resolution on Militarism and Disarmament approved at the Third (Brussels) Congress of the Labour and Socialist International (Braunthal 1967, p. 340).

III

The most effective protection of the German Republic rests on a foreign policy directed towards the reconciliation of nations and the maintenance of peace. But the power politics of imperialist and Fascist states still threatens us with counter-revolutionary interventions and new wars. Germany may be *misused* as an area of warlike conflict and drawn against its will into bloody entanglements. As long as these dangers exist, the German Republic needs a *Wehrmacht* for the protection of its neutrality and the political, economic and social achievements of the working class. The *Wehrmacht* can only fulfil its tasks if it is bound up with the people in its ideas and feelings, and is integrated into the democratic republic as a serving organ – in contrast to all militaristic tendencies, which amount to the domination of the state by the military.

In order to transform the army in this sense, the SPD makes the following specific demands:

1 The Reichstag should exercise supervision over all army matters and all contracts and agreements made by the military administration.
2 There should be no payments to private firms engaged directly or indirectly in illegal armaments.
3 Punishment for the publication of details of illegal armaments should be prohibited.
4 There should be legal provisions to make sure that recruitment is carried out without political bias.
5 Educational privileges should be removed from the Officers' Corps, and a minimum level should be laid down for promotion to the rank of Officer from the troop contingent.
6 The constitutional rights of soldiers should be secured.
7 The rights of soldiers should be protected by their own elected personal representatives.
8 Measures of discipline and military punishment should be democratised.
9 Education should be performed by republican teachers with republican books.
10 The use of military detachments in conflicts between capital and labour should be prohibited.

IV

The SPD fights against the ever more strongly apparent endeavours of leading military men in all countries to get rid of legal limitations on the conduct of war, which are the common property of mankind after thousands of years of development, and to turn future wars against the civilian population, going beyond the sphere of military operations. The SPD brands these endeavours as barbaric and demands that international law again be established on a humanitarian basis. It calls in particular for the prohibition of the use of gas and bacteria in war.

V

These socialist demands can only be made a reality through the joint and energetic action of the organised workers, through the constant enlightening of the workers about the reasons for, and the dangers of, armaments, through education in the spirit of peace in order to prepare morally for disarmament, and through a heightened political and economic struggle of the proletariat against the ruling classes until the achievement of socialism. The final goal of socialism is a society without exploitation and oppression, hence without classes and class struggles. It is a society where there is no attempt to expand areas of exploitation, hence a society without armaments and wars. Socialism is the force which will bring lasting peace to the world.

Source: Sozialdemokratischer Parteitag in Magdeburg 1929, *Protokoll mit dem Bericht der Frauenkonferenz*, Berlin: J.H.W. Dietz, pp. 288–9.

Note: The official SPD standpoint on the military question, presented here, combined the call to place the army under civilian control and democratise it (in the ten points of Section III) with an insistence that until full disarmament had been achieved by international agreement Germany would retain its 'Defence Force' (*Wehrmacht*). The justification for this was given by Wilhelm Dittmann, who claimed that 'in Germany there are ten times as many socialist elements as there are in Russia', adding that 'in Germany' (unlike Russia) 'the proletariat has something to defend'.[36]

8.10   *Proposals for a Military Programme Brought Forward by the Left Opposition in the SPD and Rejected at the Magdeburg Congress, 1929*

[After an introductory section on fundamental principles, similar to that in 8.8 but concluding with the demand to 'make use of the economic and political crisis brought about by war for the overthrow of capitalist class rule' the document continues]:

---

36   *Sozialdemokratischer Parteitag* 1929, p. 115

II

In a capitalist state, Social Democracy rejects national defence, which means the defence of the class rule and class interests of the bourgeoisie. If a country in which the proletariat has conquered political power and which is in transition to the classless society is attacked by other states still under the rule of the bourgeoisie, the proletariat is obliged to defend its class interests against all attacks with all means.

III

The development of technology has made production and transport the focal point of national defence. When war is declared these branches are placed entirely at the disposition of the combatants. With this, the proletariat engaged in the process of production becomes a more and more important instrument of combat, in place of the parts of the population that have been brought together in military units. This fact guarantees that the proletarian state will be fully capable of defending itself in case the proletariat conquers political power.

The existing conception of disarmament has been rendered out of date by the development of technology. Reductions in troop numbers and in the amount of technical instruments for the conduct of war do not in themselves mean disarmament. Changes in an outdated military apparatus which rests on a pre-war technical basis may on the contrary mean a fuller utilisation of the military effectiveness of modern industry. This consequence can only be avoided, and a desirable disarmament corresponding to the resolutions of the Brussels International [Congress] can only be achieved in connection with constant and uninterrupted supervision by the organisations of the proletariat of all the country's means of production of war-related items.

IV

In a capitalist state, the army does not just have the purpose of serving the foreign-policy interests of the bourgeoisie; it is also used where there are decisive conflicts between the proletariat and the bourgeoisie.

For this reason, Social Democracy refuses to provide the means of existence for the army and it fights for its abolition.

The SPD continuously places the class antagonism in capitalist society in the forefront of the political struggle. It recognises the need to create the instruments of proletarian power which the coming socialist society needs for its foundation and its defence.

Action Programme

It is the task of the SPD to bring the German proletariat together on this basis, ideologically and organisationally. To this end, it conducts a lasting struggle:

(1) for parliamentary and trade-union supervision of all industries and forms of transport, and first and foremost those which can be directly put into action for military purposes;

(2) for parliamentary supervision of the army and the navy and of all agreements concluded by the military administration and its subordinate branches;

(3) for reductions in expenditure on the military budget leading to the complete removal of all armaments expenditure:

(4) for the abolition of the wartime navy;

(5) for a change in the existing system of recruitment, namely the introduction of a lottery system for physically able-bodied volunteers;

(6) for the removal of restrictions on entry based on education to the career of officer;

(7) for the right of soldiers to elect a personal representative to protect their rights, for securing the civil rights of soldiers, and for complete freedom of association and rights of co-determination for soldiers;

(8) against all grants of public monies to private industry;

(9) for the removal of the provisions of the criminal law which protect illegal armaments;

(10) for prohibiting the use of the armed forces in conflicts between capital and labour.

Source: *Der Klassenkampf. Marxistische Blätter* 3.12 (December 1929), pp. 372–4.

Note: This resolution was proposed at the Magdeburg Congress of the SPD by Paul Levi, Kurt Rosenfeld[37] and Max Seydewitz, on behalf of the Left opposition. There was no vote on it, because the chair ruled that the vote in favour of the Principles of Defence Policy (see 8.8) had already settled the matter. But the strength of the *Klassenkampf* group at this Congress was shown by the voting figures on the SPD's official defence policy: 242 in favour, 147 against.[38]

---

37   Kurt Rosenfeld (1877–1943), lawyer and defender in political trials, SPD, USPD, SPD, member of the Reichstag 1920–32, chair of SAP from 1931.

38   Winkler 1988, p. 632; Klenke 1987, vol. 2, p. 1105.

CHAPTER 9

Questions of Gender and Sexual Politics

Introduction

This section addresses the relation of the Weimar Left to questions of sexual politics and the movement for women's equality. The Social Democrats, under the Erfurt Programme of 1891, were already committed before 1914 to achieving equality of rights between men and women. One glaring instance of inequality was the exclusion of women from the franchise. The USPD called in 1917 for the immediate introduction of equal voting rights for women,[1] and the MSPD was happy to agree to this once the War was over. The 1919 Constitution confirmed the decision. The occasional visit to the ballot box did not change women's unequal situation in other respects, but it cannot be said that the SPD gave priority to this matter during the Weimar Republic. Its vision of appropriate gender roles did not differ substantially from the view taken in German society as a whole. For the SPD, as Adelheid von Saldern has pointed out 'gender issues remained in the background'. The Party, she says, took a 'two-faced view on women's causes' demanding equality for women but not taking any steps to make this possible'.[2] The KPD, for its part, certainly called for full equality between men and women, but as far as its membership was concerned, 'it remained a men's club' (Mallmann).[3] The involvement of the KPD in a range of campaigns on women's issues (exemplified in documents 9.10 to 9.16) did not help it to reduce the differential between its male and its female voting support. Helen Boak has called attention to this paradox: 'The party that gained least from female suffrage was the one that had the most radical platform on women's issues'.[4]

Neither party had a high proportion of female members or leaders. The SPD had more female members (ranging from 10.3 percent in 1923 to 22.8 percent in 1932) than the KPD (ranging from 9.1 percent in 1920 to 16.5 percent in 1929).[5]

---

1 Thönnessen 1973, p. 108.
2 Saldern 1998, pp. 98, 101.
3 Mallmann 1996, p. 131. For more detailed accounts of the KPD's attitude to women see Kontos 1979 and, more recently, Grossmann 1998, pp. 135–68.
4 Boak 1981, p. 159.
5 Hagemann 1990, pp. 561–74.

The SPD executive always contained one or two women (Marie Juchacz[6] and Elfriede Ryneck[7]), or at most three (Anna Nemitz[8] was added after 1922). It was through accident rather than policy that the KPD was led for a short time by women: Rosa Luxemburg in January 1919 and Ruth Fischer in 1924–25. In general, they were rarely to be found in top party positions. Only six percent of leading communists in the Weimar period were women.[9] The KPD did try to remedy this situation in 1930, instructing party branches that 'at least a third of representatives elected to District Party Conferences should be female'.[10]

In the SPD, Point 5 of the Party Statutes adopted by the Berlin Congress in 1924 provided that 'the female members of the Party are to be guaranteed a representation proportionate to their numbers in all leading bodies of the organisation and all delegations' (11.2) but no steps were taken to implement this (9.6, 9.8). In 1926 only 4 percent of Germany's SPD town councillors were female.[11] In the wider society, equality of remuneration for the same work was an ideal objective, but it was not achieved at this time,[12] nor was women's right to work recognised. Women with small children rarely went out to work, and when married women did gain employment their income formed a minute fraction of the total family income (1.9 percent for low income families earning up to 2,500 Marks annually, 8.8 percent for middle-income workers' families of above 4,300 Marks annually).[13] The gendered division of labour continued to predominate both within the SPD (9.2) and the KPD, and in society as a whole. Although the parties in theory supported full and equal participation of their female members in political activities, many ordinary members of both the KPD and the SPD preferred their wives to be at home doing the housework rather than at party meetings.[14] There were also limits on the degree to which

---

6   Marie Juchacz (1879–1956), SPD, member of the Reichstag 1920–33, member of the Party executive, head of the Women's Secretariat and chair of the Workers' Welfare organisation.

7   Elfriede Ryneck (1872–1951), SPD, member of the Reichstag 1920–24, member of the Prussian Diet 1925–33, member of the Party executive.

8   Anna Nemitz (1873–1962), USPD, SPD, member of the Reichstag, member of the Party executive 1922–33.

9   As calculated from the biographies in Weber 1969, vol. 2.

10   Weber and Wachtler 1981, pp. 128, 596.

11   Crew 1998, p. 228.

12   Skilled women workers received 65 percent of comparable men's income in 1924 (a rise from 58 percent in 1913), unskilled women workers received 62 percent in 1924 (a decline from 71 percent in 1913). Details in Petzina, Abelshauser and Faust 1978, p. 99.

13   Winkler 1988, p. 87, based on a 1928 survey of income.

14   Fromm 1980, pp. 182–8.

it was seen as practical for women to be fully involved side by side with men in party activities. For instance, in the communist case, when the RFKB (Red Front Fighters' League) was set up in 1924 it actually had a number of female members, but by 1925 the Party had decided that they should be excluded, as 'the admission of women contradicts the military character of the organisation'. It was Ruth Fischer herself who proclaimed this decision, at the 1925 Party Congress. Women, she said, would be able to join a separate organisation, the RFMB, which would soon be set up under Clara Zetkin.[15]

The other question on which documents are printed in this section is sexual relations, between partners of the same or different genders, and their physical and social consequences. Sexual reformers clearly had more to hope for from the Left than from the Right, but the SPD was very hesitant on these matters. There had always been a strand of opinion within the Party, before 1914, which favoured birth control and a freer attitude towards sexuality, although it faced strong opposition from more traditional socialists.[16] Under Weimar, many SPD leaders felt they had to stay on good terms with the (predominantly Roman Catholic) Centre Party, with which they were permanently in alliance in Prussia. Even so, there were still some occasions when they considered it worthwhile to take up sexual reform. The communists, meanwhile, particularly between 1928 and 1933, during the so-called 'Third Period', were unconstrained by alliance politics and very happy to use demands for sexual reform as an agitational tool. The renowned psychoanalyst Wilhelm Reich, who had joined the Communist Party of Austria in 1927, joined the KPD when he moved to Germany, and he developed a theory linking sexuality with the broader social context. A socialist revolution was necessary, he argued in 1932, because 'in capitalist society there can be no sexual liberation of youth, no healthy, satisfying sex life. If you want to be rid of your sexual troubles, fight for socialism'.[17] The KPD soon decided, however, that Reich's endorsement of adolescent sexuality, even though it was supposed to happen 'within the framework of the revolutionary movement,' would 'drag politics down to the level of the gutter'. His pamphlets were no longer circulated after December 1932 because they were 'contrary to the true Marxist education of youth'.[18] He was expelled from the Party soon afterwards.

---

15   Bericht, *Parteitag* 1925, 1926, p. 754. See below, chapter 10 for a more detailed discussion of this point.
16   Niggemann 1981, pp. 267–9.
17   Reich 1972, p. 274.
18   Sharaf 1983, pp. 169–70.

One of the obstacles to a healthy sex life was the unavailability of contraceptives. Both parties were in favour of making contraception more widely available, although the Social Democrats were unwilling to demand the complete repeal of Article 184 Section 3 of the Penal Code of 1871, which prohibited the advertising of contraceptive devices on the ground that they were 'objects intended for indecent use'.[19] The KPD, on the other hand, put forward a motion to the Reichstag in 1928 calling for the repeal of this law and the establishment of free sex advice centres, and it reintroduced this motion no less than three times, in 1929, 1931 and 1932, always without success.[20] The inevitable result of difficulties in obtaining contraceptive devices[21] was an increase in the use of abortion, which was strictly forbidden under Paragraph 218 of the Penal Code, which remained in force throughout the period. Some doctors considered that abortion should be legalised, and the politicians followed their lead. The KPD was more active in this respect than the SPD, although it saw abortion as a regrettable necessity forced on working-class women by the lack of an effective birth-control system (9.12) and by economic misery. Thus in the long run abortion would be rendered unnecessary by 'raising the general economic level of the working masses'. But in the short run an 'inexorable struggle against Paragraph 218' was on the agenda.[22] Many SPD leaders, on the other hand, had reservations about decriminalising abortion. According to Cornelie Usborne, *Vorwärts*, the central SPD party organ, 'had an almost pro-Paragraph 218 slant until 1924'[23] although there were some abortion law reformers in the SPD, such as Klara Bohm-Schuch[24] and Gustav Radbruch. They jointly sponsored a bill to

19   The SPD did, however, support the Law for the Prevention of Venereal Disease (passed on 8 February 1927), which allowed 'inoffensive advertisement of prophylactics' and 'removed the last impediment to contraceptive propaganda' (Usborne 1992, p. 111) although it was a step backwards in some other respects.

20   Usborne 1992, p. 117. The text is Sozialistische Einheitspartei Deutschlands Zentralkomitee 1958, pp. 697–700.

21   Sex reform organisations, with a membership of 150,000 by 1932, did much to improve this situation. Atina Grossmann refers to their 'practical success in providing…inexpensive contraceptives which contrasted sharply with their political failure' (Grossmann 1983, p. 266).

22   Emil Höllein's speech of 3 February 1929 quoted in Fölster 1978, p. 235.

23   Usborne 1992, p. 256, n. 29.

24   Klara Bohm-Schuch (1879–1936) SPD, member of the Reichstag 1920–33. Her support for abortion law reform coexisted with somewhat reactionary views on racial matters: in May 1920 she presented a resolution protesting against the use by the French of 'coloured troops' in the occupied areas because this was 'a weapon which will ultimately bring destruction to the whole of the white race'. (Winkler 1985, p. 224.)

permit abortion during the first three months of pregnancy (31 July 1920). This naturally failed to reach the statute book.

Much later on, a major campaign around the same issue was launched by the KPD, starting in 1928 with the setting up of a doctor's course in birth control and abortion techniques with the active aid of communist doctors. In October 1929 a communist-organised Reich Congress of Working Women called for the removal of Paragraph 218 from the statute-book. It started to issue a journal for women under the slogan 'Your Body Belongs to You'. As Atina Grossmann has pointed out 'the KPD presented a clearly emancipatory alternative when it categorically demanded the abolition of Paragraph 218 and all legislation regulating personal sexual behaviour.'[25] The campaign to end women's reproductive oppression moved up a gear in 1930 in response to Pope Pius XII's encylical against birth control, which the KPD described as a 'Fascist attempt to create cannon-fodder for an imperialist war against the Soviet Union'. The slogans of the International Women's Day demonstration of 8 March 1931 were 'Down with the Brüning Dictatorship, Down with Paragraph 218, We Demand Bread and Peace'. In June 1931 a broad coalition against Paragraph 218 was set up by the KPD, which included middle-class groups like the League for the Protection of Motherhood and Sex Reform and the Women's League for Peace and Freedom alongside the Party's own Committee of Working Women. This was 'the last time the KPD and the SPD publicly agitated together on the same platform'.[26] The moment did not last. The SPD wanted not to abolish Paragraph 218 but to allow certain 'socio-economic and eugenic, as well as medical' grounds for exemption, whereas the KPD stood for complete de-criminalisation.[27] A conference held in the same month ended in disagreement. The KPD abandoned its alliance policy and set up a Unity Committee for Proletarian Sexual Reform (EPS) instead. The anti-Paragraph 218 movement disappeared as rapidly as it had arisen, and abortion continued to be a criminal offence. Later on the KPD attacked the 'timid and vacillating politics of the SPD, which insisted on maintaining an abortion law on the books'[28] but this accusation was entirely unfair, as by then the majority non-socialist parties in the Reichstag were opposed to all changes in the law, so the SPD's attitude became irrelevant.

The other major issue which came up in the area of sexual politics was homosexuality. Paragraph 175 of the 1871 Penal Code outlawed 'acts of a coital

25   Grossmann 1978, p. 133.
26   Grossmann 1993, p. 119.
27   Grossmann 1978, p. 132.
28   Grossmann 1978, p. 135.

nature performed between males' and it punished these acts with jail terms of up to five years. The paragraph continued to be enforced during the Weimar period. The SPD position had been stated somewhat vaguely by Bernstein as early as 1895: 'The state and the penal law should not be the guardians of morality'. Actual campaigning against Paragraph 175 was taken up by the homosexual rights advocate Magnus Hirschfeld[29] in 1897, although his interests were much broader than this, and he continued to push for its abolition for the next 35 years. The SPD, for its part, ignored the question of homosexuality in the early-years of the Weimar Republic, but eventually, in 1927, the Kiel Congress accepted a resolution including as Point 8 'the removal of punishment for adultery and unnatural intercourse'.[30] Kurt Rosenfeld spoke in favour, on the grounds that 'abnormal sexual relations must completely cease to be treated by the criminal law in this quasi-medieval manner'. 'Homosexuality', he added, 'cannot be stamped out by penal laws. It has existed through the ages despite Paragraph 175'. The punishment for adultery, he added, 'must finally disappear from the statute book'.[31] When it came to legislation, however, in 1929, only the KPD supported the complete removal of Paragraph 175 from the statute-book. Karl Hiller, who co-chaired the Scientific-Humanitarian Committee, which was the homosexual rights pressure group set up by Magnus Hirschfeld, said in 1930 that the communists 'were the only party which represented the Scientific-Humanitarian standpoint without any reservations'. He added that he did not belong to the KPD and was critical of it in various respects, but this was the plain truth.[32] Already in June 1924 the KPD had proposed the abolition of Paragraph 175 and an amnesty for everyone condemned under it. Their proposals could not, however, be expected to have any practical effect. In May 1927 Wilhelm Koenen, a top member of the KPD leadership, attacked Paragraph 175 as 'reactionary' and called on 'all appropriate organisations' to fight against it. The communists returned to the charge in 1929, when Arthur Ewert,[33] another

---

29   Magnus Hirschfeld (1868–1935), psychiatrist and sexual reformer. He founded the Institute for Sexual Science (*Institut für Sexualwissenschaft*) in 1919, and became one of the three presidents of the World League for Sexual Reform in 1928. His institute was destroyed in 1933 by a mob of Nazi students and he moved from Germany to France, where he spent the remainder of his life.

30   *Sozialdemokratischer Parteitag* 1927, p. 264.

31   *Sozialdemokratischer Parteitag* 1927, p. 153.

32   Herzer 1995, p. 205.

33   Arthur Ewert (1890–1959), KPD, member of the Polbüro 1925–29, member of the Reichstag 1928 to 1930. A moderate and a 'conciliator' in the factional struggles of the late 1920s, he disavowed and condemned this approach in 1930. He represented the ECCI in China from 1929–34, then in Brazil until his arrest in 1935.

member of the KPD Central Committee, spoke in the Reichstag castigating the 'so-called popular feelings' of people 'who reject what is abnormal owing to their lack of understanding and knowledge of the facts'.[34] The SPD, as a party of government, took a more cautious line. The Social Democrats were keen to get a new criminal code through the Reichstag by compromising with the bourgeois parties. They therefore introduced a replacement paragraph, number 296, prescribing penalties of from 6 months to 5 years for the seduction by gay men of juveniles below the age of 21, as well as the misuse of relations of service and dependency for sexual purposes, but legalising homosexual acts outside these contexts. In the crucial vote of the Criminal Law Committee of the Reichstag on 16 October 1929 this was what was agreed, by 15 votes to 13. But the reform never took legal effect, because shortly afterwards the Grand Coalition broke down, the Müller government went out of office, and subsequent right-wing cabinets had no interest in supporting reforms in the sphere of sexual politics. Paragraph 175, like Paragraph 218, remained on the statute book.

Documents

9.1   *Women's Demands Included in the SPD's 1921 Programme*
Social Democracy fights for equal rights and equal duties for all people, without distinction of sex or origin ... Night work should be restricted to the greatest possible extent for men. Prohibition of night work for women.[35] Prohibition of the work of women and young people in particularly unhealthy enterprises, and at machines where there is a particularly high risk of accidents. Prohibition of paid work by children of school age ... Universal right of women to employment ... A systematic population policy adapted to the social needs of the working class. Special care for large families.

---

34   Arthur Ewert's speech to the 85th session of the Reichstag Committee on Criminal Justice (Eissler 1980, p. 72).

35   The SPD's Heidelberg Programme of 1925 called simply for a 'restriction of night work' without any gender specification. but its Organisational Statute made two concessions to women: it provided that 'Female members of the Party are to be given representation in all leading bodies of the organisations and in all delegations in proportion to their numbers' (Paragraph 5) and that 'If there are more than 7,500 female party members in a District one woman is to be elected to the Party Commission in addition to the District's normal quota'. (Paragraph 22). See *Sozialdemokratischer Parteitag* 1925, pp. 11–17.

Complete constitutional and practical equality for all citizens over 20 years of age irrespective of sex, origin or religion. The judiciary should be staffed by people of all social classes, and women should be involved in all judicial offices ... Combined education of both sexes by teachers of both sexes.

Source: Sozialdemokratische Partei Deutschlands 1921, *Protokoll über die Verhandlungen des Parteitages der Sozialdemokratischen Partei Deutschlands, abgehalten in Görlitz vom 18. bis 24 September 1921*, pp. IV–VI.

9.2   *Dr. Sophie Schöfer Addresses the SPD Women's Conference in 1921 on the Role of Women in Social Work*

In speaking of 'women's social work in the community' we have first to ask the question: are there in fact specifically feminine social tasks? Has not our Party always upheld the principle that we all struggle for universal human rights and hence we should not introduce specifically female-oriented demands into the Party programme? We also cannot hide the fact that many of our comrades still agree with the representatives of the bourgeoisie in excluding women from general questions affecting the community, and want to assign them exclusively to the sphere of social tasks because, they allege, social work is precisely appropriate for women to undertake. We don't want to reject this view as being narrow-minded, but would rather ask simply: why does social work appear so appropriate for women?

Social work is helping people and protecting life. Woman is the born guardian and protector of her fellow creatures. That is why social work has to appear appropriate for women. In assigning to women the task of guarding over human life, we at the same time reply positively to the question of whether the woman has any kind of role in politics. If to engage in struggle is more appropriate to the male character, then the female character has a greater understanding of how to protect and maintain human life. If the man has more understanding of the commodity economy and commodity production, the woman is more able to reach a deeper comprehension of the destiny of humanity. Hence, in the overall framework of things, the task of being the guardian and protector of human life falls to the woman. The woman's field is therefore human economy. I did not invent this expression, but no one has yet come up with a better one ... Woman's social task is only one part of this task of promoting human economy. It brings the woman into contact with all areas of public life ... We have so far had no human economy, only a commodity economy. The capitalist economic order does not pay attention to human life, which is the highest value of all ... Alongside her job of increasing the number of human beings, the woman has the task of shaping individual human lives in the most productive and felicitous way. Our most vital interest is not to increase the population of a country but to deal with individual human lives in a manner both thrifty and wise.

One word on the question of population policy. I am naturally of the view that one should not prevent people from getting married. I don't begrudge this to anyone. But what one must prohibit is the getting of children by sick human beings.[36] It is highly irresponsible for the sick to propagate their disabilities by having children. At present everyone who gets married brings children into the world without demonstrating to the state that he has the moral right to do so, without proving that he is not burdening the community...

Source: Sozialdemokratische Partei Deutschlands 1921, *Reichsfrauentag der Sozialdemokratische Partei Deutschlands am 17. und 18. September 1921 in Görlitz*, pp. 11, 43–4.

Note: Sophie Schöfer was speaking as a representative of Workers' Welfare (*Arbeiterwohlfahrt*), the mainly female organisation founded by Marie Juchacz of the SPD in 1919 to promote social welfare. By 1926 it had over 150,000 members in almost 2,000 branches.[37] As is implied by this extract the movement accepted the maternalist politics of the SPD and made no effort to challenge the gendered division of labour.

9.3   *Helene Grünberg[38] Attacks the Failure of Male Party Comrades to Oppose the Dismissal of Married Women Workers after 1918*

People are now trying to force women out of economic life, after the number of women workers has increased phenomenally in recent years. This is done via the Demobilisation Office's Decree of 12 February 1919 (as amended on 15 April 1920) according to which women in a good financial position are to be dismissed from employment. This refers in particular to married factory workers. Hundreds of thousands of married women have simply been dismissed in industrial cities. This is extraordinarily harmful to the economy of individual

---

36   This was, as Michael Schwarz points out, the next logical step after the introduction of 'obligatory pre-nuptial health certificates' called for repeatedly by the SPD in Prussia. Later in the debate another delegate, Antonie Pfülf, also spoke in favour of compulsory sterilisation (Schwarz 1995, pp. 93–4).

37   Eifert and Selwyn 1997, p. 28.

38   Helene Grünberg (1874–1928), SPD. Dressmaker by original profession. Long trade-union career starting in 1896, member of the SPD's Control Commission 1919–20. Member of the Reichstag 1919–20.

families. The Women's Conference, which dealt with this question, proposed that the Party's parliamentary group (*Fraktion*) should make an effort to get rid of this decree. We cannot continue to live like this. We are not creating free places for the unemployed but merely worsening the misery of the working class as a whole ... The employers are exploiting this opportunity to bring in a cheaper workforce and to abolish the eight-hour day. We ought to stand by the women and protect them, and I therefore ask the Congress to accept this motion.

Source: Sozialdemokratische Partei Deutschlands 1920, *Protokoll über die Verhandlungen des Parteitages der Sozialdemokratischen Partei Deutschlands, abgehalten in Kassel vom 10. bis 16. Oktober 1920,* p. 115.

Note: This is the text of Motion No. 347, calling on the parliamentary *Fraktion* to make sure that 'the decrees preventing women from working' are rescinded and to prevent 'the issuing of similar decrees in the future'. The motion was neither accepted nor rejected but transmitted to the *Fraktion,* which took no further action.

9.4 *Views of Helene Grünberg on the Reasons for the Lack of Female Support for the Party in the 1920 Elections*

We women are reproached with failing to use the ballot correctly. Big brother is scolding little sister. If more practical socialism had been implemented within the family in the 30 years during which we were able to carry on our work unhindered, women would have had more affection and understanding for socialism, and they would also have made better use of the votes they gained as a result of the [November] Revolution. It is big brother who is to blame. Formerly, women were not regarded as worthy to receive enlightenment, and now we all have to suffer as a result. But we also ought to learn from this. We should bear in mind that we ought to look back now and again, not just deal with the questions of the day. If would be very good if this question of education were examined somewhat more thoroughly. Then we would be able to move forward.

Source: Sozialdemokratische Partei Deutschlands 1921, *Protokoll über die Verhandlungen des Parteitages der Sozialdemokratischen Partei Deutschlands, abgehalten in Görlitz vom 18. bis 24 September 1921,* p. 186.

Note: There is some evidence that women, as claimed here, were less likely to vote for the SPD than men. In Cologne, in 1919, where the male and female electorate was counted separately, the SPD received 46.1 percent of the male vote, and only 32.2 percent of the female vote.[39] Generally in predominantly Roman Catholic areas of the country the Centre Party gained the greatest benefit from the extension of the franchise to women. This divergence between male and female voting behaviour lessened, however, in subsequent years, and in the 1930 elections in Leipzig and Magdeburg, the SPD actually did slightly better among women than men.[40]

9.5   Views of Marie Juchacz on the Same Subject Three Years Later

We must ask the question: how has women's right to vote worked out for the Party? Has the attitude of women not become a matter of life and death for the Party? Is not our success now and in the future dependent on whether we can win over the broad masses of women for socialism? One more question: If we fail as a party, who is then morally responsible for such an unfavourable development? We ourselves have to bear the responsibility, because we have not fulfilled the tasks history has assigned to us. The best of our women comrades found it almost depressing when women got the vote, because they were aware of the failings of their own sex ... failings which are rooted in a false kind of education ... All development rests on education and education is not only theoretical. It has to happen in practice. So it is wrong to say that it was too early for women to receive the vote, because every development needs to pass through a period of education through action, and the politicisation of women can only occur if they themselves take an active part in political life through exercising both passive and active voting rights.

Source: Sozialdemokratischer Parteitag 1924. *Protokoll mit dem Bericht der Frauenkonferenz*, p. 225.

9.6   Marie Juchacz Complains about the Under-representation of Women in the SPD's Governing Bodies

The leading bodies of our organisations are not staffed in the way they should be. We are Social Democrats, but even among us equality of rights for women has not found unconditional recognition. Male pre-eminence continues to be defended and maintained strongly. This is often shown in elections to the executive committees of organisations, where women are allowed to occupy one or two places in a group of 10 as a form of concession. If we want to give honourable and exemplary recognition to women's equal rights the dominant consideration should not be that a woman ought to be included in

---

39   Bremme 1956, p. 243.
40   Boak 1981, p. 171, n. 21.

the group, but that the most able person, whether male or female, should get a place.

Source: Sozialdemokratische Partei Deutschlands 1921, *Reichsfrauentag der Sozialdemokratische Partei Deutschlands am 17 und 18 September 1921 in Görlitz*, p. 11.

9.7 *Frau Hörreth-Menge (Munich) Complains about the Failure of the Party to Protest Against the Post-war Mass Dismissals of Women Workers and Explains Why Some Women in Bavaria Support Hitler and the DVFP*

Women were called upon at a time of need, when labour power was in short supply. Now people want to push them aside again. (Call from the audience: Very true!) This is happening without any sign of the strong protest that should have come from the ranks of Social Democracy. We ourselves are just the vanguard of the great army of women who are fighting for an equal position in the economy and for their economic freedom, which is the path towards intellectual freedom. If, as in Bavaria, ministerial decrees are issued which not only rescind the legal regulations governing the civil service but also break the constitution, and no one does anything about it; if married female civil servants who have done their duty for 30 years are dismissed, simply thrown out onto the street, without any strong protest from Social Democracy, this is a sign that women's equality in many respects only exists on paper. As the advance guard of the struggle for women's rights, we must make use of all means at our disposal to prevent that from happening ... If in Munich the DVFP has received so many women's votes, this is to be explained by their being brought up to believe in miracles, which drives them either into the arms of the Bavarian People's Party, with its religious ideology, or, if they have lost faith in that, it brings them under the suggestive influence of Adolf Hitler, who masquerades before the people as the saviour of Germany, who can bring an end to all woes.

Source: Sozialdemokratischer Parteitag 1924, *Protokoll mit dem Bericht der Frauenkonferenz*, pp. 232–4.

9.8 *Elise Scheibenhuber (Berlin-Lichtenberg) Proposes Motion 56, Adopted by the SPD Women's Conference, Calling on the SPD to Give Equal Treatment to Men and Women, as Provided for in the Party's Programme, and to Ban the Consumption of Alcohol at Party Meetings*

There is nothing in this motion which is not completely obvious and justifiable for party comrades. Even the German Constitution guarantees fundamental rights to women. The Party also allows us these rights, but in practice things always look different . . . Women are not represented in the Party's Committees to the extent we would wish in the interests of agitation and work among women. Everywhere women are forced into the background . . . Things which go without saying for men are always seen as the exception for women. I believe that no woman who is active in public life is ever spared the question: What does your family think about this? A man never gets asked this question. The attitude of the comrades is that the family comes before work. We must fight against this point of view . . . In the dismissal of civil servants and women factory workers the only consideration is always whether the woman is married or not, and whether she depends entirely on her own income. Efficiency at work plays absolutely no role. On the contrary, we ought to put efficiency at work first, and the financial situation second. The financial emancipation of women, already called for by Bebel,[41] must be implemented by the Party and not evaded by all possible means. Women's professional training must be as thorough as that of young men . . . Our motion also takes a position on the question of alcohol. I know that many party comrades find it uncomfortable even to discuss this. But it is necessary in the interests of our movement to put an end to the drinking culture in our party assemblies. Many women are turned off from party life because so much of it takes place in bars. In addition to this, a large part of men's weekly wage, inadequate as it is, is expended on alcohol. Anyone who has observed factory gates on paydays, and seen how they are besieged by women waiting for their men to come out in order to take away the money so that they don't take it into the bars will understand the bitterness of many women about the Party's failure to take up an energetic position on these matters. Comrade Heinrich Schulz[42] has said that socialism is a cultural movement and we must use all our resources for cultural purposes. But the enjoyment of alcohol is not one of those cultural goals.

Source: Sozialdemokratischer Parteitag in Heidelberg 1925, *Protokoll mit dem Bericht der Frauenkonferenz*, p. 168.

Note: Motion 56 was referred to the parliamentary *Fraktion* for further consideration.

---

41 August Bebel (1840–1913), one of the founders of the SPD and a highly-respected elder statesman of the Party. His book *Woman and Socialism*, first published in 1879, was repeatedly republished and translated into many languages.

42 Heinrich Schulz (1872–1932), SPD, State Secretary in the Ministry of the Interior, 1919–27, member of the Reichstag 1920–30, the Party's educational specialist.

9.9   *Marie Juchacz Explains Why the SPD Opposes the 'Open Door Movement'*

In the international women's movement the question of special protection for women is the subject of much dispute, and this disagreement has even made its way into the working women's movement. It was the representatives of Danish women workers who were of the view that special measures of protection for women would force them out of the best jobs. The Swedish women also supported this idea, at the International Conference of Women Workers held in Paris in 1927. In both countries women are not yet prohibited from working at night, and the leading women in the Scandinavian trade unions are opposed to the introduction of such a prohibition. They also refuse to call for the protection of women before and after childbirth, although they have given up opposing this at international conferences. The decision of the women assembled in Paris in 1927 in favour of special protection for women was accepted by the Socialist Congress in Brussels and the Danish comrades will no doubt put up with this decision. The bourgeois women's movement in Germany agrees with us on this point ... but in the international bourgeois women's movement opinions are divided ... This special protection protects woman first and foremost in her role as mother. The opposition to this idea is based on a purely formal attitude to equality of rights. These women cannot see that special protection for women is absolutely necessary ... in order to give the woman a certain financial position and thereby make her more capable of fighting ... Whether women from bourgeois circles, who have much money and a personal interest in the unrestricted exploitation of women's labour-power, take up his position, would be a matter of indifference to us if there were not a danger that the opinions of these women might have a powerful influence on international decisions. That is why we have to take counter-measures.

Source: Sozialdemokratischer Parteitag in Magdeburg 1929, *Protokoll mit dem Bericht der Frauenkonferenz*, pp. 229–31.

9.10   *Clara Zetkin on the Communist Party and the Woman Question, 1920*

The Communist Party does not need to revise in any way its fundamental position on the woman question. It holds fast to the view that the woman question is not something that exists in and for itself, capable of being solved by reforms in favour of the female sex on the basis of the capitalist economy and within the bourgeois order of society. It is our conviction that the woman question is only a part of the great social question, and it can only be resolved, along with the social question, if the proletariat destroys capitalism and constructs communism in a common struggle of all the exploited and oppressed without distinction of gender...

Comrades, if one is of this opinion, the question arises: what then divides the communist women's movement from the socialist women's movement of the Majority SPD and the right of the USPD? For the women of both those tendencies would also subscribe to the principles we have stated. My answer is this: the communist women's movement is divided from the women's movements of other socialist tendencies and parties by everything which is decisive in this historical moment, by everything which confronts us as the need of the hour. For us communists, the goal is not the 'polar star' which is so much praised up as the light which guides us on our way, which has so often been dimmed by the clouds of opportunism and revisionism, and which has now totally disappeared from view. No, communism stands before us as a burning flame, nourished by all the present miseries with which decaying capitalism in its dissolution confronts the broad masses of women.

And we recognise one thing in the light of this flame: here there is no longer any place for haggling and bargaining, in fear and timidity, to get some small reforms for exploited women. The need of the present is to take up the struggle for the conquest of political power by the proletariat. The goal of the Communist Party's women's movement is to bring together the broadest masses of working women and to educate them to become bold and purposeful activists, ready to make sacrifices for the revolutionary struggle for the establishment of the dictatorship of the proletariat in the Council System, which is the inescapable prerequisite for the realisation of redemption through communism.

Does that mean that we reject improvements in the legal position and the situation of women? By no means. We call for these improvements, we fight for them ... But at the same time we bring home to working women the narrowly limited value of all reforms in exploitative capitalist society ... Through these struggles for reform we destroy working women's illusions about the readiness of the ruling classes and their democratic state to carry out reforms, and we replace those illusions with women's confidence in their own strength and a conviction of the necessity of the struggle for revolution in bourgeois society. Thus the struggle for political power remains the alpha and omega of our activity...

At present the philistine slogan rings out: 'Women should return to being housewives'. The trade-union bureaucrats and the parties associated with them do not fight against this slogan. On the contrary, they defend it, side by side with the most narrow-minded reactionaries. They take the view that the man has the right to employment and wages, and if there is a shortage of work the woman must give up her place to him and return to looking after the house.

They also think an unemployed woman must make do with less unemployment benefit. All the old asseverations about equal rights for women are forgotten. Unemployed men and women are forced into competition with each
other, instead of taking up the struggle against the common foe: the exploiting
capitalist. This shameful behaviour is one more proof that the opportunist
trade-union bureaucrats and their political associates have abandoned the
ground of the socialist, the revolutionary idea, and think only of compromising and bargaining with the capitalists.

Source: Vereinigten Kommunistischen Partei 1921, *Bericht über die Verhandlungen des Vereinigungsparteitags der USPD (Linke) und der KPD (Spartakusbund), Abgehalten in Berlin vom 4. bis 7 Dezember 1920*, pp. 191–206.

9.11   *General Principles for Agitation Among Women Adopted in 1920 by the KPD*

I   The Role of the Communist Party in the Liberation of Women
1 Capitalism in Germany has entered its final phase. With the shattering of its
economic foundations by the world crisis unleashed by the World War, it can
only continue to maintain itself thanks to sharper forms of economic exploitation of the proletariat through the production process, involving the sabotage
of production, profiteering and oppressive taxation. Threatened in its political
domination by the rise of the revolutionary proletariat, it endeavours to maintain its position through the deliberate expansion and ruthless application of
its apparatus of state repression, namely the bureaucracy, the judicial system
and militarism.
    The proletariat is compelled, by an impoverishment which becomes more
and more unbearable, to hasten the struggle for its complete liberation, that is
to say the rapid overthrow of capitalism and the establishment of the dictatorship of the proletariat.
2 This final phase of capitalism increasingly forces proletarian women into
the political struggle. The November Revolution brought them equal political
rights with men, thereby initiating the destruction of the illusion of formal
democracy. Bourgeois democracy was as little able to bring economic and
social freedom to proletarian women as it had been to their male class comrades. Private property in the means of production continued to exist. Hence
the basis for the exploitation of the proletariat by the bourgeoisie also
remained. Women workers are subject to severer exploitation than men: they
have lower wages, they suffer greater damage to their health, and their specific
natural inclinations and tasks as wife and mother are completely ignored. As a

proletarian housewife, the woman has to bear the heaviest burdens such as food shortages, price rises, housing shortages and children's illnesses. Private property is also at the root of a woman's complete economic and personal dependence on her husband, her lack of rights in the family and in public life. Women are completely enslaved and barred from public life by the maintenance of the outdated system of housework.

3 It is only through overcoming the capitalist mode of economic life, the basis of which is private property, and only through the establishment of the communist economy and society that women, just like men, can attain full human freedom. The fight conducted by the VKPD, which has as its goal the emancipation of all the oppressed and exploited, is necessarily also a fight for the emancipation of the proletarian woman. Proletarian women must therefore make the struggle of the proletariat for political power their own, and their highest, cause.

4 The Communist Party, as the vanguard of the proletariat in its fight for liberation, has the task of actively involving all forces for this goal. It therefore has the imperative duty of pointing out the fruits of victory to the women of the proletariat, of training them to be fighters as well and of inserting them into the fighting front of revolution. The fulfilment of this duty towards proletarian women by the Communist Party is required by the overall interest of the proletariat, because the attitude of women, who are numerically the largest part of the working class, towards the proletarian revolution will be of decisive significance, both in the struggle for the conquest and retention of political power and in the construction of the economic and social order.

5 It is the duty of the Communist Party to draw the female comrades in the Party's ranks into the most intensive party work as members with equal rights and equal duties, and to train them for all party tasks in such a way that the female comrades will always be able actively and independently to fulfill all the tasks posed by the revolution, but particularly in periods of extreme political tension.

II   Agitation Among Women within the Framework of General Party
          Work

6 In its communist agitation among women the Party pursues the same goal as it does in relation to the men of the working class: it enlightens them about their class position, it strengthens their class consciousness, it trains them to be fighters for their class. It educates women for what is most important, participation in all actions, and it involves them in all the struggles of the proletarian revolution (demonstrations, general strikes, uprisings).

7 In its agitation among women the Communist Party makes use of all the means of general agitation which are able to reach women as well, such as public and factory meetings, gatherings of the unemployed, trade unions, consumers' associations, work in the Factory Councils and the Workers' Councils, literature and the press.

8 Particular attention should be paid to work in proletarian organisations where women are strongly represented, such as the trade unions of particularly female occupations (textile workers, domestic servants, clothing workers, shop employees, health and care workers) as well as consumers' associations, parents' associations and tenants' associations.

9 In agitation among the unemployed the exceptional legislation against women – the limitations on their right to work and the reduction of their unemployment benefit – should be used to stir them up. An emphatic struggle must be waged from the communist standpoint against the view which prevails even within the proletariat, that pushing women out of jobs could solve or ameliorate the crisis of unemployment.

10 It is necessary to take care that in propaganda and in elections for Factory Councils and political Workers' Councils it is not just women working in the factories who are made aware of the Council idea and drawn into activity in the Councils, but housewives without industrial employment. They must be won over intellectually and through action, whether by sending delegations from the housewives' meetings of a locality or a proletarian town district, or from consumers', parents' and tenants' associations.

III   The Particular Character of Agitation Among Women

11 Agitation among proletarian women must be carefully adapted to their particular manner of life and thought. This means that it is necessary to have specific forms of women's agitation and appropriate to set up particular organs for the recruitment and education of women.

12 In view of women's lack of political maturity all agitation among women must be conducted in as simple and universally comprehensible a manner as possible.

13 Since a large section of women – housewives, domestic workers – cannot be contacted either through the factories or by public assemblies, house-to-house agitation is also necessary for these women.

14 In consequence of the considerable remoteness of women from public life and their exhaustive involvement in the personal concerns of the household and the family agitation must link up with their interests, and, proceeding from that basis, expand women's horizons to take in the connection between

their individual fate and the capitalist economic order. In particular, questions of food shortage, unemployment, the protection of mother and child, and of female workers, prostitution, school and church must be elucidated in detail from the class standpoint.

15 Agitation among women must be particularly directed towards overcoming the petty-bourgeois prejudices and pacifist illusions which are deeply rooted in women's intellectual world and represent a serious inhibition on revolutionary determination and ruthlessness in the class struggle. The reactionary character of the ideal of the home and the family must be demonstrated by referring to the example of the Russian Revolution and the will to overcome these forms must thereby be awakened and strengthened. The necessity for civil war using all present means must be substantiated by using the example of all previous revolutions and the portrayal of the victims of capitalism both in peace and in the imperialist World War must be used to strengthen readiness for the highest accomplishments and the greatest sacrifices for the cause of the emancipation of the proletariat.

16 Agitation among women in written form must also be adapted to these specific requirements. The Communist Party therefore needs, alongside its general communist literature, a specific literature aimed at women. This purpose will be served by:

a) The women's organ of the VKPD, '*Die Kommunistin*', which has the functions of, firstly, enlightening and recruiting women who are as yet politically uneducated, secondly, training comrades who are active in agitation, and finally, laying down the general principles of the Party and providing specific pieces of information and suggestions in the field of agitation among women.

b) The daily newspapers of the VKPD which have women's supplements.

c) Publications on particular occasions, such as leaflets and pamphlets issued by the Women's Secretariat of the Party.

IV   Organisation

17 The VKPD is against setting up a separate women's organisation ...

18 [But] it has set up a Women's Secretariat, with a director elected by the Party Congress, who will take part in all sessions of the *Zentrale* in an advisory role, although she/he will have a deciding voice in matters affecting her/his area of work.

[There follow a number of detailed instructions on the organisation and duties of a Women's Agitation Commission, directed specifically by a woman, who is made responsible for a very broad range of tasks in agitation and the publication of literature.]

Source: Zentrale der Vereinigten Kommunistischen Partei Deutschlands 1921, 'Richtlinien für die Frauenagitation', in *Bericht über die Verhandlungen des Vereinigungsparteitags der USPD (Linke) und der KPD (Spartakusbund)*, *Abgehalten in Berlin vom 4. bis 7. Dezember 1920*, pp. 261–7.

9.12   *The Attitude of the KPD in 1922 Towards Paragraphs 218 and 219 of the Criminal Code*

The *abortion paragraphs* are a shameful aspect of the old imperial Germany which the so-called November Revolution has also failed to remove. Even today the police and the courts of the German republic rage against proletarian women who are ever more frequently forced by poverty to have recourse to means of abortion.

The *Women's Reich Secretariat* of the KPD has examined this question in many sessions, and it laid down its position of principle in a memorandum to the *Zentrale* which that body adopted in its 19 April 1922 session. This is the text of the memorandum:

Paragraph 218 states: 'A pregnant woman who intentionally aborts or kills the fruit of her womb will be punished with up to five years of imprisonment. It there are extenuating circumstances, the term of imprisonment will not be less than six months. These penal provisions also apply to anyone who gives the pregnant woman the means to perform the abortion or killing or instructs her in the methods'.

Paragraph 219 states: 'Anyone who provides a pregnant woman with the means or instructs her in the method, of committing an abortion will be punished with imprisonment for up to ten years'.

The movement of proletarian women against these shameful paragraphs is on the increase throughout the country. Partly because of the reactionary attitude of the authorities, who persecute proletarian women for breaching these paragraphs, partly through our own campaign, this matter has gained increasing momentum ... *The KPD has the duty to mobilise proletarian women in the light of this concrete question and to win them for the class struggle.* We must use this persecution of working women to demonstrate the whole *swindle of democracy,* which in appearance stands for equal rights, but in reality opens the doors of the hospitals to women of polite society for abortion while delivering proletarian women into the hands of the quacks. They then go exactly to the places where police informers abound. The victims of these police persecutions are put in prison and their children are left at home to suffer hunger and neglect ... Despite the strict application of these barbaric paragraphs of the penal code, *abortion has increased immensely in the recent period*. Precise statistics cannot be obtained, as the majority of cases are unknown to the doctors. Nor can the exact number of *deaths resulting from botched abortions* be discovered. But according to medical estimates *20,000 women die every year in Germany as a result of abortions undertaken by unqualified persons*...The rise in abortions is to be explained by *the increased misery of the working class*. A large number of children exerts pressure on the whole family's standard of living...At this time of impoverishment, the working class is not in a position to reproduce itself. In this emergency it has recourse to the most obvious means of preserving its standard of life, already at the lowest possible level.

Abortion as a *way of regulating births is uneconomic and, for women, brutal.* It is only because of the hypocrisy and secretiveness of present-day society, which makes methods of birth control either unknown or unavailable to the people, that the mass of proletarian women have to adopt this ultimate method of avoiding placing children in the world for whom no bread is available.

The KPD is far from recommending abortion as an ideal. But we must emphatically oppose the way proletarian women are compelled by the capitalist social order to place children in the world for whom the state cannot create life opportunities. We must oppose the police paragraphs which forbid abortion with the demand for *maternity homes* and for *the assistance of doctors and midwives to be provided free of charge.*

Our motions in the Reichstag demand not just the abolition of Paragraphs 218 and 219 but adequate *public provision for pregnant women, babies and children.* If the state cannot provide this, we demand for women the right to have their foetuses aborted free of charge by qualified doctors in public institutions.

The USPD calls for the abolition of Paragraphs 218 and 219 without our positive proposals...The SPD wants to allow abortion in the first three months by a qualified doctor...This shows it is still caught up in the ideology of Christianity, according to which the foetus has a soul after a certain number of months of pregnancy, so that abortion then becomes murder.

We must expose the hypocrisy of bourgeois society, which gives various excuses for opposing abortion. All its excuses, whether medical or moral, are *dictated by the class interest of bourgeois society*, which sees a danger to itself in a decline in the birth rate. The bourgeoisie fears that the objects of its exploitation may diminish in number, and that the necessary labour-power may not be available at times of *strong economic expansion* while in times of crisis and depression the presence of an *industrial reserve army* is welcome to it. An even greater fear is that in the next war for the division of the world there may not be *enough cannon-fodder* available.

In its struggle against this draconian law against proletarian women, the KPD must give women themselves the right to make their own decisions, to judge for themselves whether they are in a position to bring up a new human being, as long as society is not prepared to take over the care of the mother and the bringing up of the children.

In doing this, we must *point out the dangers* of abortion for women who fall into the hands of quack doctors and often lose their lives as a result. We must also not forget that *an acceleration of the fall in the birth rate* ultimately reduces the number and strength of the working class, hence *does not serve the interests of the class struggle* ... We use this concrete case to show the hypocrisy and baseness of bourgeois society, the contradiction in this society, which wants to bring humans into the world who are condemned to a miserable life and an early death.

Present-day capitalist society is no longer in a position to secure life itself for its slaves, it is no longer able to guarantee them the most basic *right of humans to reproduce themselves*.

We are fighting for the *removal of these shameful paragraphs*, which are directed specifically against women. We want to mobilise proletarian women *against the present order of society*, to win them for the class struggle. The contradiction which lies in the whole social order and which comes to the surface in this matter can only be removed completely with the removal of the capitalist social order itself. *In this way, we mobilise women for the struggle against the whole social order of capitalism.*

Source: *Die Internationale*, 1922, 20, pp. 462–5.

9.13   *Aims and Tasks of the League of Red Women and Girls (RFMB43), 1926*

Origins of the League

Tens of thousands of proletarians rushed to join the RFB (League of Red Front Fighters) when it was formed. With its lively methods of agitation, its marches, its Red Days, its festivals, the RFB also acted to shake up and activate proletarian women who had remained passive until then. Women demanded to be accepted into RFB groups, and in most cases their wishes were granted. But the RFB was not in a position to include and retain large numbers of women. The great mass of women saw the RFB as an organisation of proletarian soldiers, whose special tasks and military colouring hardly corresponded to their specific interests and feelings as women. The RFB for its part feared that by organising women it might blur its character as an organisation of front fighters ... On 29 November 1925, therefore, the RFMB was founded, at a

43   In German: *Rote Frauen- und Mädchenbund.*

conference of women from all parts of Germany. The RFBM reflects a need strongly felt by broad strata of proletarian women. They feel the need to fight against their total impoverishment, in view of the terrible deterioration in the economic position of the working class, women in particular. Capitalist rationalisation, which leads to ever-sharper methods of exploitation, ever greater involvement of women in the process of production, drives more and more women to revolt. But the vast majority of women still shrink from joining the Party or a trade union. Women have often only just entered the production process, having grown up in the isolation and deadening monotony of housework. They are politically unenlightened and uneducated.

In general, the proletariat has not so far understood how to win over women for the class struggle. Moreover, large numbers of proletarians are still imprisoned in bourgeois attitudes, and do not recognise women as fully equal to them. The bourgeoisie, in contrast, has understood very well how to involve women in bourgeois, Fascist and Christian women's organisations, in which proletarian women are alienated from their class. In the course of a year, the RFMB has developed into an auxiliary organisation for the proletarian class struggle, and it now embraces tens of thousands of proletarian women. Through its educational work it will now convince women of the need to be organised politically and in trade unions.

I   The Goals of the RFMB

To bring together in a proletarian women's organisation, without distinction of party or religion, women of the proletariat who are still either standing aside or have strayed into bourgeois women's organisations, with the purpose of:

1 enlightening them about their class position;

2 educating them systematically in theory and practice and training them up to be class warriors;

3 involving them in the struggle for the emancipation of the working class, particularly women workers, from exploitation and disenfranchisement;

4 involving them in the common fighting front of the proletariat, particularly by organising them in the Free Trade Unions, the Workers' Cooperatives and Red Aid;

5 convincing advanced proletarian women of the need for them to be organised in the political Party.

II   The Tasks of the RFMB

In line with the overall goals of the League, they have the following tasks on the basis of the present economic and political situation in Germany and the world:

1 to fight against capitalist rationalisation and its devastating consequences for the female proletariat;

2 to fight against imperialist wars, particularly against the encirclement of the Soviet Union;

3 to fight against bourgeois women's organisations, which endeavour to draw the female proletariat into the camp of the class enemy.

[There follows an analysis of capitalist rationalisation and its impact]

The following specific demands are to be raised in the day-to-day struggle against the employers:

a) for unemployed women:

1 The closest association with employed women;

2 The fight against strike breaking by unemployed women;

3 The fight for a 50 percent increase in unemployment benefit;

4 Job creation for women too;

5 The fight against the unemployment insurance law[44] and against the sliding scale for unemployment payments, which means a reduction in support for unemployed women in particular.

b) for mother and child:

The reduction of social care is part of the employers' rationalisation programme. We are fighting for the following demands in opposition to this:

1 Measures for the protection of health in the factories;

2 Weekly payments to be extended to eight weeks before and eight weeks after the birth; establishment of state maternity hospitals, crêches and children's homes;

3 Abolition of Paragraph 218 and an amnesty for convicted women;

c) for the proletarian housewife:

1 Adequate, cheap dwellings for all working people;

2 Abolition of taxes for those without property;

3 Reductions in the price of provisions.

[Section Two covers the fight against imperialist war and the encirclement of the Soviet Union]

---

44   This was the law eventually passed on 7 July 1927 against KPD opposition. It was regarded by the SPD as one of its greatest achievements (1.16). Various compromises with the bourgeois parties made it unacceptable to the communists, even in 1927 when they were at their most moderate.

Section Three: The Fight Against the Bourgeois Women's
Organisations

These can be placed in four groups, based on their characteristics:

a) General women's associations
b) Christian women's associations
c) Fascist women's organisations
d) Pacifist and feminist women's organisations

The majority of the general bourgeois women's associations entice proletarian women with all kinds of apparent advantages, such as job opportunities, the chance to get cheaper food and articles required in the home and the provision of charity. In line with their ideology they are predominantly concerned with questions of housework and bourgeois child-rearing.

The Christian women's organisations dominate and stupefy women through their religious teachings.

The Fascist women's organisations nourish the spirit of nationalism and militarism, demand the restoration of the monarchy and propagate the idea of obligatory female labour service. They proclaim a very sharp struggle against the working class.

The pacifist women's organisations call for a fight against war and for reconciliation and peace between nations. With this they awaken the dangerous illusion that a perpetual peace can be achieved even in the age of capitalism.

A number of women's organisations have set themselves the task of making demands specifically for women, such as for example the protection of mothers, limitations on the number of births etc. Raising such partial demands, in isolation from the proletarian class struggle, will also alienate proletarian women from their class and from the class struggle.

The task of the RFMB is:

1 to enlighten women about the true character of the bourgeois women's organisations and to prevent them from entering them;

2 to induce proletarian women in the bourgeois women's organisations to leave them and to win them for the class struggle;

3 to go a part of the way together with left-inclined, sympathising bourgeois women's organisations in the struggle, for instance to hold joint demonstrations with pacifist women's organisations against war, naturally maintaining our own slogan of the fight against imperialist war, and to hold joint demonstrations and meetings with the League for the Protection of Mothers (*Bund für Mutterschutz*) for the improvement of social care for mother and child, while maintaining our fundamental positions.

The RFMB has certain deficiencies which it must work to overcome. These deficiencies are:

1 The military appearance and attitude of the group;

2 Exaggeration of the demonstrative character of the group by taking part in Red Days and Red Meetings;

3 Excessive imitation of the RFB;

4 Failure to form connections with sympathising, left-inclined women's organisations;

5 Too few public demonstrations, meetings and recruitment campaigns;

6 Excessively superficial educational work among the members, which tends to be a result of the above-mentioned deficiencies.

Source: Sozialistische Einheitspartei Deutschlands Zentralkomitee 1926, *Dokumente und Materialien zur Geschichte der deutschen Arbeiterbewegung*, Bd. VIII, pp. 381–6.

9.14 *Resolution of the Eleventh Party Congress on the Work of the KPD Among Women, March 1927*

In the course of the relative stabilisation of capital in Germany at the expense of the proletariat, women, as the cheapest and most biddable object of exploitation, are drawn increasingly into the process of production. The employers are trying to create a female labour army which will play a strikebreaking and wage-undercutting role alongside the army of the unemployed. Capitalist rationalisation, with its simplification of the labour process, makes it easier to replaced skilled workers with unskilled women. The rapid increase in the number of female workers employed in important branches of industry, and the simultaneous rise in male unemployment heightens the significance of female workers in the process of production, and this means that the KPD's work among broad strata of women also becomes more significant.

The fight of the proletariat against the worsening of the situation of the working class owing to capitalist rationalisation and against capitalist exploitation in general can therefore only be pursued with success if it is able to include women workers alongside men in the fighting front … It is therefore important for women workers to be mobilised in the factories.

The Party Congress notes that the Party's work among working women is inadequate, it stresses the need for the whole Party to take up systematic work, constantly reinforced, among the female masses, with the objective of winning them for the revolutionary movement.

I   Work Among Women: The Party's Tasks

1 To involve women, particularly working women, in the struggle against the worsening of the situation of the working class resulting from capitalist rationalisation. To mobilise working women in factories and trade unions

against wage cuts, longer hours, and speed-up, for wage increases, the eight-hour day, equal pay for equal work, the extension of protection for working women, in particular when pregnant, and against child labour...

2 To win over women to work in the Free Trade Unions. Propaganda for the entry of women into the trade unions; women to be brought into the work of the trade unions, and into trade union functions and elections; promotion of the formation of women's committees; the existing committees and functions to be staffed with oppositionists; working women to be won over to the opposition.

Particular attention must also be paid to women in office employment.

3 The fight for the specific interests of women out-workers, agricultural work-ers and small farmers. Home-workers and agricultural workers to be brought into trade unions; fight against the involvement of women industrial workers in out-work; very sharp propaganda against out-work by children. Fight against obligatory labour by the women and children of agricultural workers, against payment in kind and the system of tied cottages.

Involvement of women agricultural workers and small farmers in the legislation on social insurance; improvement of hospitals, extension of the system of midwives in the countryside, and extension of professional training.

4 The mobilisation of unemployed women. The fight against the unemploy-ment insurance law, in particular against grading according to wage classes; for an increase in unemployment benefit; for men and women to have an equal right to benefit; job creation; a joint struggle with women still in work; election of women to Committees of the Unemployed.

5 Winning over proletarian women to the cooperative consumers' associa-tions, to active participation in the life of the cooperatives, for the struggle of the opposition in the cooperatives against the reformist bureaucracy.

6 A greater involvement of women in the struggle for general social and politi-cal demands. Involvement of proletarian housewives in all the struggles of the working class. Protection for mother and child in line with the demands in the KPD's legislative proposals; the fight against child labour; the extension of the health system; the fight against the housing shortage and rent increases; the fight against taxes on articles of mass consumption; the fight against the handing over of schools to the political reaction and the Church; an ideological struggle against the disparagement and oppression of women in the family and in society.

7 Fight to abolish all discriminatory laws applying to women.

8 Involvement in the struggle against imperialist wars and for the defence of the Soviet Union. Concretisation of the Party's slogans in accordance with the ideology as well as the experiences of women in the past World War.

9 Support for the sending of women's delegations to Soviet Russia. Spreading information about the achievements of Soviet Russia, in particular in all areas which are of interest to women.

10 Strengthening of the proletarian mass organisations outside the Party (RFMB, Cooperatives, Red Aid, International Workers' Aid, Sports Organisations, Tenants' Organisations, Free Thinkers).

11 Fight against bourgeois and reformist women's organisations ... by demonstrating their anti-working class character and their actual attitude towards the interests of working women.

II   The Organisation of Work Among Women
[To win women over the Party needs to have special organs for work among women. This section describes their structure and responsibilities, concluding with a section on issuing a special journal for women, which must be 'the organ of oppositional women workers in the factories and the trade unions'.]

III   Forms and Methods of Work Among the Female Masses
Specific forms and methods of revolutionary work are needed to win over the female masses of the proletariat for the revolutionary class struggle. The most important of these are the meetings of female delegates ... They are the most appropriate method of organising and influencing women workers in the class struggle. They are composed of elected delegates, predominantly working women, and take place periodically. The particular significance of these meetings consists in the following:

1 the creation through the delegates of a permanent connection between the Party and the previously unenlightened and inactive strata of working women ...

2 the training of new female functionaries and active forces from the female proletarian masses for the trade unions and the factories and winning over the most advanced women workers to the Communist Party;

3 the establishment of a close connection and cooperation between women who stand in the production process and both their unemployed colleagues and proletarian housewives.

[In addition to this, there are two other important organisations.]

First, the RFMB a proletarian women's organisation sympathising with the KPD made up of 80 percent non-party women and 20 percent members of the Party, and divided 50/50 between women workers and others ... The RFMB applies particular methods of agitation and propaganda to win over working women, always linking its agitation to the daily needs and concerns of women and treating all questions of the day-to-day class struggle from the angle of the interests of proletarian women.

Second, the Workers' Committees. The party leadership must use its influence to make sure that representatives of proletarian women are elected to the Workers' Committees, and that Sub-Committees for work among women are set up within the Committees. The same thing applies to all appropriate unity organisations of the working masses.

Source: Zentralkomitee der KPD 1927, *Thesen und Resolutionen des XI. Parteitags der KPD, Essen, 2–7 März 1927*, pp. 72–82.

9.15 *Martha Arendsee*[45] *(KPD) on the Struggle for the Protection of Mothers, 7 July 1927*

Ladies and Gentlemen! In its time, the communist group of deputies supported the demand for ratification of the Washington Agreement,[46] not because it regarded the content of the agreement as adequate, but only because it wanted to use every opportunity to bring the question of the protection of mothers onto the agenda. The significance of this international agreement is best characterised by the fact that eight years have passed since 1918, when we took a position in the Reichstag on the ratification of this agreement. Very few countries have ratified this agreement (Continuous uproar, the chair of the assembly has to call the deputies to order). My point is, that the capitalist powers have not ratified this agreement but Russia, which does not take part in negotiating such agreements is today the only country which has implemented genuine protection for mothers (Cries of disagreement from the Social Democrats; 'Very true' from the communists). It is not the international agreements which are decisive for us but their actual implementation (Objections from the Social Democrats). You will not be able to deny, even if you try, that the most far-reaching protection of mothers has been carried through in

---

45 Martha Arendsee (1895–1953), joined the SPD in 1906, the USPD in 1917 and the KPD in 1920. Member of the Reichstag from 1924–30. Editor of the KPD women's journal *Die Kommunistin*. Left Germany for the Soviet Union in 1934.

46 The Washington Convention of 1919, an international agreement signed by representatives of the International Labour Organisation, prescribed six weeks' paid maternity leave before and after childbirth. The Reichsrat failed to ratify the Convention in 1922 because of a lack of funds. From 1925 the SPD began again to call for ratification, which was the subject of the debate in which Martha Arendsee was speaking for the KPD. The Washington Convention came into force in Germany on 19 July 1927.

Russia. And if the Reich Labour Minister stands here and declares that Germany has gone furthest of all with this law, then he has deliberately told an untruth. He knows that the Russian regulations go further, that in Russia the woman is given two months off work before and after the child is born, on full pay, and that no woman can be dismissed during this period, and that nursing money is paid for nine months. This not only fits in with the Washington Agreement but anticipates the future regulations of the law on workers' protection ...

It is very regrettable that Social Democracy has abandoned the old fighting demands of socialist women, instead of raising them with the utmost energy. The discussion of this law would have been the ideal opportunity. Today the time has come when proletarian women must again raise their old demands; the more so because the number of working women grows ever larger. The results of the industrial census show that their numbers have risen by three million since 1907 ... This makes it all the more necessary energetically to support an extension of the protection of mothers, for the combination of professional labour and housework is particularly damaging to the female organism. In addition, present working practices make it completely impossible to make allowances for pregnancy ...

The memorandum of Professor Martin[47] expresses the desires of the entrepreneurs in a crude form. He uses the fact that 50 percent of women workers stay at their machines until the five days before, and 21 percent until the day before childbirth to show how happy the women are in their work. These statistics show rather that many pregnant women are forced to work at their machines until the last minute ... This has its consequences for the birth itself: the German Textile Workers' Union's investigations have shown that 64.4 percent of these women had complications in childbirth ... The proposed law excludes women employed in agriculture and forestry from any protection if the firm employs up to three people. This applies to mills, distilleries etc., where female workers do not fall under the protection of the law. But it is precisely the female agricultural workers who are in a situation which requires especially thorough protection. If the government says today that it too considers it needful to protect women workers in agriculture but that because this is not practicable within the framework of this law, a new law will be drawn up, we already know how long one has to wait for such legislation ... It will therefore take at least three or four years before we even have the beginnings of a new law ... We demand the inclusion of protection for female agricultural

---

47   Professor Eduard Martin, a gynaecologist, and head of the Rhineland District Midwives' College, wrote a counterblast to the 1925 Memorandum of the German Textile Workers' Union, which started off the agitation for maternity benefit.

workers and also those in domestic service. For in the domestic economy too no one has the slightest consideration for a pregnant woman. Protection from dismissal in particular would be appropriate for domestic servants in very many cases. For if a housemaid shows signs of pregnancy, the so-called 'lady of the house' immediately puts her out into the street. In many cases, these are girls from the countryside who have come into the big city and now have nowhere to live. They must then seek admission to public maternity hospitals where they very often have their babies under very undignified circumstances.

We are also calling for an extension of the period of maternity benefit. We demand that pregnant women be given leave from their employment three months before and until two months after the birth. This is also in line with the demands of the Textile Workers' Union. But since Frau [Anna] Nemitz described this demand as 'agitational' I must assume that the executive of the Textile Workers' Union was not serious, and only put the demand forward in order to create a good atmosphere at the congress of Women Textile Workers ...

We also demand that all insured pregnant women receive their weekly benefit payments. At present some pregnant women are completely excluded, because of the provision that they need to have belonged to the sickness insurance scheme for at least ten months in the last two years. The Washington Convention, however, provides that 'every woman' should receive support. So here too your legislation does not tally with the Washington Convention.

We also demand that in addition to the breast-feeding pauses of half an hour twice a day, the mothers should be given an appropriate area for this, and crèche facilities should be available. The crèches should be administered jointly by the local muncipalities, the trade unions, the factory councils and mothers from the factories. Russia is exemplary in this regard in that it does not break the connection between mother and child even during working hours ... On the question of protection from dismissal, we demand the extension of the period of protection to one year. The whole of the nursing period needs to be brought under protection from dismissal, which the limitation to six months does not achieve. If a woman is in a position to breast-feed for a longer period she must be given the opportunity to do so, having regard to the child. The entrepreneur must not be allowed to get out of his obligations by simply dismissing the woman.

When the government says, in Paragraph 4 Section 3, that 'the validity of dismissals occurring for important reasons unconnected with pregnancy or birth is not affected by these provisions' it renders illusory the protection from dismissal in the previous two sections; for if the entrepreneur wants to get rid of a pregnant woman he will always be able to find another reason than her pregnancy. So it is just like the nursing pauses: the protection is only on paper. If the other women workers in the factories do not stand side by side with those who are pregnant, the entrepreneur will find a way of throwing them out onto the street despite this law. The Reichstag committee did not discuss these questions at all thoroughly. The government representative did no more than make a few remarks, and some of the government parties did not express an opinion at all. We cannot describe this as a law which genuinely secures protection for motherhood. We are therefore unable to vote for it. To women workers, we say this: you must get into a trade-union organisation. Only in this way will you attain the protection which mothers need if they are not to perish under the present conditions.

Source: Speech by Martha Arendsee in the Reichstag on the employment of women before and after the birth of their children and on the ratification of the Washington Agreement, Deutsches Reich 1924, *Verhandlungen des Reichstags, III. Wahlperiode, 1924, Bd. 393, Stenographische Berichte*, pp. 11368–372.

9.16   *The KPD's Proposed Law to Protect and Give Full Equality of Rights to Working Women, 15 October 1931*

We call on the Reichstag to demand that the government introduce a bill to protect and give full equality of rights to working women according to the following principles:

1 Establishment of complete economic, social, cultural and political equality of rights between women and men. All laws and emergency ordinances that contradict this are to be abrogated with immediate effect.

2 Women in all enterprises in industry and agriculture, doing the same work as men, are to be paid wages at the same level as men. The longest daily working time for women is to be set at seven hours, with full wage equality, while for unhealthy and heavy work, as well as for young females below the age of 18, it is to be set at six hours.

[3: Similar provisions for office workers]

4 Working women are to have a fully equal right to occupy all posts in all professions. Women workers, office employees and civil service officials are not to be dismissed because they are married. All working women are to receive free professional training appropriate to their professional capacity.

5 All unemployed women must have a legal right to full unemployment insurance payments without means testing or reference to the income of family members. Every kind of compulsory labour or compulsory re-training is prohibited. The right to receive social insurance during the whole period of unemployment is to be guaranteed.

6 All working women employed in industry, agriculture, commerce and transport and domestic work as well as women in the so-called free professions, housewives and the female relatives of working peasants are to be included in the social insurance system.

7 Dismissal of pregnant women is legally prohibited up to the 12th month after the birth of the child. The pregnant woman is to receive full pay and be exempt from work from eight weeks before until eight weeks after the birth. Nursing mothers are to receive half an hour twice a day for breast-feeding their children, without any reduction in wages.

Maternity homes in sufficient number are to be made available to all working women, also crêches for babies and children up to three years old, nurseries for children from three to school age. These services are to be provided free of payment. They are to be directed and supervised by control committees made up of delegates from the working population, mainly women.

8 The interruption of pregnancy is to be permitted by law. The contrary paragraphs of the Penal Code (184 Section 3 and 218) are to be abolished. All persons condemned under the previous abortion paragraphs are to be amnestied immediately, and all current cases are to be terminated. Abortion carried out by a doctor and the provision of the means to avoid pregnancy count as medical help in the national system of insurance.

9 When entering marriage, the woman retains her right to decide independently in all legal and personal matters. She is not dependent on the husband in any of her decisions. After marriage, the woman may take the name of her husband, but she may also continue to be known under her maiden name. She has the same parental power over her children as the man.

10 All exceptional provisions dealing with the unmarried mother and the illegitimate child are removed. Every unmarried woman has the right to bear the title of 'Frau'. In mixed marriages the choice of nationality is left to the woman.

Berlin, 15 October 1931

Torgler, Frau Overlach, Frau Gropper, Frau Ahlers, Frau Augustat, Frau Blum (Thuringia), Frau Esser (Westphalia), Frau Himmler (Chemnitz), Frau Körner, Frau Mildenberg, Rädel, Frau Sandtner, Schröder (Merseburg), Frau Zetkin, Frau Zinke

Source: Deutsches Reich 1930, *Verhandlungen des Reichstags, V.Wahlperiode 1930, Bd. 451*, Berlin, 1933, Anlage Nr. 1201, also printed in Hans-Jürgen Arendt 1969, 'Das Schutzprogramm der KPD für die arbeitende Frau vom 15 Oktober 1931', in *Beiträge zur Geschichte der Arbeiterbewegung*, Berlin, Heft 2. pp. 309–11.

CHAPTER 10

Long-term Political Objectives: Similarities and Differences

Introduction

The similarities in the party programmes of the SPD, USPD[1] and KPD resulted from their common origin in pre-1914 German Social Democracy. We shall first examine the programmes of the KPD, then those of the SPD.

The Communist Party of Germany's first programme, described as the Spartacus Programme, was adopted at the first congress of the Party on 1 January 1919. It was drawn up by Rosa Luxemburg and it bore the distinctive imprint of her conception of the revolution. It stressed that the transformation of society would be the work of 'the mass of the people themselves'. It would not happen through the actions of a 'small minority', as had been the case with previous revolutions (such as the French Revolution of 1789). The instrument of the people's rule would be, not a parliamentary body, but the Workers' and Soldiers' Councils. These already existed in Germany, although by January 1919 they had shown a distinct lack of radicalism. The Communist Party was not placed in the forefront of the Spartacus Programme. In fact it is not mentioned until the end, and then in rather negative terms: 'the Party is not a party which wishes to obtain power through or over the mass of workers'. It is simply 'the section of the proletariat which is most conscious of its goal', and its aim seems to be reduced here to giving advice and exhortations: 'it indicates to the working class its historical tasks' and 'it advocates the socialist final goal at every stage of the revolution'. Finally, most telling of all, victory will only come 'at the end of the revolution, not the beginning'. The victory of the Party is identical with the victory of the class; if the Party wins in any other way it is no victory. It followed from this view that putschism was out of the question, and the pregnant phrases in which this is expressed were repeatedly quoted in subsequent disputes between Paul Levi, who became party leader after the death of Rosa Luxemburg and Karl Liebknecht, and the leftist wing of the Party, which later set up the KAPD (Communist Workers' Party of Germany).[2]

---

1 See 12.1 and 12.2 for the USPD programmes.
2 See 12.3 for the KAPD's programme.

The Spartacus Programme was not a completely consistent document. Its contradictions reflected the fact that it was a compromise between three groups: the small but influential group of the leaders of the Spartacus League, the majority of their followers, who were inclined towards syndicalism or anarchism, and the International Communists of Germany (IKD), the Bremen group which was more in tune with the ideas of the Bolsheviks. Thus the programme at first appeared to rule out violence and terror: 'the proletarian revolution has no need of terror' and 'hates and abominates murder'. But it went on to say that the resistance of the ruling classes would be broken 'with an iron fist and ruthless energy' and the revolution would turn into a 'tremendous civil war'. This is what had just happened in Soviet Russia. The proletariat would exercise 'revolutionary violence', the programme continued, and there would be a 'proletarian dictatorship' which was however 'true democracy'. In terms of the specific German situation in 1919, the KPD naturally included a number of demands which were unrealistic within the context of capitalism, but in this the Party was consistent with the 'maximum programme' of pre-war German and international Social Democracy. The 'united German socialist republic' was one such traditional demand. There were also more realistic slogans: the calls for a reduction in the length of the working day and the expropriation of the large landed estates were long-standing Social Democratic demands which could be realised within capitalism.

The Spartacus Programme remained until 1924 the only party programme the German communists had. Then the Action Programme was issued (10.5). This was not really a long-term party programme but rather a set of instructions for dealing with a very specific situation: the aftermath of the October 1923 defeat. It was replaced in 1930 by yet another programme tailored to a specific situation. The 'Programme for the National and Social Liberation of the German People' (10.12), was the fruit of Heinz Neumann's attempt (supported by Stalin[3]) to deal with the rising Nazi threat by outbidding Hitler in nationalist demagogy. The origin of the 1930 Programme was a draft directive of 18 July 1930 'to be sent to Thälmann' calling for 'an energetic and consistent struggle against the Nazis, side by side with a struggle with Social Democracy, exposing them (the Nazis) as an element capable of selling themselves to the makers of Versailles, although they oppose it in words, and emphasising that the liberation of Germany from the Versailles Treaty and the Young Plan is

---

3 Bert Hoppe argues that Stalin had already concluded in September 1929 that the best way to deal with the rising Nazi agitation in Germany was for the KPD itself to turn towards 'national populism' and mount a campaign against the Young Plan (Hoppe 2007, pp. 183–4).

possible only with the overthrow of the bourgeoisie'.[4] The Programme issued shortly afterwards reflected this approach.

The Social Democrats were initially in the difficult situation of having a Marxist programme adopted almost 30 years earlier (the Erfurt Programme of 1891) which no longer fitted their political practice or their situation as the chief pillar of the Weimar Republic. The Erfurt Programme was drawn up when the Social Democrats were in absolute opposition to the German Imperial state, expecting its ultimate overthrow by revolution. Now a kind of 'revolution' had taken place, bringing Social Democracy, if not into power, at least into a position of influence and responsibility. In fact, the SPD had already been granted a share of power (or at least responsibility) during the War by the Imperial government, which it accepted without worrying about how this fitted in with the Party programme. After 1918, however, and in view of the need to mark off the Social Democratic position against opponents further to the left, the Party felt obliged to give itself a new programme. At the October 1920 Kassel Congress Adolf Braun[5] called for a modification of the Erfurt Programme to reflect the fact that the SPD was now no longer just a party of industrial workers. 'We are a party of intellectual and manual workers of every kind' he said. 'The workers in this hall range from university professor to unskilled labourer'.[6] All shades of opinion in the SPD were agreed that the Erfurt Programme had to be revised.[7] The revisionist thinker Heinrich Cunow[8] was given the job of producing a draft of a new programme. His view was that 'without winning over the peasantry, the office employees and the major part of the intellectuals it will be impossible to make socialism a reality'. Hence it was necessary 'to take their interests into account, and not to proclaim that we represent the industrial workers' interests and nothing more'.[9] Moreover, the Party's new programme should stress practical actions. It did not need a theoretical introduction.[10] Cunow's draft, approved by the Party's Programme Commission, contained no mention of 'class struggle' or 'socialisation', but this open disavowal of the Marxist tradition was too much for many people. From

---

4   Komolova 1999, p. 235.

5   Adolf Braun (1862–1929), centrist SPD theorist, member of the Party Executive with responsibility for press and publicity from 1920–29.

6   Sozialdemokratischer Parteitag 1920, pp. 187–92.

7   Fischer 1987, p. 55.

8   Heinrich Cunow (1862–1936), SPD, editor of Die Neue Zeit.

9   Cunow 1921, pp. 433–41.

10   Cunow 1920, p. 364.

without, the USPD remnant[11] reproached the Programme Commission with 'abandoning the basis of Marxism', while within the Party there was tremendous opposition from local party branches. Hans Marckwald,[12] an influential left Social Democrat from Frankfurt, pointed out that they would be presenting the USPD with a *fait accompli* if they accepted the programme, and this would make the task of politically reunifying the working class (in other words, joining the USPD remnant and the SPD together) much more difficult. The Commission was compelled to revert to the notion that 'the class struggle' was the basis of the SPD's activity.[13] Hence the new programme, adopted at the Görlitz Party Congress in 1921, bore a compromise character. While it maintained the idea of a 'class struggle' it abandoned the suggestion that the SPD was purely a 'class party' of the working class. Instead it was proclaimed to be a party of 'the working people in town and country', defined as 'all material and intellectual producers who are dependent on the product of their own labour'.[14]

The adoption of the Görlitz Programme, although well-nigh unanimous,[15] did not end disagreements about tactics, or even about fundamental objectives. There was a continued division between those Social Democrats who remained attached to Marxist concepts (such as Hilferding, Naphtali,[16] and Kautsky) and the revisionists, who were explicitly anti-Marxist, 'equated socialism with social policy'[17] and wanted the SPD to become a 'people's party' working within the capitalist system with no perspective of its eventual overthrow or collapse.[18] The latter group were associated with the journal *Sozialistische Monatshefte*, while the former dominated *Die Neue Zeit* (later replaced by *Die Gesellschaft*). These differences of view became much more pronounced after 1922 when the USPD remnant rejoined the SPD, bringing in a more emphatically Marxist group led by Paul Levi. These people were a constant thorn in the

---

11   The minority on the right wing of the USPD which refused to join the KPD in 1920. Often referred to in the literature in a somewhat derogatory manner as the 'Rump USPD'.

12   Hans Marckwald (1874–1933), editor of the Frankfurt SPD newspaper; insisted that a coalition with the bourgeois parties was only permissible if they fulfilled certain strict conditions.

13   These discussions are examined thoroughly in Winkler 1982, pp. 9–54.

14   It was impossible to reach a compromise over the agrarian parts of the programme, for which see below.

15   There were just five votes against it.

16   Fritz Naphtali (1880–1961), SPD, economic journalist, directed the ADGB's institute for research into economic policy, 1926–33.

17   Fischer 1987, p. 41.

18   The most prominent members of this group were Max Schippel, Gustav Radbruch, Eduard David, and Ernst Heilmann.

side of the Party leadership. The Görlitz Programme was in any case made out of date by the decision of the two parties to merge, since this was done on the basis of a separate Action Programme drawn up in September 1922. The Action Programme laid great stress on the united Party's duty to conduct the class struggle, and the need for the proletariat to achieve political power. In terms of concrete political objectives, however, this programme, like the preceding one, was modest: all its specific demands could be fulfilled within the existing Weimar context.

The Action Programme of 1922 was not intended to be permanent. The Party soon appointed a Programme Commission, chaired by Karl Kautsky, to work out a replacement, and he produced the draft of a new 'definitive' programme in 1924. There were considerable delays in bringing this to fruition, however, partly because Kautsky fell ill and retired to Vienna, taking no further part in the discussions, but mainly because the Party's leaders were in no hurry themselves, allegedly because they had urgent practical problems to deal with (when did they not?). In 1925, finally, the Programme Commission set to work again. The final version followed Kautsky's views closely. It described the Party's tasks as being 'to fight for the emancipation of the proletariat', 'to fight against capitalist exploitation' and 'to transform capitalist private property in the means of production into social property'. The programme was criticised from the right by Auer[19] and David, but thanks to Hilferding's mediation disagreements were smoothed over and the 1925 Heidelberg Congress accepted it with very few dissenting votes.

There was a curious mismatch in the Heidelberg Programme between its stress on the class struggle of the working class and the appeal made by Hilferding to the 'middle strata' of society, including the office employees and the peasantry.[20] The continued presence within the SPD of two widely divergent strategic perspectives can be shown by comparing Hilferding's remarks with those of Robert Dissmann (another former Independent) to the Berlin Congress in 1924. Dissmann said: 'The proletarians who vote for the Communists would come over to us if we pursued a policy of irreconcilable class struggle'.[21] The Marxist manner of forming concepts and conducting a political argument continued to be a hallmark of the SPD, despite the efforts of the revisionists. This did not affect its political practice, but it helped to alienate the possible middle-class supporters Hilferding hoped to encourage. The ambiguity of the SPD's position has been well described by Eric Weitz: 'The SPD ... abandoned

---

19   Erhard Auer (1874–1945), chair of the Bavarian SPD, on the right of the Party.
20   *Sozialdemokratischer Parteitag 1925*, pp. 272–83.
21   *Sozialdemokratischer Parteitag 1924*, p. 188.

socialism to some distant future' but at the same time it 'idealised the prole-tariat' and constantly talked of 'the class struggle'.[22]

Both parties had agrarian programmes (10.2, 10.9). Germany was a highly industrialised country, with a large urban proletariat, so the agrarian question was inevitably secondary. It was nevertheless very significant in certain less industrialised regions, and even more so in political terms: the growth in the hostility of the peasantry towards the Weimar Republic was one reason for its collapse, while the preservation of the large estates of the Prussian nobility was another. The communists, for their part, had little hope of securing peas-ant support, because they were not prepared to make any concessions to the bourgeoisie, a group which covered most of the peasantry, given their posses-sion of property in the shape of land, and because they saw the peasantry as a class which was doomed to disappear as capitalism took hold in the country-side. They could of course call for the expropriation of the big estates, and they did so, but since these would become collective property in one form of another instead of being handed over to the peasantry, this was also not very attractive to the latter. The KPD's programmes were therefore largely directed towards securing the support of the agricultural workers.

The situation of the SPD was much more complex. Ever since the 1890s there had been attempts to modify the Party's Marxist beliefs to take account of the continued existence of the peasantry despite the theoretical superiority of large-scale agriculture.[23] The revisionist right of the Party was very promi-nent in these debates. One might think that after 1918 and the departure of the left of the Party in the direction of the USPD and the KPD the revisionists would now have a free hand to produce an attractive pro-peasant agrarian pro-gramme. It was not so. There were several reasons for this. The SPD was always uncomfortably caught between the traditional Marxist ideas that the small peasant producer was doomed to disappearance, and that the solution of the agrarian problem lay in the socialisation of the land, and the Party's desire to appeal to the peasantry, who were property owners. Moreover, the SPD made no attempt to introduce any land reforms when it was in power after 1918, partly because they wanted to avoid disrupting the production of food at a time of severe shortages.[24] A 'Settlement Act' was passed instead (11 August 1919) under which big estate owners could be bought out by the government, which would then transfer the land to the peasants. This did in fact result in a

---

22   Weitz 2007, p. 85.

23   The SPD's pre-war debates on agrarian policy have been examined in detail by H.-G. Lehmann (1970); see also Hussain and Tribe 1980, pp. 72–101.

24   See Gerschenkron 1989, pp. 94–102.

slow decline in the area covered by large estates, which fell by 4.6 percent in Prussia between 1925 and 1933.[25] The SPD conceded in 1920 that it had made no progress in solving the agrarian question since 1895 owing to differences of view about the 'economic significance of the size of an agricultural enterprise', in other words the argument over the traditional Marxist claim that the productivity of large-scale estates was superior to that of small farms. At the Kassel Congress it adopted some 'Principles of Agrarian Policy' which included a call for the 'socialisation of agricultural and forestry enterprises where they are ripe for this' but also the reassurance that 'other property relations would not be affected'. Much of the SPD's agitation in the years of inflation was directed towards defending consumers rather than producers, who generally did well during those years. Some Social Democrats even accused the farmers of taking advantage of the situation to extort exorbitant profits. It was hard to appeal to the farmers with this sort of rhetoric. Eduard David's objections that the Heidelberg Programme was likely to alienate the peasantry were ignored; Hans Marckwald considered that it would be wrong to make too many concessions to win over the peasantry: 'When I have to deal with petty bourgeois and peasants, I say: our party defends your interests better than any other, but where petty-bourgeois interests are in conflict with proletarian interests, we cannot support petty-bourgeois interests'.[26]

From 1925 onwards the SPD again began to consider the issue seriously, with the encouragement of Hilferding, who proposed that 'the needs of the peasant farm' should be recognised and addressed in a special Agrarian Programme. Finally, in 1927, the Party issued an Agrarian Programme (10.9), directed both to peasants and to agricultural workers. This stated bluntly that the small-scale agricultural enterprise was not likely to disappear, in other words it accepted what the revisionists had claimed since the 1890s.[27] It also called for a 'systematic land reform', involving the gradual redistribution of large estates among the peasantry. The SPD's rural agitation was, however, hindered by the anti-clerical approach of many committed Social Democrats, expressed in the movement of 'free thinkers', which did not go down well in the countryside.[28] In addition to this, there was a conflict of interest between the SPD, as a party of urban consumers, and the peasantry. The main demand of the agricultural pressure group the 'Green Front' was for tariffs on imported foodstuffs to be

---

25   The statistics are presented in Gerschenkron 1989, p. 130.
26   Protokoll SPD 1921, p. 310.
27   The 1927 Agrarian Programme is discussed in Leuschen-Seppel 1981, pp. 206–10.
28   See in detail Pyta 1996, pp. 273–7.

increased, as a way to protect German agriculture from the acute crisis which had already set in by 1927. In June 1929 the SPD voted against these tariffs, although its coalition partners supported them; in December, however, the Party changed its mind and voted in favour, partly to keep the coalition in being but partly to secure an improvement in the Party's rural prospects. As Heinrich Winkler concludes, 'no-one could reproach the Social Democrats with unfriendliness to agriculture'. Not only had they abandoned the interests of the consumer, they had even supported the maize monopoly which the big landowners of East Prussia were demanding.[29]

Documents

10.1   *The Spartacus Programme, 1 January 1919*

I

On the ninth of November workers and soldiers destroyed the old regime in Germany ... On the ninth of November the German proletariat arose and threw off the shameful yoke. The Hohenzollern were driven out, and Workers' and Soldiers' Councils were elected. But the Hohenzollern were never anything more than the managers of the affairs of the imperialist bourgeoisie and the Junkers ... The World War has placed society before the alternative: either a continuation of capitalism, new wars and very soon a collapse into chaos and anarchy, or the abolition of capitalist exploitation ...

From this bloody chaos and this yawning abyss there is no salvation except in socialism. Only the world revolution of the proletariat can bring order into this chaos ... Down with the wage system! That is the slogan of the hour. Cooperative labour must replace wage labour and class rule. The means of labour must cease to be the monopoly of a class, they must become the common property of all. No more exploiters and exploited! Regulation of the production and distribution of products in the interests of the whole people ... Only in such a society will servitude and hatred between the peoples be uprooted. Only when such a society is made a reality will the land cease to be desecrated by murder. Only then will it be possible to say: this war was the last one. Socialism is now the sole salvation of humanity. The words of the *Communist Manifesto*, 'socialism or decline into barbarism' blaze forth in letters of fire upon the collapsing walls of capitalist society.

---

29   Winkler 1988, p. 759.

II

This transformation of society cannot be decreed by any official body, commission or parliament. It can only be taken in hand and carried through by the mass of the people themselves.[30]

In all previous revolutions the revolutionary struggle was led by a small minority of the people, who used the masses merely as an instrument... The socialist revolution is the first revolution which can only attain victory in the interests of the great majority of the population, and through the actions of the great majority of working people. The essence of socialist society consists in this, that the great mass of working people cease to be ruled by others and instead live their whole political and economic life for themselves and direct it in conscious, free self-determination. From the topmost summit of the state to the tiniest local council the proletarian mass must replace the outmoded organs of bourgeois class rule ... with their own class organs: the Workers' and Soldiers' Councils.

The economic transformation too can only be accomplished as a process borne along by proletarian mass action. The bare decrees of the supreme revolutionary authorities on socialisation are in themselves empty words. Only the working class can make the word become flesh with its own deed. In dogged struggle with capital ... the workers can achieve control over production and finally take over its actual direction ...

The emancipation of the working class must be the work of the working class itself.

III

In bourgeois revolutions bloodshed, terror and political murder have been the indispensable weapons in the hands of the rising classes. The proletarian revolution has no need of terror to achieve its goals. It hates and abominates murder. It does not need this means of struggle because it is not fighting individuals but institutions, because it does not step into the arena with naive illusions for the collapse of which it would have to take a bloody revenge. It is not the desperate attempt of a minority to mould the world by force according to its ideal but an action by the great million-strong mass of the people who are called to fulfil their historical mission and to turn historical necessity into reality ...

---

30   This implies a rejection of the SPD conception of a constitutional revolution. Whether subsequent references to 'mass action' imply a rejection of current Bolshevik practice is more doubtful.

It is an insane delusion to believe that the capitalists would obligingly submit to the socialist verdict of a parliament or a National Assembly, that they would calmly give up their possessions, their profits and their right to carry on exploitation. All ruling classes have fought to the last with the most dogged energy to retain their privileges... The imperialist capitalist class, as the last generation of the exploiting classes, outdoes its predecessors in brutality, open cynicism and meanness. It will defend its holy of holies, profit and exploitation, with tooth and nail, using the coldly vicious methods it has already displayed in colonial affairs and during the recent World War. It will set heaven and hell in motion against the proletariat... It would rather turn the country into a smoking heap of ruins than voluntarily give up wage slavery.

All this resistance must be broken step by step, with an iron fist and ruthless energy. The violence of the bourgeois counter-revolution must be confronted with the revolutionary violence of the proletariat... The danger threatening from the counter-revolution must be confronted by arming the people and disarming the ruling classes... The struggle for socialism is the most tremendous civil war world history has seen, and the proletariat must make ready the necessary arsenal for this civil war; it must learn how to use its arms – for combat and for victory.

The dictatorship of the proletariat is a way of arming the compact mass of the working people with the whole of political power for the task of revolution, and it is therefore true democracy... Where the mass of the proletarian millions seizes the whole of state power with its horny hands in order to smite the ruling classes on the head with its hammer... there alone can we speak of a democracy which is not a deception of the people.

[There follows, first, a list of 'immediate measures to safeguard the revolution' involving the placing of all military and political power in the hands of the Workers' and Soldiers' Councils and the complete disarmament of the representatives of the old regime and second, a full list of political, social and economic demands: abolition of the individual German states and creation of a united German Socialist Republic; abolition of all parliamentary assemblies and their replacement by Workers' and Soldiers' Councils; radical social legislation, including a six-hour maximum working day; the reorganisation of the system of food supply, housing and education in the spirit of the proletarian revolution; the expropriation of all large and medium landed estates; the formation of socialist agricultural cooperatives; the expropriation of all large industrial and commercial enterprises by the Republic of Councils; the annulment of all war loans and state debts; the election of Factory Councils to supervise production and later to take over the running of the factories; and finally

the setting up of a central strike committee to give unified direction to the
strike movement throughout the Reich.][31]

IV

This is what the Spartacus League stands for. And because it stands for these
things ... it is hated, persecuted and slandered by all the open and secret enemies of the revolution and the proletariat ...

The Spartacus League is not a party which wishes to obtain power over or
through the mass of workers. The Spartacus League is simply the section of the
proletariat which is most conscious of its goal; the section which indicates at
every step to the broad mass of the working class its historical tasks, which
advocates the socialist final goal at every individual stage of the revolution,
and in all national questions puts forward the interests of the proletarian world
revolution ...

The Spartacus League will ... refuse to come to power simply because the
Scheidemanns and Eberts have become bankrupt and the Independents have
entered a blind alley ... by cooperating with them. The Spartacus League will
never take over the government in any other way than through the clear, unambiguous will of the great majority of the proletarian mass in Germany, never
otherwise than by virtue of the proletarians' conscious assent to its ideas, goals
and methods of struggle. The proletarian revolution can only win through to
full clarity and maturity by stages, step by step, by taking the road to Golgotha,
through its own bitter experiences, through defeats and victories.

The victory of the Spartacus League stands not at the beginning but at the
end of the revolution: it is identical with the victory of the great mass of the
millions of the socialist proletariat ...

Source: *Die Rote Fahne*, Nr. 20, 14 December 1918; and Kommunistische
Partei Deutschland 1919, *Bericht über den Gründungsparteitag der KPD
(Spartakusbund)*, pp. 49–56.

Note: This is Rosa Luxemburg's programme for the Spartacus League, adopted
two weeks later at the founding congress of the KPD (Communist Party of
Germany). Her refusal to support a minority coup is clearly evident, and her

---

31   No distinction is made between an immediate programme to be implemented before the
     revolution (e.g. the Strike Committee and the social legislation) and a programme which
     a revolutionary government would carry through (e.g. the expropriations, which are to be
     made by the Republic of Councils). In foreign policy, the programme demands the estab-
     lishment of links with brother parties abroad, but does not refer to relations specifically
     with Soviet Russia.

constant concern to stress the role of the working class shines through this programme, as well as her refusal to counterpose the working class to its political Party.

10.2   *The 1920 Agrarian Programme of the KPD*
I   Introduction
[After giving an account of the economic collapse after the First World War and the conflict between capital and labour since Germany's political revolution of November 1918, the document continues:]

It is clear that the conflict between capital and labour cannot remain limited to the towns. The rule of capital weighs yet more heavily on the rural proletariat than it does on the urban workers. It also threatens the petty bourgeoisie with destruction.

The agricultural proletariat and the small-scale peasantry are hindered in their fight against capital by local fragmentation and rural isolation. The only way to overcome these disadvantages is the closest cooperation with the urban proletariat.

In the large-scale agricultural enterprise, capital itself provides the model for socialist production. All that is needed here is the destruction of the barriers of private property, the appropriation of the country ... by society, and close cooperation with socialised industry and trade, and then here too the socialist mode of labour can develop. The petty bourgeoisie suffers not less than the rural proletariat from the pressure of capitalism. But the large-scale enterprise is not yet a model for the socialist system. It cannot be imposed by force. The bourgeois economy has undermined small peasant property over the last century by a process of violent economic deracination and fraud. This process has either completely converted the small peasant into a proletarian or made him lead a twilight existence between the industrial and the agricultural proletariat ... It has separated him from the instruments of his labour and placed him under the sway of the big landowner or the industrial entrepreneur ... Once it has attained power, the working class will behave in an entirely different way towards the small peasant. Its method of action can only be to give help and education to the small peasant so that he finds the way to socialism on his own initiative ... The small peasant must be freed of bureaucratic tutelage, and the incipient cooperation between the small peasants must be extended so that they advance stage by stage to cooperative production. To attain the goal of the emancipation of the rural proletariat and the small peasant from capitalist exploitation and the introduction of the socialist form of management into agriculture, we propose [the following measures.]

II

[This section divides agricultural enterprises into a number of categories, each of which is considered to require different treatment. The categories are: (1) large enterprises and (2) peasant enterprises, subdivided into dwarf, small, medium and big enterprises.]

III

A   *Treatment of the Large Enterprise*

1 All large-scale landed property ... is to be expropriated without compensation by the socialist state. It becomes the common property of socialist society.

2 All previous patrimonial rights and jurisdictions, and all entails, are to be abolished without compensation.

3 Agricultural workers ... regularly employed on each large-scale agricultural enterprise are to form an Estate Council (*Gutsrat*).

4 The Estate Council is to take over the cooperative running of the large enterprise.

5 The Estate Council is to decide on the employment and dismissal of workers, the form of cultivation and the delivery of the surplus product, and it is to fix the requirements of the estate for products from outside, and its capital requirements.

[6 to 12 provide in detail for the organisation of work on the large estates]

13 Agricultural work on a very large scale (for example irrigation projects) is to be backed by the state with financial and physical assistance.

14 Large-scale agricultural property which has been subdivided into small farms is also to be expropriated without compensation. If the property has been cultivated on a large scale, it will be handed over to the local Councils of Agricultural Workers and Small Peasants.

15 Large-scale agricultural enterprises surrounded by small peasant farms and of no decisive economic significance can be divided among the small and dwarf peasants of the district.[32]

16 State domains ... are to be turned into model experimental farms directly overseen by the provincial or state centres. Agricultural colleges are to be attached to them.

17 The state should start to overcome the cultural antagonism between town and country by making all the elements of urban civilisation accessible to the country people. It should do this by setting up a dense network of railways and

---

32   This section is not in the first version of the programme and was added in 1920.

other means of transport, by supplying the country districts with electricity, gas etc., and lastly by the organised unification of large agricultural enterprises and large industrial enterprises.

B   *The Small and Medium Enterprise*
1 The private property of small and middle peasants in the land and the instruments of labour is to remain untouched. The land previously tilled by them is to be placed entirely at their disposal.
2 The small peasant administers his own affairs through the Council System. This autonomous administration will replace the bureaucratic tutelage of the capitalist state.
[3 and 4 provide for setting up of Councils of Small Peasants to collect supplies and distribute products communally.]
5 Socialist industry will provide the small peasants with the industrial goods that they need. The conversion of small farms into cooperatives is to be promoted by the provision of machinery for communal use and the extension of existing cooperatives.
[8 and 9 provide for measures to promote education.]
10 Mortgages on landed property are to be nationalised. They cannot be foreclosed and they can be extinguished by the state.
11 The private property of big peasants in the land and the instruments of labour remains untouched unless they come out as enemies of the Republic of Councils. In the latter case, their farms will be turned into state property and either divided up among the surrounding small peasants and agricultural workers ... employed on the farms, or handed over to them without division to be farmed into cooperation.[33]

C   *The Economic and Political Structure of the Estates Councils, Small*
          Peasants' Councils and Village Councils
1 The local Councils are to join together in economic districts and ultimately over the whole territory of the Reich. Each of these Council organisations is to elect an executive committee to deal with current business ... The supreme economic body for agriculture is the Central Congress of Workers' and Small Peasants' Councils. This will elect from its midst a central council, the Rural Economic Council ...
2 The village communes are to administer themselves through Village Councils. The Village Councils are to send delegates to the District Workers'

33   This section was also added in 1920.

and Peasants' Councils, which will exercise political power in their area jointly with the other Councils.

Source: *Die Internationale*, II/26/1 December 1920, pp. 26–33.

Note: The document presented here is the second version of the KPD's agrarian programme. It differs significantly from the first version, in that it bears marks of a more conciliatory attitude towards the 'middle peasant'. This coincides with a shift in Soviet policy in the same direction and was no doubt influenced by it. The first version, published in July 1919, stressed the fight between the agricultural workers of Prussia and their Junker overlords, and by implication denied the existence of the 'middle peasant', as it divided the estates into two categories, large and small.

The Fourth Party Congress (April 1920) was the scene of a lively discussion of the agrarian problem. Several speakers stressed the great numerical preponderance of peasant proprietors in rural Germany. Edwin Hörnle pointed out that 72 percent of the land was in peasant hands, and he claimed that 'even under a Soviet dictatorship we should have to treat the peasantry as a power with which to negotiate'. He called for the driving of a 'wedge' between the peasants and the big landowners. Another speaker (Emil Unfried) distinguished between the reactionary peasantry of Bavaria and the peasants of Württemberg and Baden, who might perhaps be accessible to communist ideas. Points A15 and B11 were introduced into the Agrarian Programme in order to meet the objections of these critics.

It need hardly be said that the chief supporters of the KPD in the countryside were and remained the agricultural workers rather than the peasant proprietors, whether 'small' or 'middle'.

10.3   *The SPD's 1921 Görlitz Programme*

The Social Democratic Party of Germany (SPD) is the party of working people in town and country. It strives for the gathering together of all material and intellectual producers, who are dependent on the product of their own labour, for a common understanding and common goals, for a common struggle for democracy and socialism.

The capitalist economy has brought the major part of the means of production which have received tremendous development from the application of modern techniques under the domination of a relatively small number of large-scale owners. It has separated the broad mass of workers from the means of production and turned them into propertyless proletarians. It has increased economic inequality and created the contrast between a small minority living in luxury and the broad strata of the people, eking out their existence in need and poverty. In this way it has made the class struggle for the emancipation of the proletariat a historical necessity and a moral imperative.

[There follows a description of the impact of the World War, which 'heightened this process by accelerating the concentration of industrial enterprises and capital'.]

The World War has swept away the dilapidated ruling systems that existed. Political transformations have given the masses the democratic rights they need for their social ascent. Capitalism is confronted with a greatly strengthened workers' movement as powerful as it is itself. The will is ever stronger to overcome the capitalist system and to protect humanity from fresh military annihilation through the international union of the proletariat and the creation of an international system of justice, a true league of equal nations. The SPD is determined to fight to its last breath for the protection of the liberty that has been attained [by the November 1918 political upheaval]. It views the democratic republic as the form of state irrevocably brought into existence by historical development, and it considers every attack on it to be an attack on the vital rights of the people.

The SPD cannot however restrict its activity to protecting the Republic from the attacks of its enemies. It also fights for mastery over the economy exercised by the will of the people organised in the free Republic, and for the renewal of society in the spirit of the socialist community. The transfer of the large concentrated economic enterprises into the communal economy (*Gemeinwirtschaft*) and beyond that the progressive reshaping of the whole capitalist economy into a socialist economy run for the good of the whole community is the necessary means to free working people from the bonds of capital's domination, to increase productive returns and to lead mankind towards higher forms of economic and ethical community.

It is in this sense that the SPD renews the statement of principle enshrined in the Erfurt Programme: it fights not for new class privileges but for the removal of class rule and classes themselves. It conducts this fight in the awareness that it will decide the fate of humanity both in the international and national communities and at local level, in the house, the factory, the trade union, the municipality and the state. For this fight the following demands hold good:

[The programme then indicates a series of measures under the headings of economic policy, social policy, financial policy, constitution and administration, local policy, the judicial system, cultural and educational policy, and finally international relations. The measures include placing the land and the natural sources of energy at the service of the community; the introduction of death duties; democratic local administration; the judiciary to be recruited from all social classes; the abolition of the death penalty; the separation of church and state; women's right to employment; a planned population policy appropriate to the social needs of the working class; and special consideration for large families. In international policy the programme demanded a League of Nations, which would not exclude any nation which recognised its statutes, and in which the parliaments of all countries would be represented; an international court to decide all disputes between nations; and a revision of the Versailles Treaty in the direction of the relief of economic burdens and the recognition of vital national rights.]

Note: The Party Congress accepted this programme almost unanimously. There were five opposing votes.

Source: Sozialdemokratische Partei Deutschlands 1921 *Protokoll über die Verhandlungen des Parteitages der Sozialdemokratischen Partei Deutschlands, abgehalten in Görlitz vom 18. bis 24. September 1921*, pp. III–VI.

10.4   *Karl Kautsky's Arguments Against the Görlitz Programme, 1922*

At their congress held in Görlitz in 1921 the German SPD (Majority Socialists) have got rid of the programme the united Party gave itself thirty years before at Erfurt. As a rule, a Party will only adopt a new theoretical programme ... if this constitutes an advance over the previous one. Is this the case with the general section of the Görlitz Programme? Our objections to the programme adopted at Görlitz are related less to what it says ... than to what it *does not contain*.

The basis of the Erfurt Programme was the materialist conception of history, the view that economic development takes place with the inevitability of a law of nature and determines the changes in people's social ideas and institutions ... For over half a century this conception of history has determined the goal and methods of German Social Democracy ... The materialist conception of history is not rejected in the Görlitz Programme, but it is pushed into the background. It is not expressed as sharply or as precisely. The new programme begins not by presenting the necessary economic development but by expressing an aspiration: The SPD 'strives for the gathering together of all material and intellectual producers, who are dependent on the product of their own labour' into a community which will 'struggle for democracy and socialism'. This formulation blots out any recognition that socialism is the product of a new economic development and that its vehicle is the new class which is emerging from this development. The Erfurt Programme stressed that socialism would be the work of the propertyless working class alone, because all other classes would hold fast to private property.

This idea was dropped at Görlitz. Socialism is now the work of all the producers, hence for example it is the work of the peasants of Bavaria and Mecklenburg too. One looks in vain for any suggestion that socialism arises from an entirely new situation and an entirely new class ...

The fact that small enterprises are being driven out by large ones, the growing concentration of the means of production in a few monopolistic hands, the growth in the productivity of labour – these processes form the only secure basis for our striving towards socialism ... yet they are not mentioned in the Görlitz Programme.

What has changed fundamentally since 1891 is not the nature of capitalism, and the way it should be understood theoretically, but the *historical situation*. This new situation has rendered the old programme inadequate. But what is required is not an *alteration* but an *extension* of the programme ... This work remains to be done.

Source: K. Kautsky 1968, *Texte zu den Programmen der deutschen Sozial-demokratie 1891–1925*, ed. by A. Langner, Cologne: Verlag Jakob Hegner. pp. 181–2.

10.5   *The KPD's Action Programme of April 1924*

The Party Congress is taking place at a moment when the German proletariat finds itself in a situation of unheard-of difficulty and danger, economically and politically, thanks to the joint offensive of the *Deutschvölkische*, the capitalists and the reformists. The Congress therefore places on all Party comrades the obligation to move without delay to the mobilisation of proletarian forces against the offensive of capital, and to make the rescue programme of the communists the starting point and the centre of the daily struggles of the working class in town and country, in the factories and among the unemployed. The KPD's watchwords must animate the broadest masses of the working population. For this purpose the organs of the united front must be formed from below and associated together for struggle. Every member, every functionary, every local group, every district organisation must immediately take up this work with heightened strength and energy. In the present epoch of an intensified capitalist offensive against the German working class the KPD presents the following watchwords: fight against the dismantling of the eight-hour day, starvation wages, the compulsory labour of the unemployed, the laying off of workers, salaried employees and officials, the closure of factories, the reductions in social insurance, the miserable housing of the proletariat, class justice and white terror, and the despoilment of small investors, poor peasants and the proletarianised lower middle classes by the state of the capitalists and exploiters.

The KPD fights for:

the eight-hour day as a normal working day;

the six-hour day for heavy work and work in industries dangerous to health;

adequate wages;

unemployment benefit at the level of an average wage;

the insertion of the unemployed into the process of production;

raising the pensions of war victims to the level of an average wage;

the conversion of the Factory Councils into revolutionary organs with the threefold task of economic struggle, politicisation of the factory and the introduction of workers' control;

the freeing of political prisoners;

the setting up of political Workers' Councils;

the arming of the proletariat for protection against the White Guards;

the disarming of the counter-revolution.

The masses must be educated and made ripe for the final revolutionary struggle. To this end, the economic strikes and movements for increased wages, the fury over mass dismissals, the tax burden, the increase in the cost of living, high rents, class justice etc., must all be heightened by energetically conducted campaigns of demonstrations and meetings, and, in association with the rising mass movement, by direct action, by the rejection of overtime in the factories, by refusal to do compulsory labour on the part of the unemployed, by the withholding of rent and tax payments, by the lowering of prices and the confiscation of commodities by the Control Commissions, by the control of the factories, routes of communication and dwellings, by the liberation of revolutionary prisoners, by the disarming of both the legal and the illegal organs of the bourgeois state, and by clearing out the bourgeois munitions depots.

All these struggles will only be able to save the proletariat from its misery and wretchedness if they broaden into struggles for political power. The dictatorship of the German bourgeoisie will only be ended by the dictatorship of the proletariat. The task of the Communist Party is to prepare and organise the struggle for the dictatorship of the proletariat. This is the task it must now fulfil.

The Congress calls on all party comrades: cease wailing and moaning about the October defeat! We have looked back enough to lost opportunities and struggles. The German working class is following its road under very great difficulties and dangers. The German working class is following the road of proletarian revolution through victories and defeats ...

This Congress marks the end of the discussion over the October defeat, it has drawn the lessons of the October defeat. The communists will lead the

German working class against the capitalists, the *Völkische* and the reformists to victory over the bourgeoisie and the establishment of Soviet power.

Source: Kommunistische Partei Deutschland 1924, *Bericht über die Verhandlungen des 9.Parteitages der KPD (Sektion der Kommunistischen Internationale), abgehalten in Frankfurt am Main vom 7. bis 10.April 1924,* pp. 387–9.

10.6   *The KPD View of Trade Unions in 1924*

Only where the Amsterdamers have already caused a split and the expelled workers remain in mass organisations can immediate steps be taken towards the formation of industrial unions (as in Ludwigshafen and similar cases)... The Amsterdamers will then bear full responsibility for the split. The Party must warn the masses against the illusion that industrial unions 'in themselves' can bring an improvement in the living conditions of the working class. Victory does not depend only on the way the trade unions are organised, although a more effective form of organisation than the previous one may strengthen and further the workers' struggle... The Party must begin to organise the unorganised in Factory Councils, Revolutionary Councils of the Unemployed, and Wage Committees of Agricultural Workers... They should be combined together in industrial groups.

The Party must conduct a broad and intensive propaganda campaign for the systematic and planned transformation of the German trade union movement from its present form into a unified organisation based on the factory and grouped together by branch of production. The Factory Councils must be the basic pillars of the trade union movement. The aim of trade union work is to free the working masses from the influence of the Amsterdamers and bring them under the leadership of the Communist Party.

Source: Sozialistische Einheitspartei Deutschlands Zentralkomitee 1924, *Dokumente und Materialien,* vol. VIII, (from 1924 9th Congress resolution on trade union work), pp. 73–7.

10.7   *Heinrich Peus (Dessau) Advocates Turning the SPD into a Labour Party*

The Party Congress should be representative of the German people. I would therefore give districts that are weakly represented on account of inadequate organisation a much stronger degree of representation, independently of the number of members organised in the district. Then fewer people from the big cities, fewer from Berlin, would come to the Congress, perhaps fewer from Saxony too: there would be fewer representatives of the industrial workers. But I should regard that as a tremendous improvement. We are at present still to far too great an extent a party of industrial workers. The English Party calls itself not 'The Workers' Party', as it is always incorrectly translated, but 'The Party of Labour', 'The Labour Party'. The greater success of the English Party in comparison to ours has been achieved above all thanks to this circumstance. We must become a 'party of Labour'. Representatives of the small craftsmen and small peasants must sit here too. As yet we have only one or two small peasants. These people will not disappear in the foreseeable future, we shall instead have to reckon with them if we want to win a majority of the people. I will not put any motion to this effect because I do not want to cause you the embarrassment of rejecting such a sensible idea. But I want it to be at least voiced. We must become a party of the labour of the whole people, a labour party. Everyone who does not live from interest and rents but from work belongs in this party.

Source: Sozialdemokratischer Parteitag 1924. *Protokoll mit dem Bericht der Frauenkonferenz*, p. 148.

10.8   *The Heidelberg Programme of the SPD, 1925*
Part 1: Basic Principles

Economic development, operating with the inner necessity of a law of nature, has led to the strengthening of large capitalist enterprises, and in industry, trade and communications this has increasingly forced the small enterprise into the background and lessened its importance. With the ever-stronger development of industry, the industrial population grows constantly in proportion to the agricultural population. Capital has deprived the mass of producers of ownership over their own means of production, and it has turned the worker into a propertyless proletarian. A large part of the land is in the hands of big landowners, who are the natural allies of big capital. Thus the economically decisive means of production have become the monopoly of a relatively small number of capitalists, who have thereby obtained economic domination over society.

At the same time ... there has been an increase in the numbers and significance of office employees and intellectuals of all types. In the socialised labour-process, these people carry out the functions of management, supervision, organisation and distribution ... As their numbers have grown, they have increasingly lost the chance of rising into a privileged position, and their interests are to an increasing degree in accordance with the interests of the rest of the working class ...

The capitalist drive towards monopoly leads to the integration of different branches of industry, the joining together of successive stages of production and the organisation of the economy in cartels and trusts. This process unifies industrial capital, commercial capital and bank capital into finance capital ...

The number of proletarians becomes ever larger. . . . and the class struggle between the capitalist rulers of the economy and those under their domination becomes ever more bitter ... The proletariat's will to overcome the capitalist system becomes more powerful than ever ...

The goal of the working class can only be attained by the transformation of capitalist private property in the means of production into social property. The transformation of capitalist production into socialist ... production will have the result that the development and the increase of the productive forces becomes a source of the highest level of welfare and all-round perfection ...

The fight of the working class against capitalist exploitation is not only an economic struggle; it is necessarily also political. The working class cannot conduct its economic struggle or fully develop its economic organisations without political rights. In the shape of the democratic republic, it possesses the form of state whose maintenance and extension are an irreplaceable necessity for its struggle for emancipation. It cannot effect the socialisation (*Vergesellschaftlichung*) of the means of production without coming into possession of political power ... The task of the SPD is to make the working class's struggle for emancipation conscious and united and to indicate to the working class its necessary goal. It strives for the final goal by engaging in constant struggle and activity in the political, economic, social and cultural spheres.

Part 2: Action Programme

[The provisions of the Action Programme can be summarised as follows:

1 Constitution: a united, democratic republic

2 Administration: democratisation of the administration

3 Justice: elected lay magistrates are to share in the administration of justice

4 Social Policy: the eight-hour working day to be laid down by law; factory inspectors; wage contracts to have the force of law

5 Cultural and Educational Policy

6 Finance, Taxes, Economic Policy: land, mineral resources and natural sources of power are to be removed from capitalist exploitation and handed over to the service of the community; the system of Economic Councils (*Wirtschaftsräte*) is to be extended in order to implement the right of the working class to co-determination in the organisation of the economy; this is

to be combined with the maintenance of close cooperation with the trade unions.]

7 International Policy[34]

Note: This programme was worked out by a commission chaired by Karl Kautsky, who had been severely critical of the 1921 Görlitz Programme (see above, Doc. 10.4).

Source: Sozialdemokratischer Parteitag 1925, *13–18 September 1925 in Heidelberg. Protokoll mit dem Bericht der Frauenkonferenz*, pp. 5–10.

10.9   *The SPD's Agrarian Programme of 1927*

It is in the common interest of the working people of the countryside and the towns to raise the yield of human labour by a constant increase in the utilisation of science and technology. *In industry* capitalism has brought about a constant and rapid growth of the forces of production through the socialisation of the labour process in the large enterprise and the removal of backward forms of enterprise. *In agriculture, too* conditions have been revolutionised from top to bottom by capitalism. It has removed the bonds and fetters of feudalism for the most part. It has torn asunder the old connection between handicrafts and agricultural labour and embedded the rural enterprise in the market network ... Commercial and banking capital have taken possession of a large part of agricultural production. Technology and science have overturned century-old modes of enterprise in agriculture.

But in agriculture, unlike in industry, capitalism allows the *property relations* and the *existing sizes of the enterprises* to remain fixed. The natural limits to soil fertility and the impossibility of achieving an unrestricted increase of agricultural production on a given land area are the reason why backward enterprises are able to remain in existence in agriculture alongside progressive ones. The laws of the capitalist market compel technical and organisational progress in agricultural production to a much lesser degree than they do in industry. Thus regulation by the market must be replaced by the conscious intervention of society and its organs in order to *raise and intensify agricultural production.*

Land Reform

The landowners compensated themselves for the abolition of serfdom in the eastern and northern parts of Germany by *stealing the land from the*

---

34   For this part of the programme, see 7.12, above.

peasants... The landowner's [current] monopoly prevents the rural producer, the peasant's son and the agricultural worker from having free access to the land.

Social Democracy therefore demands a fundamental change in property relations, a *systematic land reform*. This must entirely remove the relations of dependency which have developed in the countryside owing to the century-old subjection of the rural population to the yoke of big landed property.

[A list of specific demands follows, including:]

1 The *genuine abolition of the entailed estates* and similar concentration of landownership in the hands of individual families. Large agricultural holdings, i.e. holdings which exceed the optimum economically appropriate size, which is to be determined according to local conditions, and in the East amounts to some 750 hectares, are to be forced to hand over the excess land to public ownership *in return for compensation*.

2 Forests over 100 hectares in area are to be confiscated on the same principles.

3 The *needs of settlement* in its various forms are to be the primary consideration in determining the utilisation of the lands falling into the hands of the Reich through the implementation of point one above... The existing land area of the peasant farms is to be protected to its fullest extent. The workers employed on land confiscated under point one are to be given priority in determining claims to settle on that land. Large estates which have been confiscated can also be taken into public or cooperative use if there is a guarantee that this form of management will be appropriate to the situation...

8 The landed property owned by the Reich... must be increased in a planned and organised fashion. To this end, the Reich is to be granted a legal right of pre-emption where uncultivated land is being sold.

[There follow a number of further demands: measures for the promotion of agricultural production, the regulation of the sale of agricultural products, support for the direct exchange of products between producers' and consumers' cooperatives, the setting up of a state monopoly on the import and export of grain with the intention of establishing stable prices, the raising of the tax threshold, better housing and working conditions and higher wages for workers in agriculture and forestry, the establishment of the right to strike, and finally obligatory sickness and old-age insurance for peasant farmers.]

The SPD calls on all working people in the countryside to fight for these demands, in order in association with the working masses of the towns to burst free from the bonds imposed on them by feudalism and capitalism. *A deep solidarity of interest binds the working class to the self-employed peasants.* For the peasants the meaning of the struggle for democracy within capitalist society is self-government for the village, the abolition of manorial jurisdiction, and the transformation of the dominant state of landlords and capitalists into a state of workers and peasants, which will bring to them welfare and civilisation...The increase in the purchasing power of the industrial workers raises the demand for the most important products of the peasant farms and makes it certain that they will be sold ... The victory of the working masses in town and country subjects big landed property and big capital to the rule of society and frees agriculture from the uncertainty and the fluctuations of the market and speculation. Far from wishing to drive the peasant from his plot of land or to confiscate his property, socialist society secures to the peasant masses their property and place of work...A community of interest links all working people in the struggle against the economy of profit. Recognising this fact, Social Democracy views it as one of its most urgent tasks to *bring the rural masses into its ranks*; for this union of the working masses of town and country hastens victory and makes it an unquestionable certainty.

Source: Sozialdemokratischer Parteitag in Kiel 1927, *Protokoll mit dem Bericht der Frauenkonferenz*, pp. 273–82.

10.10   *Rudolf Hilferding's 1927 Speech on 'Organised Capitalism'*

When we ask ourselves what the situation is in reality, we have to look at it much more concretely, and find a more precise characterisation than is provided by for example the expression 'late capitalism'. The factor which is decisive is that we are at present in a period when the era of free competition, of a capitalism dominated purely by the blind laws of the market, has come to an end, and we are moving towards a capitalist organisation of the economy, hence the movement is from the *economy of the free play of forces to the organised economy*.

The organised economy has the *technical* feature that alongside steam and electricity it is *synthetic chemistry* that is increasingly coming to the forefront. After roughly half a century of scientific development it is now ripe for manufacturing applications. This application of chemistry is something that is in principle new. It makes the capitalist economy independent of the availability of specific raw materials, because it consists in the artificial creation of important raw materials out of inorganic matter which present everywhere in large quantities. I would like to mention the production from coal and lignite of oils which are of significance for industrial purposes ... and the production of artificial silk by a chemical process. This is something new, which will transform the whole basis of our technology in capitalist production with colossal, explosive strength.

The second characteristic of the organised economy is the endeavour of capitalist industry to exploit the new possibilities in an *organised* manner. The artificial silk industry, for example, is not only a monopoly in Germany: in essence it constitutes a single international capitalist concern, which is closely connected with other trust formations in Germany and in England. The third characteristic is the *internationalisation* of capitalist industry, that is to say the endeavour to convert the national monopolies, cartels and trusts into international associations. Anyone who comes into contact with capitalist economic circles – and this is very useful, because it is important to understand the psychology of the opponent – is astounded at the eagerness with which these circles, which before the war were nationally limited in economic conceptions, now seek international connections, and what an active drive there is towards international organisation . . .

The endeavour to organise capitalism means that it has given up its main objection to socialism, and the last psychological obstacle to socialism thereby falls away. Organised capitalism means the replacement of the capitalist principle of free competition by the socialist principle of planned production. This form of economy, planned and directed deliberately, is much more open to the possibility of *conscious intervention by society*, which is nothing other than the intervention of the sole conscious organisation of the society with the power to compel, namely intervention by the *state.* Our generation has the task, with the help of the state, and conscious social regulation, of transforming this economy directed and organised by the *capitalists* into an economy directed by the *democratic state* . . .

If the situation is as I have described it, our first task is . . . to raise the working class to the level of a political party, finally to get rid of the situation in which thousands of proletarians do not stand on our side. At present they vote DNVP or Centre. The DNVP is the most anti-working class party in any European city. Before the War they were limited to the lands east of the Elbe. Now they are the strongest bourgeois party in Hamburg, Leipzig and many other cities, because thousands of genuine proletarians, confused by the inflation and the post-war events, have voted for them. It is an important task to prise them away. Then there is the Centre Party. The whole strength of the Centre Party rests on the fact that we have in Germany, unlike in any other country with a strong workers' movement, *a trade union movement split into* Christian and Free. I have shown that this division is out of date and lacks any sense. We must ask the Christian workers: why is there no split among the industrial employers or the landowners? You talk about Christian solidarity. But where does the policy of the Catholic industrialists differ from that of the Protestant factory-owners? So what is needed is to constitute the *whole* working class as a political party.

Source: Sozialdemokratischer Parteitag in Kiel 1927, *Protokoll mit dem Bericht der Frauenkonferenz*, pp. 166–8, 183.

Note: Hilferding's speech stressed the need to win over the whole German working class, and in particular to loosen the hold of the Centre Party over strongly Christian workers. He did not mention the KPD, despite its strongly working-class constituency. Nor did he suggest an appeal to the lower-middle classes (the *Mittelstand*) even though it was clear that a number of middle class groups already voted for the SPD. The discontented and embittered *Mittelstand*, such a pronounced feature of the Weimar scene, was in the process of going over to the extreme right, ending up later on the Nazi camp. Hilferding's prescriptions did not address this problem. In fact he failed to draw any conclusions about political strategy from this theory of 'organised capitalism', which thus became simply a form of wish-fulfilment for socialists who were keen to believe that economic forces were working in their favour.

10.11 *Fritz Naphtali on the Consequences of Capitalist Rationalisation*
In the capitalist economy rationalisation necessarily has a dual aspect for the working class. The aim of any rationalisation is to reduce the costs required to achieve a given labour product. In so far as this reduction in costs is based on technical progress, on raising the productivity of labour by a superior organisa-tion of the enterprise, an improved association of forces, the workers assent to it in principle. This is because we know that only the greatest possible increase in the productivity of labour can create the economic conditions for realizing labour power in the world, and that only in this way can the economic prereq-uisites of a cultured life for all mankind be brought forth. We must therefore approve these tendencies towards technical and organisational progress even when we see that they give rise at first, at certain points, to an increase in unemployment, which produces suffering among the workers. This suffering can be reduced by the extension of unemployment insurance, but it cannot be removed completely.

In the economy of capitalism, however, the slogan of rationalisation, the tendency to cut costs, is not only a matter of improved technique, it is also a tendency to exert pressure on the workers, to speed up their work, to expend their labour power recklessly, without regard to whether the ongoing increase in strain will lead to a premature consumption of the workers' strength. From the point of view of capitalist profitability, it may be a matter of indifference whether costs are forced down by improved techniques or by a more ruthless utilisation of labour power. From the point of view of the working class, there are two fundamentally different tendencies at work here. The workers accept technical and organisational progress as a necessary development, even where it has a darker side which cannot at first be entirely done away with. But they naturally add to this the demand for a direct share in the benefits of rationalisation, a share which must be expressed in wage increases and reductions in the length of the working day. On the other hand, the workers must fight emphatically against the ruthless acceleration of the tempo of labour and the compulsion to an excessive expenditure of labour-power, for methods of this kind have nothing to do with a genuine and progressive rationalisation. I would like to characterise them as 'pseudo-rationalisation'. Faced with the capitalist way of thinking, which only sees the cost account and its relation to profit, and nothing else, the working class and in particular the trade unions must make their point of view prevail, namely that human beings occupy the central point in the economy, that they must not be degraded to the level of instruments, but on the contrary that the maintenance of their labour power and their vital forces must be the most important goal of the whole economic system.

It would be reactionary for the workers and the trade unions to seek to obstruct technical economic progress; but it is absolutely not reactionary, but progressive in a far higher sense, when they oppose with all their strength the methods of a pseudo-rationalisation which is nothing but a more extreme way of squeezing out labour-power. These two forms of rationalisation, which for short-sighted and brutal employers might mean the same thing, are diametrically opposed to each other from the point of view of the national, and above all the human, economy. But it is precisely because in practice they run parallel and interpenetrate each other that the trade unions must urgently fight to achieve their demand for the workers' right of co-determination, both at enterprise level (where the Factory Councils will implement this) and higher up (where the trade unions will represent them) in relation to all alterations in working practices and all processes of rationalisation.

Source: Allgemeiner Deutscher Gewerkschaftsbund 1928, *Protokoll der Verhandlungen des 13.Kongresses der Gewerkschaften Deutschlands (3.Bundestag des ADGB), abgehalten in Hamburg vom 3.bis 7.September 1928*, Berlin, 1928, pp. 185–6.

Note: This speech is a clear indication of the ambiguous attitude of Social Democrats towards rationalisation. As a capitalist strategy it threw people out of work and intensified the labour of those still employed, but as an aspect of modernisation it 'powerfully captured the imagination of the left-leaning intelligentsia'.[35]

10.12   'Programme for the National and Social Liberation of the German People', Issued by the Central Committee of the KPD, 24 August 1930

The German Fascists (National Socialists) are at present undertaking a very strong offensive against the German working class. At a time when Germany is enslaved by the Versailles Treaty, the growing crisis, unemployment and mass misery, the Fascists are trying to win over significant strata of the petit bourgeoisie ... by putting out a flood of demagogic and radical phrases ...

The KPD confronts this National Socialist demagogy with its programme of struggle against Fascism and its policy of genuine advocacy of the interests of the toiling masses of Germany.

We Communists alone fight against both the Young Plan and the robbers' peace of Versailles, the starting point of the enslavement of all the toilers of Germany. We Communists are against all payment of reparations or international debts. In the case of our seizing power, we shall declare all obligations arising out of the Versailles Treaty to be null and void ...

The Fascists (National Socialists) claim that they are against the boundaries drawn at Versailles. In reality Fascism oppresses the peoples under its domination wherever it is in power. The leaders of the German Fascists, Hitler and his accomplices, do not raise their voices against the misery of the German peasants of South Tyrol, who are groaning under the yoke of Italian Fascism. Hitler has concluded a sordid secret agreement with the Italian Fascist government, handing over the German parts of South Tyrol to the foreign conqueror. With this shameful deed, Hitler and his Party have sold out the national interests of the toiling masses of Germany to the victors of Versailles.

We ... call upon the working masses of Germany to fight above all against the enemy in our own country, to overthrow capitalist rule and to set up Soviet power in Germany, in order to tear up the Versailles Peace Treaty ... We Communists alone are against all cooperation with the bourgeoisie and in favour of the revolutionary overthrow of the present capitalist social order ... After the setting up of the proletarian dictatorship in Germany we shall tear up the plundering Versailles Treaty ... work for the full right of self-determination for all nations, and make it possible for those German areas which wish to do so to be incorporated in a Soviet Germany. We shall conclude a firm alliance between Soviet Germany and the USSR ... expropriate the industrial enterprises, banks, and large houses and the estates of the big

35   Eley 1998, p. 330.

landowners without compensation. We shall set up Soviet farms...abolish unemployment by introducing the seven-hour day and the four-day week and by making a firm economic alliance with the Soviet Union.

Only the hammer of the proletarian dictatorship can break the chains of the Young Plan and national oppression. Only the social revolution of the working class can solve Germany's national question...We therefore call upon all working people who are still under the spell of the cunning Fascist deceivers of the people to break decisively and definitively with National Socialism and enter the ranks of the army of the proletarian class struggle.

Down with the Young Plan!

Down with the government of capitalists and Junkers!

Down with Fascism and Social Democracy!

Long live the dictatorship of the proletariat!

Long live Soviet Germany!

Berlin, 24 August 1930

The CC of the KPD (Section of the CI)

Source: *Die Rote Fahne*, 24 August 1930.

10.13   *Fritz Tarnow Ponders Social Democratic Strategy 'At the Sickbed of Capitalism' in 1931*

Our demand...for the forty-hour week is not a temporary measure to solve the crisis, it is rather a long-term demand, and we should like to say publicly today that it is the most important objective of the working-class struggle, both in political and trade-union terms, for the coming years. (Enthusiastic applause) What conclusions should we draw from the present economic crisis about the prospects for the further existence of the capitalist system? Some comrades think that we are confronted with its decisive crisis, the final crisis, which must end with the collapse of capitalism... The present crisis is doubtless more extensive and its impact has been deeper than in all previous crises. But the economy will find the path to its own restoration, and in saying this I find myself in agreement with almost all economic theorists in our own ranks. The considerable decline in the rate of interest and the fall in the prices of raw materials are visible indicators that a turnaround is in the offing, though this naturally does not tell us how long the process will take.

We stand at the *sickbed of capitalism* not just as diagnosticians, however, but as – how shall I put it? – the doctor who wishes to heal the patient? – or the joyous heir who cannot bear to wait for the end and would prefer to help it along a bit with a little poison? (Laughter) This image expresses our whole situation. We are, it seems to me, condemned to be the doctor who wants to heal ... and to feel in our hearts that we are heirs who would rather take over the whole inheritance of the capitalist system today than wait until tomorrow. This dual role, of doctor and of heir, is a confoundedly difficult task. We could save ourselves some arguments in the Party if we constantly kept this dual role in mind ... We are not particularly sorry for the patient, but we are concerned for the masses he represents. If the patient enters his death throes the masses outside go hungry. If, knowing this, we come upon a medicine that at least soothes the agony, so that the masses outside get a little more to eat, then we give him the medicine and momentarily ignore the fact that we are the heirs who are waiting for his life to end ... The organised working class desires the fall of the capitalist system but not the collapse of the economy. It wants socialism to be an improvement of its situation, not a further deterioration. I have never found any clear explanation of what those who dream of a total collapse actually understand by this. The concrete answer they can make is to point to the Russian economy ... If one wants to establish socialism, one must act as they did in Russia. But what does this mean for us, comrades? ... The Russian people have been led for fourteen years into a hell-hole of wretchedness which is worse than the misery of the capitalist economy.

Source: Sozialdemokratischer Parteitag in Leipzig 1931, *Protokoll vom 31.Mai bis 5.Juni im Volkshaus*, pp. 45–6, speech by Fritz Tarnow.

CHAPTER 11

The Parties, their Supporters and the Proletarian Milieu

Introduction

This section deals with the way the parties of the Weimar Left were structured, but also presents some evidence on the socio-economic and geographical bases of their support. In studies on this topic the concept of the 'social milieu' has been applied in recent years. This can be defined as a complex consisting of social and organisational networks, shared intellectual positions and collective engagement in certain periodic ritual activities.[1] According to Rainer Lepsius there were four stable social *milieux* in Imperial Germany – Socialist, Catholic, Conservative and Liberal – which dominated political behaviour.[2] Karl Rohe in a later study reduced this to 'three camps': Socialist, Catholic and National, arguing that Conservatives and Liberals were essentially in the same 'National' camp. In his view, this configuration remained politically stable despite the constitutional and social changes of the subsequent period.[3] What made the 'Socialist camp' a milieu was the plethora of independent cultural and sporting associations already attached to it by the early twentieth century. The list is long: it includes sport leagues, friends of nature, chess clubs, choirs, associations of free thinkers, Esperantists and nudist clubs. Most important of all, of course, were the free trade unions.[4] Many of these groups were 'created by rank and file workers'[5] rather than by the SPD as a political party. Under the emperor William II they were hindered in their growth by the hostile attitude of the authorities, and developed in a situation of isolation. They were, to use Geoff Eley's words, 'confined within a self-referential, ghettoised subcultural space'.[6] The SPD was above all a party of industrial workers with few links with

---

1 This definition is close to, but not identical with, Kolb 2005, p. 168.
2 Lepsius 1993, pp. 25–50.
3 Rohe 1992, pp. 92–7, 121–39.
4 The Free Trade Unions deserve to be treated separately from the political parties, but no attempt has been made to cover this gigantic subject here.
5 Weitz 1998, p. 282.
6 Eley 1998, pp. 320–1.

the wider society outside the Party. It has been estimated that over 90 percent of the members were industrial workers before 1914.[7]

The situation changed in several ways after 1918. Firstly, a public space became freely available for the growth of a socialist culture.[8] This development was exceedingly disturbing to traditionalists, the Christian churches and people on the political Right. Hence the Weimar Republic was the scene of what have been described as 'culture wars', conflicts over secularism, over the religious content of education, over education in general, and over freedom of expression. A strong movement for disaffiliation from the church developed in the 1920s. It has been estimated that one million people formally left the Protestant churches, while 200,000 abandoned the Roman Catholic church. Many of those who left were teachers, and in the Rhineland, where the movement was particularly strong, they set up a League of Free School Societies dedicated to secular education. There was also a link between this educational movement and the defence of the Republic: the Free Schoolers claimed that the confessional schools were disloyal to the republican constitution and bred undemocratic attitudes.[9] After 1924, with the return of the political Right to power, the traditionalists went over to the offensive, endeavouring in 1927 to pass a law that 'granted equal standing to confessional, interconfessional and secular elementary schools' and ensured 'the right of parent to choose the school type for their children'.[10] Although the law did not pass the Reichstag there continued to be an atmosphere of cultural conflict, which was exacerbated by the KPD's decision to give the agitation for secular schools and church disaffiliation a more militant tone after 1929. There was also the issue of freedom of expression. A strong movement had been building up on the cultural right against the 'pornography' and 'filth' allegedly rampant in the Weimar period. This agitation culminated in the passing in December 1926 of the 'Law to Protect Youth Against Trash and Filth', which was opposed by both the KPD and the SPD as they felt it could very easily be used to suppress left-wing literature.[11]

The second change after 1918 was that there was no longer a unified socialist camp. The events of the November Revolution brought about deep political

---

7   Sperber 1998, p. 188. This did not mean that the people who voted for the SPD were all industrial workers. Regression analysis has shown that 35 percent of the Party's 1912 vote came from the middle classes, broadly defined (Sperber 1998, p. 182).

8   For workers' culture and the relationship of the Weimar Left to it, see Guttsman 1991.

9   Lamberti 2002, p. 77.

10   Lamberti 2002, p. 170.

11   See in detail Stieg 1990.

divisions, so that three rival camps emerged: the Majority Social Democrats (MSPD) the Independents (USPD) and the minority group of extreme leftists around the KPD. After the disintegration of the USPD in 1920 and the establishment of a mass communist party a two-way division between Social Democracy and Communism developed. In this context the question has been raised of the extent to which Social Democracy under Weimar was a 'class party' of the German working class, rather than a broader 'people's party'? The Party was predominantly urban,[12] and remained so, despite a temporary breakthrough into some rural areas in 1919, particularly among the agricultural workers. It continued to receive the support of many working farmers in parts of Hesse throughout the Weimar period, though this was an exceptional case.[13] The SPD's image was largely working class, but in electoral terms it made a considerable breakthrough into various middle-class groups, particularly schoolteachers and office employees, during the Weimar period. The proportion of the SPD vote provided by the middle classes 'rose from 35 percent in 1924 to 43 percent in 1932'.[14] This statistic naturally depends on a broad definition of 'middle-class' which includes office staff and all employees of public institutions, and it applies to voting figures, not to party membership. Any further penetration into the middle classes was rendered more difficult, it has been argued, by the existence of what has been called 'the social democratic milieu': the many associated organisations mentioned earlier exercised a constant psychological pressure against any further integration into the broader society.[15] In 1926 73 percent of the male members of the SPD in three large towns (Bremen, Hanover and Hamburg) were manual workers. The SPD remained a predominantly proletarian party under Weimar, although it has been calculated that the working-class proportion of its vote declined progressively from 65 percent in 1924 to 57 percent in 1932.[16]

---

12   This reflected the urbanisation of the country as a whole. It did not mean that town-dwellers were more likely to vote for the SPD than other parties. In fact multiple regression analyses by Jürgen Winkler have shown that there was only a weak correlation between the variables 'urbanisation' and 'working class' and a vote for the SPD. (Winkler 1989, p. 167).

13   Henning 1989, pp. 119–51.

14   Falter and Bömermann 1989, p. 302.

15   Büttner 2008, p. 68.

16   Winkler 1988, p. 348. For precise voting figures, see Falter and Börnemann 1989, table 5, p. 302.

Was the social democratic milieu in decline during the Weimar Republic, as claimed by some authors?[17] The membership figures for the organisations which formed part of the milieu actually show very healthy increases. The number of Worker Cyclists rose from 148,000 in 1914 to 314,000 at the end of the 1920s; the Proletarian Free-Thinkers from 6,500 to 600,000, the Workers' Gymnastics and Sports League from 170,000 to 570,000, the Workers' Singing League from 150,000 to 280,000. There were similar increases in the numbers of socialist Chessplayers, Samaritans, Athletes, Lovers of Nature, and so on. Membership in the Free Trade Unions also held up well, taking the Weimar period as a whole (11.12). The *Reichsbanner*, which had between one and two million members, organised in 5,618 local groups, and was largely composed of Social Democrats, should also be included (11.5).[18] So there is little sign, super-ficially at least, that the milieu was eroding.[19] It has, however, been argued that the influence of the milieu was becoming weaker because of the rise of mass culture, particularly the expansion of the cinema, which presented a seductive supra-class ideological message.[20] As James Wickham has put it: 'Now for the first time since the 1890s the working-class movement's members were becom-ing ideologically marginal within the working class'.[21] This idea has a long his-tory, going as far back as 1926 when Hendrik de Man advanced the theory of the 'bourgeoisification of the proletariat', by which he meant that proletarians were beginning to aspire to rise into the middle classes, or at least imitate their behaviour.[22] There was a long controversy about this alleged process at the time, in which the sociologist Theodor Geiger adopted a middle position. He conceded in 1931 that there was some ideological bourgeoisification, but he added that it was limited to the adoption of the outward symbols of bourgeois culture, which was inevitable in capitalist society. The workers, he said, 'still held on firmly to their proletarian and socialist attitudes towards the economy and the society'.[23] Hence the social function of milieu organisations remained

---

17   This view has been taken by Dieter Langewiesche (Langewiesche 1982, pp. 359–402). Peter Lösche and Franz Walter have argued as against this that the Social Democratic milieu did not decline but rather expanded in the 1920s (Lösche and Walter 1989, pp. 511–36). They then went on to back up their view with a large research project, which has yielded sev-eral individual studies of specific organisations.

18   Ziemann 1998, p. 370.

19   Lösche and Walter 1990, p. 164. See also the detailed examination by Hartmann Wunderer (1980).

20   Mallmann 1996, p. 175; Saldern 1993, pp. 44–57.

21   Wickham 1983, p. 342.

22   Winkler 1987, p. 100.

23   Geiger 1931, pp. 534–53.

THE PARTIES, THEIR SUPPORTERS AND THE PROLETARIAN MILIEU

intact, and the workers continued to be able to avoid meeting the bourgeoisie and interacting with members of other sub-cultures. Whether this was a good thing in the long run is another matter; Detlef Lehnert and Klaus Megerle suggest that this continued separation from the bourgeois social milieu contributed to the fragmentation, and ultimately the collapse, of the Weimar Republic.[24] Moreover, some of the SPD's leaders regarded these leisure-time activities with mixed feelings, as they tended to divert their supporters from directly political events.[25]

If the SPD remained predominantly urban and proletarian, the same was true of the KPD, only more so.[26] The ideal seedbed for a German communist was 'a purely Protestant terrain with a high level of industrialisation and urbanisation, deeply rooted Social Democratic pre-war traditions, and a high proportion of wage-labourers' (Mallmann).[27] The analysis of KPD membership carried out in 1927 by the Party itself (at the behest of the ECCI) revealed that 98 percent of the members lived in towns and cities; 68 percent of the members were industrial workers; 10 percent were craftsmen; and 11 percent were 'others'. These figures changed after 1927, but only in the sense that there was a considerable increase in the proportion of unemployed party members. This rose from 21 percent in 1927 to perhaps 85 percent at the end of 1932.[28] In the early 1930s the typical German communist was an unemployed worker. A question often raised in this connection is the following: was the political split between the SPD and its opponents in the working-class movement, most of whom had coalesced by 1921 to form the KPD, paralleled by a split in the socialist milieu? Did the SPD and the KPD represent 'two irreconcilably opposed social and moral *milieux*'?[29] For a long time it was assumed that this was the case, but in 1995 Klaus-Michael Mallmann argued strongly against this view, setting off a fierce controversy.[30]

---

24   Editorial introduction to Lehnert and Megerle 1989, p. 9.

25   Winkler 1988, p. 121.

26   The KPD vote in 1924 was strongly correlated with these variables in both cases (+ 0.5 for 'working class' and + 0.4 for 'urbanisation') (Winkler 1989, p. 167).

27   Mallmann 1996, p. 249.

28   Bahne 1960, pp. 661–2. There is some uncertainty about this figure.

29   Michael Rück, in a review of Winkler's trilogy on the history of the workers' movement during the Weimar republic (Rück 1993, p. 519).

30   Mallmann 1995, pp. 5–31. This article was followed in 1996 by a book on the same subject, *Kommunisten in der Weimarer Republik. Sozialgeschichte einer revolutionären Bewegung.* Mallmann takes the line that there were many 'left-proletarian' (in other words, socialist and communist) milieux rather than two rival ones, or one single milieu. But he also sometimes refers to 'milieu' in the singular: 'Communists continued to live in the

The idea of a separate communist milieu is far more convincing for the period from 1928 onwards, when the communist groups which had previously joined united workers' sporting and cultural associations linked loosely to the SPD decided, in line with the Comintern's 'left course', to set up their own organisations.[31] To prevent fragmentation the KPD also set up two umbrella groups to coordinate what eventually became a very large and varied range of organisations. One, set up in October 1927, was called the Working Group of Social and Political Organisations (ARSO).[32] Its aim was 'to join together the proletarian forces which are now scattered over a broad area of social policy' and to 'fight against reactionary social policies'. It included 14 organisations.[33] The other umbrella group was the Association for Workers' Culture (IfA), set up in 1929, which controlled the cultural sphere, including the Proletarian Freethinkers alongside the cultural activists organised in the various literary, theatrical and artistic groups.[34] It too was a rival to an SPD organisation, the Socialist Culture League, which had roughly the same purpose of 'initiating and coordinating cultural activities'.[35] The drive for separation was carried to extremes: even the associations of wounded war veterans split, with the Social Democrats staying in the 640,000 strong National League of War Wounded and Former Participants in War and the communists establishing an International League of Victims of War and Work. This point is to some extent admitted by Mallmann, who says that in June 1929 'the 12th Congress of the KPD finally cut off the common thread of the working-class movement' and 'fundamentally put in question the requirements of the milieu context'.[36] It should be added

---

inherited socialist milieu', he wrote in 1999 (Mallmann 1999, p. 405). His rich study of Weimar communism covers much more ground than this, however, offering his critics many points of attack. See in particular Andreas Wirsching (1997, pp. 449–68), and Mallmann's reply (1999, pp. 401–13).

31 It should be noted, though, that the trade union movement stayed united throughout, despite intermittent attempts by the KPD to divide it. The RGO (Revolutionary Trade-Union Opposition) was set up in 1929 with this purpose, and it recruited an increasing number of members in the next three years, but even at its height in 1932 membership was estimated at only 322,000, less than a tenth of the membership of the ADGB (Weber 1969, vol. 1, p. 366).

32 Crew 1998, p. 235.

33 Fölster 1978, pp. 222–36.

34 Guttsman 1990, pp. 76–8, 101–6.

35 Guttsman 1990, p. 67.

36 Mallmann hastened to add, however, in line with his general thesis, that remnants of the milieu continued to exist, and that 'the rise of the NSDAP between 1930 and 1932 restored the connections' which had been cut off in 1929. (Mallmann 1995, pp. 19–20)

that the proliferation of separate organisations founded by the KPD after 1929 probably did not increase its influence. At least, that is the verdict delivered by Osip Piatnitsky on behalf of the ECCI in 1934, in the bitterness of defeat: 'There was a great variety of organisations[37] but they all had a roughly identical membership, that is to say, workers who were close to the KPD were simultaneously members of all these organisations'.[38] The apparently impressive rise in the number of members of the Party over the period after 1929 also had a hidden weakness: the ECCI was well aware that this rise concealed considerable fluctuations in membership. Many people joined the Party, but they didn't usually stay in it for long. To use Mallmann's striking expression, the KPD 'resembled a transit-camp rather than a fortress'.[39]

This point applies to the Party's leaders as well as its ordinary members. There were frequent changes of leadership in the KPD until 1929 (11.10). This was partly a result of changes in policy. Each time the party line changed, the leaders who had implemented the previous policy either made themselves unacceptable by opposing the new line, or were suspected of covert opposition even if they accepted it. The resulting factional struggles have been analysed in several books about the KPD over the years.[40] There were far fewer changes of leadership during the 'Third Period', when the line remained essentially unchanged. For the SPD, in contrast, the story is much simpler. The SPD leadership was marked by a tremendous degree of continuity (11.9). The only major change was the addition of former members of the USPD in September 1922, which was obviously necessary, given the merger between the two parties. This continuity was not, however, entirely beneficial. New potential leaders had to wait, and the full spectrum of opinions within the Party was not represented.

37　For example: RHD (Red Aid) had 370,000 members in 1932; IAH (International Workers' Aid) had 56,000 members in Germany; the KJVD (Communist Youth League) had 50,000; the Association of Proletarian Freethinkers had 163,000; the Fighters for Red Sporting Unity had 114,000; the International League of Victims of War and Work had 71,000; the Fighting League against Fascism had 106,000 in December 1931 but had declined to roughly 60,000 by June 1932 (Weber 1969, vol. 1, pp. 364–6; Rosenhaft 1983, p. 95).

38　Mallmann 1996, p. 179. This was an excessively pessimistic retrospective view, however. Moreover, one could probably say the same of the SPD's subsidiary and associated organisations (though not of the trade unions). Otto Wels told the party congress held in 1927 that there were 'over 40 different types of association in which members can be active' adding that 'all these groups' sought to 'attract more men and women members to the party' (*Sozialdemokratischer Parteitag 1927*, pp. 34–5).

39　Mallmann 1996, p. 92.

40　Flechtheim 1969; Weber 1969; Fowkes 1984; Weitz 1997.

Documents

11.1   *Statutes of the KPD, 1919*
1   Membership
Any person who has attained the age of 14 can gain membership of the Party provided he or she recognises the programme and statutes of the Party.

Anyone who acts in a way which contradicts the principles and the decisions of the Party will be expelled. The Local Group (*Ortsgruppe*) is responsible for expulsions, and appeals against its judgments are to be decided in the first place by the District Party Assembly, and in the last resort by the Congress of the whole Party.

2   Local Groups
The local groups carry on their organisational work autonomously within the framework of party principles and party decisions. They should draw up their own statutes, on the basis of factory organisation and residential district organisation.

3   Districts
The Local Groups are to be associated together in Economic Areas, and latter are to be grouped together in Agitational Districts. The higher instance of every District is the District Conference. This appoints a District Committee the main task of which is organisational and propagandist activity within the District. It also has the task of directing joint actions.

4   The Party Congress
The Party Congress is composed of representatives of the Districts, elected by the members of the Party in each District. Each District has the right to send one representative to the Congress for every 1,000 members ... The names of the representatives to be elected are to be put forward by the Local Groups.

The Central Committee will summon a Party Congress at least once a year. In addition to this, a Party Congress must be called if a majority of the Districts wish it.

The decisions of the Party Congress are mandatory for all the Party's members and organisations.

5   The Central Committee
The conduct of the Party's business is entrusted by the Party Congress to a Central Committee, consisting of twenty members. Seven of these are to be elected directly by the Party Congress, and they must take up residence at the

headquarters of the *Zentrale*.[41] The other 13 members are to be elected by the Congress for the various regions of the country from the names proposed by the Districts or the representatives of the Districts at the Congress. The members of the Central Committee all have equal rights. The members directly elected by the Congress [who form the *Zentrale*] are to conduct the current business of the Party. The directors of the secretariats for agitation among women and young people are to be present as participants with voting rights at the sessions of the narrower *Zentrale* [in other words, the *Zentrale*]. The Central Committee is to exercise supervision over the *Zentrale's* conduct of business. Its sessions must be regular and it must be associated with all important decisions.

6   Dues
The level of party dues for each locality is to be decided by the corresponding Local Group. It must be at least 15 pfennigs a week for female members and young people, and 30 pfennigs a week for the rest. 30 percent of the receipts must be handed over to the Agitational District, which is then to deliver a third of that sum to the Central Committee. The settlement of accounts is to take place every quarter.

7   Officials
Paid officials in leading positions in the Party are elected by its highest instances (the Local Group Assembly, the District Conference and the Party Congress) and they can be recalled at any time by these bodies. They must put themselves up for re-election every year. They must be confirmed in their position by the next Party Congress. The following people count as officials in this sense: party secretaries, editors, agitators and business managers.

---

41   The *Zentrale*, the body which actually led the KPD for the next five years, is introduced here for the first time in this indirect way. In its narrow composition (seven or eight members at most) and its wide powers it was the German analogue to the Soviet Politbureau, and it was responsible for day-to-day policy. In fact the *Zentrale* turned out to be responsible for overall policy as well, since the *Zentralausschuss* (Central Committee), the KPD's other governing body, met infrequently (five or six times a year at most) and was dominated by the *Zentrale*, as the latter was usually a homogeneous group bound by its own inner discipline. The Central Committee was much larger in size (over 20 members) and is analogous to the Central Committee of the Russian Communist Party after 1921, although it represented an element of federalism which was foreign to the Bolshevik system of organisation. The *Zentralausschuss* was abolished in 1925 in the course of the KPD's process of Bolshevization. The *Zentrale* was itself then renamed *Zentralkomitee* (Central Committee).

Source: Kommunistiche Partei Deutschlands 1919, *Bericht über den 2 Parteitag der KPD (Spartakusbund), 20–24 Oktober 1919*, pp. 67–8.

11.2   *The SPD's Organisational Statute of 1924 (Selected Provisions)*

3 The basis of the organisation is the District Association, the boundaries of which are demarcated by the Party Executive according to what is politically and economically appropriate. The District Association is built up on the basis of local groups.

5 The female members of the Party are to be guaranteed a representation proportionate to their numbers in all leading bodies of the organisation and all delegations.

10 The Party Congress is the supreme representative body of the Party. It is composed of

a) Delegates, no more than 300 in number, elected from the District Associations.

The proportion of delegates from each district is determined by the number of members who have handed over their membership dues to the Party Executive in the previous financial year

b) Representatives of the Reichstag fraction, to number no more than one fifth of the total membership of the fraction.

c) The members of the Party Executive, the Party Committee (*Parteiausschuss*) and the Control Commission.

d) The speakers appointed by the Party Executive.

12 The Party Congress takes place every year. It may be postponed for a year with the consent of over three quarters of the Party Committee if there are important reasons to do this.

14 The tasks of the Party Congress are:

a) To receive reports on the business conducted by the Party Executive and the Control Commission, and the parliamentary activities of the Reichstag fraction.

b) To determine where the Party Executive is to have its headquarters.

c) To elect the Party Executive and the Control Commission.

d) To make decisions about the organisation of the Party and questions touching party life.

e) To take a position on the resolutions put before it.

15 An extraordinary Party Congress can be called
   a) By a three-quarters majority of the Party Executive
   b) By a unanimous decision of the Control Commission
   c) If at least 15 District Directorates call for it.

17 The leadership of the Party is the responsibility of the Party Executive, which has three chairs, two treasurers and a number of other members, to be laid down by the Party Congress. At least two women must belong to the Party Executive.

18 The Party Executive conducts the business of the Party and controls the basic line taken by the Party's press organs.

19 The Party Executive in being at the relevant time is the owner of the whole of the Party's monies and property.

20 The Party Executive can at all times check up on all party organisations and their activities, recognise expulsions and demand a financial accounting. It has the right to sit in an advisory capacity on all meetings of all party organisations, and to advise on the presentation and recall of candidates for the State Diets and the Reichstag.

22 The Party Committee consists of one representative of each District Association. The representatives are elected in the Districts. If there are more than 10,000 female members in a District, a female member must be elected in addition.

23 The Party Committee, together with the Party Executive, discusses important political questions touching the Party as a whole, the setting up of any central party institution which lays a lasting financial burden on the Party, and the establishment of an agenda and speakers for the Party Congress.

24 The Party Committee is to be called together every three months by the Party Executive as a rule, and in case of need more frequently. An extraordinary session must take place if one third or more of the District Executives propose this.

25 The Party Congress elects a nine-member Control Commission to control the Party Executive and to act as a court of appeal for complaints against it. The control operation must take place at least four times a year.

26 The central organ of the Party is *Vorwärts* (Berlin), the people's paper. Official party proclamations are to be published in a prominent position in the editorial section.

27 A Press Commission of a least 20 members is elected by party comrades in Berlin and suburbs to control the central organ's attitude in questions of principle and tactics and to administer it. The Press Commission, together with the Party Executive, decides on all affairs relating to the central organ... If there are differences of opinion between the Party Executive and the Press Commission, the Control Commission, the Party Executive and the Press Commission acting together have the power to resolve them.

28 Anyone who has seriously infringed the principles of the Party programme or been guilty of a dishonourable act cannot be a member of the Party... A member can in addition to this be expelled if his persistent defiance of the decisions of his party organisation or of the Party Congress harms the interests of the Party. Only a local group can propose expulsion. Where someone belongs to another political party, or supports it financially, or works for it against the Social Democratic Party, the Party Executive can pronounce his expulsion with immediate effect.

29 The expellee can appeal to a court of arbitration against the decision of the District Executive.

30 The expellee can appeal to the next Party Congress against the decision of the court of arbitration.

Source: Sozialdemokratischer Parteitag 1924, *Protokoll mit dem Bericht der Frauenkonferenz*, pp. 7–11.

11.3 *Statutes of the KPD (1925 version)*

I   The Name of the Party

1 The Communist Party of Germany is the Communist International's section in Germany, and it is called 'The Communist Party of Germany, Section of the Communist International'.

II   Party Membership

2 Membership is open to anyone who accepts the programme and the statutes of the Communist International (Comintern) and the Communist Party.

A member of a primary unit of the Party is someone who actively participates in its work, submits to all decisions of the Comintern and the Party, and regularly pays membership dues.

III   Party Structure

6 The Communist Party of Germany, like all sections of the Comintern, is built up on the basis of democratic centralism. Its main principles are:

a) The election of party organs at all levels by full meetings of the Party membership, at conferences and congresses.

b) A periodic rendering of accounts by party organs to their electors.

c) Mandatory acceptance of the decisions of higher party organs by lower ones, strict party discipline, and a precise implementation of the decisions of the ECCI and leading party organs...Discussion of party questions by the membership takes place only until they have been decided by the appropriate party organ. When a decision has been taken by a Comintern congress, a party congress or a leading party organ, it must be carried out unconditionally, even when some of the members or local organisations are not in agreement with the decision...

8 On local questions party organisations are autonomous, within the framework of existing decisions by the Comintern or the Party.

9 The highest instance of any party organisation is the full assembly of its members, the conference or the congress.

10 The full assembly, the conference or the congress elects the leadership, which serves in the interval between meetings as the leading organ and carries on the current work of the relevant organisation.

11 The structure of the Party in outline is as follows:

a) for individual factories, worships, streets: cell meeting – cell leadership

b) for a small town, village etc.: local cell conference (village cell conference) or full local assembly (full village assembly) – local leadership

c) for part of a town: urban area conference – urban area leadership

d) for the territory of a sub-district: sub-district conference – sub-district leadership

e) for the territory of a district: district conference – district leadership

f) for the whole territory of the Reich: Party Congress – Central Committee (*Zentralkomitee*)

IX   The Party Congress
32 The Party Congress is the highest party instance and is as a rule summoned once a year by the Central Committee in agreement with the ECCI. Extraordinary party congresses may be summoned by the Central Committee either on its own initiative or on the initiative of the ECCI, or at the request of organisations which represented a third of the Party membership at the previous Party Congress. An extraordinary congress cannot, however, be held without the consent of the ECCI ... Every delegate to the congress must have been a member of the Party for three years. The basis of representation at the congress is decided either by the Central Committee or by the Party Conference held before the congress.

X   The Central Committee
35 The Party Congress elects the Central Committee, which consists of members who all have equal rights. The number of members is determined by the Party Congress. Members of the Central Committee and political officials of the Central Committee must have been members of the Party for at least three years.

36 The Central Committee is the highest party organ when no Party Congress is in session. It represents the Party towards other Party institutions, sets up various Party organs, directs their entire political and organisational work, appoints the editorial board or the central press organ, which works under its guidance and control, organises and directs those undertakings which are of importance to the Party as a whole, distributes the Party's forces and manages the Party's central finances ... The Central Committee directs the work of fractions within those organisations which have a central character.

37 The Central Committee elects from among its members a political bureau to take charge of political work, an organisation bureau to conduct organisational work, and a secretariat (the Secretary) for all current work ...

39 The Central Committee undertakes the division of the country into districts, altering their boundaries where necessary. The Central Committee has the right to unite or subdivide existing organisations according to political or economic yardsticks, corresponding to the administrative division of the country.

XI   The Central Audit Commission

40 The Party Congress elects a central audit commission to supervise the Party's finances, keep its books and run the business affairs of the Party as a whole.

XII   Party Discipline

41 The strictest party discipline is the highest duty of all Party members and all Party organisations. Decisions of the Communist International, the Party Congress, the Party Centre[42] and all the higher Party bodies must be carried out quickly and precisely. All questions which provoke differences of opinion may be discussed freely as long as no decision has been reached on them.

42 A breach of party discipline involves punitive measures by the relevant Party organ... In regard to individual members the following punitive measures may be applied: party reprimand, public reprimand, dismissal from post, expulsion for a stated period, definitive expulsion from the Party.

43 The disciplinary procedure is implemented by the Party instances. Appeals against measures of discipline are permissible as far up as the Party Centre and the Party Congress.[43]

44 The question of the expulsion of a member from the Party is put forward by a meeting of the relevant Party organisation (cell) to the Party leadership above it. The decision on expulsion enters into force when ratified by the district leadership. Appeals may be made up to the highest instance. While confirmation of expulsion is pending the member concerned must be withdrawn from Party work...

Source: Kommunistiche Partei Deutschlands 1926, *Bericht über die Verhandlungen .des 10. Parteitages der Kommunistischen Partei Deutschlands (Sektion der Kommunistischen Internationale), Berlin, vom 12. bis 17.Juli 1925,* pp. 232–9.

---

42   This expression presumably refers to the Central Committee, but it could also refer to the Political Bureau.

43   This appears to rule out an appeal to the ECCI or a Comintern Congress.

Note: These statutes were adopted at the 10th Party Congress. They are based on the 'model statutes' intended to apply to all communist parties, drafted by the organisation department of the ECCI, ratified by that body in April 1925, and gradually implemented throughout the world.[44] What was distinctive about them in the German context was that they abolished the Central Commission (*Zentralausschuss*), which was the last trace of the federalism of the early KPD. It had exercised a certain controlling function over the decisions of the *Zentrale* but it was now replaced by a completely toothless biannual Party Conference. There was some opposition to this from Herbert Müller, representing the Rhine-Saar district of the Party, on the ground that 'the present leadership is not yet unconditionally infallible',[45] but he did not actually go so far as to vote against the proposal. As a result of the new party statutes the *Zentrale's* replacement, the Central Committee (*Zentralkomitee*), gained much more power. The election of district leaderships now needed its confirmation, and no one could be employed by a district without its consent.[46] The most important party bodies, however, where the real decisions were made, were not the Central Committee but the Political Bureau (*Polbüro*), the Organisation Bureau (*Orgbüro*) and the Secretariat mentioned in paragraph 37 of the statutes. The top leadership of the KPD endeavoured to exercise close control over the activities of its members, but it did not always succeed. Meetings of the local district leadership bodies were rarely attended by representatives from the centre, and a party which had only about 190 paid employees[47] could not hope to supervise all the activities of its 100,000 members.

11.4 Circular from the Red Front Fighters' League (RFKB), before 25 April 1925, 'On the Significance, Tasks and Organisation of the RFKB'

1 Our organisation was named the Red Front Fighters' League (RFKB) in order sharply to characterise its antagonism to the existing bourgeois Front Fighters' organisations and to place in the foreground the proletarian class character of our League.

2 Red is the historic colour of the international class struggle and of international solidarity. The banners and colours of the RFKB are therefore red.

3 The purposes of the League are to educate all its members to proletarian class consciousness, to defend against and prevent new imperialist wars, and to defend against all reactionary measures directed against the working class.

---

44   Degras 1960, p. 172.
45   Bericht KPD 1925, p. 474.
46   Mallmann 1996, p. 147.
47   Mallmann 1996, p. 150.

4 The RFKB gathers together, ideologically and organisationally, all Front Fighters who stand for the proletarian class struggle, as well as all other workers of Germany without distinction of party or sex.

5 Any worker who is over 16 years old and who agrees to the rules of the League can be a member.

Tasks of the RFKB

1 One of the main tasks of the League is to maintain and strengthen the class-consciousness of all its members.

2 Another task is to reject all attempts to impose a new kind of militarism on the working class.

3 The RFKB is the organisation of proletarian self-defence and it must assist all proletarian organisations and parties in the struggle against Black-White-Red and Black-Red-Yellow reaction and protect them against attacks by the capitalist White Guards.

4 Members of the RFKB must constantly approach proletarian comrades of the *Reichsbanner* to ask them to participate in demonstrations by the RFKB against the Black-White-Red reaction (*Stahlhelm* etc.).

5 The RFKB aims to join together locally and nationally with all proletarian organisations in so far as they stand on the ground of the class struggle, in order to ward off anti-working class machinations. For this purpose the RFKB may take part in meetings of other proletarian organisations, while maintaining its own character. At these meetings the local director of the League must be given the opportunity to stress the character of the RFKB and its significance for the whole working class.

Source: Schuster 1975, *Der Rote Frontkämpferbund 1924–29*, pp. 263–4.

Note: The RFKB was founded in July 1924, against the wishes of the leaders of the M (Military) and N (Intelligence) apparatuses of the KPD, Karl Retzlaw [Karl Gröhl] and Wolfgang von Wiskow, who preferred to retain the small military cadre organisation they headed rather than allow it to be swamped in a large, legal, uniformed and weaponless mass movement. Since the seizure of power was no longer on the agenda the KPD leadership decided to proceed with the plan. Retzlaw was expelled from the Party for continuing to oppose it.[48] The RFKB was in part a reaction to the growth of the paramilitary organisations of the Nationalist Right (the *Stahlhelm* and the SA) and of Social Democracy (the *Reichsbanner*) but it was also an attempt by the Communist

---

48   Retzlaw 1976, pp. 265–56.

Party to re-activate the Proletarian Hundreds, which had continued to exist illegally since being banned in 1923. It was mainly used to protect election meetings and, where possible, to prevent right-wing intimidation of workers. There are varying figures of its numerical strength. It seems to have grown from 40,000 members in 1925 to 127,000 in August 1927, but to have declined after that.[49] The expelled leader of its youth branch, Werner Jurr, estimated membership at 80,000 in 1929. Kurt Schuster[50] gives a figure of 76,000 RFKB members and an additional 27,000 in the youth branch. There is no doubt that it recruited very successfully, owing to the existence of a military tradition based on participation of many KPD members and sympathisers in the First World War, and, it has been argued, the way it re-established gender roles which had been undermined somewhat in the earlier years of the Republic. One example of this is its attitude towards female membership. Originally the RFKB had a number of female members, but already by 1925 the Party had decided that they should be excluded, as 'the admission of women contradicts the military character of the organisation'. It was Ruth Fischer herself who proclaimed this decision, at the 1925 Party Congress. Women, she said, would be able to join a separate organisation, the RFMB, which would soon be set up under Clara Zetkin.[51] The female delegates at the 1925 Congress strongly objected to this decision to sideline them, and in fact resolutions expressing 'the sharpest disapproval' of their exclusion and demanding that the *Zentrale* should 'instruct the RFKB to reverse its decision' were passed by the women's section. It made no difference. The women were excluded, and forced to join the RFMB a few months later.[52]

In May 1929, after the Berlin events of that month (described as *Blutmai* by the communists)[53] the organisation was banned. This was a painful blow to the RFKB. It continued to operate illegally, but it lost at least half its members. Moreover, the KPD Central Committee's proclamation of November 1931 against 'individual terror' led to a loss of morale in the organisation, and it attempted no serious resistance to the Nazi seizure of power in 1933.

---

49   Weber 1969 vol. 1, p. 364.

50   Schuster 1975.

51   Bericht KPD 1925, p. 754.

52   Mallmann 1996, pp. 194–5.

53   See the introduction to Chapter Six of this collection.

11.5 *The Statutes of the* Reichsbanner Schwarz-Rot-Gold (*adopted on 26 May 1926*)

1

The purpose of the league is to bring together all German men, particularly war veterans and young males, who stand unconditionally and unreservedly on the ground of the republican constitution.

The colours of the league are the constitutional colours of the German Reich: black, red and gold.

The headquarters and seat of the executive of the league is Magdeburg.

2

The league has the following tasks:

a) to cooperate in a non-party fashion in the social, economic and political reconstruction of Germany;

b) to engage in sport and physical exercise and in caring for young people;

c) to educate all its members in the spirit of the constitution and the republic and to enable them to spread the idea of the republican-democratic state in town and country;

d) to train its members in setting up disciplined marching formations to enable political demonstrations to be carried through in an orderly fashion and to defend against eventual attacks by political opponents on the constitution and the existence of the republic;

e) to train the league's formations in the rapid provision of first aid in case of floods, mine and railway accidents, explosions, fires, the collapse of buildings and other events;

f) to support with all its strength the republican governments, officials, parties, trade unions and other organisations which declare themselves openly in favour of the social democratic republic, and support international concord and a strong League of Nations;

g) to form relationships with organisations inside and outside Germany for the maintenance of common interests and the achievement of similar goals.

3

The league will arouse and nurture comradeship and republican attitudes, protect the constitution of the Reich and the republican state constitutions and place itself at the disposal of republic governments and officials in case of need;

it will represent the interests of the war veterans, the bereaved dependants and those wounded in the war in a strong and emphatic manner;

it will fight and rebut attacks against republicans, republican parties and trade unions will all the means at its disposal.

5

Engaging in party politics on one side or another is strictly forbidden in the league, as is the discussion of religious matters of any kind and illegal armament.

7

The league extends over the whole of the German Reich. It is divided into 32 districts, each with its own executive.

25

All executives must be composed of members of all the parties which stand on the ground of the Weimar constitution ... A one-sided political composition of any of the executives is impermissible if a broader composition is possible.

Source: Hörsing 1929, 'Das Reichsbanner Schwarz-Rot-Gold' in Harms, Bernhard (eds.) 1929, *Volk und Reich der deutschen*, vol. 2, pp. 181–3.

Note: The *Reichsbanner* was set up in 1924 with the aim of defending the Weimar Republic against threats from the Right. It was intended to be supra-class and supra-party, but in fact the vast majority of its ordinary members were workers who voted Social Democrat at election times. Members of the DDP and the Centre Party sat on its executive board, but their function was largely symbolic. How big the organisation was is uncertain, but one estimate is that it had three million members.[54] What was unusual about it was that a number of intellectual theorists, revisionist opponents of Marxism, around the journal *Neue Blätter für den Sozialismus*, were strongly committed to the *Reichsbanner*, as the organisation most likely to be able to defend the Republic against the Nazis and Nationalists after 1930. Self-defence involved not so much violent street confrontation as effective election propaganda through mass demonstrations. This line of approach was even more evident after the formation of the Iron Front in December 1931, which was intended by its founders (who were members of the *Reichsbanner*) to be a different organisation but was really a continuation of the old one. The difference lay more in the method

54   Harsch 1998, p. 254.

of agitation, which involved copying the clearly successful Nazi approach, with its 'symbolically rich ceremonies, art of staging and military construction'.[55]

11.6 *The Proletarian Free-Thinkers' Journal Criticises the Hold of the Church over Education, March 1925*

The Bavarian Concordat is a Cultural Document

Just as one can occasionally glean a quite remarkable political insight into the economic contradictions of capitalist society from examining the attitudes of the various political parties to the Dawes Plan, so the Concordat, that is to say the contract between the Roman Catholic Church and the Bavarian government which had just been accepted by the Bavarian Diet after many weeks of debate provides us with an education in cultural politics, and illuminates the cultural level of the present capitalist epoch with particular clarity.

That the adoption of this Concordat represents a cultural step backwards can already be seen when one compares its text to the wording of the old Bavarian Concordat which was concluded in 1817 after long and passionate discussion. Whereas then only one ambiguous phrase referred to the right of the Church to exercise surveillance over education, in the new Concordat the rights of the Church are enumerated in nine long articles. One can say that in Bavaria the elementary schools have been handed over to the Church, while the state only retains the right.... to pay for everything!

The organs of the state must provide the school buildings, and, through the system of compulsory school attendance, the children, but the rights of the state cease abruptly at the door of the schoolhouse... Any teaching that offends the religious feelings of Catholic parents is to be outlawed... The teachers themselves want nothing to do with this Concordat, and they have protested against it in mass meetings. But in vain. The Bavarian Prime Minister, Held, and his Education Minister, Matt, are angry with the teachers for forgetting their duty of subordination and trying to defend themselves. And it is the comparison between the attitude of the present Bavarian government and that of the government of 1817 which shows the culturally regressive character of our epoch. In 1817 the representatives of the Bavarian government fought a stubborn and determined battle to uphold the secular character of the modern state, and only after the fall from office of the main supporter of secularism, Count Montgelas, were the ecclesiastical parties able to push through a Concordat relatively favourable to the Church. But the present government was prepared to grant the Church all its demands in advance, and

---

55 Harsch 1998, p. 260.

that institution would have been foolish not to exploit the favourable situation to its own advantage.

Source: *Der Atheist: Illustrierte Wochenschrift für Volksaufklärung* 21, 3, March 1925

Note: 'The Atheist' was the leading journal of the movement of Socialist Free Thinkers, which expanded very considerably during the Weimar period, eventually numbering half a million members, most of them Social Democrats, but it was unusual in that it contained 45,000 communists in 1927. The Freethinkers' stress on atheism was not in line with the views of official SPD spokespersons, who endeavoured to appeal to religious voters by praising the 'ethical values' upheld by religion. The 1929 Congress of the SPD proclaimed that one could be a good socialist and at the same time a good Catholic or Protestant. This was a constant source of tension between the Socialist Freethinkers and their political Party.[56] There were even a case where an SPD member of the Prussian government (Severing) confiscated leaflets issued by the Socialist Freethinkers.[57] It is not surprising that when after 1928 the communists began to separate from the united organisation they were able to pull considerable numbers away from the parent body. Eventually they formed their own Union of Proletarian Freethinkers of Germany, which claimed a membership of 170,000 when it was prohibited in May 1932.[58]

11.7   *Peter Maslowski Gives the Communist View of the Freethinkers' Movement (June 1932)*

'The dissolution of the Union of Proletarian Freethinkers (*Verband proletarischer Freidenker*) is also necessary for the maintenance of freedom of religion and conscience as guaranteed by the Constitution'. Where is that written? In the official statement justifying the prohibition of the Freethinkers! In its endeavour to retain the semblance of democracy, cultural Fascism does not perceive how mendacious its sham liberalism sounds, how far the poverty of ideas displayed by brutal violence compels it to utter the most ridiculous phrase to provide a basis for this prohibition.

Provocative displays? Are the Proletarian Freethinkers even permitted to display themselves in any numbers in public? Their theatre groups have long since been forbidden. In fact, what do the authorities think they can achieve by

---

56   Wunderer 1980 vol. 2, pp. 1–33.
57   Wunderer 1980 vol. 1, p. 147.
58   *Internationale Pressekorresponden*, 37, 7 May 1932, p. 1127.

confronting a godless population such as that of Berlin? Will the policeman's truncheon drive the masses back into the Church? Even Bishop Schreiber, freshly appointed Bishop of Berlin by the grace of Otto Braun, who is the actual leader of the crusade against the Freethinkers, cannot hope for this. You only have to look at the number of people leaving the Church: since 1918 *half a million Berlin proletarians have left it* ... And just who is impressed by the remarks about the 'need to preserve Christian culture and morality from a Bolshevik revolution'? Ridiculous as all this is, the assertion by the cultural Fascists that the Proletarian Freethinkers only know how to wound the feelings of believers reaches the heights of mendacity.

We know that the way religion is anchored in the masses is not a result of *great stupidity* or *clerical deception* but of *social oppression*. We consider it completely pointless to wound the religious feelings of our class comrades who are still inclined that way. We want to win them over, to *prove* to them that religion is an instrument of class rule over them ... The motive force of our action is the recognition of the need to mobilise the masses for the proletarian revolution through the medium of anti-religious agitation. This attitude distinguishes us both from the *religious socialism* of the SPD which is nothing but a whipper-in for the official Concordat policy of Braun and Severing, and from *bourgeois liberalism* which has now almost completely capitulated to cultural Fascism.

Source: Maslowski 1932, 'Wir Gotteslästerer' in *Die Linkskurve* 4.6 (June 1932), pp. 4–8.

11.8   *A Utilitarian SPD View of the Purpose of Workers' Education, 1929*

Let us imagine a seminar in a People's University in which academics, officials, employees and workers sit alongside each other ... The theme of the seminar should be chosen in such a way that all the members of the group are interested in it, and are not taking part in order to get to know each other, but for the sake of the theme. After a while one person after another stays away and the seminar increasingly shrinks.

What has a school to do with education? One thing should be stressed. The school can provide absolutely no education. The school can provide knowledge, but knowledge is not education. Knowledge is one of the prerequisites of education but by no means the most important one ... If education means forming a consistent approach to life, one gains one's education from life itself ... Any school, in the best case, can only provide the starting-point for a person's education ... How can the People's University train the worker for his tasks in life? ... There are very narrow limits to the possibility of giving the adult worker intellectual training. Life and work hold him in their grip so firmly that a conscious educational intervention can hardly touch him. Even the amount of time during which the worker is subjected to the influence of the People's University is extremely short. For half a year, a year, or at most a couple of years, he comes to a lecture or a seminar once or twice a week ... In any case, only 1 percent of workers and employees come into contact with these establishments.

We stand before the working class holding fragments of culture and we ourselves no longer believe that the transmission of these fragments can be of any use ... We must find the purpose of education within the working class itself ... The worker must be trained to take up his own tasks. And there are plenty of these ... Workers' education must train the worker to be a functionary of the working class. This includes not just employees of the trade unions or the parties,[59] but anyone who fulfils any function in the service of the working class.

Perhaps the institutions which serve to entertain and divert the worker in his free time, such as the cinema, might later provide new points of linkage. But today the workers' education establishments fail to reach the vast majority of the workers. The People's Universities should no longer dream of following the humanist ideal of the all-round development of the personality, or believe they can create this sort of personality by the transfer of cultural values. Their pointless attempts to bridge the chasm between the German working class and 'our culture' will otherwise lead even where they are superficially successful to providing the worker with a petty-bourgeois cultural façade, Where the People's University and the working class cooperate openly and actively, the old ideal of education is increasingly being abandoned, and education is instead directed towards preparing the worker for his social tasks. The most active this cooperation, the more the People's Universities will have to make up their minds to train the workers who come to them to become functionaries of the working class.

Source: Hermberg 1929, 'Volkshochschule und Arbeiterbildung' in *Die Arbeit*, 6.9., September 1929, pp. 572–3, 579–80.

11.9 *The Party Leadership of The SPD, 1917–1933*
October 1917: Friedrich Bartels; Otto Braun; Friedrich Ebert; Eugen Ernst; Marie Juchacz; Hermann Molkenbuhr; Hermann Müller; Wilhelm Pfannkuch; Philipp Scheidemann; Otto Wels.

---

59   In the plural in the original.

June 1919: Friedrich Bartels; Otto Braun; Otto Frank; Marie Juchacz; Hermann Molkenbuhr; Hermann Müller; Wilhelm Pfannkuch; Adolf Ritter; Elfriede Ryneck; Philipp Scheidemann; Heinrich Schulz; Otto Wels.

October 1920: Friedrich Bartels; Adolf Braun; Otto Braun (between September 1921 and September 1922); Richard Fischer; Otto Frank; Otto Heinrich; Karl Hildenbrand; Marie Juchacz; Franz Krüger; Hermann Molkenbuhr; Hermann Müller; Wilhelm Pfannkuch; Adolf Ritter; Elfriede Ryneck; Heinrich Schulz; Johannes Stelling (until September 1921); Otto Wels.

September 1922: the same, with the addition of Arthur Crispien; Wilhelm Dittmann; Rudolf Hilferding; Franz Künstler; Carl Ludwig; Julius Moses; Anna Nemitz; and Emil Stahl.

June 1924: the same, without Otto Heinrich, Wilhelm Pfannkuch, Franz Krüger, Adolf Ritter and Franz Künstler.

September 1925: the same as in June 1924 with Friedrich Stampfer.

May 1927: the same as in September 1925, without Richard Fischer and with Hans Vogel and Max Westphal.

May 1929: the same as in May 1927, without Heinrich Müller, Hermann Molkenbuhr, Adolf Braun and Rudolf Hilferding.

June 1931: the same as in May 1929, with Rudolf Hilferding, Rudolf Breitscheid and Carl Litke.

11.10   Members of the KPD Leadership, 1919–1933[60]
January 1919: Hermann Duncker, Käte Duncker, Hugo Eberlein, Paul Frölich, Leo Jogiches, Paul Lange, Paul Levi, Karl Liebknecht, Rosa Luxemburg, Ernst Meyer, Wilhelm Pieck, August Thalheimer.

October 1919: Heinrich Brandler, Hugo Eberlein, Paul Frölich, Paul Levi, Ernst Meyer, August Thalheimer, Clara Zetkin

February 1920: Heinrich Brandler, Hugo Eberlein, Paul Frölich, Ernst Meyer, Wilhelm Pieck, August Thalheimer, Clara Zetkin.

---

60   Up to 1925: members of the *Zentrale*. After 1925: members of the *Polbüro*.

April 1920: Heinrich Brandler, Hugo Eberlein, Paul Levi, Ernst Meyer, Wilhelm Pieck, August Thalheimer, Clara Zetkin.

December 1920: Heinrich Brandler, Otto Brass, Ernst Däumig, Otto Gäbel, Kurt Geyer, Fritz Heckert, Adolf Hoffmann, Wilhelm Koenen, Paul Levi, Wilhelm Pieck, Hermann Remmele, Walter Stoecker, August Thalheimer, Clara Zetkin.

February 1921: Paul Böttcher, Heinrich Brandler, Hugo Eberlein, Paul Frölich, Otto Gäbel, Kurt Geyer, Fritz Heckert, Wilhelm Koenen, Ernst Meyer, Wilhelm Pieck, Hermann Remmele, Max Sievers, Walter Stoecker, August Thalheimer, Paul Wegmann.

August 1921: Paul Böttcher, Bertha Braunthal, Hugo Eberlein, Ernst Friesland (until January 1922), Fritz Heckert, Edwin Hoernle, Ernst Meyer, Wilhelm Pieck, Hermann Remmele, Felix Schmidt, August Thalheimer, Jakob Walcher, Rosi Wolfstein, Clara Zetkin.

January 1923: Karl Becker, Paul Böttcher, Heinrich Brandler (until February 1924), Hugo Eberlein, Arthur Ewert, Paul Frölich (until February 1924), Fritz Heckert, Edwin Hoernle, August Kleine (Samuel Haifiz, also known as Guralski), Wilhelm Koenen, Rudolf Lindau, Hans Pfeiffer, Wilhelm Pieck, Hermann Remmele, Felix Schmidt, Georg Schumann, Walter Stoecker, August Thalheimer (until February 1924), Walter Ulbricht, Jakob Walcher, Clara Zetkin (until February 1924).

May 1923: the same as January 1923, with the addition of: Ruth Fischer, Ottomar Geschke, Arthur König, Ernst Thälmann.

February 1924: Hermann Remmele and four other Centrists, Ernst Thälmann and one other leftist.

April 1924: Ruth Fischer, Iwan Katz, Arkadij Maslow (until May 1924), Arthur Rosenberg, Paul Schlecht, Werner Scholem, Max Schütz, Ernst Thälmann.

May 1924: Hermann Remmele added.

July 1925: Philipp Dengel, Ruth Fischer, Ottomar Geschke, Arkadij Maslow, Hermann Remmele, Paul Schlecht, Ernst Schneller, Werner Scholem, Ernst Thälmann.

November 1925: Konrad Blenkle, Philipp Dengel, Arthur Ewert, Ottomar Geschke, Fritz Heckert, Hermann Remmele, Ernst Schneller, Wilhelm Schwan (until March 1926).

March 1927: Philipp Dengel, Hugo Eberlein (until November 1928), Arthur Ewert, Fritz Heckert, Paul Merker, Ernst Meyer, Ernst Schneller (until November 1928), Hermann Remmele, Ernst Thälmann.

June 192: Franz Dahlem, Leo Flieg (until May 1932), Wilhelm Florin, Fritz Heckert, Paul Merker (until April 1930), Heinz Neumann (until May 1932), Wilhelm Pieck, Hermann Remmele (until October 1932), Fritz Schulte, Walter Ulbricht, Jean Winterich, Ernst Thälmann.

11.11   *Membership Figures for the SPD, USPD AND KPD 1919–1932*

Date	SPD Members	USPD Members	KPD Members
1919	1,012,299	c. 300,000	106,656
1920	1,180,208	893,923	78,715
1921	1,221,059	340,057	359,613
1922	1,174,106	300,659	255,863
1923			294,230
1924	940,078		121,394
1925	844,495		122,755
1926	823,520		134,248
1927	867,671		124,779
1928	937,381		130,000
1929	1,021,777		118,957
1930	1,037,384		149,000
1931	1,008,953		213,554
1932			252,000

Sources: for the SPD, Sozialdemokratischer Parteitag 1919–31, *Protokolle der Parteitage der SP*; Sozialdemokratischer Parteitag 1924–31, *Jahrbücher der deutschen Sozialdemokratie:* for the USPD, Krause 1975, *USPD. Zur Geschichte der Unabhängigen Sozialdemokratischen Partei Deutschlands* Frankfurt. p. 303; for the KPD, Fowkes 1984, *Communism in Germany under the Weimar Republic*, p. 205.

11.12   *Membership Figures For the Free Trade Unions (ADGB)*

Date	Number of Members	Percent of workers organised
1918	1,664,991	11.5
1919	5,479,073	38.0
1920	7,890,102	54.7
1921	7,567,978	52.4
1922	7,895,065	54.7
1923	7,138,416	49.5
1924	4,618,353	32.0
1925	4,156,451	28.3
1926	3,977,309	27.6
1927	4,150,160	28.8
1928	4,653,586	32.2
1929	4,906,228	34.0
1930	4,821,832	33.4
1931	4,417,852	30.6
1932	3,790,748	25.4

Source: Potthoff 1987, *Freie Gewerkschaften 1918–1933: Der Allgemeine Deutsche Gewerkschaftsbund in der Weimarer Republik,* p. 348.

11.13   *Performance of the Weimar Left In National Elections, 1919–1933*

Date	19.1.1919	6.6.1920	4.5.1924	7.12.1924	20.5.1928	14.9.1930	31.7.1932	6.11.1932	5.3.1933
SPD %	37.9	21.7	20.5	26.0	29.8	24.5	21.6	20.4	18.3
SPD seats	165	102	100	131	153	143	133	121	120
USPD %	7.6	17.9	0.8	0.3	0.1				
USPDseats	22	84							
KPD %		2.1	12.6	9.0	10.6	13.1	14.3	16.9	12.3
KPD seats		4	62	45	54	77	89	100	81
Total %	45.5	41.7	33.9	35.3	40.5	37.6	35.9	37.3	30.6
Total seats	187	190	162	176	207	220	222	221	201

CHAPTER 12

The Parties and Groups of the Dissident Left

Introduction

Factional division was a significant aspect of the Weimar Left, even though both the major parties abhorred it. The list of factions is long, and not all groups have been included here.[1] The dissident Left was relatively small in numerical terms, but not unimportant towards the end of the Weimar Republic. Hans Mommsen has even claimed, surely with some exaggeration, that 'virtually all activist elements in the German labour movement left the SPD and KPD and reorganised themselves as splinter groups'.[2] The documents in this section cover both socialist and communist groups, some of which remained factions, while others set themselves up as political parties. The first two documents here originate from the USPD, which was by far the largest of the dissident parties, although only a fragment of it survived beyond 1922. It split from the SPD in 1917 over the question of whether to continue supporting the German war effort during the First World War, but it soon developed a distinctive approach over a whole range of issues.[3] In that sense it is hard, for once, to agree with Arthur Rosenberg, who claimed that after the First World War had ended there was no longer any reason for the division between the SPD and the USPD to continue.[4] The USPD saw itself as upholding the traditions of pre-war Social Democracy, but in addition to this the November Revolution of 1918 and the revolutionary disturbances of the next two years provided it with a new political programme. It stood for proletarian power exercised through the system of Councils (12.1, 12.2). To that extent it did not differ from the communists. But it wanted to combine the Councils with elected parliaments, which was not the KPD's intention at all. The USPD was very successful in its agitation in 1920, and it ran the SPD close in the Reichstag elections of that year, before splitting into two groups. The larger group decided

---

1 One group not treated here is the 'Old Social Democratic Party of Germany' (ASPD), a group of right-wing Social Democrats expelled from the SPD in 1926, who played a certain role in Saxon politics in the late 1920s but failed in their attempt to establish themselves more widely. See Lapp 1995, pp. 291–310.

2 Mommsen 1991, p. 59.

3 See in detail Morgan 1975.

4 Rosenberg 1936, p. 18.

to merge with the KPD (in December 1920); a slightly smaller group, which rejected this option, stayed independent for less than two years, after which it rejoined the SPD (in September 1922). An even smaller group, finally, refused to rejoin the SPD in 1922 and continued through the 1920s on its lonely path until it too gave up the ghost.

The other significant dissident socialist party, the SAP (Socialist Workers' Party), emerged from the group organised and inspired by the ex-communist Paul Levi in the mid-1920s,[5] which was at first committed to working within the SPD to shift it to the left, but decided to leave in 1931 because it considered that the official SPD policy of toleration of the Brüning government was leading the Party and the country to disaster. The SAP was the main oppositional group to emerge from the SPD in the later Weimar years. Two other significant groups need to be mentioned here, however. The ISK, or 'Nelson League', had a distinctive ethical approach to socialism, and it gained considerable support in one part of Germany. Finally, the Red Fighters (*Die Roten Kämpfer*) should be mentioned. They remained in the SPD until 1931, although their ideas were actually close to the Left Communism of the KAPD. 'The intellectual leaders' of the Red Fighters 'were all communists, but communists within the SPD, because they thought the Moscow-oriented KPD was even more harmful to the working-class movement than the Social Democrats'.[6] In fact their political trajectory had taken them from the SPD to the KPD in 1918, from the KPD to the KAPD in 1920, and from the KAPD back to the SPD in 1924.

All other documents in this section relate to communist factions. They are strongly represented here simply because there were more of them; successive changes of line by the KPD led one group after another to peel off (not always voluntarily) from the 'official' party either to the 'left' or to the 'right'. The decision to go it alone was always motivated by deep-seated disagreements on questions of strategy and tactics, and in the case of the KAPD on the very nature of a political party. The party, the Left Communists of the KAPD said, must be limited to the 'most advanced sections of the working class' who reject all existing parliaments and trade unions (10.3). The adoption of this view by the Communist Party would have made it impossible to win over the mass of adherents of the USPD. This is why Paul Levi, the leader of the KPD, forced

---

5   The journal *Sozialistische Politik und Wirtschaft*, which appeared between 1923 and 1929, and was edited by Levi, was the main intellectual driving force behind the SPD Left. From 1928 a second journal, *Klassenkampf*, continued on the same lines. See in particular Klenke 1987.

6   The most prominent activists of this group were Alexander Schwab, Bernhard Reichenbach and Karl Schröder. See Rothfels 1959, pp. 438–60, and the more detailed 1969 study by Olaf Ihlau.

them out in October 1919. They went on in April 1920 to found the KAPD, which however declined very quickly as a political force once the revolutionary upheavals of the early 1920s had come to an end.[7] Having thrown out the Left Communists, Levi was himself forced to leave the KPD in 1921 because of its refusal to disavow the March Action and punish those responsible. He set up the KAG (Communist Working Group) which can be regarded as a 'right communist' group, and intentionally avoided calling itself a party because it hoped to bring the KPD round to its point of view. It entered the USPD once it became clear that this was impossible; the reunification of the USPD and the SPD in 1922 brought its members, including Levi, back into the Party most of them had left five years before.

The next bout of communist political disintegration took place not after the defeat of October 1923 which brought the leftists Ruth Fischer and Arkady Maslow to power in the KPD but after the ECCI's interventions of 1925 and 1926, first to enforce a return to 'united front' policies and then to remove the incumbent leftist Party leaders on the grounds of their alleged disloyalty and failure to implement the new Comintern line. This second intervention sparked off a furious discussion in the ranks of the KPD, and led to the formation of an astonishing range of leftist and ultra-leftist factions.[8] We print here the programmatic documents of some of the major groups. It should be noted that one ultra-left faction (known as the 'Intransigent Left' or the 'Schwarz[9] Group') found itself to be so close ideologically to the KAPD, which was still in existence, that the two groups joined together.[10] Another group aligned itself with Leon Trotsky, now in exile from the Soviet Union.[11]

One final group emerging from the KPD needs to be mentioned: the KPD (O). This resulted from yet another change of tactics by the Party, the return in 1928 to a left line under the slogans of 'Class against Class' and 'Social Fascism'. The treatment of Social Democratic trade unionists as 'Social Fascists' was too much for a number of KPD trade union leaders, and they joined with Heinrich Brandler, the former KPD leader who was blamed for the fiasco in 1923 and had

---

7   Smart 1978, pp. 40–1.

8   See Bahne 1961, pp. 359–83, Zimmermann 1978, and Langels 1984.

9   Ernst Schwarz (1886–1958), KPD, member of the Reichstag 1924–28, criticised 'Red imperialism' and the 'opportunism' of 'rightist' leaders of the Party, expelled from the Party in 1926 for leftist deviation, formed the Group of International Communists in the Reichstag. See below, note 25.

10   See below, note 15.

11   See on this group Alles 1994.

been kept in cold storage in Moscow during the mid-1920s, in setting up the KPD (O) (Communist Party of Germany, Opposition).[12] As the name suggests, they didn't want to burn their bridges with the KPD entirely, hoping that the Party would see sense and abandon its leftist line so that they could rejoin it. The hope was vain, of course, and about 1,000 members of the KPO recognised this in 1931 when they decided to merge with the left-wingers who had just been expelled from the SPD to form the SAP, as mentioned earlier. The rest of the KPO retained its separate identity. After the Nazis came to power in 1933 none of these dissident groups was able to function openly.[13] They did, however, engage in underground activities against the Nazi regime, at the cost of great sacrifices, and some resurfaced after 1945 as small political organisations.

Documents

12.1   USPD Programmatic Declaration, adopted 6 March 1919

In November 1918 the revolutionary workers and soldiers of Germany conquered state power. But they have not secured their power firmly, or overcome capitalist class rule. The leaders of the right-wing socialists have renewed the pact with the bourgeois classes and abandoned the interests of the proletariat ... Under the capitalist social order, democratic legal forms are illusory. As long as political emancipation is unaccompanied by economic emancipation, true democracy does not exist. Socialisation, as pursued by the right-wing socialists, is a cunning imposture. The class-conscious proletariat knows that it alone can conduct its fight for emancipation, making use of more than the existing organisations. A new fighting organisation of the proletariat is required. The proletarian revolution has created this fighting organisation for itself in the *Council System*, which associates the working masses together in the factories for revolutionary action, creates the right ... to proletarian self-government in factories, local councils and the state, and implements the transformation of the capitalist economic order into a socialist one.

---

12   Theodor Bergmann has traced the history of the KPO (Bergmann 1987).

13   The relative strength of the dissident groups on the eve of Hitler's appointment as Chancellor in January 1933 was: SAP, 15,000; KPO 3,000; ISK 200, Left Opposition of the KPD (Trotskyists) 700; Red Fighters (former KAPD) 400; FAUD (Anarcho-Syndicalists), 4,300 (Ulrich 2005, pp. 54–73.)

The Council System is developing in all capitalist countries out of the same economic conditions ... It is the historical task of the USPD to carry the banner of the class-conscious proletariat in its revolutionary fight for emancipation. The USPD places itself on the ground of the Council System. It supports the Councils in their struggle for economic and political power. It aims at the dictatorship of the proletariat, representing the great majority of the people, which is a necessary prerequisite for the achievement of socialism. Socialism alone will bring the removal of class rule and dictatorship, socialism alone will bring true democracy.

The USPD will make use of all political and economic means of struggle to attain this goal *including parliamentary bodies*. It rejects purposeless acts of violence. Its aim is not the annihilation of individuals but the abolition of the capitalist system. The immediate demands of the USPD are:

1 The integration of the Council System into the constitution. The Councils are to make a decisive contribution to legislation, administration at the local and state levels, and the running of the factories.

2 The dissolution of the old army. The immediate dissolution of the mercenary army that has been set up in the form of the Volunteer Corps. The disarming of the bourgeoisie. The setting up of a People's Militia recruited from the ranks of the class-conscious working class. The People's Militia will administer itself and its leaders will be elected by the rank and file. The abolition of military jurisdiction.

3 A start must be made immediately with the socialisation of capitalist enterprises. This is to be done without delay in the following areas: mining and the production of energy (coal, water, electricity), concentrated iron and steel production, other highly developed industries, and the banking and insurance systems. Large-scale landed property and forests must be converted immediately into social property ... The ownership of urban land is to be transferred to the municipalities, and adequate housing is to be provided by the municipalities at their own expense.

4 The election of officials and judges by the people. The immediate establishment of a Supreme Court of Justice to call to account those guilty of starting the World War and delaying the conclusion of peace.

5 War profits are to be completely confiscated through taxation. A part of every large property is to be handed over to the state. Public expenditure is to be funded by the imposition of progressive taxes on income, wealth and inheritance. The war loans are to be liquidated, though compensation is to be provided for those in need ...

6 The extension of social legislation. Care and protection for mother and child ... A fundamental reorganisation of public health provision.

7 The separation of church from state and church from school. Public schools of a non-ecclesiastical character are to be set up, to be organised on socialist educational principles. Every child must have the right to an education appropriate to his or her ability ...

8 The introduction of a legal public monopoly for advertisements, to be handed over to the municipal associations.

9 The establishment of friendly relations with all nations. We must enter immediately into diplomatic relations with the Russian Soviet Republic and with Poland. The Workers' International must be restored on the basis of revolutionary socialist policies and in the spirit of the international conferences of Zimmerwald and Kienthal.

It is the conviction of the USPD that the integration of all proletarian forces which is the Party's objective will accelerate the complete victory of the proletariat and guarantee its lasting character. However, the necessary prerequisite for the unification of the working class is the adoption in word and deed of the principles and demands of this declaration.

Source: Unabhängige Sozialdemokratische Partei Deutschlands 1919, *Protokoll über die Verhandlungen des ausserordentlichen Parteitages vom 2. bis 6. März 1919 in Berlin*, pp. 3–4.

Note: The compromise character of this declaration was clear from the debates at the March 1919 USPD Congress. Clara Zetkin, for the Left, complained that the Councils had been treated ambiguously. The question was, were they the *sole* fighting organisation of the proletariat? Is so, why were they merely to be 'integrated' into the Constitution? Haase replied, on behalf of the Right, that the question 'Council System or National Assembly' should not be posed at all. What was needed was a combination of the two. This idea of combining both systems together was in fact what distinguished the USPD position from that of the Spartacists (who had left the USPD by then), and the fact that only eight people voted against the resolution shows that the USPD was able to unite on the basis of the compromise advocated by Haase. The narrow margin (68 to 61 votes) by which Däumig's amendment which looked forward to the 'final overthrow of bourgeois parliamentarism by the Council System' was rejected gives some indication of the strength of the Left within the USPD at this stage.

12.2 *The USPD Action Programme of December 1919*

There are two great epochs in the proletarian revolution: the struggle for the conquest of political power, and the maintenance of that power for the period of the transition from capitalism to socialism.

The emancipation of the working class can only be the work of the class itself, because all other classes ... stand upon the ground of private property in the means of production and have as their common goal the maintenance of the foundations of capitalist society.

The interests of the workers are the same in all countries. With the extension of the world capitalist economy the situation of the workers of every country becomes ever more dependent on the situation of workers in other countries. The emancipation of the working class therefore requires an international association and a joint struggle by the workers of the whole world. The USPD is at one with the class-conscious workers of all countries in recognising this fact ... The class-conscious proletariat of all countries opposes imperialist capitalism with international socialism.

The conquest of political power by the proletariat begins the emancipation of the working class. To carry through this struggle the working class needs three things. It needs independent Social Democracy, which stands without reservation on the ground of revolutionary socialism, it needs trade unions which are dedicated to the unadulterated class struggle and must be transformed into fighting organisations of the social revolution, and it needs the revolutionary Council System, through which joins the workers together for the purpose of revolutionary action.

The USPD stands on the ground of the Council System. Even before the conquest of power it upholds all endeavours to extend the organisation of Councils as the organ of the proletarian struggle for socialism, to integrate together within the Councils all workers by hand and brain and to train them to exercise the dictatorship of the proletariat.

With the conquest of political power by the proletariat the capitalist state's organisations of political rule are smashed. They are replaced by the political Workers' Councils, which function as the proletariat's organisation of political rule. The Workers' Councils combine legislation and administration. When they enter into operation the whole capitalist administrative apparatus, including the local councils, is transformed and reshaped; this also means that the working class's right of self-determination becomes a reality ... The USPD counterposes the proletarian organisation of political rule to the capitalist one, and it counterposes the revolutionary Congress of Councils to the bourgeois parliament, for the latter is the expression of the bourgeoisie's will to power. The transformation of the economic anarchy of capitalism into the planned economy of socialism is to be implemented by the economic Council System.

The following measures are to be taken to abolish capitalism and bring socialist society into existence:

1 The dissolution of every counter-revolutionary mercenary force; the dissolution of all military, civil and police formations, local defence forces (*Einwohnerwehren*) in town and country, Emergency Technical Assistance forces (*Technische Nothilfe*), militarised police forces; the disarming of the bourgeoisie and the landowners; the setting up of a revolutionary defence force.

2 The conversion of private property in the means of production into social property. Socialisation is to be implemented without delay in the areas of banking, insurance, mining and energy production (coal, water, electricity), concentrated iron and steel production, transport and communication and other highly developed industries.

3 Large landed estates and forests are to be transferred immediately to social ownership.

4 In towns and industrial districts private property in the land is to be converted into municipal property; the municipalities are to provide adequate dwellings.

5 Planned regulation of food supply

6 Socialisation of public health.

7 Socialisation of all public educational establishments.

8 Religion is to be declared a private matter. The complete separation of church and state . . .

9 A socialist financial policy, through a progressive income tax and wealth and inheritance taxes to cover all public expenditure . . . The abolition of all indirect taxes and other financial measures which sacrifice the interests of the proletariat to those of a favoured minority.

10 The repeal of all laws which disadvantage women.

11 The introduction of a public monopoly for advertising.

12 The reconstruction of the whole system of public law on socialist principles.

13 Obligatory labour for all those capable of working. Protective measures for the maintenance of labour-power.

14 The establishment of friendly relations with all peoples. Immediate steps towards alliances with socialist republics.

The dictatorship of the proletariat is a revolutionary means to the abolition of all classes and the removal of class rule, and to the attainment of socialist democracy. The dictatorship of the proletariat will cease once socialist society is made secure, and socialist democracy is fully developed.

The organisation of socialist society is to take place through the Council System . . . The deepest meaning of the Council System is that the workers, the

people who keep the economy afloat, create social wealth and advance civilisation, must also be the responsible managers of all legal institutions and the
possessors of all political power.

To achieve this goal, the USPD makes use of all political, parliamentary and
economic means of struggle in a planned and systematic way, together with
the revolutionary trade unions and the proletarian Council organisation. The
decisive means of struggle is the action of the masses. The USPD rejects violent
actions by isolated groups and persons. Its goal is not the destruction of the
instruments of production but the abolition of the capitalist system.

The historic task of the USPD is to give the working-class movement a content, a direction and an objective, and to lead the revolutionary proletariat in
its struggle for socialism ...

The prerequisite for the unification of the working class is adherence in
word and deed to the principles and demands of this programme.

Only the proletarian revolution can overcome capitalism and realise socialism, thereby achieving the emancipation of the working class.

Source: Unabhängige Sozialdemokratische Partei Deutschlands 1919, *Protokoll
über die Verhandlungen des ausserordentlichen Parteitages vom 30. November
bis 6. Dezember 1919 in Leipzig*, pp. 3–5.

Notes: This programme, which committed the USPD to the 'dictatorship of the
proletariat' and the 'Council System', was very much to the left of the March
1919 programme. At this congress, held in Leipzig, the USPD demonstratively
broke with the Second International and made an approach to the Communist
International with a view to joining it. The West European Secretariat of the
Communist International, based in Berlin, replied favourably, saying that the
Leipzig Programme marked 'a victory of the proletarian element' in the USPD
over its 'opportunist right-wing leaders'. But the Bolshevik leaders in Moscow
found the programme highly unsatisfactory, and an uncompromising reply
was drafted by Lenin in December 1919, attacking the USPD as a whole as
a 'petty-bourgeois' party; this was eventually issued in a slightly softer form on
5 February 1920, perhaps under the influence of Radek. Now only the 'errors
of the right' of the USPD were attacked, not the whole Party, thus opening the
way to winning over as large a group of the left tendency as possible for
communism.[14]

---

14   Wheeler 1975, pp. 195–8.

**12.3   *Programme of the KAPD (Communist Workers' Party of Germany),
May 1920***
       Preface

The foundation of the KAPD was completed in the midst of the tempest of
revolution and counter-revolution. Its true date of birth, however, is not Easter
1920. It coincides rather with that phase in the development of the KPD (S)
when an irresponsible, egoistic handful of leaders endeavoured to impose its
personal conception of the 'death' of the German Revolution ... and on that
basis was able to replace the previous revolutionary tactics of the Party with
reformist ones. This treacherous attitude of the Levis, the Posners and Co. justi-
fies afresh the perception that the radical removal of all leadership politics
must form the prerequisite for the rapid advance of the proletarian revolution
in Germany ... The idea of heightening the revolutionary will of the masses so
that it becomes the decisive factor in the tactical establishment of a really proletarian organisation is the guiding motive for the organisation of our
Party ... The Marxist recognition of the *historic necessity of the dictatorship of
the proletariat* remains an irreplaceable guiding light for us. Our will to lead the
struggle for socialism in the spirit of the *international class struggle* remains
unshakeably firm.

Berlin, mid-May 1920

[There follows an outline of the general world situation, claiming that 'the
fiasco of capitalism' presents the workers with the alternative of 'relapse into
barbarism or the construction of a socialist world'.]

The economic and political situation in Germany is overripe for the outbreak of the proletarian revolution ... Everything depends on helping the proletariat to achieve the *consciousness* which is the only thing it needs to act
energetically to make use of the power it actually possesses already ... At this
moment, when the *objective* conditions for the outbreak of the proletarian
revolution are given ... reasons of a *subjective* nature must be present, standing
in the way of the accelerated progress of the revolution ... These subjective
aspects are playing a decisive role in the German Revolution. The problem of
the German Revolution is the problem of the *development of the German proletariat's consciousness of itself*...

The KAPD, in pursuing its maximalist objectives, has also decided in favour
of rejecting all reformist and opportunist methods of struggle. In a state which
bears all the hallmarks of capitalist collapse, participation in parliamentarism

is a reformist and opportunist way of proceeding...To participate in bourgeois parliamentarism signifies nothing other than *to sabotage the Council
idea*...The fight for the recognition of revolutionary Factory Councils and
political Workers' Councils...grows logically out of the struggle for the dictatorship of the proletariat...Council System or parliamentarism? That is the
question of world-historical significance.

Aside from bourgeois parliamentarism, the other main bulwark against the
further development of the proletarian revolution in Germany is formed by
the trade unions...The trade unions are one of the main pillars of the capitalist class state. The history of the trade unions in the last year and a half has
proved that this counter-revolutionary structure cannot be transformed from
within in a revolutionary sense...From the recognition of this fact there arises
the logical conclusion that only the *destruction of the trade unions* can clear the
way for the advance of the social revolution in Germany.

The Factory Organisation has arisen from the struggles of the masses. This is
the pure organisation of the proletarian struggle...The Factory Organisation
has two aims. First, the destruction of the trade unions, of their whole background and the complex of un-proletarian ideas concentrated in them...The
second aim is to prepare for the construction of the communist society. Every
worker who declares himself in favour of the dictatorship of the proletariat can
be a member of the Factory Organisation[15]...Separation from the trade unions
will have to be the touchstone for entry into the Factory Organisation...but
whereas a political party like the KAPD can never be quantitatively large, the
revolutionary masses will be united in the Factory Organisation through their
consciousness of their proletarian class solidarity. The Factory Organisation
will become the foundation for the communist party of the future.

The political organisation[16] has the task of assembling together the most
advanced elements of the working class on the basis of the party programme.
The relation of the Party to the Factory Organisation emerges from the nature
of the latter. The KAPD will conduct tireless propaganda within the Factory
Organisation. The cadres in the factory will become the mobile striking force
of the Party...In the phase of the seizure of political power the Factory
Organisation itself becomes an element of the proletarian dictatorship implemented in the factory by the Factory Councils, which base themselves on the
Factory Organisation...The Factory Organisation is an economic prerequisite

---

15   Note the narrowness of the criterion; this is what the KPD meant when it accused the
      KAPD of turning the Factory Councils into the churches of a sect. But the subsequent
      sentences appear to show that the KAPD's intention was actually the opposite of this.

16   The KAPD itself is meant here.

for the construction of the communist community. The Council System is the political form of organisation of the communist community.

[There follows a series of concrete demands of a political, economic, social and cultural nature, the most characteristic one being that for the 'dissolution of all parliaments and town councils'.]

The KAPD directs its attacks on the whole of bourgeois ideology . . . A decisive factor for the hastening of the social revolution lies in revolutionizing the whole mental world of the proletariat. In recognition of this fact, the KAPD supports all revolutionary tendencies in knowledge and the arts which correspond in their character to the spirit of the proletarian revolution. In particular the KAPD supports endeavours to bring the youth of both sexes towards self-expression. The KAPD rejects any form of tutelage over young people.

The KAPD is conscious that the final struggle between capital and labour cannot be fought out within national boundaries. Capitalism is hardly inclined to halt at national boundaries or allow its world-wide expeditions of rapine to be limited by any national scruples; equally, the proletariat is not permitted to lose sight of the fundamental idea of international class solidarity under the hypnotic effect of national ideologies. The sharper the proletariat's grasp of the idea of the international class struggle, the more consistently it is elevated to the main theme of proletarian world policy, the more rapidly and emphatically will the blows of the world revolution smash to pieces world capital, which is already in the process of dissolution. High above all national peculiarities, high above all fatherlands, the beacon of the slogan 'Proletarians of all countries, unite!' shines its everlasting glow upon the proletariat.

Source: Bock 1993, *Syndikalismus und Linkskommunismus von 1918 bis 1923*, pp. 407–8, 416–17.

Note: This programme represents the views of the Left Communists of the KAPD. There is a clear distinction, as Hans-Manfred Bock has pointed out, between the Left Communists, with their stress on the importance of the political party, and the Syndicalists, who considered political parties harmful and unnecessary. In December 1919 the latter set up the FAUD (S) (Free Workers' Union of Germany, Syndicalists), which claimed a membership of over 110,000 – if true this would make it larger than the KPD (S) at that time.[17] The KAPD itself claimed that it had 30,000 to 40,000 members when it was founded in April 1920.[18] The main points over which the KAPD and the KPD (S)

---

17   Bock 1993, p. 156.
18   Bock 1993, p. 227.

disagreed were the former's insistence on a regional, de-centralised structure for the Party, its refusal to take part in parliamentary elections, its refusal to enter the Free Trade Unions dominated by the SPD, and finally its aspiration towards the establishment of a united workers' organisation, or 'Union'. The last point brought the KAPD close to the Syndicalists in practice, although they continued to be divided by the issue of the need for a political party. The KAPD view was that a political party was essential for 'securing the revolution' but once that had been done political power 'would become unnecessary, and 'to the extent that the dictatorship of the proletariat changes into communist society the party will vanish'.[19] As the above document makes clear, it is entirely wrong to suggest that the KAPD was a 'National Bolshevik' party, although speakers from the official Communist Party sometimes tried to present it in this way. Laufenberg and Wolffheim[20] admittedly played a big part in setting up the new party, but they were expelled from the KAPD, along with the whole 'Hamburg tendency', at its second congress, held in August 1920. The Berlin organisation of the KAPD had already condemned the Laufenberg-Wolffheim tendency in a series of articles published in the *Kommunistische Arbeiter-Zeitung* in May 1920.[21]

12.4 Resolution Passed by the First Reich Conference of the KAG (Communist Working Group,[22] 20 November 1921)

The KAG is not attempting to found a party of its own; it believes rather that in view of the self-inflicted fate of the KPD and the decline in the prestige of the Communist International the impending formation of the *great revolutionary mass party* will occur not through splits but through a gathering together of forces. If the KPD holds fast to the policy it adopted at the last meeting of its ZA,[23] if it implements this policy honourably and not in order to obtain tactical party advantages, it will in the long run leave no margin between itself and

---

19   Reichenbach 1928, p. 130.

20   Fritz Wolffheim (1888–1943), member of the IWW in America before 1914, organised the left socialists in Hamburg during the War, joined the KPD 1918, expelled from the KPD in 1919, moved towards National Bolshevism, expelled from the KAPD in 1920, in contact with the Strasser wing of the NSDAP, arrested after 1933, died in a concentration camp.

21   Bock 1993, p. 280.

22   German: *Kommunistische Arbeitsgemeinschaft*.

23   The Central Committee (ZA) of the KPD, meeting on 16–17 November 1921, had adopted a resolution (5.6) supporting 'mass movements of the working class for the defence of the republic and the realization of democracy' and promising to support 'a socialist government which sets itself the goal of implementing the demands put forward by the masses'.

what is desired by the great majority of the USPD workers and a large section of the SPD workers who are genuinely revolutionary.

If the great revolutionary party is to arise in an organised sense from this situation, and if the KPD is to play a decisive part in this process, it must fulfil the following requirements, which will restore to it the necessary prestige and confidence of the masses:

1 Complete material independence from the Communist International.

2 All literature from foreign communist organisations (including organs of the Communist International and the Red International of Labour Unions) is to be placed under the joint control of the German party leadership.

3 A firm guarantee against all open or concealed interventions by the ECCI which occur alongside, outside or against the German Party.

4 A programme is to be drawn up, laying down a policy to make possible the co-ordination of all revolutionary work in Germany, and involving the explicit abandonment of all putschist endeavours of the kind exemplified by the March Action.

5 The establishment of a policy towards the German trade unions which maintains their organisational unity and their homogeneity, notwithstanding all revolutionary objectives.

Source: *Unser Weg*, Jg.3, Heft 15, Dezember 1921, pp. 415–16, also printed in *Die Internationale*, Jg.3, Heft 17, 1 Dezember 1921, p. 616.

12.5   *Platform of the Left (Korsch)*[24] *Group, 1926*

The whole world economy is at present in a period of depression, which forms the dark background to the specific crises of greater or lesser severity currently shattering the economies of particular countries. These crises cannot be stabilised... The Dawes Plan does not mean, as Trotsky and the official leadership of the Comintern think, that American capitalism has set up its hegemony over the world economy and is implementing a plan to control Europe in order to secure markets for its excess commodities and export its money capital... The Dawes Treaty means a sharper attack by world capital on the German proletariat... The League of Nations and the Treaty of Locarno are not directed at a pacification of Europe and the world... and similarly the Dawes Treaty and the penetration of American capital into all European countries does not mean a *stabilisation* of Europe and the world economy. All the talk about

---

24   Karl Korsch (1886–1961), Marxist philosopher, KPD, Professor of Law at Jena University, 1923, Minister of Justice in the Thuringian government, October 1923, member of the Reichstag 1924–28, expelled from the KPD 1926.

stabilisation, complete, partial or relative ... serves only to mask the liquidation of the Comintern's revolutionary perspective, and the abandonment for a
whole epoch of any attempt to prepare or organise a revolutionary struggle
for power ... For the foreseeable future the German economy will be in a state
of collapse, marked by increased economic, social and political antagonisms,
and heightened oppression and impoverishment of the working class and
the proletarianised strata of the population ... This situation contains all the
objective elements for a concretely revolutionary policy ... The task of the
Communist Party is to broaden the defensive struggles of the masses against
their increasing impoverishment ... and to prepare and organise the offensive
resistance of the proletariat against capital ... The proletariat must counter
the murderous plans of the capitalist class ... with the struggle for the *revolutionary control of production* ...

The question of power must be placed in the foreground. The Party must
use every opportunity to lay bare the character of the Referendum Campaign[25]
as a final parliamentary-democratic illusion ... The compromised and ambiguous slogan of the 'Workers' and Peasants' Government' is worthless in the present period. We must counterpose the slogan of 'The Exclusive Rule of the
Revolutionary Workers' Councils' to the purely bourgeois and bourgeois-
reformist governmental combination ... The KPD ought not to make pacts or
alliances with parties which abandon the revolutionary class struggle in word,
like the Right SPD leaders, and in deed, like the left SPD leaders, who abandon
the struggle in fact despite uttering revolutionary phrases ...

The theory and practice of the present leadership of the Comintern stands
in ever sharper contradiction to the clear revolutionary class policy of communism ... The 14th Congress of the Russian Communist Party[26] has revealed
to the whole world that *opportunism* has already gained the upper hand in our
Russian brother party. The March 1926 resolutions of the Enlarged ECCI show
that this opportunism is to be transferred to the whole of the Comintern.
Instead of attacking the NEP[27] (1926 version) they idealise it as 'the only
correct economic policy of the victorious proletariat'. Instead of warding off

---

25   This refers to the campaign conducted jointly by the KPD and the SPD for a referendum
      against the government's decision to compensate the former German princes. See above,
      5.13.

26   The 14th Congress of what was now called the All-Union Communist Party (Bolsheviks)
      (AUCP (B)) was held in December 1925. Stalin reported at the Congress that there was a
      temporary 'stabilization of capitalism' in Europe.

27   The New Economic Policy is considered to have reached its height in the Soviet Union in
      1926.

the exploitation of the Russian agricultural workers and poor peasants by the kulaks, they declare the middle peasant to be 'the central figure'...

A similar opportunism is expressed in the slogan of the United States of Europe, in the implementation of the liquidation of the RILU and in the impending negotiations for a merger with the parties of the Second International... The deep-going internal transformation of the Comintern and its leading party has strengthened all rightist and centrist tendencies, particularly in the German party... United Front tactics are degenerating into a policy of alliance or merger with the SPD ... An open alliance with 'broad circles of the bourgeoisie' is being propagated by the KPD. The Central Committee of the KPD, in an official proclamation entitled 'Face the Village!', has openly abandoned the call for an eight-hour day for agricultural workers in the interests of the property-owing middle and big peasants.

The whole membership of the KPD must undertake a decisive struggle against these opportunist and reformist tendencies. It must demand the genuine implementation of the often-promised intra-party democracy, including elections to leading party functions and complete freedom of discussion... In particular, it must demand a thorough and open discussion on the question which is vital for the proletarian revolution at the present time, namely the question of the Russian Party and the Communist International.

Source: 'Die Plattform der Linken. Resolution zur Politik und Taktik der KPD und der Komintern angenommen auf der Reichskonferenz der "Entschiedenen Linken" in Berlin am 2.4.1926', *Kommunistische Politik*, No. 2, April 1926.

Note: The view taken by Karl Korsch and his group in 1926 was that the 14th Congress of the Russian Communist Party had seen the victory of its opportunist, peasant-influenced wing under Stalin and Bukharin over the proletarian standpoint of the Leningrad workers, led by Zinoviev. Korsch realised that Stalin's victory in the Soviet Union could not be reversed, but he hoped to prevent the imposition of Stalin's (and Bukharin's) line on the Comintern's member parties. He had few allies internationally (the most famous of them being the Italian Left communist Bordiga) and within Germany his group, the 'Intransigent Left', was hardly more than a sect. The Korsch group became even smaller when in autumn 1926 the majority of the 'Intransigent Left' group separated from it, retaining the name, under Ernst Schwarz.[28] Despite the

---

28   The Schwarz group was close in its ideas to the KAPD, as it rejected work in the trade unions and called for 'All Power to the Councils', and in fact it merged in June 1927 with the KAPD. See Bahne 1961, pp. 379–81.

similarities between Korsch's analysis and that of Ruth Fischer and Arkady Maslow (see below, 12.6) he was divided from them by his insistence on linking the Party's policy in Germany with the internal situation in the Soviet Union and the international regime in the Comintern. This document clearly shows the combination of acute insight and wild exaggeration so characteristic of Korsch. His appeal to the 'members of the KPD' to fight against their leaders naturally had no effect, both because it ran counter to the fact that capitalism *was* undergoing a period of apparent stabilisation, and because the implied total rejection of the Soviet example and Stalin's leadership required too great an intellectual leap for ordinary party members to take. Korsch's own intellectual evolution soon led him away from communism completely.

12.6   Platform of the Left (Fischer-Maslow) Opposition of the KPD, 1927
Theses on the Situation in the German Party

1 The manifestations of crisis in the whole Communist International have become permanent.

2 Seen from the outside, the years 1924 and 1925 brought a turn to the left in the Communist International, which appeared to allay the anxieties of the Left.

3 This turn to the left was very soon replaced by a complete swing to the right, in that revisionist theories were put forward and leading anti-liquidationist elements were expelled.

4 The crisis of the Communist International cannot be explained by phrases about 'deviations' or by reference to the characteristics of individual persons or groups; it reflects rather the relative stabilisation of capitalism, with its multiplicity of contradictory tendencies.

5 The particularly difficult situation of the Soviet Union in the period of relative stabilisation produces revisionist opinions and liquidationist intentions among those who secretly regard this stabilisation as absolute.

6 In spite of all the grandiloquent reports of victory and the 'unanimous' votes for its resolutions the Communist International's official policy has got into a blind alley which it can only emerge from if the whole of its policy is changed radically.

7 It is the duty of every communist to work with all his or her strength for the necessary change of course, in order to prevent the liquidation of the Communist International.

The Development and Situation of the Comintern and the KPD
A   *The Russian Discussion as a Symptom of Crisis*
1 This is the deepest crisis the Communist International has ever experienced. The official optimism has nothing to do either with the facts or with Marxism.

2 The 'conclusion' of the discussion in Russia by mechanical means changes nothing in the objective causes of the crisis.

3 The far-reaching differences in the so-called Russian Question are essentially differences on all questions of the proletarian revolution. The Comintern is faced with the decisive question of whether it will tolerate the revision of Marxism and Leninism already openly undertaken by Stalin ... or it can summon up the strength to defeat the revisionists.

4 The theory of the possibility of constructing full socialism in Russia alone is equivalent to the practice of the abandonment of proletarian revolution in the advanced industrial countries. That is to say, it is the theory and practice of liquidationism ...

B   *The Development of the KPD*

5 Liquidationism emerged in the KPD as early as the period just after the unification of the Spartacus League with the Left USPD. It is only thanks to the constant, stubborn struggle of the Left against the liquidators (Levi, Friesland, Brandler, Thalheimer) that the revisionist, Social Democratic and liquidationist tendencies in the KPD did not come out sooner and more strongly than they have now, indeed that they appeared to have been defeated temporarily.

6 After the defeat of the German proletariat in the autumn of 1923, and given the complete bankruptcy of the official policy of the KPD led by Brandler and continuously supported by the ECCI, the Left alone gathered together the fragments of the Party, re-organised it, and restored it under the most difficult and unfavourable circumstances.

7 The period from the Frankfurt Party Congress until the beginning of 1925 was the sole period in the existence of the KPD during which the Party could live without splits and without crises.

8 During the period of Left leadership the Party also attempted to imbue the membership with the consciousness of its leading role ('the communist party, the only workers' party'), something which was doubly necessary and remains so in view of the defeat and the widespread feeling that the SPD is 'superior'. The Party also made serious attempts to cooperate internationally with fraternal parties. All that ceased completely with the Open Letter.[29]

9 The great success of the KPD during the period of Left leadership ... would without doubt have continued if the Party and its leadership had not been destroyed from above. However, the fact that the ECCI was able to remove the

---

29   The Open Letter of 1 September 1925 from the ECCI to the KPD condemned the conduct of 'certain leaders of the Left' and called for the abandonment of various Left policies and a return to the united front line. See above, 6.9.

Left leadership shows that mistakes were made, and these mistakes had their own objective roots.

[10]

11 Since the Open Letter the policy pursued by the KPD has deviated more and more from the class line. This deviation is shown in:

a) trade-union work, which is more and more openly a policy of tailing behind the reformists

b) the abandonment of any independent organisation of the unemployed movement

c) the policy of supporting bourgeois or Social Democratic governments,[30] which does not even amount to a consistent policy of opposing the bourgeois state, on the 'left Social Democratic' model.

d) the decision to draw up state-capitalist transitional slogans for capitalist countries in the present period

e) the abandonment of the line of splitting the SPD and breaking up the *Reichsbanner*.

12 The Party's present course is shown plainly by the kind of intra-party leadership, 'preparation of the Party Congress'[31] and discussion, which has now become possible with the sanction of the ECCI. They did not dare to do against the Right even a fraction of what is now being forced through against the Left, against the will of the communists in the Party, to the accompaniment of hypocritical declarations about the Left's alleged 'petty bourgeois' and 'Social Democratic' deviations.

Source H. Weber (ed.) 1963, *Der deutsche Kommunismus: Dokumente,* pp. 285–8.

Note: This was the political platform of the expelled Fischer-Maslow leadership of the KPD, issued as a pamphlet at the beginning of 1927. It criticised Moscow and the Comintern, firstly, for abandoning the leftism of 1924–25, which is presented in Point 7 of the platform as a kind of golden age of party harmony, although this was hardly true, given the witchhunt at the time against the 'right wingers' associated with Brandler and Thalheimer, and secondly, for instituting a reformist course which turned the KPD into a practically Social Democratic party; a course which corresponded in their view to the pro-peas-

---

30   In the Diets of Mecklenburg and Prussia.

31   The 11th Party Congress of the KPD, held in March 1927, concluded the fight against the Left Opposition within the Party, excluding the Left from all positions in the apparatus.

ant course pursued by Stalin and Bukharin in the Soviet Union.[32] In April 1928 the Fischer-Maslow group consolidated itself organisationally as the Lenin League (*Leninbund*) although many of its prominent leaders, including Fischer and Maslow, left a month later, after Zinoviev's capitulation to Stalin. They executed a similar capitulation in the hope of being readmitted to the KPD after six months. The Lenin League itself continued to exist, however, and some of its members later formed part of the 'United Left Opposition of the KPD' (set up in March 1930) which was associated with Leon Trotsky.[33]

12.7 Platform of the KPD-O (*Communist Party of Germany – Opposition*), 1930

What is the Communist Opposition?

1 In what ways does the policy of the Communist Opposition differ from the policy of the KPD? Answer: it differs not in principles and goals but in tactics... The only genuine guarantee of faithfulness to principles is the application of the correct means to realise communist principles and goals...

[2], [3]

4 What kind of organisation is the KPD-O? Answer: the KPD-O is not a new party. It is an organised communist *tendency*. It is not a new party because its principles and goals do not differ from those of communism...

5 What are the aims of the KPD-O? Answer: the KPD-O's aims are (1) to win over the majority of members of the KPD and the sections of the Comintern to the correct communist tactics... (2) at the same time, however, to lead the struggles of the working class *independently* as long as the Party and the Comintern still stick to their incorrect tactics... (3) if the incorrect tactics of the KPD are continued indefinitely, leading thereby... to the destruction of the Party's connection with the working class and its activities, the KPD-O will itself become the Communist Party of Germany. The communist opposition is well aware that only one communist party can exist in each country. The rulers of official communism are splitting the communist movement. The communist opposition, however, wants to save and strengthen the KPD...

7 What is the relationship between the KPD-O and Social Democracy? Answer: the KPD-O stands in very sharp, irreconcilable and principled opposition to the SPD. Its goal is to overcome Social Democracy and reformism...

95 Is the present leadership of the KPD right to assert that the Social Democratic workers are 'Social Fascists'? Answer: this assertion is absolutely

---

32 See the brief comments on the Fischer-Maslow group in Bahne 1961, p. 363. and in more detail Zimmermann 1978, pp. 99–111.

33 Weber 1969, vol. 1, p. 184.

wrong as regards the ordinary Social Democratic *workers*. It is also wrong in relation to the lower levels of reformist functionaries, who stand under the direct pressure of the members. It is only true of the middle- and upper-ranks of functionaries...

172 Must Communists always work for the unity of the trade unions? Answer: yes, because every split in the trade unions weakens the economic struggle of the workers, and ultimately their political struggle as well. Even if the reformists succeed in splitting a trade union, the communists are still obliged to uphold the unity of the trade unions...

189 What phenomena demonstrate the crisis in the KPD? Answer: 1) Internally, the split in the Communist movement, the unending factional struggle within the Party, the secret and open battle of cliques within the leadership, the increasing tendency towards place-hunting, bureaucratic irresoluteness, corruption in the middle- and upper layers of the apparatus, and the withdrawal from the Party of the old revolutionary cadres as well as the best of the younger cadres. 2) Externally, the inability of the Party to lead the day-to-day struggles of the working class and to combine with this an effective propaganda for communism. The consequences of this are: a *decline in the influence of the Party* on the working class, and a strengthening of *reformism*, despite favourable objective conditions for its defeat; the loss of almost all important positions held by the Party in the trade unions and the other proletarian mass organisations; the strengthening of Fascism; the decline in the number of party members; the growing passivity of Party members and lower-level functionaries; the decline in the standard of the party press and the impediments placed in the way of any theoretical work...

191 What are the specific causes of the crisis in the KPD? Answer: the main cause is the Party's increasing reversion to 'the infantile disease of leftism', in other words to *ultra-left tactics*. The chief manifestations of this are 1) the abandonment of the tactic of the United Front, 2) the rejection of revolutionary transitional slogans, and thereby of any concrete revolutionary propaganda for communism, 3) the incorrect line on the trade unions, the main features of which are a) the abandonment of the fight for the *unity* of the trade union movement, b) the abandonment of the policy of *conquering the trade unions* and its replacement by the course of *splitting* them and forming special 'revolutionary' trade unions, c) the attempt to lead trade union struggles directly through the party apparatus, d) the transfer of the centre of gravity to the *unorganised workers,* and e), as a general consequence, the breeding up of an anti-trade union attitude on the part of members of the Party and its working-class sympathisers; 4) the course towards a split in all proletarian mass organisa-

tions (the sporting movement, the association of free-thinkers etc.); and finally 5) the suppression of *intra-party democracy,* the bureaucratic despotism and decay of the middle- and upper party apparatus, and the replacement of democratic centralism by bureaucratic centralism ...

[A sickness has taken hold of the Party]. The main features of this sickness are: 1) the suppression of participation by the Party membership in working out the policy of the Party. The role of the members is restricted to the implementation of orders issued from above ... [Criticism of Party functionaries by Party members] has been replaced by a *mechanical drill system*; 2) the appointment of Party functionaries by the higher Party authorities and their subordination to the leading organs by means of mechanical discipline and financial modes of pressure or inducements; 3) the way the composition of Party congresses etc. is determined not by the members on the basis of free discussion but by the Party apparatus, so that supervision and participation by the members has become merely apparent; 4) the same method is applied in selecting delegations to international congresses ... 5) the *misuse of the fundamentally correct* principle of factory cell organisation to atomise the party members and deliver them over to the Party apparatus ...

192   Where will the crisis in the KPD lead, if it is not brought to an end? Answer: the Party will cease to be the instrument of communism, and it will turn into a self-sufficient apparatus, revolving in the void, having no further connection with the real struggles of the working class, and collapsing at the first serious revolutionary test through its own internal emptiness ...

Source: Kommunistische Partei Deutschlands (Opposition) 1930, *Was will die Kommunistische Partei Deutschlands: Opposition? (Verbesserte Entwurf der Plattform der KPD-O)*, 1930, pp. 5–69.

12.8   *Declaration of Principles Adopted at the First Congress of the SAP (Socialist Workers' Party) on 25 March 1932*
The Aims of the SAP

I   The Socialist Workers' Party's objective is a state of society in which private property in the means of production has been abolished and ownership has been transferred into the hands of society; it is a society in which there is therefore no longer any exploitation of man by man and there are no longer any classes, and the state, as the organised power in the hands of the ruling class, has been abolished.

State and Proletariat

II The state is always an instrument for the oppression of one class by another. Its form is adapted to ... the needs of the ruling class. The bourgeois state is therefore nothing but an instrument for implementing bourgeois class rule over the proletariat, not only under the monarchy or a Fascist dictatorship, but also in the democratic republic ... The immense bureaucratic and military organisation of the capitalist state and the parliamentary system ... cannot be taken over by the victorious working class. The proletariat must destroy this state, the organ of bourgeois domination, and build its own state, based on the Soviets of the working masses and led by the revolutionary Party.

Socialism or Barbarism?

III The present economic crisis is distinguished from all previous ones not just by its extent, seriousness and length but because it is at the time an expression of the fact that world capitalism has entered its period of decline ... In this situation, the bourgeoisie's methods of parliamentary-democratic domination are no longer enough; it is compelled to resort to open dictatorship over the working class in order to maintain the capitalist system, and with the drive towards alterations in the division of the world market the danger of war grows ever stronger. Human society is faced with the alternative: socialism or decline into barbarism. The conquest of political power by the proletariat has become the task of the present day.

Our Attitude Towards the SPD and the KPD

IV The idea of winning political power in the manner of parliamentary democracy, i.e. without the destruction of the apparatus of bourgeois power, was always an illusion. So much the more is this the case now that an open dictatorship has been set up and parliamentarism destroyed.[34] Reformist politics therefore runs counter to both the future and the day-to-day interests of the proletariat. It leads to a widening of the chasm in the working-class movement. Its character as the tool of reaction is revealed in the most direct way.

By its previous policy, the SPD is indissolubly bound up with the capitalist state and the capitalist system and it is thereby the prisoner of its own policy. For the SPD, the way back to the class struggle has been permanently closed off. Its policy can and must be even more harmful to the working class to the

---

34   This probably refers to Papen's coup against the SPD government of Prussia in July 1932 rather than the appointment of Brüning as Chancellor without a parliamentary majority in March 1930.

degree that capitalism in its period of decline assigns it the role of an instrument for holding down that class...

The SAP is therefore irreconcilably opposed as a matter of principle to the SPD and the Second International. It regards the winning over of Social Democratic workers to revolutionary politics as one of its most important tasks. The Communist Party...has not performed this task and has shown itself to be incapable of giving leadership to the proletarian masses in the revolutionary crisis. Despite its principles, and in contradiction to Lenin's teachings, it is pursuing a policy which confuses and weakens the working class, encourages its divisions, and thereby hinders the realisation of its own goals. The KPD's decisive errors are threefold: they consist in the abandonment of the united front policy (this rests in turn on the fateful theory of Social Fascism), in the RGO-course,[35] and in the policy of petty-bourgeois nationalism.[36] These errors have been worsened and in part caused by the monopoly position held by the Russian Communist Party in the Communist International. The result of this monopoly is not only erroneous directives, but also a schematic application of Russian experiences to other countries... The SAP has set itself the task of bringing the fateful consequences of these errors to the awareness of communist workers by pursuing a revolutionary policy, and thereby creating the prerequisites for a unified revolutionary organisation on a national and international basis.

We Protect the Soviet Union!
V ... The objective difficulties in the way of the construction of socialism are worsened by the errors of the present leadership of the Soviet Party. Its construction is endangered by the anti-Leninist theory that it is possible to complete the building of socialism in a single country and by that Party's failure to respect the principles of democratic centralism. Notwithstanding this necessary proletarian criticism of the leadership of the CPSU[37]... it must always be stressed that the tremendous superiority of the planned economy of socialism over the economic anarchy of capitalism has been proved in the Soviet Union... The SAP sees the Soviet Union as the bastion of the international

---

35   The decision by the KPD to set up a separate trade-union organisation, the RGO (Revolutionary Trade-Union Opposition). This held its first congress at the end of November 1929.

36   See above, 10.12.

37   This is the way the Soviet Communist Party is described in the text of the document. The title is not strictly correct. The AUCP (B) (All-Union Communist Party (Bolsheviks)) was not renamed the CPSU (Communist Party of the Soviet Union) until 1952.

proletariat. It is the duty of the working class of the whole world to defend the Soviet Union against all onslaughts mounted by the capitalist counter-revolution.

> The Tasks of the Revolutionary Workers' Party in the Struggle for Power

VII The liberation of the working class can only be achieved by the working class itself. This fight for liberation needs to be prepared and organised by a revolutionary party. The Party's task is to give direction to the struggle and to organise the tactics of the struggle in such a way that in every phase the whole of the available strength of the proletariat is brought into play . . . The tactics of the Party should be so decisive and sharp that they never fall below the level of the actual relationship of forces; they should instead constantly alter this relationship in favour of the proletariat. The revolutionary Party must be the vanguard of the working class. As such it must neither give way to the weaknesses of backward strata nor become separated from the proletarian mass by actions which do not correspond to its level of maturity.

In order to do justice to its tasks, the revolutionary Party must put democratic centralism into effect within its ranks. This consists in a unity of basic conceptions combined with initiative and responsibility on the part of the leadership, within an organisational structure which secures constant control and influence by the members and the grass-roots organisations over the leading organs, right up to the summit of the Party, as well as a disciplined implementation of all actions. The Socialist Workers' Party wishes to give the working class this kind of leadership.

Source: *Was will die SAP* in H. Weber (ed.) 1963, *Der deutsche Kommunismus: Dokumente,* pp. 307–11.

Note: The Socialist Workers' Party (SAP) was set up by left-wing members of the SPD on 4 October 1931, after they had been expelled from the Party for their continuous criticism of its leadership. Its most prominent members were Anton Grylewicz,[38] a former left-oppositionist member of the KPD expelled in 1927, and Kurt Rosenfeld, and its main strength was located in Saxony. It was joined by several other splinter groups including the remnant of the USPD around Georg Ledebour which had refused to rejoin the SPD in 1922 and a

---

38   Anton Grylewicz (1885–1971), KPD, member of the Reichstag 1924, member of the KPD *Zentrale* 1924–25, helped to found the Lenin League after his expulsion from the Party, Trotskyist in 1930.

section of the KPO led by Paul Frölich and Jacob Walcher. It was also briefly supported by the renowned physicist Albert Einstein.[39]

12.9 Proclamation by the International Youth League, November 1925
We have revealed the commercial secret on which the rule of the Party bosses is based. The rule of the bourgeoisie in the bourgeois republic is also based on this. The commercial secret the 'entrepreneurs' of both types have in common is the swindle they are engaged in with democracy. Anyone not absolutely blind can see from what the SPD does every day how true the words were that Comrade Nelson[40] dared to utter: democracy is 'not the grand arena from which the most capable people emerge as victors, but a theatre of the absurd on which the craftiest or the most corruptible chatterers outdo the man of character who loves justice and relies only on the rightness of his cause. In short, comrades, what were we really guilty of was the attempt to make the SPD into a *revolutionary, socialist* party by working within it . . . Anyone who remains in the SPD will bear joint responsibility for that Party's treacherous policy. Like the Christian church, that 'party church' will now have to be fought from out-side . . . We hold out our hands to anyone who is ready to risk the struggle against priestly domination in all its forms, who is prepared to exert the whole of their strength to prevent the work of our great predecessors from perishing. We have the courage to think for ourselves, we have the courage to engage in socialist action, we are true to the words of Karl Marx: the emancipation of the workers can only be achieved by the workers themselves. Comrades! Workers! Close your ranks! Help in building up the International Socialist Fighting League!

Source: *Mitteilungsblatt der Sozialdemokratischen Partei Deutschlands*, 2, 1925, Nr. 12, pp. 3–4.

Note: The International Youth League (IJB), later *Nelsonbund* or International Socialist Fighting League (ISK), a group of radical, anti-clerical socialists, founded by Leonard Nelson, existed at first within the SPD. It was particularly strong in the city of Göttingen, because the local SPD's strong anti-clerical tra-dition made the IJB attractive to young Social Democrats there.[41] In November

---

39   The main works on the short life of the SAP are Drechsler 1965, and Niemann 1991.
40   Leonard Nelson (1882–1927), Professor of Philosophy at Göttingen University. He advo-cated an ethical view of socialism, and he founded the International Youth League during the First World War on that basis.
41   Saldern 1998, p. 221 n. 83.

1925 membership in this group was declared incompatible with membership in the Party, because the SPD wanted to preserve its coalition with the Centre Party in Prussia, and, in addition to its anti-clericalism, the IJB had called upon socialists not to vote for Marx, the Centre Party's presidential candidate.[42] There were also more deep-seated differences, as the ISK was highly critical of the Weimar democratic system, with which the SPD was strongly identified. With the above proclamation the ISK really burned its boats. It was impossible to return to the SPD, and even the Marxist-inclined wing of the Party, previously benevolently disposed towards Nelson's group, now broke with it.

A further important dissident group should finally be mentioned: the socialists of the 'Young Right' around the journal *Neue Blätter für den Sozialismus,* which started to appear in 1930. Their leading figures were Carlo Mierendorff[43] and Theodor Haubach.[44] This group emerged from the Hofgeismar Circle, which was formed in 1923 in the context of the Ruhr occupation crisis by Young Socialists who wanted to 'combine an ethical socialism with a firm commitment to the democratic state and the German nation'.[45] They were associated with the religious socialists Paul Tillich[46] and Eduard Heimann.[47] The *Neue Blätter* group advanced a confused model of 'national socialism' involving notions of *Volksgemeinschaft* (or 'people's community') which appeared to some critics to bring them dangerously close to the ideology of the Nazis.[48] They were not, however, nor did they ever become, supporters of Hitler. They stayed within the SPD. They were most closely involved with the SPD's war veterans' association, the *Reichsbanner.* Their aim, they said, was to confront the Nazis with an alternative model of 'national socialism' which would stand for peace.

---

42   Link 1961, p. 92.

43   See above, 5.20, for his article on the lessons to be drawn from the September 1930 elections.

44   Theodor Haubach (1896–1945), SPD, helped to found the *Reichsbanner* 1924, member of the German resistance to Hitler after 1933, executed by the Nazis in 1945.

45   This is Heinrich Winkler's summary of their position (Winkler 1988, p. 367).

46   Paul Tillich (1886–1965), Evangelical theologian and philosopher.

47   Eduard Heimann (1889–1967), SPD, economist.

48   As noted by Heinrich Winkler (Winkler 1988, p. 660).

Bibliography

Documents

Allgemeiner Deutscher Gewerkschaftsbund 1922, 'Resolution Proposed at the 1922 Congress of the Free Trade Unions (ADGB) Against Collaboration with the Employers and in Favour of Factory and Workers' Councils', in Allgemeiner Deutscher Gewerkschaftsbund 1922, *Protokoll der Verhandlungen des elften kongresses der Gewerkschaften Deutschlands, Leipzig, 19–24 June 1922*, Berlin: Verlagsgesellschaft des Allgemeinen Deutschen Gewerkschaftsbundes.

———— 1931, 'Resolution of the Federal Executive of the ADGB on the Crisis in the Economy and the Forty-Hour Week, September 1931', in Michael Schneider 1975, *Das Arbeitsbeschaffungsprogramm des ADGB*, Bonn-Bad Godesberg: Verlag Neue Gesellschaft.

Allgemeiner Deutscher Gewerkschaftsbund, Allgemeiner freier Angestelltenbund and Deutscher Beamtenbund 1920, 'The Nine-Point Programme of the ADGB, the AfA and DBB 18 March 1920', in Könnemann, Berthold and Schulze (eds.) 1971, *Arbeiterklasse siegt über Kapp und Lüttwitz*, Berlin: Glashütten im Taunus Auvermann.

Allgemeiner Deutscher Gewerkschaftsbund and Allgemeiner freier Angestelltenbund 1921, 'The Ten Demands of the ADGB and the AfA, November 1921', from 'Forderungen der Gewerkschaften zur Rettung der deutschen Wirtschaft', in *Correspondenzblatt des ADGB*, 31: 48, 26 November 1921.

Arendsee, Martha 1927, 'Martha Arendsee (KPD) on the Struggle for the Protection of Mothers, 7 July 1927', in Deutsches Reich 1927, *Verhandlungen des Reichstags, III. Wahlperiode, 1924, Bd. 393, Stenographische Berichte*, Berlin: Reichsdruckerei.

Aufhäuser, Siegfried 1927a, 'Siegfried Aufhäuser's resolution of 1927 calling for opposition instead of coalition', in Sozialdemokratischer Parteitag in Kiel 1927, *Protokoll mit dem Bericht der Frauenkonferenz*, Berlin: J.H.W. Dietz.

———— 1927b, 'Siegfried Aufhäuser replies to Hilferding', in Sozialdemokratischer Parteitag in Kiel 1927, *Protokoll mit dem Bericht der Frauenkonferenz*, Berlin: J.H.W. Dietz.

Berlin Executive Council 1918, 'Proclamation by the Berlin Executive Council, calling for the Setting up of a Red Guard, 12 November 1918', in G.A. Ritter and S. Miller (eds.) 1975, *Die deutsche Revolution 1918–1919: Dokumente*, second edition, Hamburg: Hoffman und Campe Verlag.

Berlin Workers' and Soldiers' Councils 1919, 'Demands of the Berlin Workers' and Soldiers' Councils, 3 March 1919', in Sozialistische Einheitspartei Deutschlands Zentralkomitee 1958, *Dokumente und Materialien zur Geschichte der deutschen Arbeiterbewegung, Reihe II: 1914–1945, Band 3, 115*, Berlin: J.H.W. Dietz.

Bernstein, Eduard 1919, 'Eduard Bernstein's Speech on the Need to Accept the Versailles Treaty, June 1919', in Sozialdemokratische Partei Deutschlands 1973 [1919], *Protokoll über die Verhandlungen des Parteitages der SPD in Weimar*, Berlin: Glashütten im Taunus.

Brandler, Heinrich 1923, 'Heinrich Brandler on His Discussions with the Leaders of the Comintern During the Summer of 1923', in Ben Fowkes, 'Letter from Heinrich Brandler to Isaac Deutscher', in 'The Brandler-Deutscher Correspondence', *New Left Review*, 105, September–October 1977: 56–81.

Braun, Adolf 1919, 'Adolf Braun's 1919 Speech on the Relation Between Nationalism and Socialism', in Sozialdemokratische Partei Deutschlands 1919, *Protokoll über die Verhandlungen des Parteitages der SPD, abgehalten in Weimar, vom 10. bis 15. Juni 1919*, Berlin: J.H.W. Dietz.

Braun, Otto 1932, 'Otto Braun (SPD) Writes from Berlin to Karl Kautsky in Vienna, 19 February 1932 about his Decision to Support Hindenburg as Presidential Candidate', in *Vierteljahrshefte für Zeitgeschichte*, 8, 1, January 1960.

Breitscheid, Rudolf 1929, 'Rudolf Breitscheid (SPD) Suggests in May 1929 that the Party May Have to Withdraw from the Grand Coalition and Defend Democracy from Outside', in Sozialdemokratischer Parteitag in Magdeburg 1929, *Protokoll mit dem Bericht der Frauenkonferenz, vom 26. bis 31. Mai in der Stadthalle*, Berlin: J.H.W. Dietz.

Brüning, Heinrich et al. 1931, 'Discussion between the Leaders of the SPD and the German Chancellor, Heinrich Brüning, on their Conditions for Parliamentary Support, 17 March 1931', in Tilman Koops (ed.), *Die Kabinette Brüning I u.II, Bd.2.,1. März 1931 bis 10. Oktober 1931*, Boppard am Rhein: Boldt.

Central Council of the German Socialist Republic 1919, 'Proclamation by the Central Council of the German Socialist Republic Handing Over its Power to the National Assembly 4 February 1919', in Kolb and Rürup (eds.) 1968, *Der Zentralrat der deutschen sozialistischen Republik 19.12.1918–8.4.1919*, Leiden: Brill.

Cohen, Max 1920, 'Max Cohen's Plea for Reconciliation with France, Delivered at the 1920 Congress of the SPD', in Sozialdemokratische Partei Deutschlands 1920, *Protokoll über die Verhandlungen des Parteitages der SPD, abgehalten in Kassel vom 10. bis 16. Oktober 1920*, Berlin: J.H.W. Dietz.

Communist International Executive Committee 1924, 'The ECCI's Resolution on the Lessons of the German Events, 19 January 1924', in Communist International Executive Committee 1924, *Die Lehren der deutschen Ereignisse*, Berlin-Schöneberg: Verlag d. Jugendinternationale.

Communist Worker's Party of Germany 1920, 'Programme of the KAPD (Communist Workers' Party of Germany), May 1920', in Bock 1993, *Syndikalismus und Linkskommunismus von 1918 bis 1923*, 2nd ed., Darmstadt: Wissenschaftliche Buchgesellschaft.

Communist Working Group 1921, 'Resolution Passed by the First Reich conference of the KAG (Communist Working Group, 20 November 1921', in *Die Internationale*, Jg.3, Heft 17, 1 Dezember 1921.

Council of People's Representatives and the Berlin Executive Council 1918, 'Agreement Between the Council of People's Representatives and the Berlin Executive Council, 22 November 1918' from Ritter and Miller (eds.) 1975, *Die deutsche Revolution 1918– 1919. Dokumente. Zweite Auflage*, Hamburg: Hoffmann und Campe.

Cunow, Heinrich 1918, 'Die Diktatur des Proletariats', in *Die Neue Zeit. Wochenschrift der Deutschen Sozialdemokratie* 1.8. 22 November 1918.

Däumig, Ernst 1918, 'Sitzung des Vollzugsrats der Arbeiter- und Soldatenräte, 16. und 17.11.1918', in Institut für Marxismus-Leninismus beim ZK der SED, *Beiträge zur Geschichte der Arbeiterbewegung*, Berlin: J.H.W. Dietz.

David, Eduard 1919, 'Speech Praising the Weimar Constitution, July 1919', in *Die Deutsche Nationalversammlung im Jahre 1919 in ihrer Arbeit für den Aufbau des neuen deutschen Volksstaates*, Bd. 7, Berlin: Norddeutsche Buchdruckerei und Verlagsanstalt.

Der Atheist 1925, 'The Proletarian Free-Thinkers' Journal Criticises the Hold of the Church over Education, March 1925', in *Der Atheist: Illustrierte Wochenschrift für Volksaufklärung* 21, 3, March 1925.

Dissmann, Robert 1924, 'Robert Dissmann's resolution of June 1924 on the Need for the SPD to Conduct an Uncompromising Opposition to the Government', in Sozialdemokratischer Parteitag 1924, 'Resolution 243 (Dissmann and Comrades)', Berlin, J.H.W. Dietz.

Deutsches Reich 1918a, 'Demobilization Office Ordinance Establishing a Maximum Working Day of Eight Hours for Industrial Workers, 23 November 1918', in Deutsches Reich 1918, *Reichsgesetzblatt 1918*, Berlin: Verlag d. Gesetzsammlungsamts.

———— 1918b, 'The Agreement for Co-operation Made on 15 November 1918 between 21 Employers' Associations and 7 Trade Unions', in Deutsches Reich 1918, *Reichsanzeiger*, 273, 18 November 1918, Berlin: Verlag d. Gesetzsammlungsamts.

———— 1918c, 'Law Providing for the Establishment of a Voluntary People's Militia, 12 December 1918', in Deutsches Reich 1918, *Reichsgesetzblatt*, Berlin: Verlag. d. Gesetzsammlungsamts.

———— 1919, 'Law for the Establishment of a Provisional Reichswehr, 6 March 1919', in Deutsches Reich 1919, *Reichsgesetzblatt*, 57, Berlin: Verlag. d. Gesetzsammlungsamts.

Ebert, Freidrich, Hugo Haase et al. 1918, 'Proclamation of the Council of People's Representatives, 12 November 1918', in Deutsches Reich 1918a, *Reichsgesetzblatt*, Berlin: Verlag. d. Gesetzsammlungsamts.

Ebert, Friedrich, Wilhelm Dittmann et al. 1918, 'Discussion in the Council of People's Representatives About Relations with the Berlin Executive Council, Afternoon

Session, 13 December 1918', in Miller and Potthoff (eds.) 1969, *Die Regierung der Volksbeauftragten 1918/19* Volume 1, Düsseldorf: Droste.

Ebert, Freidrich and Rudolf Wissell 1919, 'The "Socialisation Law" of 23 March 1919', in *Deutsches Reich* 1919, *Reichsgesetzblatt*, 68, Berlin: Verlag. d. Gesetzsammlungsamts.

Ebert, Friedrich 1919, 'People's Representative Friedrich Ebert Calls on the Central Council of Workers' and Soldiers' Councils to Establish Democracy and the Rule of Law in Germany, 16 December 1918', in *Deutscher Geschichtskalender* 1919, *Deutscher Geschichtskalender 35, Ergänzungsband 1.1. Die Deutsche Revolution. Erster Band. November 1918–February 1919.*

———— 1920, 'Friedrich Ebert's Address to the Opening Session of the Constituent National Assembly, 6 February 1919', in Nationalversammlung 1920, *Stenographische Berichte über die Verhandlungen der verfassunggebenden deutschen National-versammlung*, Volume 326, 6 February 1919, Berlin: J.H.W. Dietz.

Executive Committee of the Communist International 1923, 'The ECCI's confidential letter to the KPD *Zentrale*, Sent in late November or early December 1923', in Internationale Pressekorrespondenz 1924, *Internationale Pressekorrespondenz*.

———— 1925, 'Open Letter from the ECCI to all Organisations and Members of the KPD, August 1925', *Die Rote Fahne*, 1 September 1925; *Inprekorr*, 128, 4 Sept. 1925.

———— 1931, 'Resolution by the Political Secretariat of the ECCI on the Referendum in Germany (Moscow, 16 September 1931, Secret)' N.P. Komolova (ed.) 1999, 'Rezoliutsiia Politsekretariata IKKI o referendume v Germanii', in *Komintern protiv Fashizma. Dokumenty*, Moscow: Nauka.

First Council of Workers' and Soldiers' Councils 1918, 'The Seven Hamburg Points, adopted 18 December 1918 by the First Congress of Workers' and Soldiers' Councils', in R. Müller 1925, *Geschichte der deutschen Revolution*, Volume 2, Berlin: Verlag Olle & Wolter.

Fischer, Maslow et al. 1927, 'Platform of the Left (Fischer-Maslow) Opposition of the KPD, 1927', in Hermann Weber (ed.) 1963, *Der deutsche Kommunismus: Dokumente*, Cologne: Kiepenheuer und Witsch.

Franz, Karl 1921, 'Karl Franz in 1921 on the Need to Defend German National Territory in Upper Silesia', in Sozialdemokratische Partei Deutschlands 1921, *Protokoll über die Verhandlungen des Parteitages der SPD, abgehalten in Görlitz, vom 18. bis 24. September 1921*, Berlin: J.H.W. Dietz.

Geyer, Curt 1921, 'Report to the *Zentrale* of the VKPD from Curt Geyer on his Experiences in Moscow as German Delegate to ECCI, February 1921' from *Archiv der sozialen Demokratie der Friedrich-Ebert-Stiftung, Bonn. Nachlass Paul Levi.*

Grünberg, Helene 1918, 'Helene Grünberg Attacks the Failure of Male Party Comrades to Oppose the Dismissal of Married Women Workers after 1918', in Sozialdemokratische Partei Deutschlands 1920, *Protokoll über die Verhandlungen des*

Parteitages der Sozialdemokratischen Partei Deutschlands, abgehalten in Kassel vom 10. bis 16. Oktober 1920, Berlin: J.H.W. Dietz.

———— 1929, 'Views of Helene Grünberg on the Reasons for the Lack of Female Support for the Party in the 1920 Elections', in Sozialdemokratische Partei Deutschlands 1921, *Protokoll über die Verhandlungen des Parteitages der Sozialdemokratischen Partei Deutschlands, abgehalten in Görlitz vom 18. bis 24 September 1921*, Berlin: J.H.W. Dietz.

Heilfron, Eduard ca. 1920, *Die deutsche Nationalversammlung im Jahre 1919 in ihrer Arbeit für den Aufbau des neuen deutschen Volksstaates* Volume 4, Berlin: Norddeutsche Buchdruckerei und Verlagsanstalt.

Hermberg, Paul 1929, 'A Utilitarian SPD View of the Purpose of Workers' Education, 1929', *Die Arbeit*, 6, 9, September 1929.

Hilferding, Rudolf 1918, 'Speech at the First Congress of Workers' and Soldiers' Councils Arguing Against the Immediate Socialisation of Industry', in Allgemeiner Kongress der Arbeiter- und Soldatenräte Deutschlands 1918, *Vom 16. bis 21. Dezember 1918 im Abgeordnetenhause zu Berlin. Stenographische Berichte*, Berlin, 1919, cols. 312–321, 9th session, 18 December 1918, morning, Berlin: J.H.W. Dietz.

———— 1920, 'Rudolf Hilferding's Arguments Against Joining the Communist International, at the USPD Congress of October 1920', in Unabhängige Sozialdemokratische Partei 1920, *Protokoll über die Verhandlungen des ausserordentlichen parteitages in Halle, 12–17 Oktober 1920*, Berlin: Verlagsgenossenschaft.

———— 1927a, 'Rudolf Hilferding's 1927 speech on "Organised Capitalism"', in Sozialdemokratischer Parteitag in Kiel 1927 *Protokoll mit dem Bericht der Frauenkonferenz*, Berlin: J.H.W. Dietz.

———— 1927b, 'Speech on the Importance of the Defence of Democracy for Socialists', in Sozialdemokratischer Parteitag in Kiel 1927, *Protokoll mit dem Bericht der Frauenkonferenz*, Berlin: J.H.W. Dietz.

———— 1932, 'Rudolf Hilferding (SPD) on the Need to Preserve Parliament and Fight against Left and Right Simultaneously, November 1932', in Hagen Schulze (ed.) 1975, *Anpassung oder Widerstand?: aus den Akten des Parteivorstands der deutschen Sozialdemokratie 1932/33*, Bonn: Neue Gesellschaft.

Hörreth-Menge, Edith 1924, 'Frau Hörreth-Menge (Munich) Complains about the Failure of the Party to Protest against the Post-War Mass Dismissals of Women Workers and Explains Why Some Women in Bavaria Support Hitler and the DVFP', in Sozialdemokratischer Parteitag 1924. *Protokoll mit dem Bericht der Frauenkonferenz*, Berlin: J.H.W. Dietz.

Hörsing, Friedrich Otto 1929, 'The Statutes of the *Reichsbanner Schwarz-Rot-Gold* (adopted on 26 May 1926)', in Bernhard Harms, Bernhard 1929, *Volk und Reich der deutschen*, Volume 2, Berlin: Verlag von Reiner Hobbing.

International Youth League 1925, 'Proclamation by the International Youth League, November 1925', *Mitteilungsblatt der Sozialdemokratischen Partei Deutschlands*, 2, 12, 1925.

Juchacz, Marie 1921, 'Marie Juchacz Complains about the Under-Representation of Women in the SPD's Governing Bodies', in Sozialdemokratische Partei Deutschlands 1921, *Reichsfrauentag der Sozialdemokratische Partei Deutschlands am 17 und 18 September 1921 in Görlitz*, Glashütten: Auvermann.

——— 1924, 'Views of Marie Juchacz on the Same Subject Three Years Later', in Sozialdemokratischer Parteitag 1924, *Protokoll mit dem Bericht der Frauenkonferenz*, Berlin: J.H.W. Dietz.

——— 1929, 'Marie Juchacz Explains why the SPD Opposes the "Open Door Movement"', in Sozialdemokratischer Parteitag in Magdeburg 1929, *Protokoll mit dem Bericht der Frauenkonferenz*, Berlin: J.H.W. Dietz.

Kautsky, Karl 1919, 'Speech on The Socialisation of Economic Life at the Second Congress of Councils, April 1919', in Centralrat der Sozialistischen Republik Deutschlands 1975 [1919], *II .Kongress der Arbeitern, Bauern- und Soldatenräte Deutschlands am 8. bis 14. April 1919 im Herrenhaus zu Berlin, Stenographisches Protokoll*, Berlin: Glashütten im Taunus.

——— 1922, 'Karl Kautsky's Arguments against the Görlitz Programme, 1922' from Berlin: Glashütten im Taunus Kautsky 1968, *Texte zu den Programmen der deutschen Sozialdemokratie 1891–1925*, edited by Albrecht Langner, Cologne: Verlag Jakob Hegner.

Keil, Wilhelm 1930, 'Wilhelm Keil (SPD) Advocates Keeping Contact with "Healthy National Consciousness" in a Speech Made in August 1930' Berlin: Glashütten im Taunus Wilhelm Keil 1948, *Erlebnisse eines Sozialdemokraten*, Volume 2, Stuttgart: Deutsche Verlagsanstalt.

Kommunistische Partei Deutschland Spartakusbund 1918, 'The Spartakus Programme, 1 January 1919', *Die Rote Fahne*, 14 December 1918; and Kommunistische Partei Deutschlands Spartakusbund 1918, *Bericht über den Gründungsparteitag der KPD (Spartakusbund)*, Berlin: Vereinigung Internationaler Verlagsanstalten.

Kommunistische Partei Deutschland 1919, 'Statutes of the KPD, 1919' from Kommunistiche Partei Deutschlands 1919, *Bericht über den 2 Parteitag der KPD (Spartakusbund), 20–24 Oktober 1919*.

——— 1919, ' "Guidelines on the Peace", issued by the KPD Zentrale, 19 May 1919', *Die Internationale*, 1, 2/3: 28–32.

——— 1920a, 'General Principles for Agitation among Women Adopted in 1920 by the KPD' Berlin: Glashütten im Taunus from Kommunistiche Partei Deutschlands, *Bericht über die Verhandlungen des Vereinigungsparteitags der USPD (Linke) und der KPD (Spartakusbund), Abgehalten in Berlin vom 4. bis 7. Dezember 1920*, Berlin: Vereinigung Internationaler Verlagsanstalten.

———— 1920b, 'Proclamation by the KPD *Zentrale* Opposing the General Strike', *Die Rote Fahne*, Number 30, 14 March 1920.

———— 1920c, 'The 1920 Agrarian Programme of the KPD', *Die Internationale*, 2, 26, 1 December 1920.

———— 1921a, 'Theses on the March Action' Berlin: Glashütten im Taunus *Die Internationale*, 3, 4, 13 April 1921: 122–7.

———— 1921b, 'Resolution on the Campaign for a Tax on Property, adopted by the CC of the KPD, 17 November 1921', in *Die Internationale*, 14 November 1921.

———— 1923a, 'The KPD's Theses on the United Front Tactic and the Workers' Government, February 1923', in Kommunistiche Partei Deutschlands 1923, *Bericht über die Verhandlungen des III (8) Parteitages der Kommunistischen Partei Deutschlands (Sektion der Kommunistischen Internationale), 28 Jan.–1 Feb. 1923*, Berlin: Vereinigung Internationaler Verlagsanstalten.

———— 1923b, 'Down with the Government of National Shame and Treachery Proclamation of 29 May 1923 by the KPD *Zentrale*', *Die Rote Fahne*, 29 May 1923.

———— 1923c, 'Military Lessons of the October 1923 Struggles in Hamburg', *Vom Bürgerkrieg*, Number 6, in Weber (ed.) 1963, *Der deutsche Kommunismus: Dokumente*, Cologne: Kiepenheuer und Witsch.

———— 1923d, 'KPD Resolution on the Victory of Fascism over the November Republic and the Tasks of the KPD', 3 November 1923 from *Internationale Pressekorrespondenz*, 3, 172, 7 November 1923.

———— 1924a, 'The KPD View of Trade Unions in 1924', Sozialistische Einheitspartei Deutschlands Zentralkomitee 1924, *Dokumente und Materialien* Volume 8, Berlin: J.H.W. Dietz.

———— 1924b, The KPD's Action Programme of April 1924', in Kommunistische Partei Deutschlands 1924, *Bericht über die Verhandlungen des 9.Parteitages der KPD (Sektion der Kommunistischen Internationale), abgehalten in Frankfurt am Main vom 7. bis 10.April 1924*, Berlin: J.H.W. Dietz.

———— 1925, 'Statutes of the KPD (1925 version)', in Kommunistiche Partei Deutschlands 1925, *Bericht über die Verhandlungen .des 10. Parteitages der Kommunistischen Partei Deutschlands (Sektion der Kommunistischen Internationale), Berlin, vom 12. bis 17. Juli 1925*, Berlin: J.H.W. Dietz.

———— 1930a, 'Programme for the National and Social Liberation of the German People issued by the Central Committee of the KPD, 24 August 1930', *Die Rote Fahne*, 24 August 1930.

———— 1930b, 'The KPD analysis of the September 1930 elections', *Internationale Presse-Korrespondenz*, 78, 16 September 1930.

———— 1930c, 'Instructions from the Secretariat to the District Leaderships (15 November 1930)', in Hermann Weber and Johann Wachtler (eds.) 1981, *Die*

Generallinie Rundschreiben des Zentralkomitees der KPD an die Bezirke 1929–1933, Düsseldorf: Droste.

───── 1931, 'The KPD's Proposed Law to Protect and Give Full Equality of Rights to Working Women, 15 October 1931', in Deutsches Reich 1933, *Verhandlungen des Reichstags, V. Wahlperiode 1930, Bd. 451*, Berlin, Anlage Number 1201.

───── 1932, 'The KPD's Guidelines for its Anti-Fascist Action (26 May 1932)' from Weber, Herman and Johann Wachtler (eds.) 1981, 'Rundtelefonat des ZK zur Antifascistische Aktion', in *Die Generallinie. Rundschreiben des Zentralkomitees der KPD an die Bezirke 1929–1933*, Düsseldorf: Droste.

───── 1933, 'Members of the KPD Leadership 1919–1933' from Fowkes 1984, *Communism in Germany under the Weimar Republic*, London: Macmillan.

Kommunistische Partei Deutschlands (Opposition) 1930, 'Platform of the KPD-O (Communist Party of Germany – Opposition), 1930', in Kommunistische Partei Deutschlands (Opposition) 1930, *Was will die Kommunistische Partei Deutschlands: Opposition? (Verbesserte Entwurf der Plattform der KPD-O)*, Berlin: Junius-Verlag

Korsch, Karl et al. 1926, 'Platform of the Left (Korsch) Group, 1926', in 'Die Plattform der Linken. Resolution zur Politik und Taktik der KPD und der Komintern angenommen auf der Reichskonferenz der "Entschiedenen Linken" from Berlin am 2.4.1926', *Kommunistische Politik*, Number 2, April 1926.

Krause, Hartfrid 1975, *USPD. Zur Geschichte der Unabhängigen Sozialdemokratischen Partei Deutschlands*, Frankfurt: Europäische Verlagsanstalt.

Krüger, Franz 1921, 'Franz Krüger Gives Reasons why the SPD Should Not Continue to Stay Out of Office', in Sozialdemokratische Partei Deutschlands 1921, *Protokoll über die Verhandlungen des Parteitages der Sozialdemokratischen Partei Deutschlands, abgehalten in Görlitz vom 18. bis 24.September 1921*, Glashütten: Auvermann.

Laufenberg, Heinrich 1918a, 'Heinrich Laufenberg Defends his Resolution of 16 December 1918', in Allgemeiner Kongress der Arbeiter- und Soldatenräte Deutschlands 1919, *Allgemeiner Kongress der Arbeiter und Soldatenräte Deutschlands vom 16. bis 21 Dezember 1918. Stenographische Berichte*, Berlin: J.H.W. Dietz.

───── 1918b, 'Heinrich Laufenberg's Resolution Calling on the First Congress of Councils to Take Power, 16 December 1918', in Allgemeiner Kongress der Arbeiter- und Soldatenräte Deutschlands 1919, *Allgemeiner Kongress der Arbeiter und Soldatenräte Deutschlands vom 16. bis 21 Dezember 1918. Stenographische Berichte*, Berlin, J.H.W. Dietz.

Leber, Julius 1928, 'Thoughts on the Prohibition of German Social Democracy, June 1933', in Julius Leber 1952, *Ein Mann geht seinen Weg. Schriften, Reden und Briefe*, Berlin: Mosaik-Verlag.

Ledebour, Georg 1918, 'Speech Defending the Authority of the Berlin Executive Council at a Joint Session with the Council of People's Representatives, 18 November 1918', in Miller and Potthoff (eds.) 1969, *Regierung der Volksbeauftragten* Volume 2, Berlin: Verlag Olle & Wolter.

Liebknecht, Karl 1919, 'Despite Everything', in *Die Rote Fahne*, 15 January 1919.

Leipart, Theodore 1925, 'Theodore Leipart Advocates a More Political Standpoint for the Trade Unions in 1925', in Kongreß der Gewerkschaften Deutschlands 1925, *Protokoll der Verhandlungen des 12.Kongresses der Gewerkschaften Deutschlands, abgehalten in Breslau vom 31.August bis 4.September 1925*, Berlin: Verlag-Ge.

Levi, Paul 1919a, 'Paul Levi's Fight against Putschism' from *Nachlass Paul Levi (NPL)*, 19/1, circular from the Central Secretariat, 11 June 1919; (2): *NPL*, 50/16, Kommunistische Partei Deutschlands 1919, circular from the Central Secretariat, 13 June 1919; (3): *NPL*, 50/13, Kommunistische Partei Deutschlands 1919 circular from the Central Secretariat, 19 June 1919; Kommunistische Partei Deutschlands 1919 *Kommunistische Räte-Korrespondenz*, 5, 20 June 1919.

———— 1919b, 'Declaration of Communist Principles and Tactics drawn up by Paul Levi and adopted by the Second Congress of the KPD (S), October 1919', in Kommunistische Partei Deutschlands 1919, *Bericht über den 2.Parteitag der KPD (Spartakusbund), 20–24 Oktober 1919*, Berlin: Vereinigung Internationaler Verlagsanstalten.

———— 1920a, 'A Communist View of Military Questions (Paul Levi's speech of April 1920)', in Kommunistische Partei Deutschlands 1920, *Bericht über den 4. Parteitag der Kommunistischen Partei Deutschlands (Spartakusbund) am 14. und 15. April 1920*, Berlin: Berliner Buch und Kunstdruckerei.

———— 1920b, 'Critique of the Line Taken by the KPD *Zentrale* Towards the Kapp Putsch', *Die Kommunistische Internationale*, 1920, Number 12, col. 2145–48.

Levi, Paul, Kurt Rosenfeld and Max Seydewitz 1929, 'Proposals for a Military Programme Brought Forward by the Left Opposition in the SPD and Rejected at the Magdeburg Congress, 1929', *Der Klassenkampf. Marxistische Blätter* 3.12.

Maslowski, Peter 1932, 'Peter Maslowski Gives the Communist View of the Freethinkers' Movement (June 1932)', *Die Linkskurve* 4.6.

Müller, August 1919, 'Views of Dr. August Müller on the Economic Disadvantages of the Council System at the Cabinet Session of 21 January 1919', Miller and Potthoff (eds.) 1969, *Regierung der Volksbeauftragten* Volume 2.

Müller, Hermann and Arthur Crispien 1920, 'Letter of 11 June 1920 from the SPD Chancellor, Hermann Müller, to the Chair of the USPD, Arthur Crispien, with Crispien's Reply', *Schulthess' Europäische Geschichtskalender, Neue Folge* Jg. 61, 1920.

Müller, Hermann 1920, 'Hermann Müller's Speech to a Joint Session of the Party Executive, the Party Committee and the Parliamentary Party Explaining why the Social Democrats are No Longer in the Government, 13 June 1920', in Dowe, Dieter (ed.) 1980, *Protokolle der Sitzungen des Parteiausschusses der SPD 1912 bis 1921. Band II*, Reprint, Berlin: J.H.W. Dietz.

———— 1921, 'Hermann Müller on the Way to Revise the Versailles Treaty,' in Sozialdemokratische Partei Deutschlands 1921, *Protokoll über die Verhandlungen des Parteitages der SPD abgehalten in Görlitz, vom 18. bis 24. September 1921*, Berlin: J.H.W. Dietz.

—— 1923, 'Hermann Müller on the French and Belgian Invasion of the Ruhr, January 1923', in Deutsches Reich 1923, *Verhandlungen des Reichstags. Stenographische Berichte*, Volume 357, p. 9424, Session 286, 13 January 1923, Berlin.

—— 1924, 'Hermann Müller's Resolution on the Continuing Need for Coalition Agreements', in Sozialdemokratischer Parteitag 1924, *Protokoll mit dem Bericht der Frauenkonferenz*, Berlin: J.H.W. Dietz.

—— 1928, 'Hermann Müller (SPD Chancellor of Germany) Addresses the General Assembly of the League of Nations on 7 September 1928 on Disarmament', in *Schulthess' Europäischer Geschichtskalender. Neue Folge. Vol. 44 (1928)*, Munich: Beck.

Naphtali, Fritz 1928, 'Fritz Naphtali on the Consequences of Capitalist Rationalization', in Allgemeiner Deutscher Gewerkschaftsbund 1928, *Protokoll der Verhandlungen des 13.Kongresses der Gewerkschaften Deutschlands (3.Bundestag des ADGB), abgehalten in Hamburg vom 3.bis 7. September 1928*, Berlin: J.H.W. Dietz.

Noske, Gustav 1918, 'Gustav Noske (SPD Minister of Defence) Defends his Decision to Use Career Officers to Restore Order in Germany after 1918', in G. Noske 1947, *Aufstieg und Niedergang der deutschen Sozialdemokratie*, Zürich: Aeroverlag.

Peus, Heinrich 1924, 'Heinrich Peus (Dessau) Advocates Turning the SPD into a Labour Party', in Sozialdemokratischer Parteitag 1924, *Protokoll mit dem Bericht der Frauenkonferenz*, Berlin: J.H.W. Dietz.

Radbruch, Gustav 1951, 'Gustav Radbruch Looks Back on the "Excessive Rationalism" of the SPD', in Gustav Radbruch 1951, *Der innere Weg: Aufriss meines Lebens*, Stuttgart: K.F. Koehler.

Radek, Karl 1921, 'Letters from Karl Radek to the *Zentrale* of the VKPD Concerning the March Action of 1921', in *Nachlass Paul Levi*.

—— 1923, 'Karl Radek's "Schlageter Speech"', 20 June 1923, in Communist International Executive Committee 1924, *Die Lehren der deutschen Ereignisse. Das Präsidium des Exekutivkomitees der Kommunistischen Internationale zur deutschen Frage, Januar 1924*, Hamburg.

Roter Frontkämpferbund 1925, 'Circular from the Red Front Fighters' League (RFKB), before 25 April 1925', from 'On the Significance, Tasks and Organisation of the RFKB', in Kurt G. P. Schuster 1975, *Der Rote Frontkämpferbund 1924–29*, Düsseldorf: Droste Verlag.

SAP 1932, 'Declaration of Principles Adopted at the First Congress of the SAP (Socialist Workers' Party) on 25 March 1932', in Hermann Weber (ed.) 1963, *Der deutsche Kommunismus: Dokumente*, Cologne: Kiepenheuer und Witsch.

Scheibenhuber, Elise 1925, 'Elise Scheibenhuber (Berlin-Lichtenberg) Proposes Motion 56, Adopted by the SPD Women's Conference, Calling on the SPD to Give Equal Treatment to Men and Women, as Provided for in the Party's Programme, and to Ban the Consumption of Alcohol at Party Meetings', from Sozialdemokratischer

Parteitag in Heidelberg 1925, *Protokoll mit dem Bericht der Frauenkonferenz*, Berlin: J.H.W. Dietz.

Scheidemann, Philipp 1919, 'Presentation of The Government Programme of 13 February 1919 to the National Assembly by the SPD Reich Chancellor', from Sozialdemokratische Partei Deutschlands 1919, *Protokoll über die Verhandlungen des Parteitages der Sozialdemokratischen Partei Deutschlands, abgehalten in Weimar vom 10. bis 15. Juni 1919*, Berlin: J.H.W. Dietz.

———— 1921, 'Philipp Scheidemann Defends the Idea of a Coalition with Other Parties', from Sozialdemokratische Partei Deutschlands 1921, *Protokoll über die Verhandlungen des Parteitages der Sozialdemokratischen Partei Deutschlands, abgehalten in Görlitz vom 18. bis 24. September 1921*, Berlin: J.H.W. Dietz.

———— 1926, 'Philipp Scheidemann's Speech of 16 December 1926 Attacking the Role of the Reichswehr as a "State Within a State"', in Deutsches Reich 1927, *Verhandlungen des Reichstags. Stenographische Berichte Bd. 391*, 3 November 1926–4 Februar 1927, Berlin: J.H.W. Dietz.

Schmidt, Robert 1922, 'Robert Schmidt (SPD) Advocates Requisitioning Material Assets as a Step Towards Socialism', in Sozialdemokratischen Parteitags in Augsburg 1922, *Protokoll des Sozialdemokratischen Parteitags in Augsburg, Gera und Nürnberg 1922*, Berlin: J.H.W. Dietz.

Schöfer, Sophie 1921, 'Dr. Sophie Schöfer addresses the SPD Women's Conference in 1921 on the Role of Women in Social Work', in Sozialdemokratische Partei Deutschlands 1921, *Reichsfrauentag der Sozialdemokratische Partei Deutschlands am 17. und 18. September 1921 in Görlitz*, Berlin: J.H.W. Dietz.

Sozialdemokratischer Parteitag 1917–33, 'The Party Leadership of the SPD, 1917–33' from Sozialdemokratischer Parteitag 1924–31, *Jahrbücher der deutschen Sozialdemokratie*, Bonn-Bad: Godesberg Kraus.

———— 1919a, 'Resolution on the Question of Councils, Adopted in April 1919 by the Second Congress of Councils', in Centralrat der Sozialistischen Republik Deutschlands 1975, *II. Kongress der Arbeitern, Bauern- und Soldatenräte Deutschlands am 8. bis 14. April 1919 im Herrenhaus zu Berlin. Stenographisches Protokoll*, Berlin: Verlagsgesellschaft des Allgemeinen Deutschen Gewerkschaftsbundes.

———— 1919b, 'The SPD Leadership Calls its Cabinet Ministers to Order in November 1919', in Potthogg and Weber (eds.) 1986, *Die SPD-Fraktion in der Nationalversammlung 1919–1920*, Number 25, 21 November 1919.

———— 1921a, 'The SPD 1921 Görlitz Programme', in Sozialdemokratische Partei Deutschlands 1921, *Protokoll über die Verhandlungen des Parteitages der Sozialdemokratischen Partei Deutschlands, abgehalten in Görlitz vom 18. bis 24. September 1921*, Berlin: J.H.W. Dietz.

———— 1921b, 'Women's Demands Included in the SPD's 1921 Programme', in Sozialdemokratische Partei Deutschlands 1921, *Protokoll über die Verhandlungen des*

Parteitages der Sozialdemokratischen Partei Deutschlands, abgehalten in Görlitz vom 18. bis 24 September 1921, Berlin: J.H.W. Dietz.

────── 1924, 'The SPD's Organisational Statute of 1924 (selected provisions)', in Sozialdemokratischer Parteitag 1924, *Protokoll mit dem Bericht der Frauenkonferenz*, Berlin: J.H.W. Dietz.

────── 1925a, 'International Policy Document Adopted by the SPD in 1925', in Deutsches Reich 1925, *Verhandlungen des Reichstags* Bd. 423.

────── 1925b, 'The Heidelberg Programme of the SPD, 1925', in Sozialdemokratischer Parteitag 1925, *13–18 September 1925 in Heidelberg. Protokoll mit dem Bericht der Frauenkonferenz*, Berlin: J.H.W. Dietz.

────── 1927, 'The SPD's Agrarian Programme of 1927', in Sozialdemokratischer Parteitag in Kiel 1927, *Protokoll mit dem Bericht der Frauenkonferenz*, Berlin: J.H.W. Dietz.

────── 1929, 'SPD Principles of Defence Policy, Adopted in May 1929' from Sozialdemokratischer Parteitag in Magdeburg 1929, *Protokoll mit dem Bericht der Frauenkonferenz*, Berlin: J.H.W. Dietz.

Sozialdemokratischer Parteitag in Heidelberg 1925, 'Resolution Calling on the SPD Parliamentary Group to Pursue a Policy of Determined Opposition to the Bourgeois Parties (September 1925)', in Sozialdemokratischer Parteitag in Heidelberg 1925, *Protokoll mit dem Bericht der Frauenkonferenz*, Berlin: J.H.W. Dietz.

Sozialistische Einheitspartei Deutschlands Zentralkomitee and Kommunistische Partei Deutschlands 1926, 'The Joint SPD-KPD Proposal for the Expropriation of the Former German Princes, 28 April 1926', in Sozialistische Einheitspartei Deutschlands Zentralkomitee 1975, *Dokumente und Materialien zur Geschichte der deutschen Arbeiterbewegung*, Berlin: J.H.W. Dietz.

Tarnow, Fritz 1931, 'Fritz Tarnow Ponders Social Democratic Strategy "at the Sickbed of Capitalism" in 1931', in Sozialdemokratischer Parteitag in Leipzig 1931, *Protokoll vom 31.Mai bis 5.Juni im Volkshaus*, Berlin: J.H.W. Dietz.

Thälmann, Ewert, et al. 1928, 'The Secret Agreement of 29 February 1928 Made at a Joint Session of KPD and Soviet Communist Party Delegates', in *Vierteljahreshefte für Zeitgeschichte*, 16, No. 2, April 1968.

The First Congress of Councils 1918, 'Resolution of the First Congress of Councils on the Respective Areas of Competence of the Central Council and the Government, 18 December 1918', in Allgemeiner Kongress der Arbeiter- und Soldatenräte Deutschlands 1919, *Allgemeiner Kongress, der Arbeiter und Soldatenräte Deutschlands vom 16. bis 21 Dezember 1918. Stenographische Berichte*, Glashütten: Auvermann.

The League of Red Women and Girls 1926, 'Aims and Tasks of the League of Red Women and Girls (RFMB), 1926', in Sozialistische Einheitspartei Deutschlands Zentralkomitee 1926, *Dokumente und Materialien zur Geschichte der deutschen Arbeiterbewegung*, Berlin: J.H.W. Dietz.

The Revolutionary Shop-Stewards and Representatives of the Big Factories of Greater Berlin; the Central Leadership of the Independent Social Democratic Electoral Organisations of Berlin and Surrounding Districts; the *Zentrale* of the Communist Party of Germany 1919, 'Joint Proclamation by the Revolutionary Shop-Stewards, the Berlin USPD and the KPD *Zentrale*, 9 January 1919', in Sozialistische Einheitspartei Deutschlands Zentralkomitee 1958, *Dokumente und Materialien zur Geschichte der deutschen Arbeiterbewegung, Reihe II: 1914–1945, Band 3*, Berlin, J.H.W. Dietz.

The USPD Members of the Council of People's Representatives 1918, 'The USPD Members of the Council of People's Representatives Announce their Resignation in Protest Against the Central Council's Declaration of 28 December 1918', in Miller and Potthoff (eds.) 1969, *Regierung der Volksbeauftragten* Volume 2, Berlin: Verlag Olle & Wolter.

Unabhängige Sozialdemokratische Partei Deutschlands 1919a, 'Appeal to the Revolutionary Proletariat to Defend the Workers' Councils, *Die Freiheit*, Number 74, 11 February 1919.

———— 1919b, 'USPD Programmatic Declaration, adopted 6 March 1919', in Unabhängige Sozialdemokratische Partei Deutschlands 1919, *Protokoll über die Verhandlungen des ausserordentlichen Parteitages vom 2. bis 6. März 1919 in Berlin*, Berlin.

———— 1919c, 'The USPD Action Programme of December 1919', in Unabhängige Sozialdemokratische Partei Deutschlands 1919, *Protokoll über die Verhandlungen des ausserordentlichen Parteitages vom 30. November bis 6. Dezember 1919 in Leipzig*.

Vorwärts 1918a, 'Up with Social Democracy!', in *Vorwärts*, Number 337, 8 December 1918.

———— 1918b, 'Telegram from the Council of People's Representatives to the German High Command, 12 November 1918', *Vorwärts*, 13 November 1918.

———— 1923, 'The Proceedings of the Chemnitz Conference of 21 October 1923', *Vorwärts*, Number 495, 23 October 1923.

Wels, Otto 1919, 'Report of the MSPD Party Leadership, Delivered by Otto Wels on 10 June 1919', in Sozialdemokratische Partei Deutschlands 1919, *Protokoll über die Verhandlungen des Parteitages der SPD, abgehalten in Weimar, vom 10. bis 15. Juni 1919*, Berlin: J.H.W. Dietz.

———— 1920, 'Reasons Given by Leading Social Democrat Otto Wels for the Party's Unwillingness to Return to Office after the 1920 elections', in Sozialdemokratische Partei Deutschlands 1921, *Protokoll über die Verhandlungen des Parteitages der SPD, abgehalten in Kassel vom 10. bis 16. Oktober 1920*, Berlin: J.H.W. Dietz.

———— 1932, 'Otto Wels (SPD) on the Party's Reaction to Papen's Coup of 20 July 1932', in Hagen Schulz (ed.) 1975, *Anpassung oder Widerstand? Aus den Akten des Parteivorstands der deutschen Sozialdemokratie 1932/33*, Bonn: Neue Gesellschaft.

Wissell, Rudolf 1919, 'Speech of June 1919 to the SPD Party Congress Criticising the Record of the Government of which He was a Member', in Sozialdemokratische

Partei Deutschlands 1919, *Protokoll über die Verhandlungen des Parteitages der Sozialdemokratischen Partei Deutschlands, abgehalten in Weimar vom 10. bis 15. Juni 1919*, Berlin, J.H.W. Dietz.

Woytinsky Wladimir, Fritz Tarnow and Fritz Baade 1931, 'The Trade Union Movement Calls for Job Creation: the "WTB Plan" of 1931', in Deutsches Reich 1927, *Verhandlungen des Reichstags. Stenographische Berichte Bd. 391*, 3 November 1926–4 Februar 1927, Berlin: Reichsdruckerei.

Zentralkomitee der KPD 1927, 'Resolution of the Eleventh Party Congress on the Work of the KPD Among Women, March 1927', in Zentralkomitee der KPD 1927, *Thesen und Resolutionen des XI. Parteitags der KPD, Essen, 2–7 März 1927*, Berlin: Zentralkomitee der KPD.

Zentralkomitee der VKPD 1921, 'Open Letter of 8 January 1921 from the VKPD to Other Workers' Organisations Calling for United Action', *Die Rote Fahne*, 8 January 1921.

Zentrale of the Factory Councils of Germany, KPD and USPD 1920, 'Zentrale of the Factory Councils of Germany, The Communists and Independents (SPD and USPD) Oppose the Passing of the Factory Council Law, 12 January 1920', *Die Rote Fahne*, 13 January 1920, reprinted in Sozialistische Einheitspartei Deutschlands Zentralkomitee 1958, *Dokumente und Materialien zur Geschichte der deutschen Arbeiterbewegung, Reihe II: 1914–1945* Volume 7, Berlin: J.H.W. Dietz.

Zetkin, Clara 1921, 'Clara Zetkin on the Communist Party and the Woman Question, 1920', in Vereinigten Kommunistischen Partei 1921, *Bericht über die Verhandlungen des Vereinigungsparteitags der USPD (Linke) und der KPD (Spartakusbund), Abgehalten in Berlin vom 4. bis 7 Dezember 1920*, Berlin: Franke.

Zinoviev, Grigorii 1922, 'Grigorii Zinoviev's Letter of 18 July 1922 to the KPD Leadership about the Berlin Agreement for Joint Action', in Kommunistische Internationale 1922, *Protokoll des IV. Kongresses der Kommunistischen Internationale, Petrograd-Moskau, vom 5.November bis 5. Dezember 1922*, Hamburg: Verlag der Kommunistischen Internationale.

————— 1924, 'Grigorii Zinoviev's Letter of 31 March 1924 to Ruth Fischer and Arkady Maslow', in H. Weber (ed.), 'Dokumentation zu den Beziehungen zwischen der KPD und der KI', VJFZ, 16.

Printed Primary Sources

Adibekov, Grant Mkrtychevich et al. (eds.) 2004, *Politbiuro, TsK RKP (b)-VKP (b) i Komintern 1919–1943. Dokumenty* Moscow: Rosspen.

Allgemeiner Deutscher Gewerkschaftsbund 1921, 'Forderungen der Gewerkschaften zur Rettung der deutschen Wortschaft', *Correspondenzblatt des ADGB*, 31: 48, 26 November 1921, 679. Berlin ADGB.

————— 1922, *Protokoll der Verhandlungen des elften kongresses der Gewerkschaften Deutschlands, Leipzig, 19–24 June 1922*, Berlin: Verlagsgesellschaft des Allgemeinen Deutschen Gewerkschaftsbundes.

————— 1925, *Protokoll der Verhandlungen des 12.Kongresses der Gewerkschaften Deutschlands, abgehalten in Breslau vom 31. August bis 4.September 1925*, Berlin: Verlagsgesellschaft des Allgemeinen Deutschen Gewerkschaftsbundes.

Allgemeiner Kongress der Arbeiter- und Soldatenräte Deutschlands 1919, *Vom 16. bis 21. Dezember 1918 im Abgeordnetenhause zu Berlin. Stenographische Berichte*, Berlin: Olle und Wolter.

Arendt, Hans-Jürgen 1969, 'Das Schutzprogramm der KPD für die arbeitende Frau vom 15 Oktober 1931', in *Beiträge zur Geschichte der Arbeiterbewegung*, Berlin, Heft 2.

Brandler, Heinrich 1977, 'The Brandler-Deutscher Correspondence', *New Left Review*, 105, 72–7.

Braun, M.J., 'Die Lehren des Kapp-Putsches', *Die Internationale* 2, 23, 1 June 1920: 22–37.

Centralrat der Sozialistischen Republik Deutschlands 1975 [1919], *II.Kongress der Arbeitern, Bauern- und Soldatenräte Deutschlands am 8. bis 14. April 1919 im Herrenhaus zu Berlin. Stenographisches Protokoll*, Glashütten: Auvermann.

Communist International Executive Committee 1922, *Protokoll des IV. Kongresses der Kommunistischen Internationale, Petrograd-Moskau, vom 5.November bis 5. Dezember 1922*, Hamburg: Verlag der Kommunistischen Internationale.

Communist International Enlarged Executive Committee 1923, *Protokoll der Konferenz der Erweiterten Exekutive der Kommunistischen Internationale, Moskau 12–23 Juni 1923*, Hamburg: C. Hoym nachf L. Cahnbley.

Communist International Executive Committee 1924, *Die Lehren der deutschen Ereignisse. Das Präsidium des Exekutivkomitees der Kommunistischen Internationale zur Deutschen Frage (Januar 1924)*, Hamburg: Verlag der Kommunistischen Internationale.

Cunow, Heinrich, 'Die Diktatur des Proletariats', in *Die Neue Zeit. Wochenschrift der Deutschen Sozialdemokratie* 1.8. 22 November 1918, 170–7.

Decker, Georg 1930, 'Opposition', in *Die Gesellschaft. Internationale Revue für Sozialismus und Politik*, 7, 3, March 1930: 196–204.

Degras, Jane (ed.) 1960, *The Communist International 1919–1943. Documents. Volume 2, 1923–1928*, London: Royal Institute of International Affairs.

Der Klassenkampf 1929, *Der Klassenkampf 3.12 December 1929*, Marxistische Blätter.

Deutscher Geschichtskalender 1919, 'Der Europäische Krieg. Ergänzungsband 1.1. Die deutsche Revolution: November 1918 bis Februar 1919', in *Deutscher Geschichtskalender*, 1919, vom 35, Leipzig: Meiner.

——— 1919, 'Ergänzungsband 1.1. Die Deutsche Revolution. Erster Band. November 1918–Februar 1919', in *Deutscher Geschichtskalender*, 1919, vom 35, Leipzig: Meiner.

——— 1928, 'Section A', in *Deutscher Geschichtskalender*, 1928, vom. 44, Leipzig: Meiner.

Deutsches Reich 1918a, *Reichsgesetzblatt*, Berlin: Verlag. d. Gesetzsammlungsamts.

——— 1918b, *Reichsanzeiger und Preußischer Staatsanzeiger*, Berlin: Kessel.

——— 1919, *Reichsgesetzblatt*, Berlin: Verlag. d. Gesetzsammlungsamts.

——— 1920, *Reichsgesetzblatt*, Berlin: Verlag. d. Gesetzsammlungsamts.

Dowe, Dieter (ed.) 1980, *Protokolle der Sitzungen des Parteiausschusses der SPD 1912 bis 1921. Band II*, Reprint, Berlin: J.H.W. Dietz.

Eisner, Kurt 1919, *Die Neue Zeit*, München: G. Müller.

Freier Deutscher Gewerkschaftsbund 1930, *Die Arbeit*, Berlin: Tribüne Verlag.

Friesland, Ernst 1921, *Zur Krise unserer Partei*, Berlin: [S.N.].

Gintsberg, Lev I. (ed.) 1994 '"Politsekretariat IKKI trebuiet". Dokumenty Kominterna i Kompartii Germanii 1930–1934', *Istoricheskii Arkhiv. Nauchno-Publikatorskii Zhurnal*, 1: 148–174.

Heilfron, Eduard 1919, *Die Deutsche Nationalversammlung im Jahre 1919 in ihrer Arbeit für den Aufbau des neuen deutschen Volksstaates*, Bd.7, Berlin: Berlin Norddeutsche Buchdruckerei und Verlag.

Hermberg, Paul 1929, 'Volkshochschule und Arbeiterbildung', *Die Arbeit*, 6, 9, September 1929.

Hilferding, Rudolf 1930, 'Der Austritt aus der Regierung', *Die Gesellschaft. Internationale Revue für Sozialismus und Politik*, 1930, 1: 385–91.

Hörsing, Friedrich Otto 1929, 'Das Reichsbanner Schwarz-Rot-Gold', in Bernhard Harms (ed.) 1929, *Volk und Reich der deutschen* Volume 2, Berlin: Verlag von Reiner Hobbing.

Huber, Ernst Rudolf 1966, *Dokumente zur deutschen Verfassungsgeschichte, Band 3*, Stuttgart: W. Kohlhammer Verlag.

Institut für Marxismus-Leninismus beim Zentralkomitee 1968, 'Sitzung des Vollzugsrats der Arbeiter- und Soldatenräte, 16. und 17.11.1918', in *Beiträge zur Geschichte der Arbeiterbewegung*, 10, 1968, Sonderheft 2, Berlin J.H.W. Dietz.

Internationale Presse Korrespondenz 1923, *Internationale Presse-Korrespondenz 172*, 7 November 1923.

——— 1924, *Internationale Presse-Korrespondenz 16*, 4 February 1924.

——— 1930, *Internationale Presse-Korrespondenz 78*, 16 September 1930.

International United Secretariat, *Inprekorr*, 128, 4 Sept. 1925: 1863–70.

Kautsky, Karl 1968, *Texte zu den Programmen der deutschen Sozialdemokratie 1891–1925*, edited by A. Langner, Cologne: Verlag Jakob Hegner.

Keil, Wilhelm 1948, *Erlebnisse eines Sozialdemokraten* Volume 2, Stuttgart: Deutsche Verlagsanstalt.

Komolova, N.P. (ed.) 1999, *Komintern protiv Fashizma. Dokumenty*, Moscow: Nauka.

Kommunistische Internationale 1922, *Protokoll des IV. Kongresses der Kommunistischen Internationale, Petrograd-Moskau, vom 5.November bis 5. Dezember 1922*, Hamburg: Verlag der Kommunistischen Internationale.

Kommunistische Partei Deutschlands 1919, *Bericht über den 2. Parteitag der KPD (Spartakusbund), 20–24 Oktober 1919*, Berlin: KPD.

———— 1919a, *Die Rote Fahne*, 15, 15 January 1919, Berlin: August Scherl.

———— 1919b, *Die Internationale*, I, 1919, 2/3, 28–32.

———— 1920a, 'Zu den Betriebrätewahlen', *Die Rote Fahne* 24, 7 March 1920.

———— 1920b, *Die Rote Fahne*, 30, 14 March 1920, Berlin: August Scherl.

———— 1920c, *Bericht über den 4. Parteitag der Kommunistischen Partei Deutschlands (Spartakusbund) am 14. und 15. April 1920*, Berlin: Berliner Buch und Kunstdruckerei.

———— 1920d, *Die Internationale*, II/26/1 December 1920.

———— 1921a, *Die Rote Fahne*, 8 January 1921, Berlin: August Scherl.

———— 1921b, *Die Internationale*, Jg.3, Heft 4, 13 April 1921, 122–7.

———— 1921c, *Die Internationale III*, 14, November 1921.

———— 1923a, *Bericht über die Verhandlungen des III (8) Parteitages der Kommunistischen Partei Deutschlands (Sektion der Kommunistischen Internationale), 28 Jan.–1 Feb. 1923*, Berlin: Vereinigung Internationaler Verlagsanstalten.

———— 1923c, *Die Rote Fahne*, No. 144, Tuesday 26 June 1923, Berlin: August Scherl.

———— 1925, *Die Rote Fahne*, 1 September 1925, Berlin: August Scherl.

———— 1926, *Bericht über die Verhandlungen des 10. Parteitages der Kommunistischen Partei Deutschlands (Sektion der Kommunistischen Internationale), Berlin vom 12. bis 17. Juli 1925*, Berlin: Vereinigung Internationaler Verlagsanstalten.

———— 1927, *Thesen und Resolutionen des XI. Parteitags der KPD, Essen, 2–7 März 1927*. Berlin: Zentralkomitee der KPD.

———— 1930, *Was will die Kommunistische Partei Deutschlands: Opposition? (Verbesserte Entwurf der Plattform der KPD-O)*, Berlin: Junius-Verlag.

Kongress der Gewerkschaften Deutschlands 1931, *Protokoll der Verhandlungen des 14.Kongresses der Gewerkschaften Deutschlands 31.August bis 4.September 1931*, Berlin Verl.-Ges. des Allg. Dt. Gewerkschaftsbundes.

Könnemann, Erwin, Brigitte Berthold; Gerhard Schulze (eds.) 1971, *Arbeiterklasse siegt über Kapp und Lüttwitz* Volume 1, Berlin: Akademie-Verlag.

Koops, Tilman (ed.) 1982, *Die Kabinette Brüning I u.II, Bd.2., 1. März 1931 bis 10. Oktober 1931* (Akten der Reichskanzlei. Weimarer Republik, herausgegeben für die

Historische Kommission bei der Bayerischen Akademie der Wissenschaften von K.D. Erdmann), Boppard am Rhein: Boldt.

Krause, Hartfrid 1975, *USPD. Zur Geschichte der Unabhängigen Sozialdemokratischen Partei Deutschlands*, Frankfurt: Europäische Verlagsanstalt.

Leber, Julius 1952, 'Thoughts on the Prohibition of German Social Democracy, June 1933', in *Ein Mann geht seinen Weg. Schriften, Reden und Briefe*, Berlin: Mosaik-Verlag.

Levi, Paul 1927, 'Der Bürgerblock', in *Sozialistische Politik und Wirtschaft*, 28 January 1927.

Maslowski, Peter 1932, 'Wir Gotteslästerer', *Die Linkskurve* June 1932: 4–8.

Mierendorff, Carl 1930, 'Lehren der Niederlage', in *Neue Blätter für den Sozialismus* 1.11, November 1930: 481–4.

Miller, Susanne, Heinrich Potthoff & Erich Matthias (eds.) 1969, *Die Regierung der Volksbeauftragten 1918/19* Volume 1, Düsseldorf: Droste Verlag.

Müller, Richard 1979 [1925], *Geschichte der deutschen Revolution* Volume 2, Berlin: Verlag Olle & Wolter.

Nationalversammlung 1919, *Stenographische Berichte über die Verhandlungen der Verfassunggebenden Deutschen Nationalversammlung* Volume 327, 38th. Sitting, 12, Berlin: Druck und Verlag der norddeutschen Buchdruckerei.

—— 1920, *Stenographische Berichte über die Verhandlungen der verfassunggebenden deutschen Nationalversammlung* Volume 326, Berlin: Druck und Verlag der norddeutschen Buchdruckerei.

—— 1920, *Stenographische Berichte über die Verhandlungen der verfassunggebenden deutschen Nationalversammlung* Volume 330, Berlin: Druck und Verlag der norddeutschen Buchdruckerei.

—— 1923, *Stenographische Berichte über die Verhandlungen der deutschen Nationalversammlung* Volume 357, Berlin: Druck und Verlag der norddeutschen Buchdruckerei.

Noske, Gustav 1947, *Aufstieg und Niedergang der deutschen Sozialdemokratie: Erlebtes aus Aufstieg und Niedergang einer Demokratie*, Zürich: Aeroverlag.

Petrich, Franz 1930, 'Kritik der Opposition. Antwort an Genossen Decker', *Die Gesellschaft. Internationale Revue für Sozialismus und Politik*, 8, 5, May 1930: 454–61.

Petzina, Dietmar, W. Abelshauser and A. Faust 1978, *Materialien zur Statistik des deutschen Reiches 1914–1945 (Sozialgeschichliches Arbeitsbuch, Bd.3)*, Munich: Beck.

Pothoff, Heinrich and Hermann Weber (eds.) 1986, *Die SPD-Fraktion in der Nationalversammlung 1919–1920*, Düsseldorf: Droste.

Potthoff, Heinrich 1987, *Freie Gewerkschaften 1918–1933: Der Allgemeine Deutsche Gewerkschaftsbund in der Weimarer Republik*, Düsseldorf: Droste.

Radbruch, Gustav 1951, *Der innere Weg*, Stuttgart: K.F. Koehler.

Reichstag 1927, *Verhandlungen des Reichstags. Stenographische Berichte Bd. 391,* 3 November 1926–4 Februar 1927, Berlin.

Ritter, Gerhard Albrecht and S. Miller, S (eds.) 1975, *Die deutsche Revolution 1918–1919. Dokumente* 2nd ed., Hamburg: Hoffman und Campe Verlag.

Schneider, Michael 1975, *Das Arbeitsbeschaffungsprogramm des ADGB,* Bonn: Verlag Neue Gesellschaft.

Schulze, Hagen (ed.) 1975, *Anpassung oder Widerstand? Aus den Akten des Parteivorstands der deutschen Sozialdemokratie 1932/33, (Archiv für Sozialgeschichte, Beiheft 4),* Bonn: Neue Gesellschaft.

Schulze-Bidlingmaier, Ingrid (ed.) 1973, *Die Kabinette Wirth I. und II, 10 Mai 1921 bis 26.Oktober 1921, 26 Oktober 1921 bis 22 November 1922,* 2 Volumes, Boppard: Boldt.

Sozialdemokratische Partei Deutschlands 1923, *Protokoll des Sozialdemokratischen Parteitags in Augsburg, Gera und Nürnberg 1922,* Bonn: Verstand der SPD.

———— 1924, *Resolution 243* (Dissmann and Comrades), Berlin: J.H.W. Dietz.

———— 1925, *Mitteilungsblatt der Sozialdemokratischen Partei Deutschlands,* 2, 1925, Number 12, Berlin: Vorwärts.

———— 1931a, *Jahrbücher der deutschen Sozialdemokratie für d. Jahr 1931,* Berlin: Nendeln/Liechtenstein Kraus.

———— 1931b, *Das Gespenst der Arbeitslosigkeit und die Vorschläge der SPD zu ihrer Überwindung,* Heilbronn: [S.N.].

———— 1973 [1919], *Protokoll über die Verhandlungen des Parteitages der SPD, abgehalten in Weimar, vom 10. bis 15. Juni 1919,* Berlin: J.H.W. Dietz.

———— 1976 [1922], *Protokoll über die Verhandlungen des Parteitages der USPD in Leipzig vom 8. bis 12 Januar 1922,* Glashütten: Auvermann.

———— 1973a [1920], *Protokoll über die Verhandlungen des Parteitages der Sozialdemokratischen Partei Deutschlands, abgehalten in Kassel vom 10. bis 16. Oktober 1920,* Berlin: J.H.W. Dietz.

———— 1973b [1921], *Reichsfrauentag der Sozialdemokratische Partei Deutschlands am 17. und 18. September 1921,* Glashütten: Auvermann.

———— 1973c [1921], *Protokoll über die Verhandlungen des Parteitages der Sozialdemokratischen Partei Deutschlands, abgehalten in Görlitz vom 18. bis 24 September 1921,* Glashütten: Auvermann.

Sozialdemokratischer Parteitag, 1924. *Protokoll mit dem Bericht der Frauenkonferenz,* Berlin: J.H.W. Dietz.

Sozialdemokratischer Parteitag in Heidelberg 1925. *Protokoll mit dem Bericht der Frauenkonferenz,* Berlin: J.H.W. Dietz.

Sozialdemokratischer Parteitag in Kiel 1927, *Protokoll mit dem Bericht der Frauenkonferenz,* Berlin: J.H.W. Dietz.

Sozialdemokratischer Parteitag in Magdeburg 1929, *Protokoll mit dem Bericht der Frauenkonferenz,* Berlin: J.H.W. Dietz.

Sozialdemokratischer Parteitag in Leipzig 1931, vom 31.Mai bis 5.Juni im Volkshaus, Leipzig, Berlin: J.H.W. Dietz.

Sozialistische Einheitspartei Deutschlands Zentralkomitee 1958, *Dokumente und Materialien zur Geschichte der deutschen Arbeiterbewegung*, 1958, Second Series, Volume 2, Berlin: Dietz Verlag.

———— 1975, *Dokumente und Materialien zur Geschichte der deutschen Arbeiterbewegung* Volume 8, Berlin: Dietz Verlag.

Stalin, J.V. 1953 [1924], 'Concerning the International Situation', 20 September 1924, in *Works* Volume 6, Moscow: Foreign Languages Publishing House.

———— 1954 [1925], 'The International Situation and the Tasks of the Communist Parties', 22 March 1925, in *Works* Volume 7, Moscow: Foreign Languages Publishing House.

Stalin, J.V., et al. 2001, *Stalin i Kaganovich. Perepiska, 1931–1936*, Moscow: Rosspen.

Thälmann, Ernst, 'Zu unserer Strategie und Taktik im Kampf gegen den Faschismus', *Die Internationale* 15 (1932), Number 6 (June): 277, 279, 284.

Unabhängige Sozialdemokratische Partei Deutschlands 1919a, *Die Freiheit*, 74, 11 February 1919.

———— 1919b, *Protokoll über die Verhandlungen des ausserordentlichen Parteitages vom 2. bis 6. März 1919 in Berlin*, Berlin: Freiheit.

———— 1920, *Protokoll über die Verhandlungen des ausserordentlichen parteitages in Halle, 12–17 Oktober 1920*, Berlin: Verlagsgenossenschaft.

Verband Deutscher Gewerbegerichte 1919, *Soziale Praxis*, Leipzig: Duncker and Humbolt.

Vereinigten Kommunistischen Partei 1921, *Bericht über die Verhandlungen des Vereinigungsparteitags der USPD (Linke) und der KPD (Spartakusbund)*, *Abgehalten in Berlin vom 4. bis 7 Dezember 1920*, Berlin: Franke.

Vorwärts 1918, *Vorwärts*, New York.

Weber, Hermann (ed.) 1963, *Der deutsche Kommunismus: Dokumente*, Cologne: Kiepenheuer und Witsch.

———— (ed.) 1960, Hindenburg zwischen den Fronten' in *Vierteljahrshefte für Zeitgeschichte*, 8, 1, January 1960: 82–4.

———— (ed.) 1968, Dokumentation. Zu den Beziehungen zwischen der KPD und der Kommunistischen Internationale, *Vierteljahrshefte für Zeitgeschichte*, 16,2, April 1968: 177–208.

Weber, Herman and Johann Wachtler (eds.) 1981, *Die Generallinie. Runschreiben des Zentralkomitees der KPD an die Bezirke 1929–1933*, Düsseldorf: Droste.

Wissell, Rudolf 1930, 'Einundzwanzig Monate Reichsarbeitsminister', *Die Arbeit*, 7, 1930.

Secondary Sources

Alles, Wolfgang 1994, *Zur Geschichte der deutschen Trotskisten ab 1930*, 2nd ed., Cologne: ISP-Verlag.

Bahne, Siegfried 1960, 'Die Kommunistische Partei Deutschlands', in *Das Ende der Parteien 1933. Darstellungen und Dokumente* edited by Erich Matthias and Rudolf Morsey, Düsseldorf: Droste.

———— 1961, 'Zwischen "Luxemburgismus" und "Stalinismus". Die "ultralinke" Opposition in der KPD', *Vierteljahrshefte für Zeitgeschichte*, 9,4: 359–83.

Bayerlein, Bernhard H. et al. (eds.) 2003, *Deutscher Oktober 1923. Ein Revolutionsplan und sein Scheitern*, Berlin: Aufbau-Verlag.

Beck, Dorothea 1986, 'Theodor Haubach, Julius Leber, Carlo Mierendorff, Karl Schumacher: Zum Selbstverständnis der "militante Sozialisten" in der Weimarer Republik', *Archiv für Sozialgeschichte*, 26: 87–133.

Bergien, Rüdiger 2008, 'The Consensus on Defense and Weimar Prussia's Civil Service', *Central European History*, 41, 2: 179–203.

Bergmann, Theodor 1987, *"Gegen den Strom". Die Geschichte der Kommunistischen Partei – Opposition*, Hamburg: VSA-Verlag.

Boak, Helen L. 1981, 'Women in Weimar Germany: the "Frauenfrage" and the Female Vote', in *Social Change and Political Development in Weimar Germany*, edited by Richard Bessel and E.J. Feuchtwanger, London: Croom Helm.

Bock, Hans-Manfred 1993, *Syndikalismus und Linkskommunismus von 1918 bis 1923*, second edition, Darmstadt: Wissenschaftliche Buchgesellschaft.

Borsány, György 1993, *The Life of a Communist Revolutionary*, New York: Columbia University Press.

Bowlby, Chris 1986, 'Blut mai 1929: Police, Parties and Proletarians in a Berlin Confrontation', *The Historical Journal*, 29: 137–58.

Bracher, Karl Dietrich 1978 [1971], *Die Auflösung der Weimarer Republik*, Fifth Edition, Düsseldorf: Droste Verlag.

Braun, Otto 1949 [1940], *Von Weimar zu Hitler*, Hamburg: Hammonia Norddeutsche Verlagsanstalt.

Braunthal, Julius 1967, *History of the International, 1914–1943* Volume 2, London: Thomas Nelson and Sons.

Breitman, Richard 1981, *German Socialism and Weimar Democracy*, Chapel Hill, N.C.: University of North Carolina Press.

Bremme, Gabriele 1956, *Die politische Rolle der Frau in Deutschland* Göttingen: Vandenhoeck und Ruprecht.

Broué, Pierre 2006 [1971], *The German Revolution 1917–1923*, translated by John Archer, Chicago: Haymarket Books.

Büttner, Ursula 1985, *Politische Gerechtigkeit und sozialer Geist: Hamburg zur Zeit der Weimarer Republik*, Hamburg: Christians.

———— 2008, *Weimar. Die überforderte Republik 1918–1933. Leistung und Versagen in Staat, Gesellschaft, Wirtschaft und Kultur*, Stuttgart: Klett-Cotta.

Carr, Edward Hallett 1982, *The Twilight of the Comintern, 1930–1935*, London: Macmillan.

Carsten, Francis L. 1966, *The Reichswehr and Politics 1918 to 1933*, Oxford: Clarendon Press.

Craig, Gordon A. 1964 [1955], *The Politics of the Prussian Army 1640–1945*, New York: Galaxy.

Crew, David F. 1998, 'A Social Republic? Social Democrats, Communists and the Weimar Welfare State, 1919 to 1933', in *Between Reform and Revolution. German Socialism and Communism from 1840 to 1990*, edited by David E. Barclay and Eric D.Weitz, Oxford: Berghahn Books.

Crew, David F. 1998, *Germans on Welfare: from Weimar to Hitler*, Oxford: Oxford University Press.

Cunow, Heinrich 1920, 'Zur Kritik des Erfurter Programms', *Die Neue Zeit*, 38, 2, 16: 361–8.

———— 1921, 'Zur Kritik des Programmentwurfs', *Die Neue Zeit*, 39,2: 433–41.

Drechsler, Hanno 1965, *Die Sozialistische Arbeiterpartei Deutschlands (SAPD). Ein Beitrag zur Geschichte der deutschen Arbeiterbewegung am Ende der Weimarer Republik*, Meisenheim: A. Hain.

Eifert, Christiane and Pamela E. Selwyn 1997, 'Coming to Terms with the State: Maternalist Politics and the Development of the Welfare State in Weimar Germany', *Central European History* 30, 1: 22–47.

Eissler, W.U. 1980, *Arbeiterparteien und Homosexuellenfrage. Zur Sexualpolitik von SPD und KPD in der Weimarer Republik*, Hamburg: Verlag Rosa Winkel.

Eley, Geoffrey 1998, 'Cultural Socialism, the Public Sphere and the Mass Form: Popular Culture and the Democratic Project, 1900–1934', in *Between Reform and Revolution German Socialism and Communism from 1840 to 1990*, edited by David E. Barclay and Eric D. Weitz, Oxford: Berghahn Books.

Erdmann, Karl-Dietrich and Martin Vogt (eds.) 1978, *Die Kabinette Stresemann I u. II* Volume 2, Boppard am Rhein: Harald Boldt Verlag.

Erdmann, Lothar 1926, 'Zum Problem der Arbeitsgemeinschaft', *Dic Arbeit*, 3, 10: 641–52.

Falter, J.W. and H. Bömermann 1989, 'Die Wählerpotentiale politischer Teilkulturen 1920–1933', in *Politische Identität und Nationale Gedenktage. Zur Politischen Kultur in der Weimarer Republik*, edited by Detlef Lehnert and Klaus Megerle, Opladen: Westdeutscher Verlag.

Fayet, Jean-François 2004, *Karl Radek (1885–1939): biographie politique*, Bern: Peter Lang.

Feldman, Gerald 1993, *The Great Disorder: Politics, Economics and Society in the German Inflation, 1914–1924*, Oxford: Oxford University Press.

Fenske, Hans 1972, *Wahlrecht und Parteiensystem: ein Beitrag zur deutschen Parteiengeschichte*, Frankfurt: Athenäum Verlag.

Feucht, Stefan 1998, *Die Haltung der Sozialdemokatischen Partei Deutschlands zur Aussenpolitik währed der Weimarer Republik (1918–1933)*, Frankfurt: Peter Lang.

Feuchtwanger, Franz 1981, 'Der militärpolitische Apparat der KPD in den Jahren 1928–1935. Erinnerungen', *Internationale Wissenschaftliche Korrespondenz zur Geschichte der deutschen Arbeiterbewegung*, 17, 4: 485–533.

Fischer, Benno 1987, *Theoriediskussion der SPD in der Weimarer Republik*, Frankfurt: Peter Lang.

Flemming, Jens et al. (eds.) 1979, *Die Republik von Weimar*, 2 Volumes, Düsseldorf: Droste.

Fölster, Elfriede 1978, 'Die ARSO von 1927–1929. Zur Geschichte der Sozialpolitik der KPD', *Beiträge zur Geschichte der deutschen Arbeiterbewegung*, 20, 2: 222–36.

Fowkes, Ben 1984, *Communism in Germany under the Weimar Republic*, London: Macmillan.

———— 1989, 'Defence of Democracy or Advance to Socialism? Arguments within German Social Democracy in the mid-1920s', in *Radical Perspectives on the Rise of Fascism in Germany, 1919–1945*, edited by Michael N. Dobkowski and Isidor Wallimann, New York: Monthly Review Press.

Fromm, Erich 1980, *Arbeiter und Angestellte am Vorabend des dritten Reiches. Eine sozialpsychologische Untersuchung*, Stuttgart, Deutsche Verlags-Anstalt.

Gallus, Alexander 2006, 'Deutsche Revolution 1918/19: die Etablierung der Weimarer Republik', in *Deutsche Zäsuren: Systemwechsel seit 1806*, edited by Alexander Gallus, Cologne: Böhlau Verlag.

Geiger, Theodor 1931, 'Zur Kritik der Verbürgerlichung', *Die Arbeit*, 8: 534–553.

Gerschenkron, Alexander 1989, *Bread and Democracy in Germany*, Ithaca, N.Y.: Cornell University Press.

Geyer, Dietrich 1976, 'Sowjetrussland und die deutsche Arbeiterbewegung 1918–1932', *Vierteljahrshefte für Zeitgeschichte (VfZ)*, 24, 1: 2–37.

Geyer, Michael 1980, *Aufrüstung oder Sicherheit? Die Reichswehr in der Krise der Machtpolitik, 1924–1936*, Wiesbaden: Steiner.

———— 1981, 'Professionals and Junkers', in *Social Change and Political Development in Weimar Germany*, edited by Richard Bessel and E.J. Feuchtwanger, London: Croom Helm.

Gorlow, Sergej A., Elena Ilina and Jürgen Zarusky 1996, 'Geheimsache Moskau – Berlin. Die militärpolitische Zusammenarbeit der Sowjetunion mit dem Deutschen Reich 1920–1933', *Vierteljahrshefte für Zeitgeschichte*, 44, 1: 133–65.

Grossmann, Atina 1978, 'Abortion and Economic Crisis: the 1931 Campaign against § 218 in Germany', *New German Critique*, 14: 119–37.

—— 1983, '"Satisfaction is Domestic Happiness": Mass Working-Class Sex Reform Organizations in the Weimar Republic', in *Towards the Holocaust. The Social and Economic Collapse of the Weimar Republic*, edited by Michael N. Dobkowski, and Isdor Wallimann, Westport, Conn: Greenwood Press.

—— 1993, *Reforming Sex: The German Movement for Birth Control and Abortion Reform, 1920–1950*, Oxford: Oxford University Press.

—— 1998, 'German Communism and New Women: Dilemmas and Contradictions', in *Women and Socialism/Socialism and Women: Europe between the Two Wars*, edited by Helmut Gruber and Pamela Graves, Oxford: Berghahn Books.

Guttsman, Wilhelm L. 1990, *Workers' Culture in Weimar Germany: Between Tradition and Commitment*, New York: Berg.

Häberlen, Joachim 2010, 'Meint Ihr's auch ehrlich? Vertrauen und Missvertrauen in der linken Arbeiterbewegung in Leipzig und Lyon zu Beginn der 1930er Jahre', *Geschichte und Gesellschaft*, 36, 3: 337–406.

Hagemann, Karen 1990, *Frauenalltag und Männerpolitik*, Bonn: J.H.W. Dietz.

Harman, Chris 1997, *The Lost Revolution: Germany 1918 to 1923*, Second Edition, London: Bookmarks.

Harsch, Donna 1993, *German Social Democracy and the Rise of Nazism*, Chapel Hill: University of North Carolina Press.

—— 1998, 'The Iron Front: Weimar Social Democracy between Tradition and Modernity', in *Between Reform and Revolution: German Socialism and Communism from 1840 to 1990*, edited by David E. Barclay and Eric D. Weitz, Oxford: Berghahn Books.

Haupts, Leo 1976, *Deutsche Friedenspolitik 1918–1919*, Düsseldorf: Droste Verlag.

Heer-Kleinert, Lore 1983, *Die Gewerkschaftspolitik der KPD in der Weimarer Republik*, Frankfurt: Campus Verlag.

Henning, Eike 1989, 'Das Sozialdemokratische Milieu und seine Ausgestaltung vor Ort: Die historische Wahlanalyse kleiner Gemeinden und Stimmbezirke', in *Politik und Milieu. Wahl und Elitenforschung im strukturellen und interkulturellen Vergleich*, edited by Heinrich Best, St. Katherinen: Scripta Mercaturae Verlag.

Herlemann, Beatrix 1977, *Kommunalpolitik der KPD im Ruhrgebiet 1924–1933*, Wuppertal: Hammer.

Herzer, Manfred 1995, 'Communists, Social Democrats and the Homosexual Movement in the Weimar Republic', in *Gay Men and the Sexual History of the Political Left*, edited by Gert Hekma, Harry Oosterhuis and James Steakley, Binghamton NY: Harrington Park Press.

Hong, Young-Sun 1998, *Welfare, Modernity and the Weimar State, 1919–1933*, Princeton: Princeton University Press.

Hoppe, Bert 2007, *In Stalins Gefolgschaft. Moskau und die KPD 1928–1933*, Munich: R. Oldenbourg Verlag.

Hunt, Richard N. 1964, *German Social Democracy 1918–1933*, New Haven, Conn.: Yale University Press.

Hürten, Heinrich (ed.) 1977, *Zwischen Revolution und Kapp Putsch. Militär und Innenpolitik 1918–1920*, Düsseldorf: Droste.

Hussain, Athar and Tribe, Keith 1980, *Marxism and the Agrarian Question. Vol. 1: German Social Democracy and the Peasantry, 1890–1907*, London: Macmillan.

Ihlau, Olaf 1969, *Die Roten Kämpfer*, Meisenheim am Glan: A. Hain.

Kaes, Anton, Martin Jay and Edward Dimendberg (eds.) 1994, *The Weimar Republic Sourcebook*, Berkeley, CA.: University of California Press.

Kastning, Alfred 1970, *Die deutsche Sozialdemokratie zwischen Koalition und Opposition 1919–1923*, Paderborn: Schöningh.

Klenke, Dietmar 1987, *Die SPD-Linke in der Weimarer Republik* Volume 2, Münster: Lit Verlag.

Kluge, Ulrich 1975, *Soldatenräte und Revolution*, Göttingen: Vandendoeck und Rupprecht.

———— 1985, *Die Deutsche Revolution 1918–19*, Frankfurt: Suhrkamp.

Kolb, Eberhard 1962, *Die Arbeiterräte in der deutschen Innenpolitik 1918–19*, Düsseldorf: Droste Verlag.

———— 2005, *The Weimar Republic*, Second Edition, London: Routledge.

Kolb, Eberhard and Reinhard Rürup (eds.) 1968, *Der Zentralrat der deutschen sozialistischen Republik 19.12.1918–8.4.1919*, Leiden: Brill.

Kontos, Sylvia 1979, *Die Partei kämpft wie ein Mann! Frauenpolitik der KPD in der Weimarer Republik*, Frankfurt: Verlag Roter Stern.

Krause, Hartfrid 1975, *USPD: Zur Geschichte der Unabhängigen Sozialdemokratischen Partei Deutschlands*, Frankfurt: Europäische Verlagsanstalt.

Lamberti, Marjorie 2002, *The Politics of Education: Teachers and School Reform in Weimar Germany*, New York: Berghahn Books.

Langels, Otto 1984, *Der Ultralinke opposition der KPD in der Weimarer Republik in den Jahren 1924 bis 1928*, Frankfurt: Peter Lang.

Langewiesche, Dieter 1982, 'Politik – Gesellschaft – Kultur: Zur Problematik von Arbeiterkultur und kulturellen Arbeiterorganisationen in Deutschland nach dem I.Weltkrieg', *Archiv für Sozialgeschichte*, 22: 359–402.

Laporte, Norman 2003, *The German Communist Party in Saxony, 1924–1933*, Bern: Peter Lang.

Lapp, Benjamin 1995, 'A "National Socialism": the Old Socialist Party of Saxony, 1926–32', *Journal of Contemporary History*, 30, 2: 291–310.

Lehmann, Hans Georg 1970, *Die Agrarfrage in der Theorie und Praxis der deutschen und internationalen Sozialdemokratie*, Tübingen: Mohr.

Lehnert, Detlef and Klaus Megerle (eds.) 1989, *Politische Teilkulturen Zwischen Integration und Polarisierung. Zur Politischen Kultur in der Weimarer Republik*, Opladen: Westdeutscher Verlag.

Lepsius, Rainer M. 1993, 'Parteiensystem und Sozialstruktur. Zum Problem der Demokratisierung der deutschen Gesellschaft' in *Demokratie in Deutschland*, edited by R.M. Lepsius, Göttingen: Vandenhoeck und Ruprecht.

Leuschen-Seppel, Rosemarie 1981, *Zwischen Staatsverantwortung und Klasseninteresse. Die Wirtschafts- und Finanzpolitik der SPD zur Zeit der Weimarer Republik*, Bonn: Verlag Neue Gesellschaft.

Levi, Paul 1929, *Wehrhaftigkeit und Sozialdemokratie*, Berlin: Internationale Verlagsanstalt.

——— 2011, *In the Steps of Rosa Luxemburg: Selected Writings of Paul Levi*, Leiden: Brill.

Link, Werner 1961, *Die Geschichte des Internationalen Jugend-Bundes (IJB) und des Internationalen Sozialistischen Kampt-Bundes (ISK). Ein Beitrag zur Geschichte der Arbeiterbewegung in der Weimarer Republik und im Dritten Reich*, Marburg: A. Hain.

Longerich, Peter (ed.) 1992, *Die Erste Republik. Dokumente zur Geschichte des Weimarer Staats*, Munich: Piper.

Lönne, Karl-Egon (ed.) 2002, *Die Weimarer Republik 1918–1933*, Darmstadt: Wissenschaftliche Buchgesellschaft.

Lösche, Peter and Franz Walter 1989, 'Zur Organisationskultur der sozialdemokratischen Arbeiterbewegung in der Weimarer Republik', *Geschichte und Gesellschaft*, 15: 511–36.

——— 1990, 'Zwischen Expansion und Krise. Das sozialdemokratische Arbeitermilieu', in *Politische Teilkulturen Zwischen Integration and Polarisierung. Zur Politischen Kultur in der Weimarer Republik*, edited by Detlef Lehnert and Klaus Megerle, Opladen: Westdeutscher Verlag.

Luthardt, Wolfgang (ed.) 1978, *Sozialdemokratische Arbeiterbewegung und Weimarer Republik. Materialien zur gesellschaftlichen Entwicklung 1927–1933*, 2 Volumes, Frankfurt: Suhrkamp.

Luxemburg, Rosa 1974, 'Die Krise der Sozialdemokratie', in *Gesammelte Werke* Volume 4, Berlin: Dietz Verlag.

Mallmann, Klaus-Michael 1995, 'Milieu, Radikalismus und lokale Gesellschaft. Zur Sozialgeschichte des Kommunismus in der Weimarer Republik', *Geschichte und Gesellschaft*, 21, 1: 5–31.

——— 1996, *Kommunisten in der Weimarer Republik: Sozialgeschichte einer revolutionären Bewegung*, Darmstadt: Wissenschaftliche Buchgesellschaft.

——— 1999, 'Gehorsame Parteisoldaten oder eigensinnigen Akteure? Die Weimarer Kommunisten in der Kontroverse: eine Erwiderung', *Vierteljahrshefte für Zeitgeschichte*, 47, 3: 401–13.

Mattheier, Klaus 1973, *Die Gelben. Nationale Arbeiter zwischen Wirtschaftsfrieden und Streik*, Düsseldorf: Schwann.

Matthias, Erich 1954, *Die deutsche Sozialdemokratie und der Osten, 1914–1945*, Tübingen: Arbeitsgemeinschaft für Osteuropaforschung.

──────── 1960, 'Die Sozialdemokratische Partei Deutschlands', in *Das Ende der Parteien 1933*, edited by Erich Matthias and Rudolf Morsey, Düsseldorf: Droste Verlag.

Michalka,Wolfgang and Gottfried Niedhart (eds.) 1992, *Deutsche Geschichte 1918–1933. Dokumente zur Innen- und Aussenpolitik*, Frankfurt: Fischer Taschenbuch Verlag.

Miller, Susanne 1979, *Die Bürde der Macht. Die deutsche Sozialdemokratie 1918–1920*, Düsseldorf: Droste.

Möller, Horst 1985, *Parlamentarismus in Preussen, 1919–32*, Düsseldorf: Droste.

Mommsen, Hans 1991, 'Social Democracy on the Defensive', in Hans Mommsen, *From Weimar to Auschwitz: Essays in German History*, London: Polity Press.

Moore, Barrington, Jr. 1978, *Injustice: The Social Bases of Obedience and Revolt*, London: Macmillan.

Morgan, David W. 1975, *The Socialist Left and the German Revolution. A History of the Independent Social Democratic Party, 1917–1922*, Ithaca: Cornell University Press.

Müller, Richard 1925, *Der Bürgerkrieg in Deutschland*, Berlin: Phöbus Verlag.

Niemann, Heinz 1991 (ed.), *Auf verlorenem Posten? Zur Geschichte der Sozialistischen Arbeiterpartei*, Berlin: Dietz.

Niggemann, H. 1981, *Emanzipation zwischen Sozialismus und Feminismus: die sozialdemokratische Frauenbewegung im Kaiserreich*, Wuppertal: Hammer.

Oertzen, Peter von 1963, *Betriebsräte in der Novemberrevolution*, Düsseldorf: Droste.

Orlow, Dietrich 1986, *Weimar Prussia 1918–1925: The Unlikely Rock of Democracy*, Pittsburgh, PA: University of Pittsburgh Press.

──────── 1991, *Weimar Prussia 1925–1933: The Illusion of Strength*, Pittsburgh, PA: University of Pittsburgh Press.

Potthoff, Heinrich 1979, *Gewerkschaften und Politik zwischen Revolution und Inflation*, Düsseldorf: Droste.

Preller, Ludwig 1949, *Sozialpolitik in der Weimarer Republik*, Stuttgart: Franz Mittelbach Verlag.

Pyta, Wolfram 1996, *Dorfgemeinschaft und Parteipolitik 1918–1933: Die Verschränkung von Milieu und Parteien in den protestantischen Landgemeinden Deutschlands in der Weimarer Republik*, Düsseldorf: Droste Verlag.

Reich, Wilhelm 1972 [1932], 'Politicising the Sexual Problem of Youth', in *Sex-Pol: Essays, 1929–1934*, edited by Lee Baxandall, New York: Vintage Books.

Reichenbach, Bernhard 1928, 'Zur Geschichte der KAPD', *Archiv für die Geschichte des Sozialismus und der Arbeiterbewegung*, 13: 117–140.

Retzlaw, Karl 1976, *Spartacus – Aufstieg und Niedergang. Erinnerungen eines Parteiarbeiters*, Fourth Edition, Frankfurt: Verlag Neue Kritik.

Reuter, Elke et al. (eds.) 2003, *Luxemburg oder Stalin? Schaltjahr 1929. Die KPD am Scheideweg. Eine kommentierte Dokumentation*, Berlin: Karl Dietz Verlag.

Rohe, Karl 1992, *Wahlen und Wählertraditionen in Deutschland*, Frankfurt: Suhrkamp.

Rosenberg, Arthur 1936, *A History of the German Republic*, London: Methuen.

Rosenhaft, Eve 1983, *Beating the Fascists?*, Cambridge: Cambridge University Press.

Rother, Bernd 1990, *Die Sozialdemokratie im Land Braunschweig 1918 bis 1933*, Bonn: J.H.W. Dietz.

Rothfels, Hans 1959, 'Die Roten Kämpfer. Die Geschichte einer linken Widerstandsgruppe', *Vierteljahrshefte für Zeitgeschichte*, 7, 4: 438–60.

Rück, Michael 1993, 'Zwischen Historisierung und Aktualisierung der ersten deutschen Republik. Überlegungen zu Heinrich Winklers Trilogie', *Geschichte und Gesellschaft*, 19: 506–21.

Runge, Wolfgang 1965, *Politik und Beamtentum im Parteienstaat*, Stuttgart: Klett.

Saldern, Adelheid von 1998, 'Latent Reformism and Socialist Utopia. The SPD in Göttingen, 1890 to 1920', in *Between Reform and Revolution: German Socialism and Communism from 1840 to 1990*, edited by David E. Barclay and Eric D. Weitz, Oxford: Berghahn Books.

———— 1993, 'Massenfreizeitkultur', *Archiv für Sozialgeschichte*, 33: 44–57.

———— 1998, 'Modernization as Challenge: Perceptions and Reactions of German Social Democratic Women', in *Women and Socialism/Socialism and Women: Europe between the Two Wars*, edited by Helmut Gruber and Pamela Graves, Oxford: Berghahn Books.

Schäfer, Rainer 1990, *SPD in der Ära Brüning. Tolerierung oder Mobilisierung*, Frankfurt: Campus Verlag.

Schmädeke, Jürgen 1966, *Militärische Kommandogewalt und parlamentarische Demokratie*, Lübeck: Matthiesen.

Schöck, Eva Cornelia 1977, *Arbeitslosigkeit und Rationalisierung. Die Lage der Arbeiter und die kommunistische Gewerkschaftspolitik 1920–1928*, Frankfurt: Campus Verlag.

Schönhoven, Klaus 1989, *Reformismus und Radikalismus. Gespaltene Arbeiterbewegung im Weimarer Sozialstaat*, Munich: Deutscher Taschenverlag.

———— 1992, 'Strategie des Nichttuns', in Winkler, H.A., ed., *Die deutsche Staatskrise 1930–33. Handlungsspielräume und Alternativen*, Munich: Oldenbourg.

Schopf, Wolfgang 2008, *Theodor W. Adorno Siegfried Kracauer Briefwechsel 1923–1966*, Frankfurt: Suhrkamp.

Schröder, Wilhelm Heinz 2001, '"Genosse Herr Minister". Sozialdemokraten in den Reichs- und Länderregierungen der Weimarer Republik 1918/19–1933', *Historical Social Research*, 26, 4: 4–87.

Schulze, Hagen 1977, *Otto Braun, oder Preussens demokratische Sendung*, Frankfurt: Propyläen.

Schüren, Ulrich 1978, *Der Volksentscheid zur Fürstenenteignung, 1926*, Düsseldorf: Droste.

Schuster, Kurt G.P. 1975, *Der Rote Frontkämpferbund 1924–1929*, Düsseldorf: Droste.

Schwarz, Michael 1995, *Sozialistische Eugenik*, Bonn: Verlag J.H.W. Dietz.

Severing, Carl 1950, *Mein Lebensweg* Volume 2, Cologne: Greven Verlag.

Sharaf, Myron 1983, *Fury on Earth: A Biography of Wilhelm Reich*, London: Hutchinson.

Silverman, Dan P. 1970, 'A Pledge Unredeemed: The Housing Crisis in Weimar Germany', *Central European History*, 3, 1/2: 112–39.

Smart, D.A. 1978, 'Introduction', in *Pannekoek and Gorter's Marxism*, edited by D.A. Smart, London: Pluto Press.

Stieg, Margaret F. 1990, 'The 1926 German Law to Protect Youth against Trash and Dirt: Moral Protectionism in a Democracy', *Central European History* 23, 1: 22–56.

Stolle, Uta 1980, *Arbeiterpolitik im Betrieb*, Frankfurt: Campus Verlag.

Tenfelde, Klaus 1982, *Proletarische Provinz: Radikalisierung und Widerstand in Penzberg/ Oberbayern 1900–1945*, Munich: R. Oldenbourg Verlag.

Thönnessen, Werner 1973, *The Emancipation of Women. The Rise and Decline of the Women's Movement in German Social Democracy, 1863–1933*, London: Pluto Press.

Timm, Helga 1953, *Die Deutsche Sozialpolitik und der Bruch der Grossen Koalition im März 1930*, Düsseldorf: Droste.

Tosstorff, Reiner 2004, *Profintern. Die Rote Gewerkschaftsinternationale 1920–1937*, Paderborn: Ferdinand Schöningh.

Trotsky, Leon 1996 [1928], *The Third International After Lenin*, translated by John G. Wright, Fourth Edition, New York: Pathfinder Press.

Ulrich, Axel 2005, *Politischer Widerstand gegen das "Dritte Reich" im Rhein-Main-Gebiet*, Wiesbaden: Thurn-Verlag.

Usborne, Cornelie 1992, *The Politics of the Body in Weimar Germany*, Basingstoke: Macmillan.

Vogelsang, Thilo 1962, *Reichswehr, Staat und NSDAP. Beiträge zur deutschen Geschichte 1930–1932*, Stuttgart: Deutsche Verlags-anstalt.

Vogt, Stefan 2006, *Nationaler Sozialismus und Soziale Demokratie*, Bonn: Dietz.

Weber, Hermann 1969, *Die Wandlung des deutschen Kommunismus. Die Stalinisierung der KPD in der Weimarer Republik*, 2 Volumes., Frankfurt am Main: Europäische Verlagsanstalt.

Wehler, Hans-Ulrich 2003, *Deutsche Gesellschaftsgeschichte* Volume 4, Frankfurt: Büchergilde Gutenberg.

Weitz, Eric D. 1997, *Creating German Communism: from Popular Protest to Socialist State*, Princeton: Princeton University Press.

———— 1998, 'Communism and the Public Spheres of Weimar Germany', in *Between Reform and Revolution: German Socialism and Communism from 1840 to 1990*, edited by David E. Barclay and Eric D. Weitz, Oxford: Berghahn Books.

———— 2007, *Weimar Germany: Promise and Tragedy*, Princeton: Princeton University Press.

Wenzel, Otto 2003, *1923: Die Gescheiterte Deutsche Oktoberrevolution*, Münster: Lit Verlag.

Wheeler, Robert F. 1975, *USPD und Internationale Sozialistischer Internationalismus in der Zeit der Revolution*, Frankfurt: Ullstein Verlag.

Wickham, James 1983, 'Working-Class Movement and Working-Class Life: Frankfurt am Main during the Weimar Republic', *Social History*, 8, 3: 315–43.

Wieszt, József 1976, *KPD-Politik in der Krise 1928–1932*, Frankfurt: Materialismus Verlag.

Winkler, Heinrich August 1982, 'Klassenbewegung oder Volkspartei? Zur Programmdiskussion in der Weimarer SPD 1920–1925', *Geschichte und Gesellschaft*, 8, 1: 9–54.

——— 1985 [1984], *Von der Revolution zur Stabilisierung*, Berlin: Verlag J.H.W. Dietz.

——— 1987, *Der Weg in die Katastrophe. Arbeiter und Arbeiterbewegung in der Weimarer Republik 1930 bis 1933*, Berlin: Verlag J.H.W. Dietz.

——— 1988, *Der Schein der Normalität: Arbeiter und Arbeiterbewegung in der Weimarer Republik 1924 bis 1930*, Berlin: Verlag J.H.W. Dietz.

——— 1990, 'Choosing the Lesser Evil: the German Social Democrats and the Fall of the Weimar Republic', *Journal of Contemporary History*, 25, 2: 205–27.

Winkler, Jürgen 1989, 'Die soziale Basis der sozialistischen Parteien in Deutschland 1912–24', *Archiv für Sozialgeschichte*, 29: 137–71.

Wirsching, Andreas 1997, '"Stalinisierung" oder entideologisierte "Nischengesellschaft"? Alte Einsichten und neue Thesen zum Charakter der KPD in der Weimarer Republik', *Vierteljahrshefte für Zeitgeschichte*, 45,3: 449–468.

Wulf, Peter 1977, 'Die Auseinandersetzungen um die Sozialisierung der Kohle in Deutschland 1920–1921', *Vierteljahrshefte für Zeitgeschichte*, 25, 1: 46–98.

Wunderer, Hartmann 1980 (1), *Arbeitervereine und Arbeiterparteien. Kultur- und Massenorganisationen in der Arbeiterbewegung (1890–1933)*, Frankfurt: Campus Verlag.

Wunderer, Hartmann 1980 (2), 'Freidenkertum und Arbeiterbewegung. Ein Überblick', *Internationale Wissenschaftliche Korrespondenz zur Geschichte der deutschen Arbeiterbewegung*, 16, 1: 1–33.

Wünderich, Volker 1980, *Arbeiterbewegung und Selbstverwaltung. KPD und Kommunalpolitik. Mit dem Beispiel Solingen*, Wuppertal: Hammer.

Ziemann, Benjamin 1998, 'Republikanische Kriegserinnerung in einer polarisierten Öffentlichkeit. Das Reichsbanner Schwarz-Rot-Gold als Veteranenverband der sozialistischen Arbeiterschaft', *Historische Zeitschrift*, 267, 2: 357–98.

Zimmermann, Rüdiger 1978, *Der Leninbund. Linke Kommunisten in der Weimarer Republik*, Düsseldorf: Droste.

Index

www.ingramcontent.com/pod-product-compliance
Lightning Source LLC
Chambersburg PA
CBHW060019030426

42334CB00019B/2106